The Myth of the Fall in Nineteenth-Century Literature

The Myth of the Fall in Nineteenth-Century Literature

LINDA FREEDMAN

OXFORD
UNIVERSITY PRESS

OXFORD
UNIVERSITY PRESS

Great Clarendon Street, Oxford, OX2 6DP,
United Kingdom

Oxford University Press is a department of the University of Oxford. It furthers the University's objective of excellence in research, scholarship, and education by publishing worldwide. Oxford is a registered trade mark of Oxford University Press in the UK and in certain other countries

Published in the United States of America by Oxford University Press
198 Madison Avenue, New York, NY 10016, United States of America

British Library Cataloguing in Publication Data
Data available

Library of Congress Control Number: 2025933029

ISBN 9780198969570

DOI: 10.1093/oso/9780198969570.001.0001

Printed and bound by
CPI Group (UK) Ltd., Croydon, CR0 4YY

For my parents and children

Contents

Acknowledgements

I began to think seriously about this project in 2016, stuck on a broken down Eurostar, on Brexit day, frustratingly close to Paris, on my way to the International Emily Dickinson Conference, at which I was to present a paper on Dickinson's readings of Genesis. I made the conference, late, and not without a good sense of the symbolism, which my international colleagues appreciated. Since then, Fall moments have seemed everywhere apparent and catastrophes always upon us. But this has been a passion project and writing it was a source of pleasure throughout. I would like to thank the members of the Emily Dickinson and William Blake societies, who helped get the first ideas going. I am exceptionally grateful to my brilliant colleagues and friends at UCL; especially to Juliette Atkinson, who read an astonishing number of chapters at rough and ready stages and advised with care, warmth, generosity, and insight; to Charlotte Roberts, Anthony Ossa-Richardson, Greg Dart, Eric Langley, and Julia Jordan, who read individual chapters, counselled through difficulties, and helped shape intellectual directions; and to John Mullan, Helen Hackett, Alison Shell and Stephen Cadywold, who gave much needed practical support. Special thanks also goes to Thomas Constantinesco, Cécile Roudeau, Kristen Treen, Ben Quash, Tim Barringer, David Peters Corbett, Lawrence Freedman, and Ben Morgan, whose creative sympathy and intelligence I value hugely. Thank you to my editors, Eleanor Collins and Jack McNichol for recognizing the value of the book and seeing it through to publication. I am grateful to the Thomas Cole Archive, the William Blake Archive, the British Library, the Coloured Conventions Archive, and the Frederick Douglass Papers for making much of this research possible, and The British Museum, The Tate Gallery, The Museum of Fine Art, Boston, The Paul Mellon Foundation at the Center for British Art at Yale University, The Allen Memorial Art Museum, The Amon Carter Museum of American Art, and The Metropolitan Museum of Art, New York for the reproduction of images.

Genesis is a book about families: husbands and wives, parents and children, siblings. My greatest thanks goes to my family, mostly, thankfully, full of much happier times than the Book of Genesis. To Sam, for his love of intellectual energy, to Ava, Oscar, and Grace, for their happiness and humour, to my parents for their unwavering encouragement and my siblings for their steadfast support.

List of Figures

Introduction

Worlds we Make

> And when the woman saw that the tree was good for food, and that it was pleasant to the eyes, and a tree to be desired to make one wise, she took of the fruit thereof and did eat, and gave also unto her husband with her, and he did eat.
>
> Genesis 3: 6

> It is very unhappy, but too late to be helped, the discovery we have made, that we exist. That discovery is called the Fall of Man.
>
> Ralph Waldo Emerson, 'Experience' (1844)

In Genesis 1, time and form begin when God creates the world. When Adam and Eve eat the forbidden fruit in Genesis 3, they change. Human creativity and world-making effort are bound by different notions of time and form to those that define God's creation. In Genesis 4, Eve bears a child and her child-bearing opens a space between conception and creation. Eve says her child is 'from the Lord' but the magical moment when God could say, or touch, something, and it be, has gone.[1] Cain works the earth 'and in process of time' brings an offering to God.[2] God rejects the fruits of his labour, and thus, the Bible tells us, the first murder 'came to pass'.[3] Time becomes something we must live in, work and suffer through. It contains disappointment, desire, deceit, discord, wandering, and death. Form also changes. Bodies look different once Adam and Eve know what they are looking at, and they seek to cover themselves in shame. Their punishment is physical as much as temporal. The beguiling serpent is condemned to a debased form: 'upon thy belly shalt thou go, and dust thou shalt eat all the days of thy life'.[4] Creation becomes a tortured process as Eve is doomed to bear children 'in sorrow'.[5] The world feels different, enmity in all its forms: 'cursed is the ground for thy sake…Thorns

[1] Genesis 4: 1.

[2] Genesis 4: 3. The King James Version emphasizes the abstract shift in temporality. A more literal translation of the Hebrew is 'Now it came to pass at the end of the days'.

[3] Genesis 4: 8. [4] Genesis 3: 14. [5] Genesis 3: 16.

The Myth of the Fall in Nineteenth-Century Literature. Linda Freedman, Oxford University Press.
 DOI: 10.1093/oso/9780198969570.003.0001

also and thistles shall it bring forth to thee'.[6] Most importantly, fallen form becomes mortal: 'dust thou art, and unto dust thou shalt return'.[7]

The long nineteenth century was so steeped in Christian tradition that the Fall remained an ineluctable structure of thought and shape of time, and even those who resisted or tried to secularize its doctrinal orthodoxies tended to affirm its logic. They used it to tell an alternative history, envisage a possible future, claim a world-making force, express a libidinous energy, and develop secular ethics. For many of the writers in this book, artistic form exhibits as well as comments on the problem of fallenness—it belongs to the world of artifice, fracture, incompleteness, and human effort and yet it offers experiences of fullness. So, form helps produce the vocabulary of critique even as it is, itself, often part of what is being critiqued. This lends the nineteenth-century myth of the Fall a particularly rich literary texture. The Fall remains a dominant hermeneutic of existence and prevailing shape of time, but it is also a self-reflective artistic lens. Exploring works chosen partly for their diverse and innovative formal qualities and partly for the value, range, and importance of their ideas, I have wanted to capture the feel of some of the most theologically imaginative and aesthetically and politically interesting textures of the Fall in nineteenth-century literature.

The myth of the Fall has a longstanding place in studies of American literature. In 1950, Henry Nash Smith described the 'pull of a vacant continent' on the American imagination.[8] *Virgin Land: The American West as Symbol and Myth* emphasized new world mythology, the idea of untouched land, as the intellectual underpinning of westward expansion and established the relationship between myth, history, and literature as the principal concern of the new American studies, beginning what would become known as the 'myth and symbol' school. In 1955, R. W. B. Lewis published *The American Adam*, in which he imagined the archetypal figure of nineteenth-century American literature as a pre-lapsarian Adam, a man of 'heroic innocence and vast potentialities, poised at the start of a new history'.[9] It was, he acknowledged, 'an image crowded with illusion', subject to inevitable disillusion, but nonetheless he maintained that it was the concealed cause of every ethical polemic and the underlying structure of American literature.[10] Lewis made his study of the American Adam a plea for the hopeful and redemptive practice of literary criticism in the context of cold war scepticism and fear: 'A century ago,

[6] Genesis 3: 17–18. [7] Genesis 3: 19.

[8] Henry Nash Smith, *Virgin Land: The American West as Symbol and Myth* (Cambridge, Mass.: Harvard University Press, 2018; 1950), 3.

[9] R. W. B. Lewis, *The American Adam: Innocence Tragedy and Tradition in the Nineteenth Century* (Chicago: University of Chicago Press, 1955), 1.

[10] Lewis, *American Adam*, 1–6.

the challenge to debate was an expressed belief in achieved human perfection, a return to the primal perfection', he wrote:

> Today the challenge comes rather from an expressed belief in achieved hopelessness. We stand in need of more stirring impulsions, of greater perspectives and more penetrating controversies. Perhaps a review of that earlier debate can help us on our way. We can hardly expect to be persuaded any longer by the historic dreams of the new Adam. But it can pose anew, in the classic way of illumination as it did in the nineteenth century, the picture of what might be against the knowledge of what is, and become once more a stimulus to enterprise and a resource for literature.[11]

The epilogue of *The American Adam* defines the moral lesson of nineteenth-century literature as a willingness to take risks, an openness to experience and encounter in an age of containment, detachment, and defence.

Christopher Castiglia has recently defended the practices of cold war American literary criticism. In the wake of arguments made by Rita Felski and Jane Bennett, he positions critique as a way of enchanting rather than diminishing the world, not naïve but hopeful, measuring the past and the present against ideals in order to articulate a more desirable future.[12] 'Every critique', he writes, 'is a determined affirmation'.[13] He defends national mythologies as something more than oppression and narrowing, explores allegoric form as alternative world-making and pays close attention to style as the socially transformative power of literature, 'the extraordinary dislocations of our fixed ideas of reality that occur as we read'.[14] These attitudes are not the special province of American studies. They are implicit in recent critical studies such as Michael Hurley's *Faith in Poetry* and his edited collection with Marcus Waithe, *Thinking through Style: Non-Fiction Prose of the Long Nineteenth-Century*. Castiglia's defence of the 'myth and symbol' school therefore resonates with broader and more recent ideas about reading as imaginative encounter and form and style as alternative world-making. Imaginative idealism, as Castiglia puts it, is 'to confront "what is" with "what might be"'.[15]

[11] Lewis, *American Adam*, 9.

[12] See Rita Felski, *The Limits of Critique* (Chicago: Chicago University Press, 2015); Jane Bennett, *The Enchantment of Modern Life: Attachments, Crossings, Ethics* (Princeton: Princeton University Press, 2001).

[13] Christopher Castiglia, *The Practices of Hope: Literary Criticism in Disenchanted Times* (New York: New York University Press, 2017), 2.

[14] Richard Poirier, *A World Elsewhere: The Place of Style in American Literature* (New York: Oxford University Press, 1966), 84, cited in Castiglia, *Practices of Hope*, 181.

[15] Castiglia, *Practices of Hope*, 24.

This book suggests that ways of reading Genesis 3 in the nineteenth century might invigorate what Castiglia defines as a hopeful practice of critique further than the ideas of mid-century. The myth of the Fall had a reticular and typological structure that was both constitutive and reflective of the texture of experience. The fratricide of Genesis 4, the Flood of Genesis 7, the audacity and punishment of Babel, Jacob's wrestle with the Angel, the different origin myths of Genesis 1 and 2, and stories from the Prophets and Revelations were frequently invoked in relation to Genesis 3. The Fall retains an imaginative idealism, even as literature often questions, revalues, undermines, and resists orthodox doctrines. But it generates a mode of reading that pays attention to a variety of experience—that confronts 'what might be' with 'what is'. This book extends the canon beyond the novelists and poets valued by the 'myth and symbol' school, rethinking narratives of American exceptionalism with transatlantic and anti-racist writings, arguing that the myth of the Fall was a shaping force on the imaginative enterprises of writers and artists living vastly different lives.

The myth of the Fall was a political, social, and cultural force but it was also an aesthetic preoccupation and a formal logic, a way of reflecting on the limitations and possibilities of art and literature, driving innovations in prose, poetry, and the novel. Part I looks at the way different literary forms adapt the myth of the Fall to think about their own acts of fiction. Through Jean-Jacques Rousseau's prose genres, William Blake's composite art, Emily Dickinson's poetry, and George Eliot's novels, I explore the Fall as a shaping force on time and narrative and expose the ways in which literature shapes a living myth. The myth of the Fall makes sense of modern malaise and frames questions of responsibility, creativity, desire, and choice. Part II considers national mythologies. In the nineteenth century the sense that the nation had fallen, and the question of how it could be redeemed, fed the imagination of writers and artists in England as well as America. National mythologies were not univocal. In England, the Oxford Movement and the Catholic revival turned Protestant nostalgia towards sudden and miraculous transformation. In America, new world mythology was contested by Black writers who held the hope of redemption in visions of Black citizenship and racial equality.

The myth of the Fall survives partly because of way it adapts to the secular. George Levine observes that: 'it was characteristic of the Victorians to value some pure, authoritative, and immediately apprehended experience;...the Fall might have been from an ideal community, or from language in touch with its experiential sources, or from classical order and balance'.[16] Indeed, the story of secularization is often constructed as a fall narrative, catastrophic or fortunate. Charles Taylor follows Max Weber's story of lost enchantment in his hugely influential *A Secular Age*; George Levine counters with a fortunate 'fall upward' into secularism.[17] In both these narratives, literature, and literary criticism, have a specific role to play, offering a way of holding onto residually religious values. As Charles LaPorte observes: 'one need only think of Terry Eagleton's classic *Literary Theory: An Introduction* (2008) which claims the most obvious explanation for the "rise of English" as a scholarly discipline to be found in the "failure of religion"'.[18] But, as Colin Jager has argued, nineteenth-century secularization can also be overstated: religious participation in England actually rose in the first half of the century and in

[16] George Levine, *Realism, Ethics and Secularism: Essays on Victorian Literature and Science* (Cambridge: CUP, 2009), 118. In his study of Modernism's religious inheritance, Matthew Mutter writes that the myth of the Fall: 'has been naturalised in modernity by being recast as the alienation of subject from object (Coleridge and Marx), a fall into self-consciousness (Hegel and Emerson), a fall out of benevolent instinct into civilisation (Rousseau) or even, in the case of Nietzsche, an enemy of Christian theology, a fall from aristocratic, heroic nonchalance into the moral obsessions of the "ascetic ideal"', *Restless Secularism: Modernism and the Religious Inheritance* (New Haven: Yale University Press, 2017), 9.

[17] In his 1917 lecture 'Science as Vocation', Max Weber described what he saw as the secular disenchantment of the world over the past century. Older sources date the lecture to 1918. It was first published in 1919. Weber first uses the term *Entzauberung* (the 'de-magicking' of the world, which he took from from Friedrich Schiller's *entgötterte Natur* or 'ungodded nature' in his 1788 poem 'The Gods of Greece') in *The Protestant Ethic and the Spirit of Capitalism* (1905). See Max Weber, *The Protestant Ethic and the Spirit of Capitalism*, tr. Talcott Parsons (London: Routledge, 2005), 61. (Parsons translates this as 'the elimination of magic from the world', but the German (*Prozeß der Entzauberung*) is commonly translated elsewhere as 'disenchantment'.) See Sara Lyons, 'The Disenchantment and Enchantment of the World: Aesthetics, Secularisation and the Gods of Greece from Friedrich Schiller to Walter Pater', *Modern Language Review* 109.4 (Oct. 2014): 873–95, 873. Lyons cites the following sources for the imaginative connection between Weber's theory of disenchantment and the myth of the Fall: Jane Bennett, *The Enchantment of Modern Life: Attachments, Crossings and Ethics* (Princeton: Princeton University Press, 2011), 84; Jonathan Sheehan, 'When was Disenchantment? History and the Secular Age', in *Varieties of Secularism in a Secular Age*, ed. Michael Warner et al. (Cambridge, Mass.: Harvard University Press, 2011), 217–42, 217–19. Charles Taylor follows Weber's disenchantment theory in *A Secular Age* (Cambridge, Mass.: Harvard University Press, 2007), describing secularization as a buffering of the modern self. George Levine constructs an alternative fortunate fall or 'fall upward' into secularism in his introduction to *The Joy of Secularism: Eleven Essays for How we Live Now* (Princeton: Princeton University Press, 2011), 1–23.

[18] Charles LaPorte, 'Victorian Literature, Religion and Secularisation', *Literature Compass* 10.3 (2013): 277–87, 278. Taylor gives the nineteenth century pre-eminence in his argument for offering precisely this sort of humanist substitution for religious satisfaction: 'If the crucial story of the rise of secularity over the centuries is the creation of an exclusive humanist alternative to faith, then this is a period in which the gamut of alternatives of this range becomes richer and wider', *Secular Age*, 322. In his study of the Victorian novel, Norman Vance writes similarly: 'Christianity could still be seen and reconfigured as a religion of humanity. Its partly outmoded scriptures with their grand narrative of salvation history could now be reread or revised as narratives of the mystery of goodness, self-sacrifice and love in society and history, or they could be replaced by her own narratives on the same theme', *Bible and Novel: Narrative Authority and the Death of God* (Oxford: OUP, 2013), 113.

the US modernization closely correlated with religious vibrancy.[19] Jager, along with others including LaPorte, Richard Brantley, and Michael Hurley, has written persuasively about the Bible as a continuing source of innovative writing in the period and countered the pre-eminence of the secularization narrative in literary studies of the long nineteenth century.[20] I take seriously the religious faith that persisted, juxtaposing secular writings by Rousseau and Eliot with the fervent, unorthodox, belief of Blake and the resistant religious imagination of Dickinson, who refused to say definitively whether she believed in God. The persistence of faith comes to the fore in the ideas of nation-building explored in the second part of the book. Far from removing religious modes of thought from the world, the nineteenth century is notable for a renewed interest in religion as a social, cultural, and political force. Secular attitudes became more permissible but theological thinking was not lost nor did a fundamentally religious hope in redemption fade away.

A major nineteenth-century tension in the myth of the Fall was between providence and circumstance, events which were always going to happen and events which just happen. This had a huge influence on notions of human agency and was, to some extent, empowering, suggesting we might make our own world. But secularization also led to profound feelings of pessimism as creative efforts stumbled on what Ralph Waldo Emerson called the 'negative power' of circumstance.[21] Unorthodox thinkers like Emerson, Dickinson, and Eliot realized that circumstance was often no easier to direct than providence. For writers imagining the future of America, the hope of redemption continued to matter precisely because the unpredictable outcomes of circumstance and chance made self-actualization feel precarious. In the slippery and

[19] Colin Jager, 'Romanticism/Secularisation/Secularism', *Literature Compass* 5.4 (2011): 791–806, 792–3. Jager argues for a reconceptualization of the terms 'religious' and 'secular' in the wake of challenges to the thesis that secularization is part of modernization. For a benchmark study of that thesis, see Owen Chadwick, *The Secularisation of the European Mind in the Nineteenth-Century* (Cambridge: CUP, 1975). For revisionary histories of nineteenth-century secularization, see: Hugh McLeod, *Secularism in Western Europe, 1848–1914* (New York: St Martin's Press, 2000), Callum Brown, *The Death of Christian Britain: Understanding Secularisation 1800–2000* (London: Routledge, 2001), and Jeffrey Cox, 'Towards Eliminating the Concept of Secularisation: A Progress Report', in *Secularisation in the Christian World*, ed. Callum Brown and Michael Snape (Farnham: Ashgate, 2010), 12–26.

[20] Colin Jager, *The Book of God: Secularisation and Design in the Romantic Era* (Philadelphia: University of Pennsylvania Press, 2007) and *Unquiet Things: Secularism in the Romantic Age* (Philadelphia: University of Pennsylvania Press, 2014); Charles LaPorte, *Victorian Poets and the Changing Bible* (Charlottesville, Va.: University of Virginia Press, 2011); Richard E. Brantley, *Transatlantic Trio: Empiricism, Evangelicism and Romanticism* (Iowa: Culicidae Press, 2017); Michael Hurley, *Faith in Poetry: Verse Style as a Mode of Religious Belief* (London: Bloomsbury, 2018). This is also the intention of my earlier book on *Emily Dickson and the Religious Imagination* (Cambridge: CUP, 2011).

[21] Ralph Waldo Emerson, 'Fate' (1860), *Selected Essays* (Harmondsworth: Penguin, 1982), 361–93, 369.

contingent secular world, human agency could feel genuinely world-changing, but it also sometimes seemed to really lack the world-making force and salvific power of God. For those who entertained nostalgic ideas of an English Eden, the hope of redemption survived as a narrative of sacred return. For these writers, an unfallen England was always there, ready to be revealed: one just needed to be able to see, and feel, the hand of God.

This recourse to faith was often a matter of emotional response and not intellectual, or even religious, decision. Thomas Constantinesco observes that, in nineteenth-century America, the Christian hermeneutic of redemption through suffering was 'even more necessary to account for what would otherwise amount to senseless pain.'[22] He notes that: 'well into the era of Reconstruction, the Christian model of redemption through suffering remained one of the nation's defining secular tenets, testifying to persistence of earlier models of pain long after the invention of anaesthetics and analgesics.'[23] As Dominic Erdozain has argued, secularization was also often a matter of emotional response and not intellectual decision.[24] The doctrine of original sin became a specific source of religious rejection because it seemed so unforgivingly cruel. Herbert Spencer complained: 'how absolutely and immeasurably unjust it would be that for Adam's disobedience (which might have caused a harsh man to discharge his servant), all Adam's guiltless descendants should be damned, with the exception of a relatively few who accepted the plan of salvation.'[25] At mid-century, Emily Dickinson sardonically described 'Sin' as 'a distinguished Precipice' and the young Marian Evans, yet to take the pen name George Eliot, wrote forgivingly of 'this world of mistakes.'[26] But original sin also adapted very easily to the language of Darwinian science and proto-Freudian psychology. Christopher Herbert explains: 'In place of the myth of the Fall, secular social theory had only to set up the mystery of "instinct"...its familiar story of human nature as a bundle of unruly drives needing to be severely repressed.'[27]

[22] Thomas Constantinesco, *Writing Pain in the Nineteenth-Century United States* (Oxford: OUP, 2022), 19.

[23] Constantinesco, *Writing Pain*, 12.

[24] Dominic Erdozain, *The Soul of Doubt: The Religious Roots of Unbelief from Luther to Marx* (Oxford: OUP, 2016), 5.

[25] Cited in Dominic Erdozain, *Soul of Doubt*, 209.

[26] *The Poems of Emily Dickinson: Variorum Edition*, ed. R. W. Franklin (Cambridge, Mass.: Harvard University Press, 1998), poem no. 1577; Marian Evans to her aunt, Mrs Samuel Evans, 6 Feb. 1839, *The George Eliot Letters*, ed. Gordon S. Haight, 9 vols, (New Haven: Yale University Press, 1954–78), vol. 1, 14.

[27] Christopher Herbert, *Culture and Anomie: Ethnographic Imagination in the Nineteenth Century* (Chicago and London: University of Chicago Press, 1991), 35.

So, the Fall continued to motivate judgements made around instinctive drives and moral choice. These judgements were often gendered: Eve ate first and greed or lust remained, as John Ruskin put it, with tellingly casual misogyny, 'the old Eve-Sin'.[28] There has already been much excellent work done on the sexually deviant 'fallen woman' in nineteenth-century literature.[29] It was, as Angela Leighton has observed, a capacious trope: 'which ranges from the successful courtesan to the passionate adultress, from the destitute streetwalker to the seduced innocent, from the unscrupulous procuress to the raped child'.[30] In an early and influential study, Nina Auerbach argued that fallenness often becomes an avenue for female growth and a trope through which to explore the possibilities—or perhaps, fantasies—of female world-making power. She gives the example of *Alice in Wonderland*, which she describes as 'almost a parody of our cultural myth'. In Alice's iconic fall, Auerbach observes a metamorphosis in which Alice becomes 'both outcast in, and creator of, her newly expanded world'.[31] Beth Kalikoff notes that popular treatments of fallen women often titillated readers with stories of crime and punishment.[32] As Auerbach also comments, there is a fetishistic quality in works of art that 'could punish women more effectively for an offstage and unnamed trespass than civilised society was permitted to do'.[33] By contrast, Kalikoff suggests that the 'falling', as opposed to 'fallen' woman became a trope through which literary novelists could address more complex questions of temptation, seduction, goodness, and redemption.[34] In Elizabeth Gaskell's *Ruth*, the central character, a young orphan girl, falls for the aristocratic and rakish Henry Bellingham. Seduced and then abandoned, she has a baby out

[28] John Ruskin, 'The Stones of Venice', *Collected Works*, ed. A. T. Cook and Wedderburn (London: George Allen & Unwin, 1903–12), vol. 9, 63 and 65.

[29] See George Watt, *Fallen Women in the Nineteenth-Century English Novel* (London: Routledge, 1984); Nina Auerbach, 'The Rise of the Fallen Woman', *Nineteenth-Century Fiction* 35.1 (1980): 29–52, reprinted in *Woman and Demon: The Life of a Victorian Myth* (Cambridge. Mass.: Harvard University Press, 1982), 150–84; Nina Auerbach, *Romantic Imprisonment: Women and Other Glorified Outcasts* (New York: Columbia University Press, 1985), 149–70, 230–368; Tom Winnifrith, *Fallen Women in the Nineteenth-Century Novel* (Basingstoke: Palgrave, 1994); Beth Kalikoff, 'The Falling Woman in Three Victorian Novels', *Studies in the Novel* 19.3 (Fall 1987): 356–67; Susan David Bernstein, 'Dirty Reading: Sensation Fiction, Women and Primitivism', *Criticism* 36.2 (Spring 1994): 213–41; Lyn Pykett, *The Improper Feminine: The Women's Sensation Novel and the New Woman Writing* (London: Routledge, 2003); Mark Knight and Emma Mason, *Nineteenth-Century Religion and Literature: An Introduction* (Oxford: OUP, 2006), 141–6.

[30] Angela Leighton, '"Because Men Made the Laws": The Fallen Woman and the Woman Poet', *Victorian Poetry* 27.2 (Summer 1989): 109–27, 111.

[31] Auerbach, 'Rise of the Fallen Woman', 39.

[32] For examples, see Kalikoff, 'Falling Woman', 357.

[33] Auerbach, 'Rise of the Fallen Woman', 50.

[34] For examples, see: Kalikoff, 'Falling Woman', 358. Kalikoff includes a long discussion of *The Mill on the Floss*, observing that at the heart of Maggie's most severe temptation is a desire to be good (p. 363).

of wedlock and emerges as a redemptive figure of peace and calm, inflecting the figure of the fallen woman with the mother-idealism of the Madonna.[35]

This book revisits the fallen woman genre in a discussion of Charlotte Mew's 'Madeleine in Church' in the Epilogue. It also turns, in Chapter 4, to the related question of moral choice as an aspect of the Fall in George Eliot's novels.[36] Like Rousseau, Blake, and Dickinson, Eliot wins her place on formal as well as thematic grounds; the Fall underlies questions of moral choice, but it is also a trope which reflects on the fallible perspectivism of her realism and helps build a more forgiving aesthetic. At the beginning of this Introduction, I observed that Eve's punishment expresses a peculiarly unsettling quality of the fallen world. As she is condemned to bear children and bring them forth 'in sorrow', a gap opens between conception and creation. Instead of a magical moment, we have a tortured process. We might interpret this in artistic terms, as the agony of creative endeavour in a world of endlessly disappointing fallen forms. We might also interpret it in moral terms, as the connection between error and consequence which comes to define, and sometimes undermine, the moment of choice in the fallen world. Maggie Tulliver feels the consequences of her fall 'before the outward act was completed' and Gwendolen Harleth confesses her fear that in wishing her sadistic husband dead, she had somehow made it happen.[37] The collapsed space between conception and creation, error and consequence, stages a conflict with the egoistic will of the Creator-God, who can simply say, or touch, something, and it be. Maggie and Gwendolen have no such world-making power and the consequences of error press upon the moment of choice. Eliot's treatment of choice thus intersects with the trope of the fallen, or falling, woman and its biblical archetype—in

[35] Eric Trudgill selects this novel as a key moment in the development of the genre, arguing that with the publication of *Ruth*, the integration of magdalenism and the mother-idealism of the Madonna was complete. Eric Trudgill, *Madonnas and Magdalens* (London: William Heinemann, 1976), 290.

[36] Discussions of moral choice in Eliot have tended to focus on sympathy as the basis for ethical decision. See e.g. Patrick Fessenbecker, 'Sympathy, Vocation and Moral Deliberation in George Eliot', *ELH* 85.2 (Summer 2018): 501–32; Simon Calder, 'The Art of Conduct, the Conduct of Art and the "Mixed Science" of Eliot's Ethics: "Sympathetic Impulse" and "The Scientific Point of View" in *The Mill on the Floss*', *George Eliot Review: Journal of the George Eliot Fellowship* 41 (2010): 60–74; Jonathan Loesberg, 'Aesthetics, Ethics and Unreadable Acts', in *Knowing the Past: Victorian Literature and Culture*, ed. Suzy Anger (Ithaca, NY, and London: Cornell University Press, 2001), 121–51; Hina Nazar, 'Facing Ethics: Narrative and Recognition from George Eliot to Judith Butler', *Nineteenth-Century Contexts* 33.5 (Dec. 2011): 437–50; Annette Federico, 'Being Torn: *The Mill on the Floss*', *Literature, Interpretation, Theory* 12.4 (2001): 359–79; Suzy Anger, *Victorian Interpretation* (Ithaca, NY: Cornell University Press, 2005), 95–130. Richard Kaye has explored the Darwinian context of sexual selection and evolution in relation to female choice in Eliot's novels in *The Flirt's Tragedy: Desire without End in Victorian and Edwardian Fiction* (Charlottesville, Va.: University Press of Virginia, 2002), 118–50.

[37] George Eliot, *The Mill on The Floss*, ed. Juliette Atkinson (Oxford: OUP, 2015), 436; George Eliot, *Daniel Deronda*, ed. Graham Handley (Oxford: OUP, 2014), 586.

Genesis 3, it is the woman's body that locates the troubling space between error and consequence. But the myth of the Fall also influences broader philosophical and aesthetic issues around choice, vital to the development of her secular ethics and her generous mode of realism.

In its various applications, the myth of the Fall holds onto a sense of the fullness of time and the residually religious hope of salvation that derives from doctrines of grace and redemption. Genesis 3 was, from the start, a theory of modernity, a source for the often-wretched condition of being in time. The theological fullness of time sets it apart from other theories of modernity which focus on the temporally fleeting and spatially transitory experience of novelty: speed, fragmentation, networks, commodification, fashion, ephemera—the 'now' of the world.[38] Gillian Beer talked similarly about a 'remnant of the mythical' in her work on Darwin, George Eliot, and evolutionary narrative in nineteenth-century fiction.[39] The phrase comes from R. W. Mackay's chapter on 'The Meditation of Philosophy' and, Beer notes, was quoted by George Eliot in her review of Mackay's *The Progress of the Intellect* (1850) in the *Westminster Review* in 1851. It feels apt here:

> The true religious philosophy of an imperfect being is not a system of creed but, as Socrates thought, an infinite search or approximation. Finality is just another name for bewilderment or defeat…A remnant of the mythical lurks in the very sanctuary of science. Forms or theories ever fall short of nature, though they are ever tending to reach a position above nature, and may often be found really to include more than the maker of them at the time knew.[40]

The myth of the Fall provides structure, architecture, and foil for experience. It survives through a secularizing age as much more than a judgemental and repressive social mechanism. This is partly because of the adaptability and

[38] For a range of readings of modernity in nineteenth-century literature see Leo Marx, *The Machine in the Garden: Technology and the Pastoral Ideal in America* (Oxford: OUP, 1964); Lloyd Pratt, *Archives of American Time: Literature and Modernity in the Nineteenth Century* (Philadelphia: University of Pennsylvania Press, 2009); Jonathan Crary, *Techniques of the Observer: On Vision and Modernity in the Nineteenth Century* (Cambridge, Mass.: MIT Press, 1990); Clare Pettit, *Serial Forms: The Unfinished Project of Modernity 1815–1848* (Oxford: OUP, 2020) and *Serial Revolutions 1848: Writing, Politics, Form* (Oxford: OUP, 2022); Amelia Bonea, Melissa Dickson, Sally Shuttleworth, and Jennifer Wallis, *Anxious Times: Medicine and Modernity in Nineteenth-Century Britain* (Pittsburgh: University of Pittsburgh Press, 2019).

[39] Gillian Beer, *Darwin's Plots: Evolutionary Narrative in Darwin, George Eliot and Nineteenth-Century Fiction*, 3rd edn (Cambridge: CUP, 2009; 1983), 1–8.

[40] R. W. Mackay, *The Progress of the Intellect* (1850), cited in George Eliot, 'Mackay's Progress of the Intellect', *Westminster Review* 54 (Jan. 1851): 353–68, 367.

force of its narrative logic, and partly because it gives narrative time the feel of a quest, 'an infinite search' for meaning. It holds onto the otherworldly and the unworldly. It is, in Roland Barthes's terms, a formal metalanguage, which asserts itself as a grammar of the worlds we make.[41]

The Shape of Time

The Torah tells the story of transgression and punishment. Form and time change when Adam and Eve eat the forbidden fruit, but there is no mention of a fall from grace. This later interpretation of Genesis 3 was part of early Christian doctrines about what human beings are and what power they had over what they could become.[42] The Greek Fathers emphasized that Adam and Eve fell through a misuse of their will and that this accounts for modern misery. They are clear that the Fall unleashed evil into the world and that we are thus all involved in Adam's sin. For Athanasius of Alexandria (*c.*296-373) the wretchedness of modern man was directly traceable to the first lapse in Eden. The sin of disobedience, which he maintained was freely committed, released the destructive forces that were latent in human nature. The images he uses are of human disintegration and divine obscuration. God's perfect creation had fragmented and his Word had become encrusted with dirt, but it was always still there, ready to be revealed. Athanasius believed that we could work our way out of this state of inherited corruption. He had no doubt that we were wounded by Adam's sin, but he maintained that it was still possible to live a sin-free life and resist the forces of disintegration through continuous exertion of the will. In other words, the Fall was responsible for modern misery, but it was still possible for human beings to redeem themselves.[43] The key shift came with Augustinian theology. St Augustine is clear that is we cannot avoid Adam's sin without God's grace. Writing his *Confessions*, the converted St Augustine realizes he is not the author of his own story and that the end had been determined from the start: 'You knew, but I did not, what the outcome would be.'[44] He concludes: 'and when I forgot you, you did not forget me… Before I called to you, you were there before me.'[45] In the Augustinian

[41] Roland Barthes, 'Myth Today', in *Mythologies* (London: Vintage, 2019), 141.

[42] For a full explanation of early church doctrines of the Fall see J. N. D. Kelly, *Early Christian Doctrine* (London: Adam & Charles Black, 1968; 1955), 344–75.

[43] Kelly, *Early Christian Doctrine*, 346–8.

[44] Augustine, *Confessions*, tr. with an introduction and notes by Henry Chadwick (Oxford: Oxford World's Classics, 2008), 146.

[45] Augustine, *Confessions*, 273.

tradition, original sin was not only a sign of the depravity of man, it indicated the supreme authorship of God and the circular shape of sacred time.

Genesis 3 is also one of the founding myths of progressivism: the fortunate fall into knowledge and the liberation of sexual desire. The effect of eating from the Tree of Knowledge is not described as a downward fall but a breakthrough which suggests movement in quite a different direction: 'And the eyes of them both were opened.'[46] The passage arguably satirizes the familiar story of the over-reacher: 'And the Lord God said, Behold, the man is become as one of us, to know good and evil.'[47] As God asserts his dominance and punishes his creation, that declaration of equality was often interpreted as more sarcastic than sincere. The nineteenth-century American biblical scholar, George Bush, observed: 'The usual interpretation put upon this passage has been to consider it as an ironical mode of upbraiding Adam with the issue of his transgression.'[48] But other stories of the Ancient World suggest things might work out differently. The *Epic of Gilgamesh* gives us one such parallel. A man named Enkidu is seduced by a harlot. After having sex with her he gains '*reason*, and wide understanding'. The harlot tells him: 'You are handsome, Enkidu, you are just like a god!' She also introduces him to clothing and sends him to a land 'where young men are girt with waistbands.'[49] Progressive time leans forward. It can be teleological, but it can also be open and uncertain; there is no knowing what knowledge can bring. One version of the myth of the Fall is a coming-of-age tale, the moment when Adam and Eve grow up.

Genesis 3 therefore shapes two distinct notions of time: a nostalgic vision of redemptive return and a progressive vision of knowledge-based advancement, social development, and sexual awakening. They don't always remain distinct. The idea that we had something good, and lost it, remains a powerful nostalgic narrative, and modern political theodicies repeatedly play to it to embolden human agency, promising to 'take back control' or 'make America great again.'[50] The frustrated ambition of Genesis 3 intersects with the Greek

[46] Genesis 3: 7. [47] Genesis 3: 22.

[48] George Bush, *Notes, Critical and Practical on the Book of Genesis; Designed as a General Help to Biblical Rading and Instruction,* 2 vols (New York: Ivison, Phinney & Co., 1838), vol. 1, 90. In his account of sixteenth-century interpretations, Arnold Williams also observes: 'The general solution is that God speaks ironically. Man thinks he has become like God or the angels by eating the fruit. Actually, man had only learned to know good from evil by losing good and gaining evil.' Arnold Williams, *The Common Expositor: An Account of the Commentaries on Genesis 1527–1633* (Chapel Hill, NC: University of North Carolina Press, 1948), 135.

[49] *The Epic of Gilgamesh: The Babylonian Epic Poem and Other Texts in Akkadian and Sumerian,* tr. with an introduction by Andrew George (London: Penguin, 2000), 8–9.

[50] Campaign slogans for the Vote Leave Campaign during the EU Referendum in the UK and for the Trump Presidential Campaign in the US, respectively, both 2016, and the Reagan Presidential Campaign, 1980.

myth of Prometheus, the over-reacher who stole fire from the gods and gave humanity the gift of knowledge, only to be tied to a cliff and have his liver pecked out by an eagle for all eternity. William Blake used Promethean iconography to depict revolutionary world-making spirit fallen to terror and bound by reason.[51] Promethean imagery also married with the myth of the Fall in depictions of America's national symbol of the eagle. The eagle represented hope and ambition in the new nation, but it also depicted the violence of colonialism and enslavement: a figure for new world promise that was fallen from the start.[52]

Progressive visions frequently take hold of the origin myth and rewrite it, staking a claim to authorship which is both imaginatively utopian and historically cognizant and committed. In the seventeenth and eighteenth centuries, the first few chapters of Genesis became a source for the rewriting of civil society. The Fall remained a theodicy, an account of the moment when everything went wrong, but it also fed a residually religious tradition of prophetic writing which imagined alternative histories and possible futures in which things could get better not worse.[53] This was not a singular narrative. Edward Gibbon, for example, wrote a great history of decline.[54] But 'Origins' and 'Progress' were key terms of historical, philosophical, and scientific enquiry throughout the eighteenth century.[55] The coming-of-age story helped manage the shapelessness of evolutionary time by suggesting a developmental narrative. It was frequently reimagined in terms that deliberately posited a

[51] The most common Promethean figure in Blake's mythology is Orc, the revolutionary spirit who is also depicted as the crucified Christ.

[52] See Linda Freedman, *William Blake and the Myth of America: From the Abolitionists to the Counterculture* (Oxford: OUP, 2018), 130–1. See also my discussion of William Wilson's *Afric American Picture Gallery* in Chapter 6, 207.

[53] Ana Acosta, *Reading Genesis in the Long Eighteenth Century: From Milton to Mary Shelley* (Aldershot: Ashgate, 2006), 2–4. For an analysis of seventeenth-century readings of creationism and the new science see: William Poole, *The World Makers: Scientists of the Restoration and the Search for the Origins of the Earth* (Oxford: Peter Lang, 2010).

[54] Edward Gibbon, *The History of the Decline and Fall of the Roman Empire*, 6 vols. (London: Strahan & Cadell, 1776–89). For further reading on Gibbon and the shape of time, see: Charlotte Roberts, *Edward Gibbon and the Shape of History* (Oxford: OUP, 2014).

[55] Anna Wierda Rowland, *Romanticism and Childhood: The Infantilisation of British Literary Culture* (Cambridge: CUP, 2012), 35. Rowland cites the following examples of 'Origins' and 'Progress' in a chapter on the analogies of childhood: 'John Millar's *Origin of the Distinction of Ranks*, Jean-Jacques Rousseau's *Discourse upon the Origin and Foundation of Inequality*, Antoine-Yves Goguet's *The Origin of Laws, Arts and Sciences, and their Progress among the Most Ancient Nations*, Samuel Farr's *A Philosophical Enquiry into the Nature, Origin, and Extent of Animal Motion*, Charles Davy's *Conjectural Observations on the Origin and Progress of Alphabetic Writing*, Richard Eastcott's *Sketches of the Origin, Progress and Effects of Music*, Benjamin Barton's *New Views of the Origin of the Tribes and Nations of America*, James Tytler's *A Dissertation on the Origin and Antiquity of the Scottish Nation*, John Whitaker's *The Real Origin of Government*. A volume such as Lord Kames's *Sketches of the History of Man* includes chapters such as "Origin and progress of commerce," "Origin and progress of arts," "Origin and progress of American nations," "Progress of manners."'

different beginning, and alternative future, to the catastrophic fall in Genesis.[56]

The first generation of Black evangelicals represented chattel slavery as a fortunate fall because it exposed them to the knowledge of Christianity. Vincent Caretta explains:

> what mattered most spiritually was that pagan Africans be exposed to Christianity and be humanely treated in whatever social status they found themselves. Slavery was thus seen theologically as an effect of the fall of Adam and Eve, whereby the discomfort of the slaves' present physical life was overcompensated by the chance given them of achieving eternal salvation.[57]

But the idea of a fortunate fall also informed the conversion stories that structured narratives of personal growth and emancipation.[58] The pernicious and progressive applications of the myth were not always easily disentangled. The enslaved and educated poet, Phillis Wheatley, presented her capture as an act of divine 'mercy'—a fortunate fall because it converted her to Christianity:

[56] In 1689, John Locke published his *Essay Concerning Human Understanding*, in which he suggested a colony of children, left to themselves, would come to learn reason and understanding through experience and social interaction. In 1746, Etienne Bonnot de Condillac published his *Essay on the Origin of Human Knowledge*. He argued that speech and language were the origins of human mental life and posited an alternative to the theory that language was handed to Adam by God, suggesting that human beings might also have developed it themselves: 'Adam and Eve did not owe the exercise of the operations of their soul to experience. As they came from the hands of God, they were able, by special assistance, to reflect and communicate their thoughts to each other. But I am assuming that two children, one of either sex, sometime after the deluge, had gotten lost in the desert before they would have known the use of any sign. The fact I have just mentioned gives me the right to make this assumption. Who can tell whether some nation owes its origin only to such an event? So that I am permitted to make this assumption. The question is to know how this budding nation made a language for itself?' Etienne Bonnot de Condillac, *Essay on the Origin of Human Knowledge*, tr. and ed. Hans Aarsleff (Cambridge: CUP, 2001), 113.

[57] Vincent Caretta, 'Olaudah Equiano, Phillis Wheatley Peters and the Black Evangelical Experience', in *The Oxford Handbook of Early Evangelicism*, ed. Jonathan Yeager (Oxford: OUP, 2022), 603–21, 606.

[58] For examples of emancipation narratives, see *A Narrative of the Captivity and Restoration of Mrs Mary Rowlandson*, also known as *The Sovreignty and Goodness of God*, first published in 1682. For an edition of the narrative and other examples of the genre see Alden T. Vaughan and Edward W. Clark, eds, *Puritans among the Indians: Accounts of Captivity and Redemption 1676–1724* (Cambridge, Mass.: Belknap Press of Harvard University Press, 1981). See also Olaudah Equiano, *The Interesting Narrative and Other Writings*, ed. with an introduction and notes by Vincent Caretta (London: Penguin, 2003); *Narrative of the Life of Frederick Douglass, an American Slave* [1845], ed. Deborah E. McDowell (Oxford: OUP, 2009).

> 'Twas mercy brought me from my *Pagan* land,
> Taught my benighted soul to understand
> That there's a God, that there's a *Saviour* too:

And yet Wheatley's poem also subverts the tools of Christian pro-slavery apologia. She invokes the colour prejudice that equates whiteness with purity and Blackness with sin, but lecturing white, male, Harvard students on their moral duty, she makes it heavily ironic, clearly announcing her own moral superiority:

> Remember, *Christians*, *Negroes*, black as *Cain*,
> May be refin'd, and join th'angelic train.[59]

The free, but formerly enslaved, Olaudah Equiano similarly echoes, and subverts, the fortunate fall as he describes the taste of new knowledge. On arriving in England and wondering at snow, he first thinks it is salt and is encouraged by a new friend to set his curiosity at rest by tasting it:

> He desired me to taste it. I did so, and was surprised beyond measure. I then asked him what is was, he told me it was snow…I asked him the use of it, and who made it, and he told me a great man in the heavens called God: but here again I was to all intents and purposes at a loss to understand him…After this I went to church…they gave me to understand it was worshipping God, who made us and all things. I was still at a great loss, and soon got into an endless field of inquiries, as well as I was able to speak about such things…and from what I could understand from him about this God…I was much pleased……I was astonished at the wisdom of the white people in all things I saw.[60]

Tasting is, here, is not the transgressive savouring of forbidden fruit but an obedient act; Equiano's curiosity is guided and dutiful rather than disobedient and disruptive. The scene rewrites the Edenic narrative as one of beneficent tutelage and enlightened growth. The adult narrator manages the ignorance and innocence of his younger self with fondness, but he also

[59] Phillis Wheatley, 'To the University of CAMBRIDGE in NEW-ENGLAND', 1773, *Complete Writings* (London: Penguin, 2001), 11–12, 12.
[60] Equiano, *Interesting Narrative*, 67–8.

illustrates the way in which narratives of spiritual conversion might be turned towards paternalist pro-slavery apologia, a fortunate fall into 'the wisdom of white people'. Equiano explicitly writes against this misapplication of Christian enlightenment; he is clear that his enslavement was 'unjust and cruel'.[61]

For Wheatley and Equiano, the fortunate fall is turned towards self-authorship, promising a rewriting of origins and purpose. For Equiano, the taste of new knowledge is quickly followed by an encounter with books, which refers to Genesis, the book of beginning: 'I had a great curiosity to talk to the books, as I thought they did; and so to learn how all things had a beginning: for that purpose I have often taken up a book, and have talked to it, and then put my ears to it, when alone, in hopes it would answer me; and I have been very much concerned when I found it remained silent'.[62] Henry Louis Gates argues that the talking book is the ur-trope of the African-American tradition, carrying the idea that Black people could only become speaking subjects by inscribing their voice in the written word.[63] Desiring to talk to books to find out 'how all things had a beginning', the adult narrator partly positions his encounter with books as another rewriting of Genesis, a fortunate fall into knowledge which frames his childish innocence and ignorance in affectionate terms while self-consciously positioning his adult self within a literate and knowing African-American tradition. The adult Equiano no longer talks to books because he has successfully inscribed his voice in print.

Staking his claim to an African-American literary tradition, Equiano also signals the fundamental importance of the Bible to his story of origin and progress. He ends by affirming the fortunate fall into knowledge as both a progressive forward-facing narrative and a providential good, in which the self-authorship and empowerment he derives from new knowledge and acquired literacy is framed as an act of listening to the divine authorship of God:

> I early accustomed myself to look at the hand of God in the minutest occurrence, and to learn from it a lesson of morality and religion ... To those who are possessed of this spirit, there is hardly any book or incident so trifling that it does not afford some profit, while to others the experiences of

[61] Equiano, *Interesting Narrative*, 194. [62] Equiano, *Interesting Narrative*, 68.

[63] Henry Louis Gates, *The Signifying Monkey: A Theory of African American Literature* (Oxford: OUP, 1989), 139–83. Gates traces this topos of the talking book back to the slave narrative of James Albert Ukawsaw Gronniosaw, first published in 1770.

> ages seems no use; and even to pour out to them the treasures of wisdom is throwing the jewels of instruction away.[64]

Learning to read, a fortunate fall into knowledge, became a key trope of the emancipation genre. Frederick Douglass made learning to read a turning point in his *Narrative* and the fortunate fall into knowledge continued to frame stories of self-empowerment and racial uplift right through the nineteenth century. For Equiano, the fortunate fall into knowledge retains the element of sacred return even as it structures a story of origin and progress and a claim to self-authorship. To be able to see the hand of God is a blessing; without divine grace all the effort and learning, the wisdom and knowledge of the world, is wasted.

We might think of the division between the catastrophic and fortunate fall as one of sacred and secular shape. Secular has come to mean the opposite of sacred, and to some extent that is how I have used it in this book, but I am also responding to Colin Jager's call to recognize the way literature disrupts those categories. Literature, he rightly argues, can belong within religion and stand beside it; 'religion' and 'the secular' are not objective things in the world, or stable categories of meaning, but historically constructed, shifting, and contingent terms.[65] Secular once meant the work of God in the world, a present-facing notion. It evokes the feeling of an age, civil, lay, temporal (Latin *saeculum*; generation, age, in Christian Latin 'the world'). George Levine enthusiastically declares that that the secular is about 'the here and now': 'the point is not that secularism is a falling away, a necessary loss but that (and I'll sneak the word in again) it's a damned good thing.'[66] By contrast, the shape of sacred time is circular, longing to return to primordial origin. Writing in the third volume of *Time and Narrative*, Paul Ricoeur juxtaposed what he termed Augustine's 'time of the soul' with Aristotle's 'time of the world.'[67] The 'time of the soul' proceeds from memory and interiority, whereas

[64] Equiano, *Interesting Narrative*, 236.

[65] Jager, 'Romanticism/Secularisation/Secularism', 796–800. See also Colin Jager, 'The Secular and the Literary', *Christianity and Literature* 67.3 (2018): 411–18, *The Book of God: Secularisation and Design in the Romantic Era* (Philadelphia: University of Pennsylvania Press, 2007), and *Unquiet Things: Secularism in the Romantic Age* (Philadelphia: University of Pennsylvania Press, 2014). By contrast, in his study of the Victorian novel, Norman Vance describes a replacement theory, where literature becomes part of the narrative of nineteenth-century secularization, *Bible and Novel: Narrative Authority and the Death of God* (Oxford: OUP, 2013).

[66] Levine, 'Introduction', *Joy of Secularism*, 12.

[67] Ricoeur is responding to, and in dialogue with earlier philosophers of time and narrative, particularly Henri Bergson and Maurice Merleau-Ponty. For a full discussion of these inter-relations, see Mark S. Muldoon, *Tricks of Time: Bergson, Merleau-Ponty and Ricoeur in Search of Time, Self, and Meaning* (Pittsburgh: Duquesque University Press, 2006).

the 'time of the world' proceeds from external things. For Ricoeur, any theory of narrative must respond to both these notions of time, and particularly to the tension they create. He explains: 'The aporia of temporality, to which the narrative operation replies in a variety of ways, lies precisely in the difficulty of holding onto both ends of this chain, the time of the soul and that of the world.'[68] Augustine finally remembers himself in God. Aristotle's sense of time is rooted in the present: 'For what is bounded by the "now" is thought to be time—we may assume this', he says.[69] If the 'time of the soul' holds onto sacred origin, the 'time of the world' is avowedly secular. The myth of the Fall disturbs that dichotomy, exposing secular forms of nostalgia as much as it holds onto the sacred as something that matters to present and forward-facing time.

Selected Readings

I begin with Rousseau because he recognized one of the fundamental paradoxes of modernity; disasters feel as if they come upon us with unexpected suddenness precisely because the moment of collapse is so hard to find. He makes it clear that the Fall is a narrative construct, something we use to shape our sense of time and our restless desire for authenticity in a world of cultural sophistication. One of the most striking things about Rousseau's portrayal of his own life story is just how often he says he has fallen. Each imagined fall exposes some innate good in his own character, a pre-lapsarian fantasy of the self that exists only as an authorial construct. For Rousseau, this is the catch-22 of the fall into culture: writing takes him away from original innocence, into sophistication and artifice, but it also keeps the idea of purity alive in a world that has no hope of redemption.

The second chapter sets up a contrast with Rousseau's secular nostalgia through William Blake's profoundly religious investment in creative art as a fallen but potentially redemptive practice. Like Rousseau, Blake was appalled by the catastrophic world he thought we had made and energized by a desire to do good. Blake drew his models of creative artistry from the first two chapters of Genesis, looking to claim an original world-making force for imaginative art. He championed sexual desire and wrote against the misogynist reception of Genesis 3, making an emotional case for the Eden that was aborted when the church buried female sexuality in darkness and called it

[68] Paul Ricoeur, *Time and Narrative*, vol. 3 (Chicago: University of Chicago Press, 1988), 14.
[69] Aristotle, *Physics*, cited in Ricoeur, *Time and Narrative*, 16.

'Sin'. But he stumbled repeatedly on the problem of fallen form. How could the artist give redemptive form to creation when creative forms turn repeatedly on the conditions of fallenness? Blake drew hope from the idea that we could make ourselves vulnerable in our creative endeavours, defining them as friendships not projects. He saw value in encounter, risks that open the self to forces beyond its control and resist the monomaniacal drives of will and power that result in solipsistic and self-closed worlds. For Blake, redemption ultimately relied on the gift of grace, but it was received in the condition of energetic effort. By these efforts, he suggested we might allow the gift of grace to enter the creative imagination and inspire human authorship; we could never get there by work alone.

Chapters 3 and 4 show how evolutionary theory continued to shape the myth of the Fall after the publication of Darwin's *On the Origin of Species* in 1859. Chapter 3 turns to Emily Dickinson, who staged a dynamic tension between design and chance from the perspective of someone who would never commit to believing or disbelieving in God. Dickinson saw that hermeneutics create as well as reflect ways of being in the world. She indulges the idea that poetry can be a form of revisionary exegesis, a subversive, playful, and rebellious practice, which takes pleasure in errancy and challenges authority. But she also had a more solemn sense of the limits of human agency in the face of circumstance and chance and she sometimes satirized poetic power as another pre-lapsarian fantasy, making fun of its little dominion. Like Blake, Dickinson valued risk and her version of the fortunate fall abandoned those forms of knowledge associated with stability and certainty. In Dickinson's writings, the Fall became more than a narrative through which to make sense of the slow processes of evolutionary time; it became a creative coming-of-age story, a traumatic breakthrough which lands on more uncertain, unstable, and exciting poetic ground.

Chapter 4 turns to the novels of George Eliot and the question of moral choice. Eliot was taught to see the Fall as a failure of the will, a sinful choice. By the time she came to write fiction she had abandoned her early evangelical belief in absolute right and absolute wrong, but she continued to play on the idea that a woman's choice might be a world-making or world-breaking event. She was interested in the way in which people drift into error, either through inaction or through the decision to play a part and try to author their own existence. Her novels are full of difficult choices and dreadful mistakes, especially those made by women subject to the cruel social consequences of a double-standard. Although she developed a generous and forgiving form of realism, strongly influenced by Darwin's theories of adaptation and growth, she never absolved her characters, or herself, from moral responsibility. In her novels, the myth of the Fall continued to underlie, but not define, the ethics of choice in a world where social judgements were severe and tragedies often those of circumstance.

Part II discusses national mythologies. Chapter 5 revisits the myth of America as a New Eden. In the precarious decades of the early to mid-century, white American artists and writers renewed the colonial myth with a mixture of enthusiasm and increased anxiety. As Andrew Jackson pursued violent policies of westward expansion and slavery continued in full force in the South, the dream of perfect beginning seemed ever more of a fallacy. But the possibility and potentiality of new world mythology remained a powerful influence on ideas of authorship, inspiring the idea that America was yet unwritten. In 1844, Emerson could still claim: 'America is a poem in our eyes. Its ample geography dazzles the imagination, and it will not wait long for metres.'[70] But Emerson also knew that he was too late for this possibility and potentiality. His investment in pre-lapsarian fantasy is countered by an ever-rising scepticism, a feeling of being shut out and detached from original world-making force. This chapter traces the tension between faith and scepticism through volatile shifts in texture: smooth myths and rough histories, fluid force and sliding surface, integration and disintegration of form. The world yet to made emerges always already undone.

For Black Americans, fighting for freedom and civil rights, the hope of redemption from oppression turned struggle and suffering into sacrifice: a story that was yet to have its meaning fulfilled. In this context, the myth of the Fall was not Genesis 3 but Genesis 4: the fratricide which set brother against brother, white against Black, in the violent beginnings of American history. The story of Cain and Abel, the first murder, is a new point of origin in Genesis and a second, catastrophic, fall. It was common, in the nineteenth century, for white Europeans and Americans to preach that Black skin was the mark of Cain, and Ham his direct descendant. But Black Americans regularly described the white man as Cain, in a deliberate subversion of white tools of oppression. Chapter 6 shows how the Cain myth emphasized the violent injustice underpinning white narratives of self-making, growth, prosperity, and progress. For Black writers, the dream of a new beginning was not carried by the spotless landscape of Eden; it was rooted in resurrection from sin. The fratricide represents the origin and continuity of evil, but it also holds the hope of redemption in Abel, a type of Christ, whose blood becomes

[70] Ralph Waldo Emerson, 'The Poet' (1844), *Selected Essays*, 259–85, 281.

symbolic of shared foundational sacrifice in the new republic and vocal resistance to white supremacy as it cries from the ground.

If the American story was yet to be written, an English Eden was to be recovered. The final chapter moves back to England and mythologies of national fall and redemption that emphasize a narrative of sacred return. In the English myth of the Fall, absolutes seemed to have been lost or forgotten but were always still there, ready to be revealed. This fed the pernicious work of empire with a belief in the innate supremacy of Englishness but it was also, paradoxically, a mindset that valued humility. Chapter 7 looks at the way the English myth of the Fall particularly feared the sin of idolatry—the crime of the misplaced absolute. If the Fall began with disobedience, and the result was deception and falsehood, then truth could only be recovered through obedience. Whereas other mythologies of the Fall celebrated a daring and playful disobedience, these writers did not. But neither did they like conformity. Like Blake, the writers in this chapter maintain that revelation comes as a gift of grace but is received in the condition of energetic effort and willingness to change. Effort lifts obedience from an attitude of mindless conformity to a sincere commitment to truth. The English Eden reflected a faith in sacred time, wholeness, and uncorrupted origin. Through effort, and by grace, one might still see and feel the hand of God.

The Epilogue offers some brief reflections on the myth of the Fall at the turn of the century, drawing examples from Walter Pater, James McNeill Whistler, Oscar Wilde, Charlotte Mew, Robert Louis Stevenson, T. S. Eliot, and Sigmund Freud. Decadent *fin-de-siècle* writers played obsessively and ambiguously with the myth of the Fall, idealizing the sensual moment of pleasure and fantasizing about atavistic darkness. The myth of the Fall survived as a self-reflective artistic lens and residually, and sometimes explicitly, religious aesthetic. It continued to make sense of time, generate creative and political energy, and drive questions of desire and choice. It could express profound pessimism, but also keep the hope of redemption alive. In its various iterations the Fall remained what it was from the start, an origin myth of modernity and a source for being in time.

PART I
FICTION

1

The Fall into Culture

Rousseau, Writing, and Catastrophe

In the summer of 1749, on the way to visit his incarcerated philosopher friend Denis Diderot in Vincennes, Jean-Jacques Rousseau experienced what he recalled as a transformation, a dramatic turning point in his life:

> Vincennes is some two leagues distant from Paris. In no position to pay for a carriage, I would set out on foot at two o'clock in the afternoon on days when I was on my own, to arrive sooner. The trees along the road, which, as is the fashion in this country, had been severely pollarded, gave almost no shade, and often, overcome by heat and fatigue, I would stretch myself out on the ground unable to go any further. In order to moderate my pace, I hit upon the idea of taking a book with me. One day I took the *Mercure de France* and, scanning it as I walked, happened upon the following question proposed by the Academy of Dijon for its prize the following year: *Has the progress of the sciences and arts contributed to the corruption or the purification of morals?*
>
> The moment I read these words I saw another universe and I became another man…[Diderot] urged me to give free reign to my ideas and to enter the competition. I did so, and from that moment on I was lost. The whole of the rest of my life, and all of my misfortunes were the inevitable effect of this aberration.[1]
>
> (On compte deux lieues de Paris à Vincennes. Peu en état de payer des fiacres, à deux heures après midi j'allais à pied quand j'étais seul, et j'allais vite pour arriver plus tôt. Les arbres de la route, toujours élagués, à la mode du pays, ne donnaient presque aucune ombre, et souvent, rendu de chaleur et de fatigue, je m'étendais par terre n'en pouvant plus. Je m'avisai, pour modérer mon pas, de prendre quelque livre. Je pris un jour le *Mercure de*

[1] Jean-Jacques Rousseau, *Confessions*, tr. Angela Scholar and ed. Patrick Coleman (Oxford: Oxford World's Classics, 2000), 341–2. Diderot was one of many political prisoners, incarcerated for his criticism of the government.

The Myth of the Fall in Nineteenth-Century Literature. Linda Freedman, Oxford University Press.
 DOI: 10.1093/oso/9780198969570.003.0002

> *France* et tout en marchant et le parcourant, je tombai sur cette question proposée par l'académie de Dijon pour le prix de l'année suivante: *Si le progrès des sciences et des arts a contribué à corrompre ou à épurer les moeurs.*
>
> À l'instant de cette lecture je vis un autre univers, et je devins un autre homme... [Diderot] m'exhorta de donner l'essor à mes idées, et de concourir au prix. Je le fis, et dès cet instant je fus perdu. Tout le reste de ma vie et de mes malheurs fut l'effet inévitable de cet instant d'égarement.[2])

This is the moment that Rousseau becomes a writer and he presents it as a catastrophic fall, a single 'aberration', which is the root cause of all his unhappiness, a momentary deviation that explains 'all of [his] misfortunes'. In this moment Rousseau describes himself as 'lost'. The word carries the theological sense of damnation into the secular sense of self-alienation. Rousseau is lost because he can no longer recognize himself. He implies that, in becoming an author, he has sacrificed an original, authentic, innocent, self for a worldly, cultivated, and alienated persona. His fall is a fall into culture, leading him away from pre-lapsarian innocence into the high cultural life of Parisian salons.

But Rousseau also invokes the opposite narrative of salvation. The scene recalls two dramatic conversions to faith: Saul on the road to Damascus and Augustine in the garden in Milan. Saul, in the act of persecuting the followers of Jesus, has a revelation which exposes his error and proves a dramatic turning point in his life:

> And as he journeyed, he came near Damascus: and suddenly there shined round about him a light from heaven: And he fell to the earth, and heard a voice saying unto him, Saul, Saul, why persecutest thou me? And he said, Who art thou, Lord? And the Lord said, I am Jesus whom thou persecutest: *it is* hard for thee to kick against the pricks. And he trembling and astonished said, Lord, what wilt thou have me to do? And the Lord *said* unto him, Arise, and go into the city, and it shall be told thee what thou must do.[3]

Saul remains blinded for three days and neither eats nor drinks, an echo of the period in between Christ's death and resurrection. He is then blessed with new sight and baptized into a new life. Saul the Pharisee becomes the Paul the Christian Apostle: 'And immediately there fell from his eyes as it has been

[2] Rousseau, *Les Confessions*, ed. Bernard Gagnebin, notes by Jean Balsamo, extra notes Michèle Crogiez (Paris: Le Livre de Poche Classique, 1988), vol. 2, 125–6.

[3] Acts 9: 3–6.

scales: and he received sight forthwith, and arose, and was baptised.'[4] Collapsing on the road to Vincennes, seeing another universe and becoming another man, Jean-Jacques frames his turning point in distinctly Pauline terms.

It matters that he reads a book. Rousseau's *Confessions* pays homage to his Catholic interlocutor, St Augustine.[5] At the moment of his conversion, Augustine is weeping in agony under a fig tree in the garden in Milan and a voice tells him to read. He confesses: 'I checked the flood of tears and stood up. I interpreted it solely as a divine command to open the book and read the first chapter I might find.'[6] Augustine is reading but his reading is conveyed to us as an act of listening. The passage he lights upon is not coincidental; the accident of finding it indicates the hand of Providence. The passage comes to him as a revelation and Augustine presents his conversion to Catholicism as a sudden and unqualified moment of conviction: 'At once, with the last words of this sentence, it was as if a light relief from all anxiety flooded my heart. All the shadows of doubt were dispelled.'[7] On the road to Vincennes, Jean-Jacques has a similarly revelatory and tearful reading experience while collapsed under a tree. But rather than realizing the divine authorship of God, and with Diderot's serpentine encouragement, he himself becomes an author.

Framing this moment in terms resonant of two famous narratives of salvation is partly ironic; the good St Paul becomes the egregious Saul of Tarsus; the chaste Augustine reverts to a life led by appetite. But it is not straightforwardly ironic. Rousseau depicts a fall into culture which holds onto the possibility of salvation in two distinct ways. First, on the road to Damascus, and in the garden in Milan, Saul and Augustine discover their true author in God. But once one takes God out of the picture, self-knowledge, as opposed to divine will, becomes the shaping force of existence and writing offers itself as a potentially redemptive tool of remaking. As Patrick Riley observes, Rousseau gives us: 'a secular recasting of conversion, its reorientation away from God and toward a self so divided by experience that it can only subsist as a series of autobiographical representations.'[8] But, he argues: 'Before

[4] Acts 9: 18.

[5] Rousseau does not mention Augustine and, in fact, claims he has no literary precedent or model of the self. But the claim is generally agreed to be authorial posturing and parallels with Augustine have been widely noted. The most sustained and extreme argument has come from Ann Hartle, who sees Rousseau as systematically responding to Augustine: Ann Hartle, *The Modern Self in Rousseau's Confessions: A Reply to St. Augustine* (Notre Dame, Ind.: University of Notre Dame Press, 1983). See also Paul J. Archambault, 'Rousseau's Tactical Misreading of Augustine', *Symposium* 41 (1987): 6–14; Patrick Riley, 'The Inversion of Conversion: Rousseau's Rewriting of Augustinian Autobiography', *Studies in Eighteenth-Century Culture* 28 (1999): 229–55.

[6] Augustine, *Confessions*, 153.

[7] Augustine, *Confessions*, 153.

[8] Riley, 'Inversion of Conversion', 230.

autobiographical writing can become a potentially redemptive project, writing as such is posited as a potentially disastrous activity that puts the self at the mercy of its purely public image, so that to become an author is to die as an autonomous self and to be reborn as the fantasy one deduces from the other's writings.'[9] There is a clear religious framework here, too. The converted St Paul declares: 'I protest by your rejoicing which I have in Christ Jesus our Lord, I die daily.'[10]

Secondly, the revelation on the road to Vincennes is not completely disastrous. In answering the question proposed by the Academy of Dijon, Rousseau became a vocal social critic with an active sense of moral responsibility. He presented culture as a gilded prison and set himself against the trends and tastes of the day: '[the arts and sciences]' he declared, 'spread garlands of flowers over the iron chains, with which they are burdened.'[11] Dismayed by the growing wealth and economic inequality of Geneva, he rejected the popular theory of *commerce doux* as nothing but an excuse for worldly vanity. *Commerce doux* was rooted in a belief that a system of exchange rendered humanity sociable, as opposed to selfish. It included, but was not limited to, economic development and trade. The word *douceur* suggested all manner of gentle and mutually beneficial interests, acting as a check on the dangerous passions of the individual.[12] But Rousseau complained that politicians had lost sight of morals and virtue and spoke only of business and money. Rousseau's catastrophic fall into culture on the road to Vincennes thus exposes his innate integrity. It displays a residual innocence in his character and an energetic desire to do good, that is preserved in the very moment he is sullied.

In his *Confessions*, and throughout his writings, Rousseau brings a reading of Genesis 3 as a coming-of-age story to the fore. The moment of catastrophe is also the moment of maturity, a volatile pubescence where something might be gained as well as lost. Rousseau emerged from, and helped shape, a modern social, cultural, and educational vision profoundly invested in the relationship between childhood and adulthood. If, as Wordsworth would later claim, 'the child is father of the man', the way we treat children matters, in a

[9] Riley, 'Inversion of Conversion', 241. [10] 1 Cor. 15: 31.

[11] Jean-Jacques Rousseau, 'Discourse on the Sciences and the Arts', *Rousseau: The Basic Political Writings* (2nd edn), tr. and ed. Donald A. Cress (Cambridge: Hackett, 2011), 1–26, 6; 'les Sciences, les Lettres & les Arts…étendent les guirlandes de fleurs sur les chaînes de fer dont ils sont chargés', Jean-Jacques Rousseau, *Discours sur les Sciences et les Arts*, ed. George R. Havens (London: OUP, 1946), 101–2.

[12] See Albert O. Hirschman, *The Passions and the Interests: Political Arguments for Capitalism before its Time* (Princeton: Princeton University Press, 2013).

large part, because of the adults they become.[13] Within this secularized narrative of development, infancy is not a lost state of pre-lapsarian bliss so much as a set of impressions and experiences that exert a strong shaping force on the adult world. Infancy and maturity, nature and culture, savagery and civilization, worked as a fluid set of analogies for the origin and progress of self and world as a gradual and fortunate, rather than sudden and catastrophic, fall into knowledge.[14] This chapter focuses on that volatile and often catastrophic 'moment' of maturity as it manifests across his different prose genres. Rousseau was a deeply pessimistic thinker, animated by an overactive sense of proximity to disaster, and he draws attention to this dramatic turning point as a fiction, something we invent to make sense of the fact that disasters seem to come upon us so suddenly. He returns to the coming-of-age moment so obsessively and indulgently because writing and rewriting it becomes the only way of displaying and preserving the idea of innocence and the shape of sacred time in a world that feels profoundly corrupted.

'To Pinpoint the Moment': The *Second Discourse* (1755)

In the *Second Discourse* Rousseau identifies a key paradox of modernity: it is the extreme slowness of evolutionary change that makes disasters feel as if they are suddenly upon us. He had won first prize at the Academy of Dijon for his *Discourse on the Sciences and Arts*, and it made him notorious. The piece was published and not altogether well received: widely criticized for its attack on *commerce doux*. But Rousseau had courted controversy, anticipating that his response would cause a universal outcry. In 1751, Rousseau wrote to Toussaint-Pierre Lenieps, describing criticisms he had received for his treatment of *commerce doux* in the *First Discourse*. Lenieps was a kindred spirit, eighteen years older than Rousseau, and another Genevan brought up on Calvinism and Plutarch, living in exile in Paris. Like Rousseau, Lenieps was hugely critical of both *commerce doux* and the Genevan government, believing that it was anything but gentle. Once a perfect democracy, he thought it was now a vile oligarchy. Lenieps felt he had a moral responsibility to fight back.[15]

[13] William Wordsworth, 'My heart leaps up when I behold' [1802], *The Major Works*, ed. Stephen Gill (Oxford: OUP, 2008), 246.

[14] Rowland, *Romanticism and Childhood*, 14.

[15] Helena Rosenblatt, *Rousseau and Geneva: From the First Discourse to the Social Contract, 1749–1762* (Cambridge: CUP, 1997), 75–6.

It was on the back of his dialogue with Lenieps and the negative reception of the *First Discourse* that Rousseau entered another competition at the Academy in 1754, answering the question: 'What is the origin of inequality among people, and is it authorized by natural law?' He had also been rereading the Bible.[16] Rousseau invoked Jean Calvin's idealized Christian commonwealth when he dedicated his *Second Discourse* 'to the Republic of Geneva' and its 'magnificent, most honoured and sovereign Lords'. He continued:

> Having the good fortune to be born among you, how could I reflect on the equality that nature has placed in men and the inequality they themselves have instituted, without reflecting on the deep wisdom with which both, felicitously combined in this city-state, work together, in a fashion closest to natural law, and most favourable to society.[17]
>
> (Ayant eu le bonheur de naître parmi vous, comment pourrais-je méditer sur l'égalité que la nature a mise entre les hommes et sur l'inégalité qu'ils ont instituée, sans penser à la profonde sagesse avec laquelle l'une et l'autre, heureusement combinées dans cet État, concourent de la manière la plus approchante de la loi naturelle et la plus favorable à la societé.[18])

The lavish praise of Rousseau's dedication had a heavy and pointed irony. To his mind, eighteenth-century Geneva was a disaster—profoundly fallen and unequal—but it was also able to represent a lost utopian ideal.[19]

He began by identifying two types of inequality: one natural, the other moral or political. Of the former, he argued, it is absurd to enquire after the cause: 'one cannot ask what the source of natural inequality is because the answer is expressed by the very definition of the word'.[20] Turning to moral and political inequality, he declared his wish to identify not a cause but a point of inception. The aim was to find the elusive, but pivotal, moment of disaster:

[16] Rosenblatt, *Rousseau and Geneva*, 47.

[17] Jean-Jacques Rousseau, *Discourse on the Origin of Inequality* [1755], tr. Franklin Phillip (Oxford: OUP, 2009), 3.

[18] Jean-Jacques Rousseau, *Discours sur l'origine et les fondements d l'inégalité parmi les hommes*, ed. Gérard Mairet (Paris: Le Livre de Poche, 1996), 59.

[19] For a reading of the influence of Genesis 1–3 on Rousseau's utopian thought in the *Second Discourse* see Acosta, *Reading Genesis in the Long Eighteenth Century*, 89–127.

[20] Rousseau, *Discourse on the Origin of Inequality* [1755], 23–4; 'On ne peut pas demander quelle est la source d'inégalité naturelle, parce que le réponse se trouverait énoncée dans la simple définition du mot.' Rousseau, *Discours sur l'origine d l'inégalité*, 77.

> To pinpoint the moment in the development of events when right replaced violence and nature was subjected to law, and to explain by what sequence of marvellous events the strong could resolve to serve the weak and the people to purchase a semblance of peace at the price of true felicity.[21]
>
> (De marquer dans le progrès des choses le moment où le droit succédant à la violence, la nature fut soumise à la loi; d'expliquer par quel enchaînement des prodiges le fort put se résoudre à servir le faible, et le peuple à acheter un repos en idée, au prix d'une félicité réelle.[22])

Rousseau drew his structure from Genesis 3, imagining a happy state that had been suddenly lost. Just as Eve might be seen to have made a foolish trade in giving up Paradise for the promise that she would be like God, so he suggests the people have sold something genuinely good for something they (wrongly) hoped might be better. The French makes the shift from nature to culture more explicit: what is translated here as 'semblance' is the French *idée*, which more clearly suggests a constructed notion. People have traded a real happiness for a collective fantasy: the coded web of constructions of meaning that we call culture. Rousseau's 'sequence of marvellous events' is another reconfiguration of the exile from Eden. This is the fall into culture: the encrustation of civility on the living body of man.

The fall into culture becomes a formal as well as thematic concern of Rousseau's writing. His desire to pinpoint the moment of catastrophe enables a form of historical narrative that is pseudohistorical, setting aside facts in favour of construct. Rousseau talks openly about the need for constructs to make sense of shapeless existence. Philosophers, he says, have long talked about getting back to a state of nature (*remonter jusqu'à l'état de nature*) without ever having been able to get there. The etymology of Rousseau's French *remonter* (Old French; *re* + *monter*; climb up or ascend again) implies a quest for something out of reach. For Rousseau, the state of nature is an obvious construct of culture. But he tells us this doesn't matter: 'Let us begin by setting aside all the facts, for they have no bearing on this question.'[23] What matters to pseudohistory isn't fact but fiction. And the fiction turns on that pivotal 'moment' which Rousseau sets out to find.

[21] Rousseau, *Discourse on the Origin of Inequality*, 23–4.

[22] *Discours sur l'origine d l'inégalité*, 78.

[23] Rousseau, *Discourse on the Origin of Inequality*, 24; 'Commençons donc par écarter tous les faits, car ils ne touchent point à la question.' *Discours sur l'origine d l'inégalité*, 78.

In a typically eighteenth-century move, he makes sense of the long durée of human history by imagining it in terms of a single human lifespan: 'There is, I think, an age at which the individual would like to go on unchanged; you are going to seek the age at which you would wish your whole species had remained.'[24] He is clear that imagining this 'age' as a particular point in time is a fiction. Moreover, he accepts that such artifice is defensive.

> I proceed in a flash across many centuries, forced by the passage of time, the profusion of things I have to say, and the almost imperceptible progress of the beginnings of things—for the more slowly the events unfolded, the more rapidly they may be described.[25]
>
> (Je parcours comme un trait des multitudes de siècles, forcé par le temps qui s'écoule, par l'abondance des choses que j'ai à dire, et par le progrès presque insensible des commencements; car plus les événements étaient lents à se succéder, plus ils sont prompts à décrire.[26])

In other words, it is the very impossibility of pinpointing a single moment of disaster in the long span of evolutionary time that forces him to artificially construct it. Disasters feel as if they come upon us suddenly *because* change happens so slowly. To imagine an 'age' or a 'moment' is an exertion of authorial control. The extreme slowness of evolution makes no sense. So, Rousseau declares, we must think in terms of moments and stages, origins and progress, in order to make it make sense.

Rousseau defines the ideal state of society as a moment of pubescence—a point just before the catastrophic fall. This, he declares was the inception of the family: 'this new situation which brought together husbands and wives, fathers and children, in a common dwelling.'[27] It was family, he contends, that became the first model of society. In this state, individual power was replaced with the strength of mutual cooperation and affection: 'though each one became less fit to contend with wild beasts, it was easier, on the other hand, to cluster together to resist them jointly.'[28] And yet, even this ideal state was not

[24] Rousseau, *Discourse on the Origin of Inequality*, 25; 'Il y a, je le sens, un âge auquel l'homme individuel voudrait s'arrêter; tu chercheras l'âge auquel tu désirerais que ton espèce se fût arrêtée.' *Discours sur l'origine d l'inégalité*, 79.

[25] Rousseau, *Discourse on the Origin of Inequality*, 58.

[26] Rousseau, *Discours sur l'origine d l'inégalité*, 110.

[27] Rousseau, *Discourse on the Origin of Inequality*, 58; 'l'effet d'une situation nouvelle qui réunissait dans une habitation commune les maris et les femmes, les pères et les enfants.' Rousseau, *Discours sur l'origine d l'inégalité*, 110.

[28] Rousseau, *Discourse on the Origin of Inequality*, 59; 'mais si chacun séparément devint moins propre à combattre les bêtes sauvages, en revanche il fut plus aisé de s'assembler pour leur resister en commun.' Rousseau, *Discours sur l'origine d l'inégalité*, 110–11.

wholly defined by innocence. Like many other exegetes, he locates the seeds of human downfall in idleness and ease:

> In this new state, with its simple and solitary life, with very few needs and very few tools invented to meet them, men enjoyed a good deal of leisure and used it to procure for themselves many conveniences unknown to their forefathers; and this was the first yoke they unwittingly imposed on themselves and the first source of the evils they were preparing for their descendants.[29]
>
> (Dans ce nouvel état, avec une vie simple et solitaire, des besoins très bornés, et les instruments qu'ils avaient inventés pour y pourvoir, les hommes jouissant d'un fort grand loisir l'employèrent à se procurer plusieurs sortes de commodités inconnues à leurs pères; et ce fut là le premier joug qu'ils s'imposèrent sans y songer, et la première source de maux qu'ils préparèrent à leurs descendants.[30])

Even as Rousseau strives to identify the moment of collapse, he acknowledges that its suddenness is false. Changes that seem good turn out to be disastrous:

> From seeing each other, people cannot do without seeing each other even more. A tender and sweet disposition steals into their souls and, at the least opposition, becomes a raging fury; jealousy awakens with love; discord triumphs and the sweetest of passions receives the sacrifice of human blood.'[31]
>
> (À force de se voir, on ne peut plus se passer de se voir encore. Un sentiment tendre et doux s'insinue dans l'âme, et par la moindre opposition devient une fureur impétueuse: la jalousie s'éveille avec l'amour; la discorde triomphe et la plus douce des passions reçoit des sacrifices de sang humain.[32])

The fall into culture happens gradually—almost imperceptibly:

> As ideas and feeling succeeded one another, and hearts and minds were cultivated, the human race became more sociable, contacts increased and bonds grew tighter... Each person began to gaze on others and want to be gazed on himself, and what came to be prized was public esteem... this was the first step toward inequality and also toward vice. These first preferences

[29] Rousseau, *Discourse on the Origin of Inequality*, 59.
[30] Rousseau, *Discours sur l'origine d l'inégalité*, 111.
[31] Rousseau, *Discourse on the Origin of Inequality*, 60.
[32] Rousseau, *Discours sur l'origine d l'inégalité*, 112.

> gave rise, on the one side, to vanity and scorn, and on the other, to shame and envy; and the ferment produced by these new leavens eventually led to concoctions ruinous to happiness.[33]
>
> (À mesure que les idées et les sentiments se succèdent, que l'esprit et le coeur s'exercent, le genre humain continue à s'apprivoiser, les liaisons s'étendent et les liens se resserrent…Chacun commença à regarder les autres et à vouloir être regardé soi-même et l'estime publique eut un prix…et ce fut le premier pas vers l'inégalité, et vers le vice en même temps: de ces premières préférences naquirent d'un côté la vanité et le mépris, de l'autre la honte et l'envie; et la fermentation causée par ces nouveaux levains produisit enfin des composés funestes au bonheur et à l'innocence.[34])

The moment that Rousseau sets out to find passes unnoticed. But, in order to make sense of social inequality, the *Second Discourse* carries the fall narrative from sacred myth to secular pseudohistory. We console our modern discontent by imagining an instant where we can believe it all went wrong.

The manifestly imperfect condition of Rousseau's pre-lapsarian state leads Dena Goodman to argue that the *Second Discourse* is definitely *not* a fall narrative. There is, she rightly observes, no real fall from grace, only a loss of equilibrium.[35] In the state Rousseau imagines optimal, the golden age which follows the state of nature and precedes the state of culture, things are not faultless, they are just held in balance: 'this period in the development of human faculties, striking a good balance the indolence of the primitive state and the fervid activity of our own vanity must have been the happiest and most enduring age'.[36] And yet the architecture Rousseau imposes on this secular pseudohistory is residually religious, and clearly taken from Genesis 3: 'man can have left it only as the result of some fatal accident that, for the common good, ought never to have happened'.[37]

One of the effects of Rousseau's secularization of the Fall is to counter progressivism with nostalgia. Lost equilibrium can be seen as a secular version of

[33] Rousseau, *Discourse on the Origin of Inequality*, 60.

[34] Rousseau, *Discours sur l'origine d l'inégalité*, 112.

[35] Dena Goodman, *Criticism in Action: Enlightenment Experiments in Political Writing* (Ithaca, NY: Cornell University Press, 1989), 134–66, 155.

[36] Rousseau, *Discourse on the Origin of Inequality*, 61–2; 'cette période du développement des facultés humaines, tenant un juste milieu entre l'indolence de l'état primitif et la pétulante activité de notre amour-propre, dut être l'époque la plus heureuse et la plus durable'. Rousseau, *Discours sur l'origine d l'inégalité*, 113.

[37] Rousseau, *Discourse on the Origin of Inequality*, 62; 'qu'il n'en a dû sortir que par quelque funeste hasard qui pour l'utilité commune êut dû ne jamais arriver'. Rousseau, *Discours sur l'origine d l'inégalité*, 113.

the fall from grace at least partly because the *Second Discourse* fiercely contends progressive notions of history with a story of decline: 'all subsequent advances appear to be so many steps toward improvement of the individual but [are], in fact, towards the enfeeblement of the species.'[38] What Rousseau really wants to be able to do is to stop the clock. The desire to pinpoint a moment of catastrophe, to go back, recover an imagined golden age and make time stand still is a reaction to the onslaught of shapeless, secular, time, where disasters feel sudden and uncontrollable precisely because they happen with imperceptible, unstoppable, and irreversible slowness.

There is therefore a feeling of grim and unwanted inevitability in Rousseau's narrative:

> But from the moment one man needed help from another, and as soon as they found it useful for one man to have provisions enough for two, equality evaporated, property was introduced, and work became mandatory; vast forests were transformed into sunny open country that had to be watered with the sweat of man, and where slavery and adversity were soon seen to germinate and ripen with crops.[39]
>
> (mais dès l'instant qu'un homme eut besoin du secours d'un autre; dès qu'on s'aperçut qu'il était utile à un seul d'avoir des provisions pour deux, l'égalité disparut, la propriété s'introduisit, le travail devint nécessaire et les vastes forêts se changèrent en des campagnes riantes qu'il fallut arroser à la sueur des hommes, er dans lesquelles on vit bientôt l'esclavage et la misère germer et croître avec les moissons.[40])

The *Second Discourse* ends with an image of circular sacred time hijacked by progressive secular time. For Rousseau, inequality will eventually lead to despotism, which reinstigates a warped version of the state of nature through merciless oppression:

> This is the final stage of inequality, the extreme point that closes the circle and links up with the point from which we set out. Here, all individuals become equal again because they are nothing…everything is brought back solely to the law of the strongest.[41]

[38] Rousseau, *Discourse on the Origin of Inequality*, 62; 'et que tous le progress ultérieurs ont été en apparence autant de pas vers la perfection de l'individu, et en effet vers la decrepitude de l'espèce,' Rousseau, *Discours sur l'origine d l'inégalité*, 113.

[39] Rousseau, *Discourse on the Origin of Inequality*, 62.

[40] Rousseau, *Discours sur l'origine d l'inégalité*, 114.

[41] Rousseau, *Discourse on the Origin of Inequality*, 82.

(C'est ici le dernier terme de l'inégalité, et le point extrême qui ferme le cercle et touche au point d'où nous sommes partis. C'est ici que tous les particuliers redeviennent égaux parce qu'ils ne sont rien…tout se ramène à la seule loi du plus fort.[42])

The circle closes in a horrifying parody of pre-lapsarian return: 'the one was the state of nature in its pure form and the other the fruit of excessive corruption.'[43]

And so, Rousseau arrives at the justification for his efforts. These states look the same but, in truth, they could not be more different. What Rousseau's pseudohistory has done is expose the fiction of pre-lapsarian return and the artifice of the Fall as a construct which keeps such notions of innocence alive. There can be no turning back or stopping of the clock. Changes are real and irreversible:

the human race of one era is not the human race of another…savage and civilised man differ so much in the depths of their hearts and in their inclinations that what constitutes the supreme bliss of one would drive the other to despair.[44]

(le genre humain d'un âge n'étant pas le genre humain d'un autre âge…l'homme sauvage et l'homme policé diffèrent tellement par le fond du coeur et des inclinations que ce qui fait le bonheur suprême de l'un réduirait l'autre au désespoir.[45])

It has also exposed the fiction of positive progression:

I have endeavoured to set out the origin and progression of inequality… inequality, being almost non-existent in the state of nature, derives its strength and growth from the development of our faculties and the progress of the human mind, and eventually becomes stable and legitimate through the institution of property and laws…for it is manifestly contrary to the state of nature, however it is defined, that a child should rule over an old man, that an idiot should guide a wise man, and that a handful of men

[42] Rousseau, *Discours sur l'origine d l'inégalité*, 131.

[43] Rousseau, *Discourse on the Origin of Inequality*, 82; 'l'un était l'état de nature dans sa pureté, et que ce dernier est le fruit d'un excès de corruption.' Rousseau, *Discours sur l'origine d l'inégalité*, 131.

[44] Rousseau, *Discourse on the Origin of Inequality*, 83.

[45] Rousseau, *Discours sur l'origine d l'inégalité*, 132.

> should gorge themselves with superfluities while the starving multitude goes in want of necessities.[46]
>
> (J'ai tâché d'exposer l'origine et le progrès d'inégalité...l'inégalité, étant presque nulle dans l'état de nature, tire sa force et son accroissement du développement de nos facultés et des progrès de l'esprit humain et devient enfin stable et légitime par l'établissement de la propriété et des lois...puisqu'il est manifestement contre la loi de nature, de quelque manière qu'on la définisse, qu'un enfant commande à un vieillard, qu'un imbécile conduise un homme sage et qu'une poignée de gens regorge de superfluités, tandis que la multitude affamée manque du nécessaire.[47])

The *Second Discourse* closes with a deeply pessimistic indictment of culture which carries the mythic architecture of Genesis 3 into secular pseudohistory in order to convey the profound fallenness of civilization while simultaneously destroying any illusion of salvific return.

Getting the Moment Right: *Émile, or On Education* (1763)

Rousseau's educational treatise, *Émile or On Education*, gave more credence to the notion that maturity, if it happens at the right time, might be a fortunate, rather than catastrophic, fall into knowledge. The book begins with an allusion to Genesis 1–3: 'Everything is good as it leaves the hands of the Author of things; everything degenerates in the hands of man.'[48] Anticipating Darwin, he presents nature as an authorial principle modelled on the Creator-God of Genesis 1 and cultured man as a fallen writer, confusing the ordered creation that God called 'good' with artificial selection and monstrous miscegenation:

> He forces one soil to nourish the products of another, one tree to bear the fruit of another. He mixes and confuses the climates, the elements, the seasons. He mutilates his dog, his horse, his slave. He turns everything upside down; he disfigures everything; he loves deformity, monsters.[49]

[46] Rousseau, *Discourse on the Origin of Inequality*, 84–5.
[47] Rousseau, *Discours sur l'origine d l'inégalité*, 133.
[48] Jean-Jacques Rousseau, *Émile, or On Education* [1763], tr. Allan Bloom (London: Penguin, 1991), 37; 'Tout est bien sortant des mains de l'Auteur des choses, tout dégénère entre les mains de l'homme.' Rousseau, *Émile, ou de l'Éducation, nouvelle edition avec les variants et des notes* (Paris: Charpentier, Libraire-Éditeur, 1848), 7.
[49] Rousseau, *Émile*, 37.

(Il force une terre à nourrir les productions d'une autre, un arbre à porter les fruits d'un autre; il mêle et confond les climats, les éléments, les saisons; il mutile son chien, son cheval, son esclave; il bouleverse tout, il défigure tout, il aime la difformité, les monstres.[50])

This confusion and misapplication of creative energy is profoundly dangerous. Every attempt to give form deforms the world. But most distasteful is the relish with which cultured, modern man views his handiwork. Rousseau suggests an egotistical blindness to culture, a misplaced faith in innovation and progress, which results in chaos and horror. His sophisticated modern man is one of the antecedents of Mary Shelley's Frankenstein, the modern Prometheus, who makes a monster out of individually beautiful body parts.[51]

Education belongs to the fallen world of culture and so the most it can do is cultivate a parody of natural goodness. But Rousseau maintains that it is precisely because the world has gone so wrong that careful education, from birth, is a necessary evil:

> Were he not to do this, however, everything would go even worse, and our species does not admit of being formed halfway. In the present state of things a man abandoned to himself in the midst of other men from birth would be the most disfigured of all. Prejudices, authority, necessity, example, all the social institutions in which we find ourselves submerged would stifle nature in him and put nothing in its place. Nature there would be like a shrub that chance had caused to be born in the middle of a path and that passers-by soon cause to perish by bumping into it from all sides and bending it in every direction.[52]
>
> (Sans cela, tout irait plus mal encore, et notre espèce ne veut pas être façonnée à demi. Dans l'état où sont désormais les choses, un homme abandonné dès sa naissance à lui-même parmi les autres serait le plus défiguré de tous. Les préjugés, l'autorité, la nécessité, l'exemple, toutes les institutions sociales dans lesquelles nous nous trouvons submergés, étoufferaient en lui la nature, et ne mettraient rien à la place. Elle y serait comme un arbrisseau que le hasard fait naître au milieu d'un chemin, et que les passants font bientôt périr, en le heurtant de toutes parts et le pliant dans tous les sens.[53])

[50] Rousseau, *Émile ou de l'Éducation*, 7.

[51] Mary Shelley, *Frankenstein, or the Modern Prometheus* [1818], ed. D. L. Macdonald and Kathleen Scherf (London: Broadview, 2012), 83.

[52] Rousseau, *Émile*, 37.

[53] Rousseau, *Émile ou de l'Éducation*, 7.

Émile advocates a very careful process of readying so that the child may leave the garden of their childhood at the right time.

Rousseau draws a clear distinction between physical and mental exposure. The former is strongly encouraged:

> From the moment the child breathes on leaving its envelope, do not suffer his being given other envelopes which keep him more restricted: no caps, no belts, no swaddling; loose and large diapers which leave all his limbs free and are neither so heavy as to impede his movements nor so hot as to prevent him from feeling the impressions of the air. Put him in a large well-padded cradle, where he can move at ease and without danger. When he begins to grow stronger, let him crawl around the room. Let him spread out, stretch his little limbs. You will see them gaining strength day by day.[54]
>
> (Au moment que l'enfant respire en sortant de ses enveloppes, ne souffrez pas qu'on lui en donne d'autres qui le tiennent plus à l'étroit. Point de têtières, point de bandes, point de maillot; des langes flottants et larges, qui laissent tous ses membres en liberté, et ne soient ni assez pesants pour gêner ses mouvements, ni assez chauds pour empêcher qu'il ne sente les impressions de l'air. Placez-le dans un grand berceau bien rembourré, où il puisse se mouvoir à l'aise et sans danger. Quand il commence à se fortifier, laissez-le ramper par la chambre; laissez-lui développer, étendre ses petits membres; vous les verrez se renforcer de jour en jour.[55])

His emphasis on physical childhood freedoms is not an abandonment of parental control. The 'large well-padded cradle' provides an intermediary space between womb and world, a measured and controlled environment in which harm is kept at bay. As the child grows, sterner exposure to natural childhood illnesses is encouraged. Nature is a hard but beneficial teacher, producing toughness and resilience: 'The tests passed, the child has gained strength.'[56] Rousseau criticizes the soft, overprotective mother, whose short-term kindness is long-term cruelty: 'She preserves him for a moment from a few discomforts without thinking about how many mishaps and perils she is thereby accumulating for him to bear later.'[57] There is, for Rousseau, no such

[54] Rousseau, *Émile*, 60. [55] Rousseau, *Émile ou de l'Éducation*, 47.

[56] Rousseau, *Émile*, 47; 'Les épreuves faites, l'enfant a gagné des forces', Rousseau, *Émile ou de l'Éducation*, 25.

[57] Rousseau, *Émile*, 47; 'Elle le préserve un moment, elle accumule au loin d'accidents et de périls sur sa tête', Rousseau, *Émile ou de l'Éducation*, 24.

thing as premature physical development. 'Children', he maintains, can have 'the same agility in limbs as a man can have'.[58]

Émile's tutor, autobiographically named Jean-Jacques, is much more worried about exposing Émile to society than exposing him to the elements. He anticipates the charge of inconsistency:

> I will be told that I fall here, with respect to the body, into the mistake of premature culture of children which I criticise with respect to the mind. The difference is very great, for progress in one area is only apparent, but in the other it is real.[59]
>
> (On me dira que je tombe ici, par rapport au corps, dans le défaut de la culture prématurée que je blâme dans les enfants par rapport à l'esprit. La différence est très grande; car l'un de ces progrès n'est qu'apparent, mais l'autre est réel.[60])

In arguing against mental precocity, Rousseau was in dialogue with John Locke. In his *Essay Concerning Human Understanding* (1689), Locke had described a colony of young children who have no knowledge of God but will come to it through reason, enquiry, and social interaction.[61] The children left alone on the island was a lastingly influential image but Rousseau, sceptical of social influences, puts his faith in the isolated child not the colony of children; thus, *Robinson Crusoe*, the story of the child left alone on the island, is the only book Émile has permission to read. But Rousseau's main quarrel with Locke is a quarrel about timing:

> To reason with children was Locke's great maxim...The masterpiece of a good education is to make a reasonable man, and they claim to raise a child by reason! This is to begin at the end, to want to make the product, the instrument. If children understood reason, they would not need to be raised.[62]
>
> (Raisonner avec les enfants, était la grande maxime de Locke...Le chef-d'œuvre d'une bonne éducation est de faire un homme raisonnable: et l'on prétend élever un enfant par la raison! C'est commencer par la fin, c'est

[58] Rousseau, *Émile*, 147; 'Des enfants...avoir dans les membres la même agilité que peut avoir un homme', Rousseau, *Émile ou de l'Éducation*, 190.

[59] Rousseau, *Émile*, p. 147.

[60] Rousseau, *Émile ou de l'Éducation*, 191.

[61] John Locke, *An Essay Concerning Human Understanding* [1689], ed. Roger Woolhouse (London: Penguin, 1997), 98–107.

[62] Rousseau, *Émile*, 89.

vouloir faire l'instrument de l'ouvrage. Si les enfants entendaient raison, ils n'auraient pas besoin d'être élevés[63]).

For Rousseau, precocity, or premature exposure to reason, precipitates a catastrophic fall: 'Nature wants children to be children before being men. If we want to pervert this order, we shall produce precocious fruits which will be immature and insipid and will not be long in rotting.'[64] Thus, Rousseau affirms: 'Treat your pupil according to his age.'[65]

Adam and Eve are taught obedience through prohibition and deterrence: 'And the woman said unto the serpent, We may eat of the fruit trees of the garden: But of the fruit of the tree which is in the midst of the garden, God hath said, Ye shall not eat of it, neither shall ye touch it, lest ye die.'[66] They learn the cost of disobedience and the supreme authority of God when they transgress and lose their right to the bountiful fruit of Eden: 'thorns and thistles shall it [the earth] bring forth to thee; and thou shalt eat the herb of the field.'[67] Rousseau suggests that good parenting follows a very different route to that taken by the authoritarian Father-God of Genesis:

> let him not know what obedience is when he acts nor what dominion is when one acts for him. Let him sense his liberty equally in his actions and in yours... do so in such a way that he receives your services as a sort of humiliation and longs for the moment when he can do without them and have the honour of serving himself.[68]
>
> (Qu'il ne sache ce que c'est qu'obéissance quand il agit, ni ce que c'est qu'empire quand on agit pour lui... qu'en recevant vos services avec une sorte d'humiliation, il aspire au moment où il pourra s'en passer, et où il aura l'honneur de se servir lui-même.[69])

Children comply with authority because they don't know it exists. Instead of forcing obedience through prohibition and deterrence, he imagines it occurring naturally and effortlessly. Émile is not forced to define his freedom as an act of rebellion, and because he feels free enough, he will accept the limits of his reach. In this model of ideal development, children eventually want to

63 Rousseau, *Émile ou de l'Éducation*, 92.

64 Rousseau, *Émile*, p. 90. 'La nature veut que les enfants soient enfants avant que d'être hommes. Si nous voulons pervertir cet ordre, nous produirons des fruits précoces, qui n'auront ni maturité ni saveur, et ne tarderont pas à se corrompre:' Rousseau, *Émile ou de l'Éducation*, p. 93.

65 Rousseau, *Émile*, 91; 'Traitez votre élève selon son âge.' Rousseau, *Émile ou de l'Éducation*, 95.

66 Gen. 3: 2–3.

67 Gen. 3: 18.

68 Rousseau, *Émile*, 85–6.

69 Rousseau, *Émile ou de l'Éducation*, 85–6.

author their own existence not because they feel defiant but because they become reasonable, competent creatures who are embarrassed to be dependent on others. Rousseau suggests that maturity can be a fortunate fall into knowledge, but only if it happens at the right time. In an ideal coming-of-age, the child's eyes will be opened and he will not only know good and evil, he will be able to choose good.[70]

The potential disaster Rousseau imagines in developing Émile's mind too fast is the original version of that premature social exposure repeatedly dramatized by other Enlightenment, Romantic, and Victorian writers. Voltaire's Candide and Goethe's Young Werther are thrust into the world of experience in a comedy or tragedy of unpreparedness. Mary Wollstonecraft argues furiously against Rousseau's treatment of women but nonetheless agrees with him on the dangers of precocity:

> The female understanding has often been spoken of with contempt, as arriving sooner at maturity than the male. I... only appeal to experience to decide whether young men who are early introduced into company (and examples now abound), do not acquire the same precocity. So notorious is this fact, that the bare mentioning of it must bring before people, who at all mix in the world, the idea of a number of swaggering apes of men, whose understandings are narrowed by being brought into the society of men when they ought to have been spinning a top or twirling a hoop.[71]

Her daughter, Mary Shelley, grieving for her lost mother and her own lost infant daughter, conceives of horror manifesting in a new-born adult man, who has never had a childhood or known a mother and whose final act is to throw himself to his death in a parody of the Fall.[72] William Wordsworth begins *The Excursion* with an apology, hoping that the poem, though unfinished, and therefore imperfect, might not be thought premature.[73] George Eliot, a reader of Rousseau, Wollstonecraft, Shelley, and Wordsworth, ends book two of *The Mill on the Floss* by bringing the tragedy of prematurity into the realist novel. Forced by economic circumstance, Maggie and Tom leave the garden of their childhood too soon:

[70] 'For God doth know that in the day ye eat thereof, then your eyes shall be opened, and ye shall be as gods, knowing good and evil.' Gen. 3: 5.

[71] Mary Wollstonecraft, *A Vindication of the Rights of Woman* and *A Vindication of the Rights of Man* ed. Janet Todd (Oxford: OUP, 1993), 140.

[72] Shelley, *Frankenstein*, 221.

[73] William Wordsworth, *The Excursion*, ed. Sally Bushell, James A. Butler, and Michael C. Jaye with the assistance of David Garcia (Ithaca, NY, and London: Cornell University Press, 2007), 37.

> The two slight youthful figures soon grew indistinct on the distant road—were soon lost behind the projecting hedgerow.
>
> They had gone forth together into a new life of sorrow, and they would never more see the sunshine undimmed by remembered cares. They had entered the thorny wilderness, and the golden gates of their childhood had forever closed behind them.[74]

Echoing the end of *Paradise Lost*, Eliot emphasizes the catastrophe that inheres in prematurity and precocity. For maturity to be a fortunate fall, innocence must be protected until the child is ready to grow up.

Righting and Rewriting the Moment: *Confessions* (1769)

One of the most striking things about the *Confessions* is just how often Jean-Jacques falls. The revelation on the road to Vincennes is just one of many transformative moments in the book framed by the mythology of Genesis 3. Soon after he tells us that 'the whole of the rest of my life, and all of my misfortunes were the inevitable effect of this aberration' he presents another catastrophic fall: 'a terrible and fateful epoch in a fate of which there is no other example among mortal men'.[75] 'As the reader knows, I repeat myself' confesses Jean-Jacques, 'it must be so'.[76] But nothing is repeated with the same obsessive energy as the ever-returning moment of complete and life-changing disaster, which is then, almost as quickly, overwritten.[77] Halfway through book 1 Jean-Jacques announces the end of his childhood with an inflated allusion to the world-changing discord of Genesis 3:

> Never again did I enjoy pure happiness...We stayed on in Bossey a few months. We lived there as we are told the first man did, when he was still in his earthly paradise but had ceased to enjoy it. Everything appeared the same, but in fact belonged to quite a different order of being...we began to

[74] George Eliot, *The Mill on the Floss*, ed. Juliette Atkinson (Oxford: OUP, 2015), 180.

[75] Rousseau, *Confessions*, 342, 408; 'Tout le reste de ma vie et de mes malheurs fut l'effet inévitable de cet instant d'égarement', Rousseau, *Les Confessions*, vol. 2, 126; 'époque terrible et fatale d'un sort qui n'a point d'exemple chez les mortels'; Rousseau, *Les Confessions*, vol. 2, 221. Rousseau completed the work in 1769 but it was first published in 1782, four years after his death.

[76] Rousseau, *Confessions*, 404–5; 'Je me répète, on le sait; il le faut', Rousseau, *Les Confessions*, vol. 2, 217.

[77] D. G. Wright notes a representative though not exhaustive range of examples in the *Confessions*. D. G. Wright, 'Rousseau's *Confessions*: The Tragedy of Teleology', *Journal of Social and Political Thought* 1.4 (Jan. 2003). http://www.yorku.ca/jspot/4/rousseau.html

> dissemble, to rebel, to lie ... we stopped tending our little plot, our herbs, our flowers ... we left ... each side weary of the other, and not sorry to separate.[78]
>
> (Dès ce moment je cessai de jouir d'un bonheur pur ... Nous restâmes encore à Bossey quelques mois. Nous y fûmes comme on nous représente le premier homme encore dans le paradis terrestre, mais ayant cessé d'en jouir: c'était en apparence la même situation, et en effet une tout autre manière d'être ... nous commencions à nous cacher, à nous mutiner, à mentir ... Nous cessâmes de cultiver nos petits jardins, nos herbes, nos fleurs ... nous nous séparâmes ... rassasiés les uns des autres, et regrettant peu de nous quitter.[79])

And yet this is not the first time he has fallen. Bossey is Edenic but it is also the environment in which the child first experiences sexual desire—excited too early, and in a warped manner, by the spankings he receives from his nurse:

> Who would have believed that this childhood punishment, meted out to a boy of eight years by a young woman of thirty, should have decided my tastes, my desires, my passions, my whole self, for the rest of my life, and in a direction that was precisely the opposite of what might naturally be expected.[80]
>
> (Qui croirant que le châtiment d'enfant, reçu à huit ans par la main d'une fille de trente, a décidé de mes goûts, de mes désirs, de mes passions, de moi pour le reste de ma vie, et cela précisément dans le sens contraire à ce qui devait s'ensuivre naturellement?[81])

Like the revelation on the road to Vincennes, this early corruption exposes, perverts, and preserves an innocence in Jean-Jacques's character: 'This bizarre taste, which persisted beyond adolescence and indeed drove me to the verge of depravity and madness, nevertheless preserved in me those very standards of upright behaviour which it might have been expected to undermine.'[82]

The moment of fall proliferates in Jean-Jacques's subsequent account of his life, always with some sort of saving grace. As Avrom Fleischman writes: 'the *Confessions* can be seen as a succession of Edenesque landscapes, in each of

[78] Rousseau, *Confessions*, 20.
[79] Rousseau, *Les Confessions*, vol. 1, 47–8.
[80] Rousseau, *Confessions*, 15.
[81] Rousseau, *Les Confessions*, vol. 1, 41.
[82] Rousseau, *Confessions*, 15; 'Même après l'âge nubile, ce goût bizarre, toujours persistant et porté jusqu'à la dépravation, jusqu'à la folie, m'a conservé les moeurs honnêtes qu'il semblerait avoir dû m'ôter', Rousseau, *Les Confessions*, vol. 1, 42.

which primal innocence and happiness are partially achieved, invariably followed by a fall—merited or unmerited—and expulsion.'[83] The result is that the catastrophic fall, which Rousseau so frequently invokes, undoes itself each time. It is never completely disastrous and presented in such a way as to expose what Rousseau imagines to be natural, though regularly misdirected, goodness. If the theoretical form of the educational treatise allowed Rousseau to indulge his most optimistic vision of a possible fortunate fall, the autobiographical form of the *Confessions* enabled him to rehearse his anxieties about the authenticity and original goodness of the self in the mediated world of writing and representation.

'I was born almost dying', Jean-Jacques declares.[84] Rousseau's birth was difficult. The child was born sickly and his mother died as a result of her labour. His *Confessions* are piloted by the guilt and grief of this original trauma and Jean-Jacques presents the very moment of his origin as blighted. In Rousseau's account of his own life-story there is no perfect beginning, no uncorrupted moment of innocence and nascent possibility. He is fallen from the start: 'I cost my mother her life, and my birth was the first of my misfortunes.'[85] Arguably, Jean-Jacques never finds the right moment of maturity because he has never had the kind of protected and innocent childhood advocated in *Émile*. Brought up by his father, Jean-Jacques's childhood is prematurely, and, he claims, dangerously, but it also seems, pleasurably, adult. His early years provide a deliberate and striking contrast to the model presented in *Émile*. Émile's conditions are carefully controlled, his imaginative tendencies rigorously suppressed, but there is no wall around Jean-Jacques's childhood garden. Where Émile is allowed only one book (*Robinson Crusoe*), Jean-Jacques reads unchecked:

> My mother had left some romances. We began to read them after supper, my father and I. Our intention was simply that I should practice my reading with the help of some entertaining books; but we soon became so engrossed in them that we spent whole nights taking it in turns to read to one another without interruption, unable to break off until we had finished the whole volume. Sometimes my father, hearing the swallows at dawn, would say shamefacedly: 'We'd better go to bed now; I'm more of a child than you are.'[86]

[83] Avrom Fleischman, *Figures of Autobiography* (Berkeley, Calif.: University of California Press, 1983), 95.

[84] Rousseau, *Confessions*, 7; 'J'étais né presque mourant', Rousseau, *Les Confessions*, vol. 1, 29.

[85] Rousseau, *Confessions*, 7; 'Je coûtai la vie à ma mère, et ma naissance fut le premier de mes malheurs', Rousseau, *Les Confessions*, vol. 1, 28.

[86] Rousseau, *Confessions*, 8.

> (Ma mère avait laissé des romans. Nous nous mîmes à les lire après souper, mon père et moi. Il n'était question d'abord que m'exercer à la lecture par des livres amusants, mais bientôt I'intérêt devint si vif, que nous lisions tour à tour sans relâche, et passions les nuits à cette occupation. Nous ne pouvions jamais quitter qu'à la fin du volume. Quelquefois mon père, entendant le matin les hirondelles, disait tout honteux: 'Allons nous coucher; je suis plus enfant que toi.'[87])

In the place of the mother are her books; in the place of the father is the child. Jean-Jacques's original trauma becomes a trauma of origins: the lost parent is a continually present absence. Jean-Jacques is a vital (yet inadequate) replacement for his lost mother, just as his father's tenderness is a vital (yet inadequate) replacement for the absence of maternal love:

> He thought he could see my mother in me, without being able to forget that I had deprived him of her; he never caressed me without my sensing, from his sighs, from his urgent embraces, that a bitter regret was mingled with them, for which, however, they were the more tender... 'Ah', he would sigh, bring her back to me, comfort me for losing her; fill the emptiness she has left in my soul. Would I love you as much if you were only my son?'[88]
>
> (Il croyait la revoir en moi, sans pouvoir oublier que je la lui avais ôtée; jamais il ne m'embrassa que je ne sentisse à ses soupirs, à ses convulsives étreintes, qu'un regret amer se mêlait à ses caresses... 'Ah! disait-il en gémissait, rends-la-moi, console-moi d'elle, remplis le vide qu'elle a laissé dans mon âme. T'aimerais je ainsi si tu n'étais que mon fils?'[89])

But, of course, the mother cannot be replaced, only represented. Representation, which contains within it the sense of making something absent present again, becomes an act of mourning which seeks to mediate the gap opened by loss but can never quite close it. Rousseau makes this loss the foundation not only of his writing but of *all* writing. In this scene, reading becomes a way of mourning his mother and it also opens an imaginative world of fantasy and fiction.

One way of understanding the repeated falls of the *Confessions* is through this unresolved grief. Jean-Jacques is always looking for mother figures and his erotic desires are self-consciously framed as part of this quest. As Jacques

[87] Rousseau, *Les Confessions*, vol. 1, 30.
[88] Rousseau, *Confessions*, 7.
[89] Rousseau, *Les Confessions*, vol. 1, 28.

Derrida observes, the boy's lover also comes to represent, and supplement, the lost mother:

> '*To supply the place* of my extinguished ambition, I needed a lively sentiment which should *fill* my heart. In a word, I needed a successor to mamma... *I found in Thérèse the supplement that I needed*.'
>
> Across this sequence of supplements a necessity is announced: that of an infinite chain, ineluctably multiplying the supplementary mediations that produce the sense of the very thing they defer: the mirage of the thing itself, of immediate presence, of originary perception. Immediacy is derived.[90]

Rousseau deplores the obstacles that get in his way, but he also needs them to define his desires. Derrida's gloss emphasizes the connection between Jean-Jacques's traumatic birth and the catch-22 hermeneutics of the fall into culture. In the act of trying to recover a lost original, he finds himself further removed. And yet, that is also as close as he can get.

In the passage from which Derrida quotes, Jean-Jacques is professing his desire to 'possess' Thérèse despite her lack of wholeness (she has just admitted that her hymen had been accidentally and innocently damaged in her youth). She has lost, therefore, her *pucelage* (unpenetratedness). Rousseau writes: 'Ah my Thérèse! I am only too glad to find you, whole and healthy, and not what I was not looking for'.[91] In finding Thérèse, Rousseau implies more than sex. Vitally alive, 'whole and healthy', she is a supplement to original wholeness, or perfection which is, to use Derrida's terms, 'always already' undone and, to use Rousseau's, 'not what [he] was looking for'. In place of the mother, perfect beginning, or nature, Rousseau puts Thérèse. The chain of maternal supplementation mourns through representation something Rousseau has never really known. The birth, which is almost death, like the child, or lover, who is not quite the mother, further embeds, and empties out, the sacred model of circular time within the secular: a narrative of return directed by the continuous presence of an original absence.

These maternal supplements allow for exciting, dangerous, premature excursions into passion and imagination, while paradoxically also keeping

[90] Derrida, *Of Grammatology*, 170–1. Italics and translation are Derrida's. 'Il me fallait à la place de l'ambition éteinte un sentiment vif qui remplît mon coeur. Il fallait, pour tout dire, un successeur à Maman... Je trouvai dans Thérèse le supplément dont j'avais besoin.' Rousseau, *Les Confessions*, vol. 2, 94–5.

[91] Rousseau, *Confessions*, 322; 'Ah! ma Thérèse, je suis trop heureux de te posséder sage et saine, et de ne pas trouver ce que je ne cherchais pas', Rousseau, *Les Confessions*, vol. 2, 94.

the idea of innocence alive. Émile gets to 15 with his imagination undeveloped and his desires chaste. But, at the hands of another mother figure, Jean-Jacques experiences the spanking that prematurely awakens and paradoxically disarms sexual desire:

> in spite of an ardent, lascivious and very precocious temperament, not only did I pass beyond the age of puberty without desiring, without knowing, any sensual pleasures beyond those to which Mlle de Lambercier had quite innocently introduced me.[92]
>
> (Non seulement donc c'est ainsi qu'avec un tempérament très ardent, très lascif, très précoce, je passai toutefois l'âge de puberté sans désirir, sans connaître d'autres plaisirs des sens que ceux dont Mlle Lambercier m'avait très innocemment donné l'idée.[93])

Because spanking perversely arouses sexual desire before its time, masturbatory fetish, the supplement for sex, takes the place of the original. Puberty passes without the loss of virginity, or even ejaculation, and thus Jean-Jacques's aberration oddly preserves a warped version of innocence: 'what should have ruined me preserved me...I have thus possessed very few, but have nevertheless achieved much pleasure in my own way, that is, through my imagination.'[94]

The connection Rousseau makes between masturbatory and imaginative pleasure was typical in mid-eighteenth-century Europe. The pamphlet called *Onania*, published sometime between 1708 and 1716, influenced a growing sub-genre of hygiene literature on puberty.[95] The writers of hygiene literature emphasized that imagination should play no part in the awakening of desire. Masturbation was threatening because, as Thomas Laqueur explains: 'it entailed the wilful mobilization of the imagination engaged in the endless creation of desire—fictive desire—that had at most a tangential relation to its real counterpart...it was a sham version of real pleasure.'[96] On 8 July 1762, two months after the publication of *Émile*, the Swiss physician, Samuel

[92] Rousseau, *Confessions*, 16. [93] Rousseau, *Les Confessions*, vol. 1, 43.

[94] Rousseau, *Confessions*, 16–17; 'ce qui devait me perdre me conserva...J'ai donc fort peu possédé, mais je n'ai pas laissé de jouir beaucoup à ma manière, c'est-à-dire par l'imagination', Rousseau, *Les Confessions*, vol. 1, 43–4.

[95] *Onania; or, The Heinous Sin of Self Pollution, and all its Frightful Consequences, in both SEXES Considered, with Spiritual and Physical Advice to those who have already injured themselves by this abominable practice. And seasonable Admonition to the Youth of the nation of Both SEXES.* See Thomas W. Laqueur, *Solitary Sex: A Cultural History of Masturbation* (New York: Zone Books, 2003), 25.

[96] Laqueur, *Solitary Sex*, 220.

Auguste Tissot, sent Rousseau a copy of *Onanism*, writing: '*Onanism* will show you that finally there is a doctor who sees all the dangers of the odious practice which you have so sharply attacked and had the courage to make known.'[97]

Masturbation moved quickly and easily from medico-moral literature to other forms of writing and came to represent, for many eighteenth-century thinkers, a derangement of sociability, destructive to the body but dangerous even if it had no physically demonstrable, or discernible, effects. Rousseau had warned against masturbation in *Émile* and presented it as a potentially catastrophic fall: 'Once he knows this dangerous supplement, he is lost'.[98] The pupil becomes lost to his teacher because he is hopelessly enslaved to himself.[99] If masturbation is the supplement to sex, it is dangerous because it is both a premature and fictitious awakening, and an awakening to fiction, the limitless yet self-enclosing, iterative function of fancy. Whereas sex involves the limit of the other, masturbation can run unchecked.

Physiological and philosophical discourse made the same point: bringing a child through puberty, the process of coming-of-age, could be either a catastrophic or fortunate fall. The devil was in the timing of it. Mid-century medical literature presented premature arousal as particularly dangerous. In his 1772 treatise, titled *The Men's Doctor, from Puberty until Extreme Old Age*, the French physician, Jean Goulin, wrote: 'The seminal fluid of man is the purest and the most balsamic [health-giving] part of the blood: it is, according to Hippocrates, a substance taken from every part of our body, During the delicate years of youth, nature, eager to perfect her work, uses this liquor to vivify and to fortify the being to which she has given birth.'[100] Precocious sexual activity, especially premature ejaculation, results in malformation. In an ideal eighteenth-century world, sexual awakening would happen at the precise moment that the child was reborn into the reasonable state of adulthood. Ejaculation would occur naturally and without imaginative stimulus. The fall into knowledge would be a fortunate rather than catastrophic event; the shape of narrative time progressive and secular rather than cyclical and devoted to the myth of sacred return.

[97] Laqueur, *Solitary Sex*, 42.

[98] Rousseau, *Émile*, 334; 'S'il connaît une fois ce dangereux supplement, il est perdu', Rousseau, *Émile, ou sur l'Education*, 498.

[99] 'Whatever happens, I shall tear you more easily from women than from yourself', Rousseau, *Émile*, 334. 'Quoi qu'il arrive, je t'arracherai plus aisément aux femmes qu'à toi', Rousseau, *Émile, ou sur l'Education*, 498.

[100] Cited in Mary K. McAlpin, 'Innocence of Experience: Rousseau on Puberty in the State of Civilisation', *Journal of the History of Ideas* 71.2 (Apr. 2010): 241–61, 246.

The repeated moment of catastrophe that Rousseau rehearses in the *Confessions* is rooted in the disruption of both secular and sacred time: a failure to find the right moment of maturity or locate an origin that is not already a supplement, or representation, of innocence. But the myth of the Fall paradoxically allows Rousseau to keep the idea of an innocent and authentic self rhetorically alive *because* it exposes it as fiction. Repeatedly destroyed and preserved in the iterative moment of his fall, Jean-Jacques is able to sustain the image of original innocence corrupted by a premature and catastrophic fall into knowledge even as he exposes the authentic and innocent self as a cultivated, post-lapsarian fantasy.

After the Moment: *Émile et Sophie, ou les solitaires* (1773)

Rousseau's posthumously published and unfinished sequel to *Émile* tells another story of disaster.[101] In *Émile*, the form of the treatise had allowed him to indulge a theoretical ideal of a fortunate fall. Rousseau regularly referred to *Émile* as his most important book, though he complained that it was ill-understood. Banned in Paris and Geneva, and publicly burned in the first year of its release, its author was pilloried as a danger to religion and society and subsequently exiled from France. The first mention of a sequel occurs a year after his exile, when he was living in Môtiers in the canton of Neuchâtel in Switzerland. He had also begun to write the *Confessions*.[102]

Rousseau chose to write an epistolary novel, told from the perspective of the unhappy grown-up child, and this shift in genre seems to acknowledge the possibility that the ideal might fail. As the scene changes from carefully controlled childhood innocence to the unpredictable world of adult experience, the change in genre is key. Émile is no longer the mouldable young subject of the educational treatise but an adult character, with his own passions and interests, who has only his education to guide him. Written as two letters by Émile to his old tutor, Jean-Jacques, *Émile et Sophie* begins with a rebuttal of the ideological treatise. *Émile* ends with new world promise in the birth of a new child, the hope that a careful leading out of the garden will have

[101] Written 1773, first published 1780.

[102] He declared that he wanted to use the sequel to *Émile* to give 'a charming and striking example' of an important moral maxim: 'avoid situations that put our duties in opposition with our interests, and which show us our good in the harm of someone else'. Rousseau, *Confessions*, cited by Christopher Kelly, 'Introduction', *Émile, or On Education (includes Émile and Sophie; Or, The Solitaries), The Collected Writings of Rousseau*, vol.13 (Hanover, NH: Dartmouth College Press, 2010), p. xxiii.

established a narrative of progression and an indication that the youth has finally found the right moment of maturity. But the opening of *Émile and Sophie* reveals this to be a precarious rather than happy ending:

> I was free, I was happy, oh my master! You had made me a heart suited to savouring happiness, and you had given me Sophie. To the delights of love, to the outpourings of friendship, a growing family added the charms of paternal tenderness: everything proclaimed a pleasant life to me, everything promised me a sweet old age and a peaceful death in my children's arms. Alas! What has become of that happy time of enjoyment and hope, in which the future embellished the present; in which my heart, drunk with its joy, imbibed a century of felicity each day? Everything vanished like a dream; still young I lost everything—wife, children, friends, in sum everything—even commerce with my fellows. My heart has been torn apart by all its attachments; it no longer holds onto anything except the least of all, the tepid love of a life without pleasures but exempt from remorse. If I outlive my losses for long, my fate is to age and die alone, without ever seeing a man's face again, and providence alone will close my eyes.[103]
>
> (J' étais libre, j'étais heureux, ô mon maître! vous m'aviez fait un cœur propre à goûter le bonheur, et vous m'aviez donné Sophie; aux délices de l'amour, aux épanchements de l'amitié, une famille naissante ajoutait les charmes de la tendresse paternelle: tout m'annonçait une vie agréable, tout me promettait une douce vieillesse, et une mort paisible dans les bras de mes enfants. Hélas! qu'est devenu ce temps heureux de jouissance et d'espérance, ou l'avenir embellisait le présent; où mon cœur, ivre de sa joie, s'abreuvait chaque jour d'un siècle de félicité? Tout s'est évanoui comme un songe; jeune encore, j'ai tout perdu, femme, enfants, amis, tout enfin, jusqu'au commerce de mes semblables. Mon cœur à été déchiré par tous ses attachements; il ne tient plus qu'au moindre de tous, au tiède amour d'une vie sans plaisir, mais exempte de remords. Si je survis longtemps à mes pertes, mon sort est de vieillir et mourir seul, sans jamais revoir un visage d'un homme ; et la seule Providence me fermera les yeux.[104])

The first test that Émile has had to face is Sophie's infidelity. He is confronted, in other words, with the figure of the fallen woman. In book 5 of *Émile*, newly

[103] Rousseau, *Émile and Sophie; Or, The Solitaries, The Collected Writings of Rousseau,* vol. 13, 685–721, 685.

[104] Rousseau, *Émile, ou sur l'Education*, 739.

engaged to Sophie, the young man is confronted by his tutor holding a letter. 'What would you do if you were told Sophie is dead?' Jean-Jacques asks. Émile is angry: 'What would I do...I don't know. But what I do know is that I would never again see the man who had informed me.' The tutor reassures Émile that his fiancée is alive and well, but continues to show him how vulnerable his feeling for a woman has made him: 'how would you see the man who would take her from you while she is still living—the one who would dare to say to you, "She is dead to you. Virtue separates you from her."?'[105]

In *Émile et Sophie*, Sophie herself says just this: 'I am no longer anything to you. Another has sullied your bed.'[106] On discovering that Sophie is pregnant with another man's child, Émile, in another echo of Augustine, and of Jean-Jacques on the road to Vincennes, collapses in a public garden:

> I sought darkness under the trees; finally, finding myself out of breath, I let myself fall half-dead on a lawn...'Where am I, what have I become? What have I heard? What a catastrophe? Madam! What a chimera have you chased after? Love, honor, faith, virtues, where are you? The sublime, the noble Sophie is only a despicable woman!'[107]
>
> (Je cherchais l'obscurité sous les arbres; enfin, me trouvant hors d'haleine, je me laissai tomber à demi-mort sur un gazon...Où suis-je? que suis-je devenu? qu'ai-je entendu? quelle catastrophe ! Insensé, quelle chimère as-tu poursuivre? La sublime, la noble Sophie n'est qu'une infâme![108])

In its clichéd portrayal of the false and serpentine temptress, *Émile and Sophie* suggests that corruption inheres everywhere; the carefully nurtured child who finds the right moment of maturity still faces risk from exposure; the ideals of innocence will inevitably falter on the received narratives of experience.

Repeatedly rewriting the Fall across different secular genres, Rousseau draws attention to it as a cultural invention, a fiction we use to make sense of modern feelings of discontent and desire. He explicitly positions his own relentless rewriting of the Fall as a defensive strategy, a way of making sense of overwhelmingly slow and meaningless evolutionary time and the feeling that something has gone—or will go—wrong: social and commercial inequality,

[105] Rousseau, *Émile, or on Education*, 442, 444.

[106] Rousseau, *Émile and Sophie*, 692. 'Je ne vous suis plus rien : un autre a souillé votre lit.' Rousseau, *Émile, ou sur l'Education*, 750.

[107] Rousseau, *Émile and Sophie*, 693.

[108] Rousseau, *Émile, ou sur l'Education*, 751.

educational failures, self-alienation, displaced desires and unpredictable futures. Adapted to secular pseudohistory, educational treatise, autobiography and epistolary novel, the fall into culture suggests both a catastrophic collapse and a turning point, a coming-of-age moment where we might take control of our own story and build a better world. But Rousseau exposes this moment as a fiction when he acknowledges in the *Second Discourse* and the *Confessions* that a single pivotal point of collapse is very hard to find, and in *Émile* and *Émile et Sophie* that a fortunate fall is very hard to get right. So, his writing and rewriting of the Fall has an obsessive and relentless quality. It is through writing that Rousseau comes to know goodness because he knows evil; through writing that he encounters origin because he experiences distance; and through writing that he can keep the idea of innocence alive. Emphasizing the myth of the Fall as a narrative construct, Rousseau's secular adaptations are profoundly pessimistic, keeping the desire for purity alive in a world that has no hope of redemption.

2

Fallen Forms

Blake's Comedy of Errors

In the last year of his life, William Blake returned, as an illustrator, to the Book of Genesis.[1] The unfinished manuscript exists today in the Huntingdon Library, San Marino, California: eleven unbound leaves, each measuring about 38cm by 28cm. There are two title pages, containing the most developed, but still unfinished, drawings, done in pencil and watercolour. The first page shows a creation scene that recalls the dramatic large-scale designs of Michaelangelo, whom Blake admired. The Father-God crouches in the upper left, one hand reaching down, the other reaching out to touch the finger of Adam, who rises with muscular strength and dynamic energy out of flames. A black wash suggests smoke in the background. Blake arranges the Gothic lettering of the title, 'Genesis', over three rows, down the centre of the image, so that the 'I' hangs like a covering in front of Adam's groin, foreshadowing his fall. A flaming figure runs across the top of the page. Another bearded figure stands to the right, hand raised in priestly benediction. Rough sketches of four figures at the bottom suggest desperate, half-buried, forms, torso and arms reaching upwards. A dash of green watercolour hints that they are bound by organic matter, while scarlet flames and serpentine coils further indicate Blake's sense that creation turns on fallen, material, form.[2]

The second title page explicitly recalls the events of Genesis 3. The sketchy figures at the bottom now clearly have humanoid forms with animal heads. One, with scaly arms, a serpentine tongue, and a fiery crown of diabolical thought, points towards the tempting, rosy-coloured, fruit on the Tree of

[1] The illustrated text was probably begun on commission from Blake's friend and patron, John Linnell. W. M. Rossetti places the manuscript in the Linnell's possession, but does not state that he commissioned the work. Alexander Gilchrist, however, states that the work was 'commenced … for Mr Linnell'. The manuscript editors, Mark Crosby and Robert Essick, also think it unlikely that Blake would have begun such a project without a commission as he was already in ill health. See *Genesis: William Blake's Last Illuminated Work*, ed. with a commentary by Mark Crosby and Robert N. Essick, with an essay by Robert N. Wark (reproduced with permission of the Huntingdon Library, Art Collections and Botanical Gardens, San Marino, Calif., 2012), 28.

[2] *Genesis*, ed. Crosby and Essick, 'The Manuscript', Leaf 1.

The Myth of the Fall in Nineteenth-Century Literature. Linda Freedman, Oxford University Press.
 DOI: 10.1093/oso/9780198969570.003.0003

Knowledge. Adam is standing on a grassy mound, his posture more sedate, his finger not directly touching God.[3] The first page bears the watermark J. Whatman/Turkey Mill/1821; the second J. Whatman/1826. There is a general assumption that Blake began the first, and less complete, drawing earlier but he may have just used an older sheet of paper. The ten other illustrations in the manuscript are rough pencil sketches, interspersed with chapter and verse copied from the King James in inked Gothic lettering. Blake's main addition to the text was a series of chapter titles, which further reflect his interpretation of Creation as Fall: the division of spiritual wholeness into the fallen forms of the material world.

Chap 1: The Creation of the Natural Man.
Chap 2: The Natural Man divided into Male & Female & of the Tree of Life & of the Tree of Good & Evil.
Chap 3: Of the Sexual Nature & its Fall into Generation & death.
Chap 4: How generation & death took possession of the Natural Man & of the Forgiveness of Sins written upon the Murderers forehead.[4]

Blake is known for his outspoken criticisms of organized religion, but he was equally critical of the secularizing drives of the eighteenth century, accusing Rousseau—and other Enlightenment luminaries—of a self-righteous and unforgiving hypocrisy:[5]

> Voltaire Rousseau Gibbon Hume charge the Spiritually Religious with Hypocrisy!...We are men of like passions with others and pretend not to be holier than others...Voltaire! Rousseau! You cannot escape my charge that you are Pharisees and Hypocrites! constantly talking of the Virtues of the Human Heart, and particularly of your own, that you may accuse others & especially the Religious, whose errors, you by this display of pretended Virtue chiefly design to expose. Rousseau thought Men Good by Nature; he found them evil & found no friend. Friendship cannot exist without Forgiveness of Sins continually.[6]

[3] *Genesis*, ed. Crosby and Essick, 'The Manuscript', Leaf 2.

[4] *Genesis*, ed. Crosby and Essick, 'The Manuscript', Leaf 3, 6, 8, 10.

[5] On Blake and alternative religiosity, see Robert Rix, *William Blake and the Cultures of Radical Christianity* (Aldershot: Ashgate, 2007); Jon Mee, *Dangerous Enthusiasm: William Blake and the Culture of Radicalism in the 1790s* (Oxford: OUP, 1992).

[6] William Blake, *Jerusalem The Emanation of the Giant Albion* (1804–c.1820), in *The Complete Poetry and Prose of William Blake*, ed. David V. Erdman with a commentary by Harold Bloom (New York: Doubleday, 1988), 201. All further typographic quotations from Blake's works are to this edition, included in the text with the abbreviation E.

For Blake, Rousseau's secular myth of the Fall leads to a highly judgemental and lonely pessimism because it holds no faith in redemption and leaves no room for forgiveness and friendship. He criticizes Rousseau for attacking the corruption of modern civilization while paradoxically—and, Blake insists, hypocritically—preserving the myth of his own innate incorruptibility. By contrast the 'Forgiveness of Sins written upon the Murderers forehead' elides the difference between the judgement that banishes Cain to the wilderness and the mark of forgiveness that brings him back into the body of Christ. In Blake's profoundly religious interpretation of the Fall, judgement is tempered with mercy.

As Blake returned to the Book of Genesis in the very last stages of life, he returned to the biblical accounts of creation and corresponding ideas of fallen form that had long troubled his mythology of the artist. Blake found two different models of the artist in the two different versions of God depicted in Genesis 1 and 2. The God of Genesis 1 creates meaningful form by drawing clear lines: separating light from dark, earth from air, and bird from beast. He is a God of conflict, power, and presence. In the manuscript illustration above Genesis 1, Blake sketched the Father-God extending his finger downwards in an act of formative creation. The image has a precedent in the frontispiece to *Europe: A Prophecy*, composed in 1794 (Figure 1). In this plate, titled 'The Ancient of Days', a bearded and muscular figure reaches down into the darkness, strong shafts of light extending from his powerful fingertips. It is both a dramatic and compelling evocation of the artistry of Genesis 1, an individual figure drawing lines of meaning upon chaotic darkness, and a profoundly satirical image. Blake depicts this God as Urizen, the most fallen creature of his mythology. He is creating the material universe, the fallen form of existence, which distances us from spiritual wholeness. The shafts of light emerging from his pointed finger suggest Newtonian instruments of measurement: the calipers of the compass that maps everything by physical laws. But Urizen is still a creator, an artist, and in his story lies Blake's unhappy acknowledgement that art might be inseparable from the conditions of the fallen world. In 2019, 'The Ancient of Days' was projected onto the dome of St Paul's Cathedral, London: a reminder that, looking at this satirical image, one might still see a version of a powerful God (Figure 2).

Despite the satire of the Creator-God in the figure of Urizen, Blake is often seen as an artist who favoured the model of Genesis 1: clear and precise lines 'Drawn with a firm [and decided] hand at once' (E576). He railed against indistinct and sludgy oil paintings: the Royal Academician, Sir Joshua Reynolds, whom the Pre-Raphaelite Brotherhood later nicknamed Sir Sloshua, was the

Figure 1 William Blake, Frontispiece, *The Ancient of Days*, 'Europe: A Prophecy', 1794, copy A, Plate 1. Yale Center for British Art. Paul Mellon Foundation.

Figure 2 William Blake, *The Ancient of Days,* 1827, projected by Tate Britain onto St Paul's Cathedral 2019 Photo. © Tate (Alex Wojcik).

subject of many barbed critiques.[7] But, he also polemicized against the fashion for smoothed and heavily finished works of art, commenting wryly: 'These things that you call Finishd are not Even Begun how can they then, be Finishd'? The Man who does not know the Beginning, can never know the End of Art' (E639). *A Descriptive Catalogue*, which accompanied his self-staged, disastrously received, one-man exhibition of 1809, was his most sustained prose aesthetic manifesto: more polemical than descriptive. The theory of art in *A Descriptive Catalogue* is rooted in the pre-lapsarian creation of Genesis 1: a world in which individual parts cohere in a vision of wholeness. Spiritual unity has been lost in historical time; and the function of the artist is to restore it through the distinctive power of the visionary imagination. Thus, Blake writes: 'The artist is an inhabitant of that happy country [Eden], and if every thing goes on as it has begun, the world of vegetation and generation may expect to be opened again to Heaven, through Eden, as it was in the beginning' (E543). Beginning is what Blake understands, then, by real artistic End.

The God of Genesis 2 scoops and moulds clay from the ground, infusing it with breath: a more tactile and embedded model of artistry than the divisive illumination of Genesis 1. Unlike comparable accounts of creation in the Ancient Near East, which show the potter seated at the wheel, this God creates freestyle. The unfinished illustrations to the Book of Genesis reveal a method which recalls the process artistry of Genesis 2: the definite line began as a sensitive sketch. Blake started his career as an engraver. In the kind of engraving that he learned in his youth, multiple mark-making, sometimes hundreds or thousands of marks, builds a sense of shape, volume, texture, and tone.[8] The Genesis manuscript shows that Blake developed his drawings in the same way, working through a series of flexible pencil movements to a definite outline. If the clear line belongs to the decisive artistry of Genesis 1, the feeling sketch corresponds with the process artistry of Genesis 2, moulding form out of matter. In the manuscript illustration to Genesis 2, Blake drew the forms of Adam and Eve separating amidst cloudy, shapeless, matter.[9] At the end of the chapter, Blake loosely sketched a horizontal, bearded figure, floating, with his arms outstretched, over a prostrate, nude, Adam. Eve floats between them, her feet just touching Adam's rib-cage. Both drawings reflect

[7] See Blake's *Annotations to the Works of Sir Joshua Reynolds* (E635–62).
[8] Martin Myrone, *The Blake Book* (London: Tate, 2007), 22.
[9] *Genesis,* ed. Crosby and Essick, 'The Manuscript', Leaf 6.

the creative model of Genesis 2. Form emerges from matter as opposed to lines drawn on chaotic darkness.[10]

Form, for Blake, is a grammar of being. Mark-making has cosmological and teleological significance, and questions of draughtsmanship draw no real lines between aesthetics and ethics. Like the Creator-God of Genesis 1, Blake's preferred artist creates meaningful existence through a series of formal distinctions that are also a way of knowing what is 'good'.

> The great and golden rule of art, as well as of life, is this: That the more distinct, and sharp, and wirey, the bounding line, the more perfect the work of art; and the less keen and sharp, the greater is the evidence of weak imitation, plagiarism and bungling. Great inventors, in all ages, knew this: Protogenes and Apelles knew each other by this line. Rafael and Michael Angelo, and Albert Durer, are known by this and this alone. The want of this determinate and bounding form evidences the want of idea in the artist's mind, and the pretence of the plagiary in all its branches. How do we distinguish the oak from the beech, the horse from the ox, but by the bounding outline? How do we distinguish one face or countenance from another but by the bounding line and its infinite inflexions and movements? What is it that builds a house and plants a garden but the definite and determinate? What is it that distinguishes honesty from knavery, but the hard and wirey line of rectitude and certainty in the actions and intentions? Leave out this l[i]ne and you leave out life itself; all is chaos again, and the line of the almighty must be drawn out upon it before man or beast can exist. (E550)

The 'bounding outline', derived from the artistry of Genesis 1, is a powerful creative model. Without lines, we cannot make distinctions. But the line can also be a limiting judgment. Blake regularly derided what he saw as the inflexible and self-serving judgments of the hardened and righteous, criticizing Rousseau for precisely this reason. He was deeply satirical when it came to what he saw as 'barren mountains of Moral/Virtue': rigid forms and codified structures perpetuating divisions and oppressions while masquerading as good (E193). Urizen, drawing lines upon chaotic darkness, represents a fallen form of the Creator-God and his name echoes the self-limiting horizon of the hyper-rational intellect: one version, and definite risk, of the 'bounding line'. In Blake's prophecy of *America*, composed in 1793, Urizen is the giver of the

[10] *Genesis*, ed. Crosby and Essick, 'The Manuscript', Leaf 7.

oppressive 'stony law' that the revolutionary figure of Orc stamps to dust (E54). As a powerful creator and material and moral law-giver, Urizen helps us understand both the vision and the terror that Blake identified in the 'bounding line' of Genesis 1.

However, the 'bounding line' also reflects the influence of Genesis 2. It suggests an energetic kind of limit; reach as much as containment; process as much as judgement. As a way of encountering difference, distinguishing 'one face or countenance from another', the 'bounding line with its infinite inflexions or movements' implies resistance to the kind of judgemental attitudes Blake decried. On the one hand, Blake expresses an energetic optimism about the creative possibilities of encounter but he was also worried that all form, however it was made, was inevitably poised to fall. We can see this anxiety at work in his polemic against the weak mind, which, he declares, has 'plagiary in all its branches', endlessly copying others and thus proliferating sameness. 'Branches' suggest the organic matter of the material world and the natural man fallen from spiritual wholeness. They imply the organization of intellectual enquiry and energetic encounter into codified systems of knowledge subject to received error. But they also reflect the multiple branchy marks through which Blake built his own distinctive outlines.

Blake's different models of the artist, drawn from Genesis 1 and 2, turn on the same set of questions: how can the artist give form that is redemptive when every act of formative creation turns on the conditions of fallenness? How can the 'bounding line', the powerful and ethical artistry modelled on Genesis 1, not become a fallen 'stony law'? How can the more tactile, feeling artist, modelled on the God of Genesis 2, stop flexible branchy marks becoming fixed branches of organized thought? Blake shares with Rousseau an energetic desire to do good in a world that seems to have gone profoundly wrong. Like Rousseau he is animated by an overactive sense of proximity to disaster and, like Rousseau, he can't shake the feeling that even our best efforts are inevitably poised to fall. Blake also turned to the myth of the Fall to make sense of the catastrophic world we have made. But there is a key difference. Whereas Rousseau's secular vision had no room for redemption, Blake held that promise sacred. Fallenness, for Blake, meant separation from God and fallen forms turn on fixity and sameness because they are cut off from the ever-renewing force of divine inspiration. Redemption thus begins with the energetic, creative, and ethical effort he recognizes in the 'bounding line', but it depends on the precarious and unpredictable divine gift of grace.

Satire: *The [First] Book of Urizen* (1794)

In 1794 Blake produced a satire of Genesis, sometimes thought to be the 'Bible of Hell' promised at the end of *The Marriage of Heaven and Hell*, composed in 1790.[11] He arranged the text in two columns, mimicking standard biblical format. The title page depicts Urizen as a gowned and bearded Father-God, with long white flowing hair. He crouches on a large open book, perhaps Genesis, the 'First' Book of the Bible and the foundation of scriptural authority.[12] He is holding writing or drawing instruments in both hands; they may be quills, pencils, or etching needles. Behind him are two gravestones, which recall the stone tablets of Mosaic Law. His arms rest on two sets of rectangular stone tablets, which resemble an open, stony-leaved book in which he is writing or drawing, or, alternatively, the ends of a long, stone, coffin lid. The background is dark and suggests a graveyard setting. A willow-like tree bends its branches like a cavern over Urizen. In this caverned form, Blake was partly parodying John Locke's theory of the empirical mind as a dark closet illuminated by sensory experience:

> a closet, wholly shut from light, with only some little opening left, to let in external visible resemblances, or ideas of things without; would the pictures coming into such a dark room but stay there, and lie so orderly as to be found upon occasion, it would very much resemble the understanding of man, in reference to all objects of sight, and the ideas of them.[13]

In Blake's image tree roots sprout beneath and around Urizen's feet, suggesting parallels between stony law, the dead book, and organic matter, hard quadrangular lines and branchy empiricist caverns, which all evoke deathly, fallen, forms (Figure 3).

[11] See Robert Essick, *William Blake and the Language of Adam* (Oxford: Clarendon, 1989), 140; Leslie Tannenbaum, 'Blake's Art of Crypsis: *The Book of Urizen and Genesis*', *Blake Studies* 5.1 (Fall 1972): 141–64, 141; Christopher Rowland, *Blake and the Bible* (New Haven: Yale University Press, 2011), 86–119; Robert Rix, 'In Infernal Love and Faith: William Blake's "The Marriage of Heaven and Hell"', *Literature and Theology* 20.2 (June 2006): 107–25.

[12] For a discussion of Blake and scriptural authority in *The [First] Book of Urizen*, see Jerome J McGann, 'The Idea of an Indeterminate Text: Blake's Bible of Hell and Dr. Alexander Geddes', *Studies in Romanticism* 25.3 (Fall 1986): 303–24.

[13] Locke, *Essay Concerning Understanding*, 158. See also: Steve Clark, '"Labouring at the Resolute Anvil": Blake's Response to Locke', in *Blake in the Nineties*, ed. Steve Clark and David Worrall (Basingstoke: Palgrave Macmillan, 1999), 133–52; Harald A. Kittel, 'The Book of Urizen and An Essay Concerning Human Understanding', in *Interpreting Blake*, ed. Michael Phillips (Cambridge: CUP, 1978): 111–44; Wayne Glausser, *Locke and Blake: A Discussion across the Eighteenth Century* (Jacksonville, Fla.: University Press of Florida, 1998); Matthew I. A. Green, *Visionary Materialism in the Early Works of William Blake* (London: Palgrave Macmillan, 2005), 1–41.

Figure 3 William Blake, Title Page, *The First Book of Urizen*, 1794, copy A, Plate 1. Yale Center for British Art. Paul Mellon Foundation.

Like all origin myths *The [First] Book of Urizen* is interested in understanding the moment of creation in relation to the conditions of history.[14] In his introduction to the work, David Worrall groups it with *The Book of Los* and *The Book of Ahania*, which intersect with it in various ways, and suggests that these productions are among Blake's most politically interventionist works of the 1790s.[15] In its parody of the Book of Genesis it levels a critique at the world man has made. As he retells the creation story as a story of self-destruction, Blake mixes his satire of the self-limiting perspectives of Lockean empiricism with a satire of the faith in scriptural authority, which had bolstered centuries of false hierarchy with a belief in the Bible as the singular Word of God. This work is satirical but it is also profoundly interested in *how* these damaged worlds are made and the conditions which form the basis of their making.

[14] As Erin Goss has argued, without a relationship to history, origin stories would remain enclosed in an isolated mythic moment. Erin M. Goss, '"What is Call'd Corporeal": William Blake and the Question of the Body', *The Eighteenth Century* 51.4 (Winter 2010): 413–30, 418.

[15] William Blake, *The Urizen Books*, ed. Davis Worrall (London: Tate, 1995), 19.

In Blake's wider mythology the figure usually identified with the artist is Los, 'the Eternal Prophet', the fallen form of Urthona, whose name suggests the 'loss' of the infinite, the 'logos' of Christ, and the sun whose brightness has been reversed or eclipsed (E67). In this work, Urizen and Los are two sides of the same character. Like the creation of Eve in Genesis 2 and recalling Sin, who springs from Satan's head in *Paradise Lost*, Urizen is rent from Los's side.

Urizenic mentality is defensive. Secretive and 'self-clos'd', Urizen is a psychological portrayal of paranoid selfhood, which Blake regarded as one of the greatest social, religious, and artistic dangers (E70). Such defensiveness haunts the 'hard and wirey line of rectitude' that Blake recognizes as part of artistic world-making in the *Descriptive Catalogue*; it is the root cause of collapse from energetic and decisive encounters into the 'self-clos'd' judgements of the hardened and righteous. In *The [First] Book of Urizen*, the strong God of Genesis, who subjugates chaos and emerges victorious from conflict, becomes a nervous wreck, neurotically battling phantasmal 'shapes / Bred from his forsaken wilderness', the 'self-begotten armies' of his own solitary mind (E70 and E73). In these defensive manoeuvres, his selfhood proliferates. Every character in this work is, to some extent, a version of Urizen, fuelled by sameness and fearful of difference. The world-making that Blake satirizes is born of epistemological overconfidence, papering over the incomprehensible void of alterity. Just as scriptural authority and empiricism bolster their own limited, and self-limiting, perspectives, so Blake realizes that art can be an act of defensive self-projection.

If *The [First] Book of Urizen* is critical of the world humanity has made, it is also curious about the creative impulse. Form emerges here as tortured self-defence:

> In a horrible, dreamful, slumber
> Like the linked, infernal, chain
> A vast spine writh'd in torment
> Upon the winds; shooting pain'd
> Ribs like a bending cavern
> And bones of solidness froze
> Over all his nerves of joy. (E75)

The image of a 'bending cavern' reflects the agonized Lockean mind turned in upon itself and the spirit caged in a prison-house of fear. In one of his plates, Blake drew the caverned ribs of a skeleton bent in foetal form, implying that closed minds create rigid, stillborn worlds (Figure 4). *The [First]*

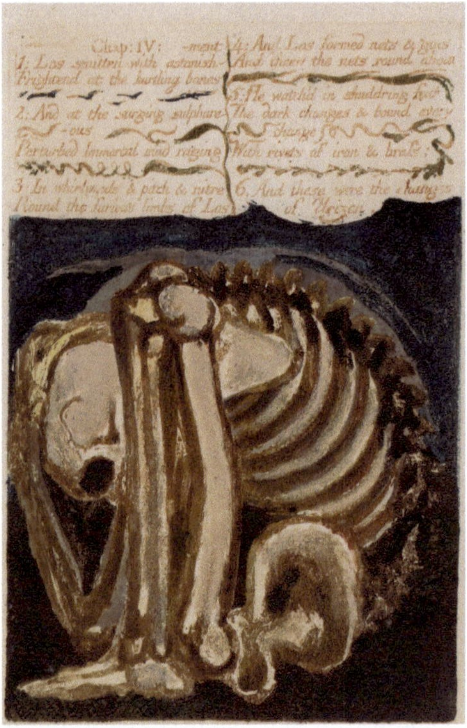

Figure 4 William Blake, Chapter IV. 'Los smitten with astonishment', *The First Book of Urizen*, 1794, copy A, Plate 12. Yale Center for British Art. Paul Mellon Foundation.

Book of Urizen is his strongest critique of the defensive world-making impulse, which he recognizes in *all* creators, including himself.

Blake suggests a kind of mimetic creativity at play in Urizen's world. On the title page, it looks as if he is copying from the book beneath his feet (Figure 3). Mimesis is both divisive and self-reflexive; Los creates art as the God of Genesis 1 fathers children by 'begetting [his] likeness, / On [his] own divided image' (E79). *The [First] Book of Urizen* abounds with such divided images. Urizen divides 'times on times' (E70). 'Eternity roll'd wide apart' (E73). Los howls 'wrenching apart' (E74). 'Pity began, / In anguish dividing & dividing…the soul' (E77). '[T]he Eternal Prophet was divided / Before the death-image of Urizen' (E78). '[T]he visions remote / Of the dark separation [sic] appear'd' (E78). When the first woman, Enitharmon, separates from Los, she emerges as his narcissistic reflection in the water, her 'female form trembling and pale / Waves before his deathly face' (E78).

The plates in *The [First] Book of Urizen* contain numerous reflexive images. Urizen is crowned with the same halo of rebellious fire as his fourth and final son, Fuzon, even as he sits bound in iron chains.[16] One plate depicts a fleshy, bloated form of Los howling into the void and recalls the image of Urizen's coarse son, Grodna, 'howling' as he 'rent the deep earth' (E81).[17] The naked youth running through the 'unquenchable burnings' of eternal fire is reborn again in a different, muscular, version of Los, who hammers at the forge, and in his infant son, Orc, who is born in an explosion of fire with arms outstretched in joy not terror.[18] The crucified form of Los, hanging upside down and bound with the coils of Urizen's serpentine thought, rises again in Urizen.[19] Most strikingly, however, the figure of the Eternal Prophet 'divided before the death-image of Urizen' shows him made in the image of both Urizen and Los (Figure 5).[20]

Figure 5 William Blake, Chapter V. 'Thus the Eternal Prophet was divided', *The First Book of Urizen*, 1794, copy C, Plate 13. Yale Center for British Art. Paul Mellon Foundation.

[16] Compare object 3 and object 4 of copy A.

[17] Compare object 10 with object 4 of copy A.

[18] Compare objects 5, 17, and 22 of copy A.

[19] Compare object 9 and 6 of copy A. In F and G these are adjacent images.

[20] Object 20 of copy A.

Behaviours are also relentlessly copied. Like the Immortal, against whose naturally 'expand[ing]' and 'contract[ing]' will Urizen rebels, Urizen seeks to impose his will as natural law. Los forms 'nets' in response to the encircling fury of the 'perturbed Immortal mad raging / In whirlwinds.../ Round [his] furious limbs' (E74). He uses these nets to bind Urizen who then constructs his own 'Net of Religion' under which the world shrinks and sickens (E82). Urizen's flaming son, Fuzon, a type of Moses, who leads an exodus at the end of the poem, comes full circle to Urizen's own act of rebellion. In the last line of the poem: 'the salt ocean roll[s] englob'd' (E83). The globe, like the cavern, represents the mind turned in upon itself. It depicts the eye that sees only in the corporeal sense and has no spiritual vision. And it recalls Blake's depiction of Creation as the Fall into material form. The globular earth, bound by organic matter, is fallen from spiritual wholeness. Far from heralding freedom, the exodus turns on another englobing, another Fall.

The world that Urizen builds is born of 'weak imitation' and has 'plagiary in all its branches'. Urizen's world first appears in a relationship with Eternity, emerging 'On the shore of the infinite ocean' (E73). But Los then presides over a terrible rupture in cosmic fabric and stands guard against the gods, fighting against, rather than for, Eternal presence, as he defends the 'globe of Urizen' as a marker of separation and exclusion:

> And Los round the dark globe of Urizen,
> Kept watch for Eternals to confine,
> The obscure separation alone;
> For Eternity stood wide apart,
> As the stars are apart from the earth (E73)

Los, hammering tirelessly at the forge, becomes suddenly still and falls into: 'A nerveless silence, his prophetic voice / Seiz'd' (E77). Urizen's world is one in which prophecy cannot function because the connection with the 'stars', the relationship with infinity, is severed.

Blake maps the downward spirals of alienation and disconnect onto the contours of the body, which begins in a state of apparent health, 'expand[ing] and contract[ing]' with the breath of divine inspiration. As we move through the six stages of creation as a withdrawal from infinity, the living, breathing body reforms as a hard and lifeless cage, 'Nerves change into Marrow / And hardening Bones' (E82). 'All flexible senses' atrophy and sicken: 'The Senses inward rush'd shrinking, / Beneath the dark net of infection' (E82). As Erin Goss has argued, Los builds Urizen's body as an obstruction, a prescriptive limitation of 'nets' which becomes the basis of the world which follows it.[21] Urizen's body is, primarily, a defensive strategy of containment, shutting out difference; a world unto itself.

Blake's parody of Genesis bodies forth a host of ugly forms, broken, bound, pained, contorted, and atomized. Alterity is ruthlessly excluded from a self whose insistence on sovereignty is, ironically, the root cause of division and disconnect. The world comes into being disembodied and dying, 'like a human heart, struggling and beating' (E73). As the world-body grows, it cannot sustain its integrity, breaking apart into 'Portions of life', and Urizen wanders through a wilderness of nonsensical forms (E81). In his late, long poem, *Jerusalem The Emanation of the Giant Albion* (*c.*1804–20), Blake gives us a glimpse of a different sort of body, and a different sort of world, in which alterity is bound into the self in a vision of redemptive form.

> I am in you and you in me, mutual in love divine:
> Fibres of love from man to man thro Albions pleasant land (E146)

Urizen's self-proliferating body contrasts strongly with this later vision of redemption.

The Immortal governs the world into which Urizen explodes. But he too is guilty of singular vision and flexes his muscular will in a show of strength and power.

> Earth was not: nor globes of attraction
> The will of the Immortal expanded
> Or contracted his all flexible senses
> Death was not, but eternal life sprung (E71)

Harmony looks very like tyranny when it is controlled by the singular will. 'All-flexible senses' imply the reach and limit of empiricist thought. And it is hard to see where creativity comes into this picture of inevitable resolution and unchallenged quiet.

It is, therefore, unsurprising that Blake, a champion of 'Mental Fight' and progressive 'contraries', first describes Urizen's rebellion as an awakening (E95 and E34):[22]

[21] Goss, 'What is Call'd Corporeal', 424.

[22] See Sarah Haggarty and Jon Mee, eds, *Blake and Conflict* (Basingstoke: Palgrave Macmillan, 2009).

The sound of a trumpet the heavens
Awoke & vast clouds of blood roll'd
Round the dim rocks of Urizen (E71)

In Revelations, the sound of the trumpet is a wake-up call to sinners on Earth and a signal for them to repent before the end of days.[23] Blake incorporates this apocalyptic imagery to heighten the melodrama of the moment. Urizen's creative act violently explodes the complacency of Eternal concord. But Urizen's creativity is ultimately fallible because, like the bad artist derided in *A Descriptive Catalogue*, he acts in 'weak imitation'. Blake presents Urizen's self-involvement as sexual and creative implosion: 'tormenting passions' that result in the 'enormous labours' of a fruitless birth (E70).

Copying the Immortal, exerting an indomitable will to power and defending nervously against difference, he rules against alterity, allowing for only:

One command, one joy, one desire,
One curse, one weight, one measure
One King, one God, one Law (E72)

Urizen's singular vision is his great flaw and, yet, in the literary quality of this great speech, Blake is sensitive to the attraction of authority. Urizen is statesman-like, offering stability and reassurance. Blake does seem to understand *why* we so often make the mistake of shutting out others and refusing vulnerability. Life sometimes feels safer that way. Blake's great skill is not just to expose the disease of Urizenic mentality but to comprehend its contagion, even as he subjects it to satire.

Leslie Tannenbaum argues that the namings in *Urizen* are perverted creations, things that should never be brought into being.[24] Certainly, no one in *The [First] Book of Urizen* wants to own the world they make. In Genesis, God's words claim possession of his creative actions: 'And God said, let there be light, and there was light'.[25] The naming of the world's parts results in God's satisfaction and ownership of his own creative mastery: 'that it was good'.[26] In *Paradise Lost*, Adam's God-given power to confer names also assists in the creation of his world.[27] But in *The [First] Book of Urizen*, naming is accompanied by fear and flight. When Urizen rises he is 'unknown', and the

[23] Rev. 8: 6–13. [24] Tannenbaum, 'Blake's Art of Crypsis', 159.
[25] Gen. 1: 3. [26] Gen. 1: 4.
[27] John Milton, *Paradise Lost*, ed. Alastair Fowler (London: Routledge, 2007), book VIII, ll. 270–3, p. 443. My reading is indebted here to Angela Esterhammer, who traces the devolution of performative

Eternals do not know how to name or make space for his being: 'Some said / "It is Urizen"' (E70). When Enitharmon, the first female form, is created, they run in fear (E78). When Orc, the first child, is born to Los and Enitharmon, he strikes a 'paralytic' blow into the heart of Eternity and produces a primal 'shriek' of abandonment and despair (E79). Aghast, they 'shudder' as they watch Los act like the self-admiring God of Genesis 'begetting his likeness / On his own divided Image' (E79). Identifying the world in terms of the bondage of slavery rather than the beauty of creation, the poem ends its satire of Genesis by invoking Exodus: 'They call'd it Egypt, and left it' (E83). This is a world that we are desperate to escape, not a paradisal land to which we might long to return.[28] Naming is a form of disowning and another defence.

Like Rousseau, Blake identifies the family as the first model of society. With the creation of family, which is a unit of likeness, the rift between earth and heaven is complete. Like Urizen, 'self-clos'd' in his bony prison, the Eternals raise their defensive barriers: 'They closed the tent /...beat down the stakes with cords /.../ [and] No more Los beheld Eternity' (E79–80). Blake attacks more than the caverned mind of Lockean empiricism in his portrait of limited, and limiting, bodies. Just as the Eternals do not know how to name Urizen, bodies compensate poorly because they are the wrong sort of body; they seek to delimit and control; they infect rather than absorb, proliferating selfhood and shutting out difference. In 2 Corinthians, Christ is described as 'God...reconciling the world unto himself'.[29] And, in his late, long work, *Jerusalem*, Blake lets us glimpse that better deity: 'not a God afar off...a brother and a friend' (E146).[30] But there is no friendship or brotherhood offered here. There is no reconciliation, mutuality, or reciprocity in the paranoid projections that uphold the sovereign self.

In Blake's satire of the seven days of creation, the period is that of the nine months of gestation and the baby is already a corpse: 'Time on times he divided, & measur'd / Space by space in his ninefold darkness' (E70). Urizen's 'ninefold darkness', like his 'enormous labours', is part of a recurrent trope in Blake's writing of creativity as monstrous, or aborted, pregnancy and tortuous labour pains. Urizen has one parallel in Enion who, in Blake's manuscript work *Vala* or *The Four Zoas* (c.1796–1807), is the feminine emanation of

language from the God of Genesis to the tyrant Urizen. Angela Esterhammer, 'Calling into Existence: *The Book of Urizen*', in *Blake in the Nineties*, ed. Clark and Worrall, 114–32.

[28] Jon Mee has argued that naming in *The [First] Book of Urizen* is an account of the world's errors and not its beauties, commenting that with each act of naming, we are further separated from the fluid world of the Eternals. Mee, *Dangerous Enthusiasm*, 186–7.

[29] 2 Cor. 5: 19.

[30] Jesus describes himself as a friend in Matt. 26: 50; John 15: 13–17.

Tharmas. She represents sexuality and sexual urges while Tharmas represents sensation. In the fallen world, Enion and Tharmas are separated and Enion takes on the role of earth mother. Like one of the Fates weaving the threads of life and death, Enion weaves for nine days and nine nights as she births a world of fear and pain:

> Nine days she laboured at her work & nine dark sleepless nights
> But on the tenth trembling morn the Circle of Destiny Complete
> Round rolld the Sea Englobing in a watry Globe self balancd
> A Frowning Continent appeard Where Enion in the Desart
> Terrified in her own Creation viewing her woven shadow
> Sat in a dread Intoxication of Repentence & Contrition. (E303)

A 'watry Globe', Enion's 'Creation' recalls the icy tears and bounded vision of Urizen's own fallen universe and blighted perceptions.[31] A 'woven shadow', it resembles Urizen's insular 'self-contemplating shadow' and the laced 'nets' in which he is caught and with which he imprisons the world (E71 and E74).

It also mirrors his frigidity. Enion's 'woven shadow' is a metonymic extension of the clothes with which Adam and Eve cover their nakedness after the Fall. She confesses:

> I thought to weave a Covering for my Sins from wrath of Tharmas
> I thought Tharmas a Sinner & I murdered his Emanations
> His secret loves & Graces (E304)

But Blake tells us that this world, with its awareness of sin and its attendant feelings of violent terror and shame, is her own 'Created Phantasm' (E303). Like Urizen, she creates a world from the 'self-begotten armies' of her own tormented mind: 'that dark and dismal infinite where Thought roams up & down' (E303). The Spectre of reason tells her: 'with one Sting of my tongue / Envenomd thou rollst inwards to the place where I emergd' (E304). Uniting the globular earth with the rational eye, Blake allows for no difference between external and internal spheres. Aligning reason with the serpent, he emphasizes the 'fall into Division' that here, as in *The [First] Book of Urizen*, reflects the drastic irony that Blake perceived in a world in which the self's

[31] Urizen has tears on his cheeks in his portrait in copies F, B, A, and G. In copy B it is Los that is weeping.

rationality was justification for its sovereignty above all else (E301). Enion's world, like Urizen's, is stillborn and immediately deconstructs with sickening plunges and destabilizing, disorienting rifts, voids, and chasms. Blake's rewriting of Genesis as stillbirth, seven days of destruction, disavowal, and coiled, reptilian form is an indictment of imitative art and monomaniacal artistry, of Creator-Gods who make reflexive images and men who make Gods of themselves.

On the final plate of the poem Blake depicts Urizen clutching his net in the same manner as he clutches his stone tablets and the dead brass book on the title page (Figure 6; Figure 3). He implies that the birth of organized religion and the failure of art spring from the same defensive self-limiting fear of the unknown. Urizen's 'Net of Religion' finds its counterpart in 'shrunken eyes clouded over' and 'bound down / To earth by their narrowing perceptions' (E82–3). As on the title page, hard and inflexible 'books formd of metals' are

Figure 6 William Blake, Chapter IX. 'They lived a period of years', *The First Book of Urizen*, 1794, copy C, Plate 25. Yale Center for British Art. Paul Mellon Foundation.

his support (E72). They represent centuries of biblical orthodoxy and scriptural authority and are the material version of his defensive postures, filled with his 'secrets of dark contemplation', putting up barriers to creative interpretation and laying the foundations of spiritual death.

The fallen form of Urizen is a judgement on organized religion as an artistic failure. When he falls into 'stony sleep', the Eternals look upon him and say: 'What is this? Death / Urizen is a clod of clay' (E74). Blake is partly borrowing his vocabulary from Milton. When Milton's Adam falls, he recognizes the fact of death in his mortal body, which he describes as a 'corporeal clod'.[32] Urizen is a fallen creature, but he is also a fallen creation. As man makes God in his own image, he does so poorly, with little skill (the clay is unformed) and even less feeling (it is lifeless and dull). Los stands howling and terrified 'At the formless, unmeasurable death' (E74) and starts to cast nets to capture and contain him. In the face of chaos, death, and violent sex, Los seeks stability. Confronted with 'formlessness', he desires form. But form is corrupted by fearful control. Bound by Los, Urizen becomes entangled in the 'Net of religion', which he casts over the world.

Encounters: *The Book of Los and The Book of Ahania* (1795)

The [First] Book of Urizen emerged at a moment the foundations of scriptural authority were beginning to be shaken. Well before the nineteenth century, and partly in response to the obvious fissures in the text, people started to wonder whether Genesis might not have been solely written by Moses. By the late eighteenth century, the textual variations, repetitions, and inconsistencies in Genesis had forced scholars to consider that it may not be a work of single authorship and that perhaps Moses may not even have written any of it. The late nineteenth-century biblical scholar, Julius Wellhausen (1844–1918) managed to synthesize, organizes, and augment centuries of biblical enquiry into a working model of textual origins that became known as the documentary, or sometimes as the Wellhausen, hypothesis. Wellhausen brought textual and historical reasoning together. He fused existing ideas that Israelite religion developed in three stages and that the source documents had been authored in three different periods and called these strands J (after the freestyling God of Genesis 2 who was known as Yahweh), E (after the Priestly God Elohim), D, and P. He concluded that J and E derived from the time when Israelite

[32] Milton, *Paradise Lost*, book X, l. 786, p. 583.

religion was basically a fertility cult. D reflected the development of the religion into a spiritual and ethical organization and P was composed during the Priestly stage of law and order. The Priestly writer (or group of writers) was a redactor, who fused the different strands into a literary whole. For the first time, the inconsistencies, doublings, and fractures in Genesis were given a historical explanation.[33]

As Jerome McGann has argued, Blake would likely have read the work of Alexander Geddes, who was part of the circle of radicals that gathered around the publisher Joseph Johnson in late eighteenth-century London.[34] Geddes was a Scottish theologian and scholar who came to London after he was suspended from the priesthood for his unorthodox views. He anticipated Wellhausen and the Higher Criticism of the nineteenth century, suggesting that we see the Bible as a work of syncretic mythography with multiple authors. Like Blake, Geddes believed that the Bible was simply an ancient text, a collection of 'poetic tales' (E38), which the political and self-interested forces of organized religion had artificially turned into doctrine. Reading Geddes, Blake would have known that Genesis was not a singular authoritative narrative but a multi-authored, densely textured composition, rich in conflict and contradiction.

Doctrinal fixity, excluding democratic participation and suffocating the creative imagination while shoring up power and privilege, was, to Blake's mind, the very definition of bad art, 'shrunken...reptile forms' of sacrilege and social evil (E82). In 1795, Blake produced two further illuminated books: *The Book of Los* and *The Book of Ahania*. These are the books that David Worrall groups together with *The [First] Book of Urizen*, and for compelling reasons.[35] The *Book of Los* retells *The [First] Book of Urizen* just as Genesis 2 retells its first chapter. *The Book of Ahania* speaks from the margins, its female protagonist directing biblical utterance away from normative male dominance. *Urizen* itself has no fixed structure as Blake arranged the plates differently in each version. Large paintings of the same period interact thematically and visually with the works.[36] As a grouping, these books resist the artistic, religious, and social implications of singular authority.

The different ordering of images across the various versions of *The First Book of Urizen*, together with the variant versions of storytelling found in *The*

[33] For an accessible and interesting account of biblical origins, see Richard Elliot Friedman, *Who Wrote the Bible?* (New York: Simon & Schuster, 2019).

[34] McGann, 'Indeterminate Text', 303–24, 309–19.

[35] *Urizen Books*, ed. Worrall.

[36] Joseph Viscomi, 'Blake's "Annus Mirabilis": The Productions of 1795', *Blake: An Illustrated Quarterly* 41.2 (Fall 2007): 52–84.

Book of Los and *The Book of Ahania,* suggest that Blake's satire of Genesis was at least partly directed at the way the book had been read and received as a divinely sanctioned narrative, and used to justify the controlling mechanisms of organized religion.[37] We can also connect the different ordering of the plates in *Urizen* and the alternative voices introduced in *Los* and *Ahania* with the 'infinite inflexions and movements' that Blake saw as the saving grace of the 'bounding line' he praised in *A Descriptive Catalogue.* The open composition, which reflects the contemporary challenge to the Bible as a singular Word of God, makes a deliberate contrast to the monistic self-projections of Urizenic artistry and the scriptural authority used to bolster church hierarchy. The books of *Los* and *Ahania* interact with the *The [First] Book of Urizen* in a way which mirrors the stranded, woven, and elliptical texture that Geddes emphasized in his account of the Book of Genesis and the various arrangements of plates in different copies further resists singularity of narrative and purpose.

In *Ahania*, the descriptions of both Urizen and his rebellious son, Fuzon, match visual portraits offered in *Urizen*:

> Fuzon...
> On Spiked Flames rose; his hot visage
> Flam'd furious! Sparkles his hair & beard
> Shot down his wide bosom and shoulders. (E84)

In his portrait in *Urizen* Fuzon is crowned with flames, which also engulf his broad chest.[38] Urizen, described in the *Book of Ahania* as a 'cloudy God, seated on waters', is painted swimming or perhaps, sinking, as his beard floats apart and knees hunch and arms rise to battle the watery element.[39] As *Los* and *Ahania* retell the narrative of *Urizen*, we are exposed to worlds which might have been, stories which could have gone another way, voices which have been suppressed and silenced. The *Book of Ahania*, for example, fills in the narrative of Fuzon's uprising, presenting it as a moment of violent but frustrated revolution, similar to those Blake witnessed in America and France. In Blake's prophecy of *America,* Fuzon's counterpart, Orc, is successful, breaking free of the 'accursed tree' to reassert the 'fiery joy, that Urizen

[37] McGann, 'Indeterminate Text', 319–24.
[38] Object 4 of copy A; object 22 of copies C, D, and F; object 21 of copy B.
[39] Object 7 of copy A; object 5 of copy C; object 11 of copy D.

perverted to ten commands' (E54). Wreathed in flames, Fuzon represents the same 'fiery joy'. But this time Urizen nails him to the 'accurs'd Tree' that Orc escapes in *America* and his youthful, fiery form becomes a 'lifeless corse' (E87). Unlike *America*, *Ahania* leaves no room for optimism.

Urizenic religion destroys the divine energy represented by Fuzon and kills it with scriptural authority:

> the rock, swift and invisible
> On Fuzon flew, enter'd his bosom;
> His beautiful visage, his tresses,
> That gave light to the mornings of heaven
> Were smitten with darkness, deform'd
> And outstretch'd on the edge of the forest
>
> But the rock fell upon the Earth,
> Mount Sinai, in Arabia (E86)

The 'rock' that fells Fuzon is the law that Moses receives on Sinai, represented in the sepulchral stone tablets on the title page of *The [First] Book of Urizen* (Figure 3) and echoed by 'Net of Religion' which he casts over the world (Figure 6). In *America*, the figure of Orc rebels by crushing these tablets to dust. But *America* is the story of a world which might have been. The *Urizen* books are a reflection on the world that we have made, offering only a glimpse of other, possible, worlds in the voices that Urizen has suppressed. Urizen's 'book of iron' is composed at the same time as the diabolical 'Tree of Mystery' forces its 'pained root' into the earth. When Urizen drives iron 'nail[s]' into Fuzon's hands and feet and crucifies him on that tree, the spirit is destroyed by the forces of organized religion, which are maintained by the singular voice of scriptural authority. Thus Fuzon's brightness is extinguished and the 'dismal shade' of mystery, which Blake thought a sham version of eternity, descends on the earth (E87).

The Book of Ahania has another comment to make on lost narratives and worlds that might have been. Ahania is Urizen's feminine portion, 'parted soul' and the embodiment of sexual desire, which he disowns. This Eve-like creature is depicted as diminutive and childlike. The plate which precedes the title page of *Ahania* shows a small fleshy woman, with curling golden locks like Milton's Eve, crouched in between Urizen's knees looking up as he leans over her, head down, fists balled, simultaneously caressing and crushing her. She represents female sexual pleasure which the church buried in darkness and called 'Sin'. Mirroring the acts of naming in *The [First] Book of Urizen* he 'call[s] her Sin' in order exclude and disown her:

> He groan'd anguished and call'd her Sin,
> Kissing her and weeping over her;
> Then hid her in darkness in silence;
> Jealous tho' she was invisible (E85)

Hiding her in darkness buries desire. Yet Blake makes her the main character. He puts her centre-stage. In this deliberate authorial subversion of Urizenic oppression, there is a further subversion of scriptural authority. Hatsuko Niimi argues that *Ahania* bears testament to the voice of change, which is supressed under the autocratic reign of the written.[40] Ahania's 'lamenting voice' speaks from the margins, 'weeping upon the Void' (E88). She is the very opposite of Urizenic fixity: 'Her voice was heard, but no form / Had she' (E88). Sundered from Urizen, Ahania is a half-life, struggling 'on the verge of / Non-entity' (E88). But she seems less the rebellious voice of change that Niimi suggests, as the embodiment of Urizen's suppressed stories and stories of suppression. Ahania is not the voice of prophecy, which Blake admired, but lamentation, which he feared. She does not offer redemption like Fuzon, which may be one reason why her story is juxtaposed with his. She sings mournfully of a time of lost desire, lost happiness, when sex was free and pleasurable. She is, in that sense, a representation of female sexuality, which the church buried in darkness and called Eve's 'Sin'. Urizen has shut her out. 'Surging sulphureous', his passions implode as sex is aligned with sin and religious chastity binds desire in shackles of ice and the 'pained root' of the Tree of Mystery forces itself into the earth in a demonstration of rapine power.

This violent suppression of female sexuality is one of the root causes of Urizen's stillborn fallen world: 'Where bones from the earth are buried / Before they see the light' (E90). If Fuzon has his parallel in the revolutionary Orc of *America*, Ahania has hers in Oothoon, 'the soft soul of America', a Black enslaved woman who is raped and then labelled a 'whore' by the white, slaveholding patriarchy in Blake's 1793 work *Visions of the Daughters of Albion* (E46, E50). Oothoon laments the lost 'moment of desire', the hope of love and happy sexual awakening that has gone unfulfilled (E50). She uses it to express a lost narrative. For Oothoon, that narrative is the promise of a

[40] Hatsuko Niimi, 'The Book of Ahania: A Metatext', *Blake: An Illustrated Quarterly*34.2 (Fall 2000): 46–54.

new world, embodied in an American continent of sexual, political, and religious freedom. But like the new world she represents, Oothoon's promise has passed, 'stampt' in the very moment of its blossoming (E46). Her lamentations form a sterile echo across the Atlantic as the realities of slavery deny her both love and liberty.

Ahania, too, speaks of lost desire as a lost narrative of possibility: 'When I found babes of bliss on my beds. / And bosoms of milk in my chambers' (E89). Like Oothoon, her sexual promise is destroyed in the moment of fullness: 'Swell;d with ripeness & fat with fatness' (E89). United with Urizen, she could have issued forth worlds of 'infant joy' (E89). Sundered, she can but 'wander on the rocks / With hard necessity…Where bones of beasts are strown / On the bleak and snowy mountains' (E89–90). Juxtaposing life with death, soft flesh with hard bones, and warm conjugal affection with frigid chastity, Ahania makes an emotional case for the world which Christianity aborted when it buried female sexuality in darkness and called it 'Sin'. In telling her story, Blake also makes his case for the unrepresented other, the suppressed voice and 'poetic tales' hidden in doctrinal 'forms of worship'.

If *The Book of Ahania* speaks against the suppression of desire and the misogyny that aligns female sexuality with 'Sin', *The Book of Los* focuses on the relationship between religion and art. Like the books of *Urizen* and *Ahania*, it recalls a time of 'unquenchable burnings' when 'flames of desire / Ran thro' heaven and earth' (E71, E91). Like them, it laments the religious institution of sex as sin and longs for a time when 'Love and Joy were adoration: / And none impure were deemed' (E90). Urizen's rebellion is retold in a way that elides the difference between religious doctrine, empirical thought, and fallen artistic form:

> Coldness, darkness, obstruction, a Solid
> Without fluctuation, hard as adamant
> Black as marble of Egypt; impenetrable
> Bound in the fierce raging Immortal.
> And the separated fires froze in
> A vast solid without fluctuation,
> Bound in his expanding clear senses (E91)

A 'Solid / Without fluctuation', the 'impenetrable Bound[ing]' of Urizenic form foreshadows the dangers of the 'bounding line' if it does not contain 'infinite inflexions and movements'. Both here and in *The Book of Ahania* the muscular 'will of the Immortal' does not feature. Urizen's quest for fixity therefore makes a much stronger contrast with the raging disembodied fires of Eternity. Los appears as the fallen form of the Immortal who, like the rebellious Orc of *America*, crushes Urizen's stones in a violent bid for freedom:

> The Prophetic wrath, strug'ling for vent
> Hurls apart, stamping furious to dust
> And crumbling with bursting sobs; heaves
> The black marble on high into fragments (E92)

But this act of creative rebellion is already fallen. Like Urizen's revolution and Fuzon's fiery uprising, it turns on yet another, more vertiginous fall, and yet another, more shattering, dislocating, fragmentation of parts:

> the innumerable fragments away
> Fell asunder; and horrible vacuum
> Beneath him & on all sides round.
>
> Falling, falling! Los fell & fell
> Sunk precipitant heavy down down
> Times on times, night on night, day on day (E92)

As the Immortal becomes indistinguishable from Los, and subject to a terrible gravity, the poem turns on what it means to live and create within conditions of irredeemable fallenness. What worlds can we make, what images can we form, to defend against the void?

Lucy Cogan argues that *The Book of Los* confronts one of the darker and most far-reaching themes of Blake's poetry; the idea that transcendent acts of the imagination can only be achieved in a fallen world and that they involve some degree of compromise and capitulation.[41] It is certainly true that the Immortal acclimatizes to his new environment:

> The Immortal revolving; indignant
> First in wrath threw his limbs, like the babe
> New born into our world: wrath subsided
> And contemplative thoughts first arose
> Then aloft his head rear'd in the Abyss
> And his downward borne fall chang'd oblique (E91)

[41] Lucy Cogan, 'William Blake's *The Book of Los* and the Female Prophetic Tradition', *Romanticism* 21.1 (2015): 48–58. See also, Lucy Cogan, *Blake and the Failure of Prophecy* (London: Palgrave Macmillan, 2021).

Blake knew that the story of the Fall belonged partly to the genre of children's literature. The disobedient children who cross their Father's wishes are only doing what all children do on the path to maturity. As the Immortal falls, he grows up, adapts to new conditions, and rallies. The initial fury of youth gives way to the 'contemplative' 'groan[ing]' of age, 'Branchy forms' and 'inflexible organs'.

'Branchy forms' look forward to Blake's polemic on the weak mind, with 'plagiary in all its branches', in *A Descriptive Catalogue* (1809). They are deeply fallen but, recalling his own process of mark-making, they are not devoid of artistic struggle:

> Many ages of groans: till there grew
> Branchy forms. organizing the Human
> Into finite inflexible organs (E91)

'Oblique' and 'Branchy' forms thus anticipate the ways in which Blake later imbricates aesthetics and ethics in his philosophy of the line. Blake suggests that fallen form is subject to a horribly tyrannical organic materialism: hijacked by insistent growth, it tends towards inflexible finity. On the title page of *Urizen* a branch forms a kind of cavern (Figure 3). In his late poem *Milton* (*c*.1804–11) Blake gives us a clearer visual illustration of these fallen 'branchy forms' in the grotesque figure of Los vegetating into branchy looking tree roots, tortuously bent over the buried form, and immobilized head, of Urizen (Figure 7).

The fallen Immortal in *The Book of Los* floats 'Sidelong on the purple air' and bends the world to his will:

> Incessant the falling Mind labour'd
> Organising itself: til the Vacuum
> Became element, pliant to rise,
> Or to fall, or to swim, or to fly:
> With ease searching the dire Vacuity (E92–3)

As the 'Vacuum [becomes] element', it becomes pliable, mouldable, like the artist's 'clod of clay'. The Immortal has become the fallen human artist. Modelled on the God of Genesis 2, he is a giver of form in the finite world.

In this fallen universe Urizen rises like Leviathan: 'writhing upon the dark void…an iron chain / Whirling about in the Deep' (E93). As in *The [First] Book of Urizen*, Blake uses cosmology at least partly to portray the neurotic, hyper-rationalizing mind locked in its own darkness and bound with its own

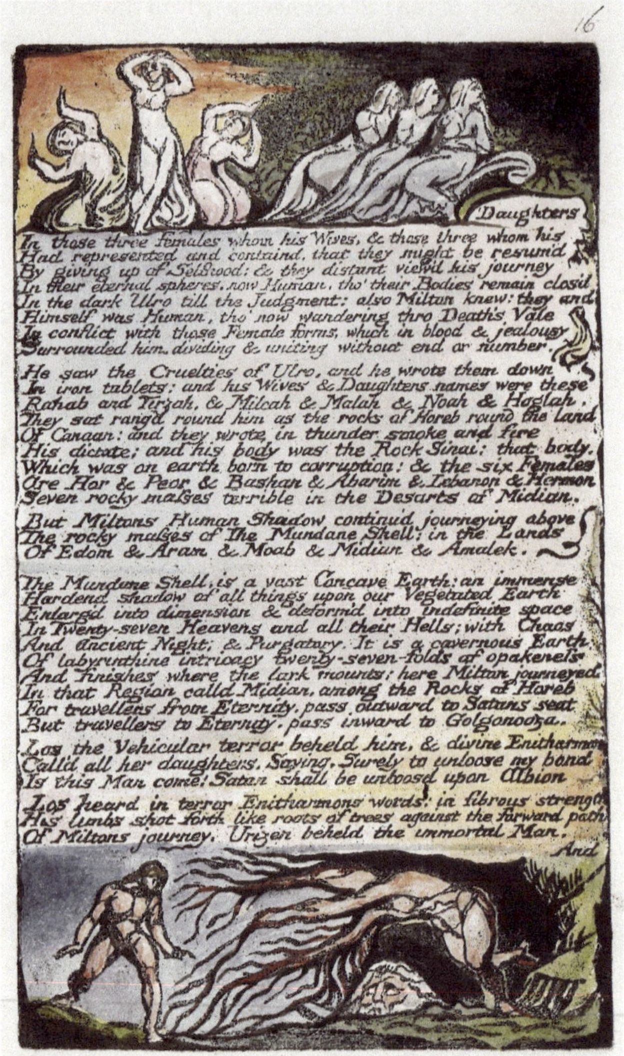

Figure 7 William Blake, 'In those three females', *Milton: A Poem in 2 Books*, 1804–11, copy A, Plate 16. © The Trustees of the British Museum.

fetters. But here, the focus of the story is Los, the prophet-artist, who battles furiously against a power he cannot control and,

> astonish'd and terrified, built
> Furnaces; he formed an Anvil
> A Hammer of adamant then began
> The binding of Urizen day and night (E94)

In *The [Frirst] Book of Urizen*, the nets which Los casts over his enemy become Urizen's own 'Net of Religion', a prison for self and world. Here, they are artworks, beautiful, burning 'orbs', forged and 'fram'd' in conditions of inescapable fallenness (E94). Through the 'nine ages', which define the seven days of creation in terms of a monstrous pregnancy, Los inextricably tethers creativity to the fallen world:

> And Los smil'd with joy.
> He the vast Spine of Urizen seiz'd
> And bound down to the glowing illusion
>
> But no light, for the Deep fled away
> On all sides, and left an unform'd
> Dark vacuity: here Urizen lay
> In fierce torments on his glowing bed. (E94)

In the fallen world, art is in bed with Urizen. Los, working tirelessly to defend against his monstrous presence, ends up as his lover, 'in darkness and deep clouds involv'd' (E94). As in the illustration of Los vegetating in *Milton*, Blake suggests that Urizen's world is the artist's bind (Figure 7).

If *Urizen* reflects the world we made, *Ahania* laments a world which might have been and *Los* bears testament to the frustrated efforts of the artist to reverse its fallen condition. Cut off from the stars, Los can only make endless fiery globes which sink, extinguished, into Urizen's 'Dark Vacuity' (E94). Blake's satire of Genesis was deeply critical of selfhood, which the Enlightenment had used reason to justify and defend, but which was also the ultimate failing of man who makes God in his image and Creators who fashion worlds unto themselves. It was damning of organized religion and profoundly political in the way it undermined the Bible as a singular narrative of scriptural authority. But it was also profoundly cognizant of his own acts of fiction-making, deeply fallen, repetitively fallible 'Orb[s] of fire… quench'd… in the Deeps' (E94). The fall that we see in *The [First] Book of Urizen* displaces its own origins and quickly proliferates. Creation is not so much identical with Fall as it is repetitively fallible. Flexible form appears as a mirage, retreating before the author in the very moment of creation. Insofar as they are satirical, the *Urizen* books involve an apparent contradiction: they simultaneously target the world-making delusions of artists and suggest that worlds *are* made in the image of the mind that makes them. They fixate on the moment of creation and immediately confine its possibility within conditions of inescapable fallenness.

Together, these three books have as much to say about encounter as creation. The horror of Urizen's fallen world is that every encounter is an encounter with the self, presented through reflexive images and mimetic creativity. But Blake's works overspill his themes and characters. The *Urizen* books, with their various arrangements of plates and intersections of voice, are also premised on an encounter with the reader for whom every authorial directive is also a point of divergence, an intersection or reordering of narrative, which folds away from received reading. The *Urizen* books counter their pessimistic portrayal of the 'self-clos'd' creative moment in which worlds are hurled forth with a sense of encounter: the ongoing conditions of history in which the moment of creation is not extinguished but subject to conflict, divergence, and possible renewal. Formally, the *Urizen* books do what their protagonist cannot. They refuse to paper over an epistemological void with certainty and they resist the fixed body as a strategy of containment and defence. They suggest, therefore, that creativity is sustained not in the self-enclosed directives of monomaniacal world-making but in the continued and divergent conditions of artistic encounter, which resist a singular narrative of experience with the erotic vulnerability of momentary capture.

The recognition of hermeneutics as a creative tool does not write the artist out. Aesthetics *are* ethics in the world-making impulse. But it does resist the kind of mimetic and self-reflexive artistry that forecloses narrative in the iterative reflections of likeness (a God who makes man in his image; a man who moulds the world to his advantage). Blake was an iterative artist, but the work changed each time. He returned repeatedly to his existing images, redrawing rather than refining. Non-identical copies resist the notion of a singular 'original' text and work against 'weak imitation, plagiarism and bungling' even as his mythology foregrounds the risk in its proliferating cast of reflexive characters.

Redemption: *Milton* (*c.*1804–1820) and *Jerusalem* (1804–*c.*1820)

By the time he died, on 12 August 1827, Blake had transcribed, and illustrated, as far as Genesis 4: 15: 'And the Lord said unto him, Therefore whosoever slayeth Cain, vengeance shall be taken upon him sevenfold. And the Lord set a mark upon Cain's forehead, lest any finding him should kill him.'[42]

[42] Blake added 'forehead' to the King James Version. In his essay on the manuscript, Robert R. Wark observes that, according to biblical scholars, this more specific indication of where the mark was set

A sketchy drawing on the final page of the manuscript depicts the mark of Cain as the kiss of forgiveness.[43] The first creator and the first destroyer are on their knees, humbled and tenderly embracing. It is not wholly clear where one form ends and another begins. It is hard to make out the details of faces or surroundings. This Old Testament God is not Urizen, shooting with compasses. He is much closer to that tender Christological figure that Blake described in his late long poem *Jerusalem*: 'not a God afar off... a brother and a friend' (E146). Blake's drawing of Cain redeemed in the very moment of his punishment reflects a combination of tenderness and severity.

In *Jerusalem*, Blake unites the Christological Redeemer with the sculptor-God of Genesis 2. Drawing on an alternative iconography that depicts Christ as the Creator of Adam and Eve, he describes the Redeemer forming Eve from Adam's rib: 'the Saviour in mercy / takes Contractions Limit, [Adam] / and of that limit he forms Woman' (E189). In the corresponding image, a figure floats, downward facing, arms outstretched, as if crucified, stigmata visible on his hands and feet. A male figure (Adam) lies unconscious on the ground. Eve's head and shoulders push out from his rib-cage, straining and staring upwards. In uniting the God of Genesis 2 with Christ, Blake suggests that a tactile, feeling, model of artistry might turn on redemption rather than irredeemable Fall. Eve might be looking into the face of her Redeemer in the very moment of her creation. The background suggests the revolutionary, fiery energy that resists stony law. But a stone-like text cuts across the middle of the plate and denotes the scriptural authority, and rule of law, which will condemn Eve, and her sex, through history. If the stone cuts across her vision, Eve is not staring into the eyes of her Redeemer but into the hard face of Moral Law. This image reveals Blake's longing for a Christological Creator in the God of Genesis 2: a model of the artist as a giver of redemptive form. But it also reveals his fear that every effort to give form might turn on conditions of irredeemable fallenness (Figure 8).

In *Milton*, Blake again invokes the artistry of Genesis 2 as a potentially redemptive model but he also worries that it might plunge us deeper into fallen conditions. He depicts the poet as the tactile sculptor-God:

> Silent Milton stood before
> The darkend Urizen; as the sculptor

may have some support in the Hebrew text. Robert R. Wark, 'Blake's Illuminated Manuscript of Genesis', in *Genesis*, ed. Wark and Crosby, 18.

43 *Genesis*, ed. Wark and Crosby, 'The Manuscript', Leaf 11.

Figure 8 William Blake, 'Then the divine hand found the two limits', *Jerusalem*, 1804–20, copy E, Plate 35. Yale Center for British Art. Paul Mellon Foundation.

Silent stands before
His forming image; he walks round
it patient labouring.
Thus Milton stood forming bright
Urizen. (E114)

Figure 9 William Blake, *Milton: A Poem in 2 Books*, 1804–11, copy A, Plate 15. © The Trustees of the British Museum.

Across the top of the corresponding plate are an ensemble of figures, thought to represent the sons and daughters of Rahab and Tirzah who lure Milton across the river with their beauty. Rahab embodies the religion of law, sin, and punishment; Tirzah represents the religion of nature and materialism (Figure 9). They personify the fallen forms of organized religion, which Blake condemned as bad art. On the one hand, Blake presents Milton as a fallen artist, who, in his artistic efforts, reinforces those fallen forms and falls further from spiritual wholeness, moulding the figure of Urizen. In Urizen's world, the redemptive function of art turns to ransom. To ransom has a double meaning: it is both the act of delivering from sin or damnation and redeeming a person or object through extorted economic transaction. Los toils tirelessly for a connection to the infinite, as if it has been ransomed for the price of his labour. He ends up building Urizen's body as obstruction. In *The Marriage of Heaven and Hell*, an early satire of organized religion composed in 1790, Blake had light-heartedly and subversively adopted the 'Voice of the Devil' as the voice of the poet and affectionately criticized Milton's Puritanism in what has become a well-known side note: 'Note: the reason Milton wrote in fetters when he wrote of Angels & God, and at liberty when of Devils and Hell, is because he was a True Poet and of the Devils party without knowing it' (E35). In *Milton*, Blake shows us the poet building his own 'fetters' as he is seduced by the sons and daughters of Rahab and Tirzah, shaping Urizen's form, and ransoming his poetic gifts in an effort to justify God's ways to man.

Yet Milton's creative poetic energy becomes manifest if we see this as an image of him resisting, rather than sculpting, the form of Urizen. Depicted against a black background with his hands at Urizen's throat, the figure recalls Jacob wrestling with a mysterious night-time deity at Peniel as much as he recalls the God of Genesis 2, moulding form out of matter. The God with whom Jacob has power has a demonic element: he is afraid of daylight and uses dark magic to try to win the fight. Jacob faces the struggle alone, with surprising success.

> And Jacob was left alone; and there wrestled a man with him until the breaking of the day. And when he saw that he prevailed not against him, he touched the hollow of his thigh; and the hollow of Jacob's thigh was out of joint, as he wrestled with him. And he said, Let me go, for the day breaketh. And he said, I will not let thee go, except thou bless me. And he said unto him, What is thy name? And he said, Jacob. And he said, Thy name shall be called no more Jacob but Israel, for as a prince thou has power with God and with men, and hast prevailed...And Jacob called the name of the place Peniel: for I have seen God face to face, and my life is preserved.[44]

Jacob becomes a figure for Blake's Milton partly because of this narrative of struggle with a morally ambiguous force and the sudden and surprising revelation of its end. Blake was not the only Romantic to take Jacob as a figure for the questing poet. For Emily Dickinson, Jacob was also a 'pugilist' and 'poet', who was 'bewildered' when he found he had 'worsted God' in the moment of inspiration.[45] Blake's Milton, wrestling with Urizen, suggests something akin

[44] Gen. 32: 24–30.

[45] Dickinson aligned herself with Jacob as a 'Pugilist and Poet' in an 1886 letter to Thomas Wentworth Higginson. Thomas H. Johnson ed., *Letters of Emily Dickinson* (Boston: Belknap Press, 1997), 903. Dickinson's description of Jacob as a 'bewildered Gymnast' who 'Found he had worsted God' occurs in an early poem (Fr145), a variant of which was first sent to her sister-in-law, Sue Dickinson, in 1860. Herman Melville also aligned Jacob with the artist, 'Art', as did Rainer Maria Rilke, 'The Man Watching'.

to this unpredictable Dickinsonian struggle. The artist battles with the forces of darkness, but, just as it is not clear whether Eve is looking into the tender face of her Redeemer or the stony face of Moral Law, it is not clear whether the outcome of Milton's struggle will be to build or destroy Urizen: to reinforce fallen form or, by creative effort, become blessed.

In a letter to Thomas Butts, dated April 1803, Blake talked about his work over the last three years, saying that the immensity of *Milton* rendered the time taken over its production non-existent:

> I have written this Poem from immediate Dictation, twelve or sometimes twenty lines at a time without Premeditation & even against my Will. the Time it has taken in writing was thus renderd Non Existent. & an Immense Poem Exists which seems which seems to be the Labour of a long Life all produced without Labour or Study. (E728–9)

Blake's feeling that greatness in some sense annihilates effort acknowledges that, as we encounter a great poem, it still 'seems to be the Labour of a long Life'. Grace is baffling, especially to those who work hard. Blake is always trying to reconcile his faith in the redemptive function of the moment of inspiration with his equal, and more energetic, faith in creative action.

In *Milton* Blake draws a distinction between election and redemption, critiquing the former and recommending the latter:

> And the Elect shall say to the Redeemd. We behold it is of Divine
> Mercy alone! of Free Gift and Election that we live.
> Our Virtues & Cruel Goodnesses, have deserv'd Eternal
> Death. (E107)

Redemption is preferable to election because it demands work as well as grace. Redemption is not a 'Free Gift', but nor is it earned. As Sarah Haggarty explains, Blake dislikes the idea of a 'Free Gift' but he also works very hard to excise Urizenic figures of debt, ransom, money, and price from his notion of redemption, even though they are present in the Bible. Thus, in *Jerusalem*, Jehovah's angel says: 'Jehovah's Salvation is without Money & without Price' (E212).[46]

Grace and inspiration arrive suddenly and unexpectedly, with the seeming effortlessness of comic resolution, but they are not to be repaid quickly or in

46 Sarah Haggarty, *Blake's Gifts: Poetry and the Politics of Exchange* (Cambridge: CUP, 2010), p. 30.

kind. For, as Haggarty has argued, to return too quickly is like paying off 'services rendered', and 'to expect quick gratitude is to pull rank'.[47] Reciprocity, as opposed to intermeasurability, is vital to the value Blake places in artistic labour. In *Milton*, only the 'Industrious' can find the redemptive moment of inspiration. They expect no payment for their labour, but their efforts function as a kind of reciprocal and voluntary giving, a deserving openness. Blake describes the moment of inspiration as something that no amount of effort can find without the grace of God and yet effort is still vital to grace:

> There is a Moment in each Day that Satan cannot find
> Nor can his Watch Fiends find it, but the Industrious find
> This Moment & it multiply, & when it once is found
> It Renovates every Moment of the Day if rightly placed. (E136)

Blake affirms industry as the condition for greatness, but it is also something in which limit inheres. You can work as hard as you like and never find inspiration or grace. In *Jerusalem*, Los builds Urizen's body as nets; his daughters work incessantly only to create more fallen, and fearful, forms:

> Other daughters of Los, labouring at looms less fine
> Create the Silk-Worm & the Spider & the Catterpiller [sic]
> To assist in their most grievous work of Pity and
> Compassion. (E209)

The gate of Los is 'by vegetations viewless': 'tho' they [Satan's Watch Fiends] search numbring every grain / of sand on Earth evry night. they never find this Gate' (E181).

Whereas other writers of the period frequently framed the ethics of encounter in terms of sympathy, Blake favoured the more volatile notion of friendship.[48] Criticizing Rousseau, he accused him of having no friends. In *Jerusalem*, Blake emphasized that friendship makes you vulnerable to injury:

[47] Haggarty, *Blake's Gifts*, 74–88.

[48] See Jonathan Lamb, *The Evolution of Sympathy in the Long Eighteenth Century* (London: Pickering & Chatto, 2009) and Ildiko Csengei, *Sympathy, Sensibility and the Literature of Feeling in the Eighteenth Century* (Basingstoke: Palgrave, 2012). For a broader discussion of intimacy and the ethics of encounter beyond sympathy in other Romantic writers, see Nancy Yousef, *Romantic Intimacy* (Stanford, Calif.: Stanford University Press, 2013). Sarah Eron argues that *The Book of Urizen* offers a commentary on the moral and structural failings of sympathy, '"Bound by their Narrowing Perceptions": Sympathetic Bondage and Perverse Pity in *The Book of Urizen*', *Blake: An Illustrated Quarterly* 46.3 (Winter 2012–13): 1–13.

'It is easier to forgive an Enemy than to forgive a Friend, the man who permits you to injure him deserves your vengeance. / He also will receive it' (E251). Blake values these risks, and they are the very opposite of Urizen's defensive postures. Friendship thus differs vastly from pity and compassion, which, Blake believes, are only ever really forms of disowning. Blake draws a parallel between the aesthetics of redemptive fiction-making and the ethics of friendship in a 'bounding line' which in its 'infinite inflexions and movements' is open and vulnerable to hurt. In Blake's comedy of errors, a happy ending comes in the condition of fallenness and only by the grace of God. Redemption arrives suddenly and unexpectedly as we make ourselves vulnerable through the erratic encounters and continuous creative efforts Blake understands as acts of true friendship and the foundation of artistic world-building. As he puts it in *Jerusalem*:

> One first in friendship & love; then a Divine
> Family &, in the midst,
> Jesus will appear. (E251)

3

Errancy, Accident, and Desire

Dickinson's Open Endings

Emily Dickinson's speakers and subjects often slip up. What is interesting is how they find their feet. A plank in reason breaks and sends consciousness into freefall, landing, finally, on more uncertain ground; a 'decoy' sends the credulous wildly and pleasurably off course; 'Faith slips—and laughs, and rallies'.[1] As one speaker puts it, we maintain a 'precarious gait' because the risk of destabilization accompanies every step we take (Fr926). Maurice Lee has noticed that Dickinson's poems are full of surprises, accidents like these little slips, which both call attention to, and resist, the stability of received narratives. A poem which begins 'Meeting by Accident' (Fr1578) sets chance against Design and destiny by describing an extraordinary unpredictable 'error' that only happens once a century. 'To interrupt his Yellow Plan' (Fr622) parodies the providential will of the Father-God in the image of the tyrannical Sun working against 'Caprices of the Atmosphere'. In 'Luck is not Chance' (Fr1360), aleatory experience dismisses, as too easy, the argument from Design, but, as Lee says, it 'cannot wholly foreclose the potential of Providence'.[2]

If Rousseau exemplifies the pessimism that accompanies the secularization of the Fall narrative, and Blake illustrates the hope that is retained by a fundamentally religious faith in redemption, Dickinson stages a dynamic nineteenth-century tension between design and chance. In this context, the Fall is either an event which happens as part of a providential plan that includes Christ's redemptive sacrifice, or it is an accident of circumstance, where futures are multiple and unknown. Like Rousseau, Dickinson recognizes the way in which the idea of the Fall helps us make sense of experience, giving narrative shape to the long span of evolutionary time and imposing

[1] *The Poems of Emily Dickinson: Variorum Edition*, ed. R. W. Franklin (Cambridge, Mass.: Harvard University Press, 1998), poem numbers: 340, 310, 373. Unless otherwise stated, all further references are to this edition, included in the text with the abbreviation Fr.

[2] Maurice Lee, *Uncertain Chances: Science, Skepticism and Belief in Nineteenth-Century American Literature* (Oxford: OUP, 2012), 167–8.

The Myth of the Fall in Nineteenth-Century Literature. Linda Freedman, Oxford University Press.
 DOI: 10.1093/oso/9780198969570.003.0004

meaning on unpredictable outcomes. Conceiving of the Fall as an everyday slip or trip becomes an instrumental part of her challenge to authority, suggesting that freak accidents and unplanned encounters might engender new ways of knowing and potentially lead to fundamental shifts in ways of being in the world.

She often sets a reading of Genesis in which the world was authored by the forbidding structures of divine dictat, the vertically positioned and strictly out of reach 'Apple on the Tree' (Fr310), against a reading in which the world might be poetically and subversively reordered by the errant structures of disobedience, desire, and play, and the serendipitous possibilities of accident in a world liberated from design. Yet there are also poems in which she imagines the poetic reordering of existence as just another childish prelapsarian fantasy. Dickinson takes pleasure in errancy, allowing poetry to become a subversive space in which she can challenge received orthodoxies and indulge a more creative form of exegetical play. But she finds it easier to satirize the authoritarian Father-God than the evolutionary forces of circumstance and chance, which seem just as much of a threat to the agency of human authorship and hold no hope of redemption.

Dickinson recognizes the way in which received readings of the Bible shape our world, governing the way we live—and sometimes even the way we die—and she often uses her Fall poems to challenge orthodox interpretations. One might theorize Dickinson's revisionary poetic exegesis as a version of what Hayden White, responding to Eric Auerbach, has called figural realism. White argues that: 'if historical discourse is to be comprehended as productive of a certain kind of knowledge, it must first be analysed as a structure of language'.[3] For White, figural methods of interpreting and ordering the world become a way not just of reading, but also potentially reconfiguring, world-shaping discourse. Dickinson invested in the idea that figures and types might be more than a way of making sense of experience. The question she asks is twofold. How far can poetic architectures, figures, and tropes provide us with meaning and pattern as teleological order is lost; and how far can revisionary exegesis shape the world anew?

She was coy about her own faith, writing in a letter four years before her death: 'On subjects of which we know nothing, or should I say *Beings*—we both believe, and disbelieve a hundred times an Hour, which keeps believing

[3] Hayden White, *Figural Realism: Studies in the Mimesis Effect* (Baltimore and London: Johns Hopkins University Press, 1999), 4.

nimble.'[4] She would never commit to believing, or disbelieving, in God and, like Blake, she was resistant to orthodox interpretations of the Bible. Drawing our attention to the Bible as a collection of stories, Dickinson emphasized the multiple ways in which the poetic teller might shape the tale. Delighting in lateral movements, alternative words, unorthodox interpretations, and erotic desires, Dickinson, like Blake, levels a critique at scriptural authority as she celebrates the discoveries that are made when we move away from received readings and land on more unstable cognitive ground.

'Not an Instant's Act': Darwin and Real Loss

In Dickinson's century, it was Charles Darwin who was credited with overturning the received reading of the world. In a late letter to Otis Philip Lord, dated 1882, she related the town gossip on the controversial Massachusetts politician, Benjamin F. Butler: 'Mrs Dr Stearns called to know if we didn't think it very shocking for Butler to "liken himself to his Redeemer".' Dickinson commented rather archly to Lord: 'We [presumably herself and her sister] thought Darwin had thrown the Redeemer away' (*Letters*, 750).[5] Dickinson's jest is playful but it makes a serious point. Darwin's disruption, as she presents it here, is a hermeneutic one. Christ is not the Creator-God imperilled by evolutionary theories; he is the figure who, in Christian theology, gives that creation meaning by promising the redemption of eternal life. Dickinson's joke recognizes that Darwin's evolutionary theories were as much, if not more, of a danger to the Christian sense of an ending as they were to an orthodox faith in the biblical account of the world's beginning.

Published in 1859, *On the Origin of Species* seriously challenged the creation story found in Genesis. But it posed an even greater threat to the Christian interpretation of Genesis 3 as the catastrophic loss of an original goodness that would be redeemed in the fullness of time. In an essay on Darwin's theological virtues, James Williams talks about Darwin's commitment to narrative shape, noting the frequent crescendos in his prose, and commenting: 'Darwin's faith is always in dialogue with, and in some ways continuous with, hope, the virtue which is at work in the accretive way his

[4] Emily Dickinson, *Letters of Emily Dickinson*, ed. Thomas H. Johnson (Boston: Belknap Press, 1997), 750.

[5] I am indebted here to Jane Donahue Eberwein, 'Outgrowing Genesis: Dickinson, Darwin and the Higher Criticism', in *Emily Dickinson and Philosophy*, ed. Jedd Deppman, Marianne Noble, and Gary Lee Stonum (Cambridge: CUP, 2013), 47–68, 47.

writing orders facts towards conclusions.'[6] In giving us the sense of an ending Darwin is partly compensating for his own anxieties, knowing the threat his observations posed to teleological order and wanting to hold on to the hope that fallen creation might be redeemed. Naturalism had origins in theology, looking to the world for evidence of God's design. As late as 1802, William Paley published *Natural Theology or Evidences of the Existence and Attributes of the Deity*, arguing that there could be no watch without a watchmaker. Between 1830 and 1833, Charles Lyell composed his *Principles of Geology*, one of the most important pre-Darwinian works on evolution. It made a strong argument, supported by extensive fieldwork and data collection, that the earth was formed by continuous, gradual processes. He maintained the value of empirical evidence in his work, arguing that our sense of the earth's history should be drawn only from what we could presently observe in its surface. In 1844, Robert Chambers published *Vestiges of the Natural History of Creation*. It mattered because, like Lyell's *Principles of Geology*, it imagined the history of the natural world in terms of developmental change instead of creation and design.

Darwin was not the first to notice that things disappeared without coming back. That idea was introduced by Georges Cuvier in the early nineteenth century, to some theological alarm.[7] But Darwin popularized the notion of extinction: real, irredeemable, loss without the hope of resurrection or redemption. 'The Things that can never come back, are several—', writes Dickinson in a late poem, 'Childhood—Some forms of Hope—the Dead' (Fr1564). Both the classical and Christian worldviews allowed that death could be rebirth. 'All things do change. But nothing, sure, doth perish', declares Pythagoras towards the end of Ovid's *Metamorphoses*.[8] 'The last enemy that shall be destroyed is death', writes St Paul in 1 Corinthians. Darwin, on the other hand, observed that things could be 'utterly lost', noting 'there will be much extinction of the less improved forms'.[9] This was a major departure in the experience of grief and Darwin felt the anxiety around it, seeking to offset his notions of extinction with a sense of benevolent

[6] James Williams, 'Darwin's Theological Virtues', in *Thinking through Style: Non-Fiction Prose of the Long Nineteenth Century*, ed. Michael D. Hurley and Marcus Waithe (Oxford: OUP, 2018), 149–161, 156. Gillian Beer has also written brilliantly on the way in which Darwin's authorial voice counters the loss of teleological order, *Darwin's Plots: Evolutionary Narrative in Darwin, George Eliot and nineteenth-Century Fiction* (Oxford: OUP, 2009), 41.

[7] Georges Cuvier, *Essay on the Theory of the Earth* [1813] (London: Routledge, 2018).

[8] *Ovid's Metamorphoses*, tr. Arthur Golding, edited with an introduction and notes by Madeleine Forey (London: Penguin, 2002), 440.

[9] Charles Darwin, *On the Origin of Species* (Oxford: OUP, 2008), 317, 83.

direction: 'old forms will be supplanted by new and improved forms.'[10] This was the aspect of Darwinian thought that led to Herbert Spencer's more insidious theory of the 'survival of the fittest', with its fascistic appeal. But it was first, for Darwin, a way of mitigating the grief that went hand-in-hand with evolutionary theory.

Extinction was also an argument against the sudden catastrophic moment of the Fall. 'That natural selection will always act with extreme slowness, I fully admit', wrote Darwin.[11] In his reworkings of the Fall, Rousseau had exposed the way disasters seem to come upon us with unexpected suddenness precisely because they happen so slowly. Dickinson, too, realized that there is often no sudden catastrophic moment of loss, just a belated feeling of emptiness and regret:

> Eden is that old-fashioned House
> We dwell in every day
> Without suspecting our abode
> Until we drive away.
>
> How fair on looking back, the Day
> We sauntered from the Door—
> Unconscious our returning,
> But discover it no more.
>
> (Fr1734)

Her erotic poems sometimes use Eden to demarcate a placeless utopia which resists the shape of time and express a hypothetical ecstasy which elides the difference between sex and death.[12] But her poems on the Fall, and her broader use of the trope of errancy, recognize the ontologically destabilizing force of accident and chance and explore our need for an organizing hermeneutic in order to make sense of a world in which losses feel so sudden because they come upon us unnoticed.

In a poem beginning 'Crumbling is not an instant's Act', Dickinson debunks the myth of a sudden and catastrophic Fall with the slow processes of evolutionary decline, drawing attention to way in which patterns of interpretation change according to the dominant worldview.

> Crumbling is not an instant's Act
> A fundamental pause

[10] Darwin, *Origin*, 350. [11] Darwin, *Origin*, 83.
[12] See 'Wild Nights—Wild Nights!' (Fr269) and 'Come slowly—Eden!' (Fr205).

Dilapidation's processes
Are organized Decays—

'Tis first a Cobweb on the Soul
A Cuticle of Dust
A Borer in the Axis
An Elemental Rust—

Ruin is formal—Devil's work
Consecutive and slow—
Fail in an instant, no man did
Slipping—is Crashe's law—
(Fr1010)

This is an exegetical poem on Genesis 3, which refracts, with characteristic irony, some of the theological anxieties around evolution. It confronts a desire to render slip-ups, and chance events, meaningful within world-ordering narratives. In this poem, the Fall becomes both the accidental 'slip' of everyday mishap and a long and mundane process which resists narrative shape. Dickinson acknowledges (and slightly parodies) our need for patterns of interpretation. Turning a crash into a 'Law' attributed to a fictional individual named 'Crashe' is a quip on the laws of physics used to explain the workings of the universe in a manner equivalent to Design and makes a joke of both accident and providence. She conceives of dilapidation in terms of 'organized Decays': this organization further reflecting (and again somewhat parodying) the need for interpretative patterns. The poem tracks shifting vocabularies, which map different intellectual orderings of the accidental process of decay; the spiritual 'Cobweb on the Soul' gives way to the corporeal 'Cuticle of Dust', which transmutes into the natural 'Borer in the Axis' and finally the scientific 'Elemental rust'. The idea of a moment where it all went wrong, the instant of failure, or the Fall, is a nonsense here: 'Fail in an instant, no man did'. But the need for hermeneutic structures, for a 'Law' or language that will render accident legible, remains intact.

The way in which accident immediately becomes subject to an organizing hermeneutic has an ontological importance because it both reflects and shapes our way of being in the world. It is, to carry Dickinson's conceit, how we find our feet when understanding slips. By the nineteenth century, the religious hermeneutic that Dickinson expresses through the 'cobweb on the soul', the philosophic materialism which can be seen, in part, in the corporeal decay of a 'cuticle of dust', and the Reformation theology which encouraged Christians to read the Book of Nature had also passed through the

Enlightenment. The 'Borer in the Axis' reflects the kind of intellectual curiosity which invests in the observation of natural phenomena as a primary site of new knowledge. Our way of being in the world was no longer rooted in the revelation of a divine plan but our own mental processes: our ability to form a hypothesis based on empirical evidence and act accordingly.[13]

Dickinson recognizes that such narratives reflect the shaping force of dominant worldviews and thus implicitly acknowledges that hermeneutic shifts are ontological shifts. Like Darwin, she was well aware that the hermeneutics of existence were always involved with questions of its authorship. Recuperating accident from the myth of the Fall while simultaneously acknowledging the long intellectual history of narrative reordering evinces an understanding that the interpretation of Genesis 3 both reflects and shapes our way of being in the world. As she reworks the myth of the Fall, Dickinson wonders about the ontological claims of poetic exegesis: the extent to which creative reading and poetic rewriting of biblical tales might be a world-making tool.

Errant Boys: Poetry and Exegetical Play

Dickinson recognized that Genesis 3 is partly a story about growing up and her poetic retellings were culturally conditioned by late eighteenth-century developments in the conception of childhood. Anna Rowland explains the way the discourse developed after Rousseau's influential writings: 'the "Romantic child" earns its sobriquet because it is essentially an idealised, nostalgic, sentimental figure of childhood, one characterised by innocence, imagination, nature and primitivism'.[14] In this vision of childhood, the exploratory child was no longer a wicked creature, in need of constant chastisement and correction, but a force for innocence and good. Dickinson inherits the Romantic conception of the child as an innocently transgressive and fundamentally creative poetic figure and her child personae frequently challenge the social hierarchies, received wisdoms, and formulaic behaviours which define being grown up. Through the figure of the child, often a 'boy' or a tomboyish girl, Dickinson adopts a voice that is both unfallen and profoundly transgressive; the boy is both an innocent and wicked creature. In a

[13] See Ross Hamilton, *Accident: A Philosophical and Literary History* (Chicago and London: University of Chicago Press, 2007), 127.

[14] Anna Wierda Rowland, *Romanticism and Childhood: The Infantilisation of British Literary Culture* (Cambridge: CUP, 2012), 9.

light-hearted and subversively silly Fall poem about disobedient fruit-picking, transgressive reaching, and the 'stain' of Sin, she identifies with this figure and sets it against a parody of the authoritarian Father-God as a scolding matron:

> Over the fence—
> Strawberries—grow—
> Over the fence—
> I could climb—if I tried, I know—
> Berries are nice!
>
> But—if I stained my Apron—
> God would certainly scold!
> Oh, dear—I guess if He were a Boy—
> He'd—climb—if He could!
>
> (Fr271)

Dickinson's 'Boy' is not a fetishized vision of the child as the oracle of truth, but it does retain a Romantic idea of childhood as a trope through which to rehearse the disruptive reordering of the adult world.

Both the figure of the child and a wandering aesthetic become central to the question of revisionary poetic exegesis.[15] She published only a handful of poems in her lifetime, most probably against her wishes, but when she died, she left a large group of manuscript poems in various stages of completion and, often, in variant versions, or with variant words recorded. Her sister Lavinia decided that these were Dickinson's letter to the world and should be published, but the first publication of a selection of poems was rather delayed and hampered by a family quarrel and the manuscripts were split up. The first half of the twentieth century saw a number of selected editions and scores of new poems come to public attention but it was not until 1955 that the first three-volume Variorum edition was published, edited by T. H. Johnson, with all known variants. This was followed, in 1998, by R. W. Franklin's Variorum edition, which is now the standard scholarly reference. Johnson and Franklin both released one-volume reading editions, more portable and affordable for the interested lay-reader, but the compromise was to exclude the wandering aesthetic that Dickinson made central to her practice.[16]

[15] Franklin notes three (one lost) variant versions of this poem, written about 1882.

[16] The scholarly debate around the publication and editing of Dickinson's poems has a long and complicated history. For Franklin's early sense of this see R. W. Franklin, *The Editing of Emily*

Playful thinking about biblical texts allows Dickinson to lampoon scriptural authority and undermine the trend towards historical scholarship. But it also makes a serious point: exegesis builds the stories that take on the currency of truth and create the fictions by which we live. Dickinson has an abiding interest in a kind of exegesis which rethinks biblical hierarchies and challenges accepted worldviews. A late poem, which she revised several times, introduces a 'Diagnosis of the Bible, by a Boy'. The Bible, as it has been received over the course of history, appears both as an object of satire, antiquated, heavy, and voluminous, and a foundational literary text.

> Diagnosis of the Bible, by a Boy—
>
> The Bible is an untold Volume
> Written by unknown Men—
> By the direction of hallowed Spectres—
> Subjects—Bethlehem—
>
> Genesis—Bethlehem's Ancestor—
> Satan—the Brigadier—
> Judas—the first Defaulter—
> David—the Troubadour—
>
> Sin—a distinguished Precipice—
> But I must desist—
> Boys that believe—are very lonesome—
> Other Boys—are lost—
>
> Had but the Tale a thrilling Teller
> All the Boys would come—
> Orpheus' sermon captivated
> It did not condemn
>
> (Fr1577)

The first line of this poem is often left out of reading editions of Dickinson's poetry.[17] But it sets the tone well: the wry introduction of the poem as biblical 'Diagnosis', offered by the subversive faux-innocent alter-ego of the 'Boy', is satirical. The poem can be read as an irreverent caricature of a text and a set of subjects Dickinson had been taught to treat with holy reverence and fear.

Dickinson (Madison, Wis.: University of Wisconsin Press, 1967).

[17] Johnson and Franklin both exclude the line from their reading editions and choose the later variant in which 'Untold' is replaced by 'Antique'.

Her juvenile speaker diagnoses many of the problems Dickinson saw in the church; here, the Bible is variously out-of-touch, antiquated, judgemental, terrifying, and alienating. But the persona is also an affectionate satire. A later version of this poem was sent to a real and beloved boy (her nephew, Ned) whom Dickinson may well have identified with the poem's speaker. The childish exegete is very sure of himself, as children often are, convinced that he has identified both problem and solution. He mimics as well as critiques the authoritarian tones of eminent biblical scholars. When her cheeky speaker throws his hands up and 'desist[s]' from his sport, as one might 'desist' from the 'precipice' of 'Sin', satire of the church and of biblical exegesis gives way to sympathy for the stories which might 'captivate' an audience. Dickinson's critique rests on the opening pun: she rescues the 'untold Volume' of stories, which may yet find its 'thrilling Teller', from the 'untold Volume' of heavy sermonizing she heard as a child.

The first stanza demonstrates a keen awareness of exegetical practice. In the Puritan tradition, which Dickinson inherited, the primary mode of biblical exegesis was typology: Old Testament figures and types had their fulfilment in New Testament antitypes. Describing 'Genesis' as 'Bethlehem's ancestor' is typology viewed backwards. The characterization of Satan as a 'brigadier' pays homage to Milton and is a tacit acknowledgement of the way our reading of the Bible is shaped by the cultural myths and literary works which surround it. Dickinson extracts certain narratives and knowingly excludes others. Casting Judas as 'the great defaulter' is deliberately ironic; Judas fulfilled his public duty but failed in his private commitments of friendship and loyalty. David, here, is not the warrior but the writer of psalms. 'Sin' is satirized as a predictable plot twist, the 'distinguished precipice', the inevitable fall.

Dickinson is also in dialogue with contemporary theories about biblical composition. The idea that the Old Testament was composed over three distinct historical periods, rather than divinely revealed to Moses, culminated in the work of the late nineteenth-century scholar Julius Wellhausen, who synthesized a century of biblical enquiry into a working theory of biblical origins. In Dickinson's poem, current notions of biblical authorship are rendered questionable even as they are given some support. This version has the authors as 'unknown', countering the sure-footed tones of historical scholarship but also upholding the idea that the author was definitely not Moses (as earlier theories had maintained). Another version has them as 'faded'. Like the 'hallowed Spectres' at whose bidding they wrote, they may be falsely venerated ghosts or increasingly irrelevant relics of a past age.

Dickinson's library included a copy of William Jenks's *Companion to the Bible*, which reflected the debates on translation and authorship that changed biblical scholarship in the nineteenth century and drew attention to the Bible as a historical and material text.[18] In 1867, Professor C. E. Stowe published his *Origin and History of the Books of the Bible*, which was reviewed in *The Atlantic Monthly*, to which the Dickinson family subscribed. The reviewer commented:

> He [Stowe] brings into prominence a theory now held, we believe, by all the best biblical critics but not, we think, very familiar to the common mind, that the Bible is not an original record, but is made up of the fragments of Hebrew literature, going back to a remote and even to an unknown antiquity. This point will be recognised as one of singular interest and of great importance; especially in connection with the Old Testament.[19]

For Jenks, Stowe, and his reviewer, the primary concern was to arrive at the truest version of the Bible. Dickinson's scepticism towards the truth-claims of historical scholarship bears comparison with those of her contemporary, the Transcendentalist minister, essayist, and poet, Ralph Waldo Emerson. Emerson grew weary of the way contemporary Christianity 'dwell[ed], with noxious exaggeration about the *person* of Jesus'.[20] For Emerson, the emphasis on the historicity of the Bible suffered from an all-too-familiar dogmatism. As his Calvinist ancestors had insisted on the authenticity and subsequent authority of the Divine Word, so his contemporaries seemed to enforce their authority through the truth-claims of historical artefacts and people. Calling for a new age in which the role of 'priest' and 'poet' was interchangeable, he united religious and poetic office.[21] Dickinson was no Transcendentalist. But, like Emerson, and like Blake, she accepted, and to some extent internalized, the destabilization of biblical authority. Like Emerson, she remained sceptical about the justifying claims of historical scholarship, even as she accepted the

[18] Jenks's *Companion* is available online in digitalized image reproduction https://archive.org/details/comprehensivecom05jenk (last accessed 31 July 2017). Dickinson's copy is in the Houghton Library, Harvard, Call No. EDR 458.

[19] *Atlantic Monthly* 21.1 (Boston: Ticknor & Fields, 1868), 123–7, 124. Available via *The Making of America* https://babel.hathitrust.org/cgi/pt?id=coo.31924079597047&view=1up&seq=6 (last accessed 18 Oct. 2022).

[20] Ralph Waldo Emerson, 'An Address Delivered before the Senior Class in Divinity College, Cambridge 1838', in Emerson, *Selected Essays*, ed. Larzer Ziff (Harmondsworth: Penguin, 1982), 107–27, 114.

[21] Emerson, *Selected Essays*, 117.

Bible as a historically produced text: 'Ararat's a Legend—now— / And no one credits Noah', she wrote in 1863 (Fr532).

Dickinson was clearly thinking about the character and qualities of storytelling when she wrote her late poem 'diagnos[ing]' the Bible because she included an astonishing thirteen variants for 'thrilling': 'typic, hearty, bonnie, breathless, spacious, tropic, warbling (*written twice*), ardent, friendly, magic, pungent, winning, mellow'.[22] Cristanne Miller has suggested, rather persuasively, that Dickinson *did* make final decisions about the ways in which her poems should be read. But this is a case where she seems to have struggled to decide, as she enumerated the messy and complex set of qualities she associated with her own craft.[23] Words like 'mellow', 'magic', 'friendly', and 'winning' suggest a seductive approach to narration. Yet 'magic' is, in many ways, the opposite of 'friendly'; it is ethereal and invisible rather than companionable and inviting. Perhaps Dickinson's 'magic' teller is closer to her 'breathless' one. In Dickinson's lexicon, 'breathless' suggests something unearthly and beyond mortality as well as something furiously racing with the life that 'hearty', 'bonnie', and 'ardent' bring to the fore. This is significant not just because it seems to be a general celebration of exegesis as storytelling but also because it emphasizes the multiple ways in which the teller may shape the tale. In other words, in a poem in which she was clearly thinking about different kinds of voices and modes of reception, and in which her boy speaker both satirizes the interpretation and moral codification of biblical texts and is affectionately satirized as another childishly overconfident exegete, Dickinson identifies exegesis as the very opposite of 'Diagnosis'; not something which uncovers meaning, but something which creates it.

In 'The Bible is an untold Volume' the boy exegete has gone deliberately, and playfully, off course: he has chosen to be 'lost'. He aligns himself with 'Orpheus', the legendary poet-prophet-musician of Greek mythology, who stands, here, as a figure of the creative fallen exegete, whose narrative movements are lateral rather than linear. For, if 'condemn[ation]' is a top-down structure, implying transgression and punishment, 'captiv[ation]' suggests something more wayward and enticing: the pull of desire as opposed to the strictures of doctrine. Darwin had been troubled by a sense of his own theological errancy but Dickinson delights in the poetic pleasure of going astray,

[22] The thirteen alternatives for 'thrilling' appear in an extra stanza at the end of the earliest recorded version of this poem, written in pencil on a discarded bifolium of stationary and addressed to her sister, Vinnie, in an unidentified hand. *Poems of Emily Dickinson*, ed. Franklin, vol. 3, 1381.

[23] *Emily Dickinson's Poems as she Preserved Them*, ed. Cristanne Miller (Cambridge, Mass.: Harvard University Press, 2016).

setting the trope of errancy against the trope of authority.[24] If the former is associated with a sort of innocent fallenness and revolves around childhood, playfulness, poetry, and desire, the latter is connected to the strict hierarchical order imposed by the prohibition in Eden.

In '"Heaven"—is what I cannot reach!', a poem in which Dickinson explicitly turns to Genesis 3, the shape of language is even more clearly linked to moral codes.

> "Heaven"—is what I cannot reach!
> The Apple on the Tree—
> Provided it do hopeless—hang—
> That—"Heaven" is—to Me!
>
> The Color, on the Cruising Cloud—
> The interdicted Land—
> Behind the Hill—the House behind—
> There—Paradise—is found!
>
> Her teasing Purples—Afternoons—
> The credulous—decoy—
> Enamored—of the Conjuror—
> That spurned us—Yesterday!
> (Fr310)

Two discourses of 'Heaven' exist in this poem. In the first instance, there is the received notion. Dickinson places that discourse within the vertical structures and reported speech on which it relies. This is what she has been told to want and told she is not good enough to have. But the poem dwells precisely in the pleasures of not having and so the authoritarian structure encodes its own undoing. The poem rejects the received notion of 'Heaven' in favour of a more personal, affective discourse of 'Paradise', which is framed in the language of erotic desire. This discourse turns away from the top-down narrative structures that uphold received worldviews. If the high-hanging apple on the tree imposes authorial control through prohibition, Dickinson suggests a counter-narrative in the twin movements of errancy and desire.

[24] Shortly after the publication of *On the Origin of Species*, Darwin wrote to Asa Gray: 'With respect to the theological view of the question; this is always painful to me.—I am bewildered.—I had no intention to write atheistically', Charles Darwin to Asa Gray, 22 May 1860, *The Correspondence of Charles Darwin*. ed. Frederic Burkhardt and Sydney Smith, 30 vols (Cambridge: CUP, 1985–), vol. 6, 504.

The spatial dynamics of this poem confirm what is implicit in Orpheus's captivating sermon: Dickinson imagined desire in lateral terms. In describing tantalizing pleasure, the poem feels outward rather than upward. The 'Cruising Cloud' is low-lying, tinged by the seductive glow or 'Teasing Purples' of the afternoon sun. 'The interdicted Land' is positioned 'behind' not above the houses and hills. These horizontal movements are wandering and indulgent. There is every sense here that desire takes one off course. The supposedly *real* 'Paradise', mysteriously located in some hidden periphery, turns out to be a 'decoy', something which distracts from a true purpose. This is both an errant quest and a quest which takes pleasure in errancy. Diverted from the reach upwards, the poem discovers, in error, the pleasures of fiction. The 'Conjuror' bears comparison with the Orphic singer. Both captivate their audience with make-believe, 'decoy[s]', which in the very act of distraction build narratives that take on the status of truth.

The narrative structures of poetic errancy, which are divergent and distracted, are opposed to the narrative structures of the Creator-God, which are ordered and commanding. Dickinson implicitly recognizes the way in which narrative structures encode behaviours and hermeneutics of interpretation have ethical and ontological implications. Like the cheeky child who confidently claims to have 'diagnos[ed]' the Bible as a 'tale' in need of a 'thrilling teller', Dickinson suggests a subversive world-making quality in exegesis that takes pleasure in errancy. It is subversive because it opposes the top-down authoritarian structures which 'condemn' rather than 'captivate'. But it is also constructive because the distractions of a 'decoy', the lures of a 'Conjurer', and the seductive 'thrill' of the Orphic tale are acts of narratological reordering, which might change our way of being in the world. As the spatial narrative shifts from the vertical to the horizontal, the world ordered by prohibition gives way to one structured by desire. As a Fall poem, this sets the seductive lateral pleasures of fiction against the controlling narrative structures of prohibition and 'condemn[ation]'. But there is also a post-lapsarian knowingness in Dickinson's writing, which exposes a naïve fallibility in her poetic voice. Once spurned, she should be twice shy. But she is still falling for the same fanciful story the next day.

It was partly Milton who taught Dickinson that the Fall could be construed as a fall into 'fancy'. Errancy could be seen as human authorship, and human authorship, with its capacity for equivocation, invention, and multidirectionality, becomes instrumental to the course of human history at the very point at which it becomes distanced from the providential plan of the

Father-God.[25] Milton is clear that God is an author: 'by His Word, the Mighty Father made / All things' (*Paradise Lost*, book V, ll. 836–7). The grammar and lineation are uncompromisingly direct: 'Word,...made / All things'. In this vision of pre-lapsarian language as a world-making tool, there is arguably no difference between word and thing.

If language is a world-making tool, world-changing narratives need new authors with new attitudes to language. Satan appears as the 'Author of Evil' when he leads the revolt in Heaven (*PL*, book VI, l. 262). Satan's narrative movements are deliberately misleading and markedly different to God's. He is 'irresolute / Of thoughts' and that convolution of mind and capacity for deception are reflected in his serpentine form: 'He swiftly rolled / In tangles, and made intricate seem straight (*PL*, book IX, ll. 87–8 and 631–2). Lapsarian history is defined by 'falsities and lies' (*PL*, book I, l. 367) and, in contrast with the strict correlation between word and thing in Eden, Milton announces that the devils were 'known to men by various names' (*PL*, book I, l. 374).

Like Milton, Dickinson saw the post-lapsarian garden as a site of duplicity, secrecy, and fiction-making, and she took a poet's pleasure in delightful words which do not lead directly to their sense. In a teenage letter to her friend, Abiah Root, written on 12 January 1846, Dickinson jokingly dubbed herself 'Eve, alias Mrs Adam' (*Letters*, 24). As marriage is a product of the fallen state, her playful name and its 'alias' bears testament to an identity founded in duplicity and deception. Milton's Eve finds that the diabolic gift of verbal fluency and the pleasure of inventing stories follows quickly upon the taste of the forbidden fruit: 'Greedily she ingorged without restraint...Thus to herself she pleasingly began' (*PL*, book IX, ll. 791 and 794). Dickinson enjoys her identification with the first storyteller.

By contrast, Milton's pre-lapsarian Adam, who knows nothing of his own origins, and cannot fathom his own story, finds God's narrative 'readily' in his mouth:

> But who I was, or where, or from what cause,
> Knew not; to speak, I tried, and forthwith spake;
> My tongue obeyed, and readily could name
> Whate'er I saw. (book VIII, ll. 270–3)

Pre-lapsarian Adam intuits language directly from God: his act of naming reiterates and reinforces preordained narrative structures. From the hierarchy

[25] As Adam and Eve gorge themselves on the forbidden fruit, Milton writes: 'As with new wine intoxicated both, / They swim in mirth, and fancy that they feel / Divinity inside them breeding wings, / Wherewith to scorn the earth', Milton, *Paradise Lost*, book IX, ll. 1008–10, p. 528.

of Heaven proceeds the status of man, who is granted dominion in a clear reflection of the celestial order. Echoing the Divine Word, which orders the world by separating light from dark, earth from sea, and man from beast, Adamic naming creates a place for everything and keeps everything in its place (including man as inferior to God).

In one poem, Dickinson assumes the name 'Nobody' in a refusal of the Adamic tradition of naming and the divine authorship it mimics. 'I'm Nobody' is most obviously read in relation to Dickinson's refusal to publish. Her denial of the name is a denial of the public sphere and the fixity that accompanies renown. Publicity, in this poem, is presented as tedious conformity, self-admiring narcissism, and an absurd quest for social status. But another way of reading Dickinson's defence of her own secrecy is through the poem's subversive invocation of a Fall narrative in which the resistant naming of 'I'm Nobody' celebrates fanciful post-lapsarian language. Naming herself 'Nobody', Dickinson's speaker subversively adopts a secret identity, which is cheeky and playful, and sets it in opposition to the 'dreary' world of fixity in which one might be thought 'Somebody'. Just as Milton's God gives Adam dominion in Eden, publication confers a certain social status, but that status comes at the cost of a 'rigid interdiction' on narrative capability (book VIII, l. 334).

Like the 'Boy' who diagnoses the Bible, Dickinson's youthful personae preserve the poet's difference from the rigid adult world of received wisdom, hierarchical status, and stale doctrine. Playful, errant, and conspiratorial, the poem delights in its subversion of top-down authority, publicity, and society.

> I'm Nobody! Who are you?
> Are you—Nobody—too?
> Then there's a pair of us!
> Don't tell! They'd banish us—you know!
>
> How dreary—to be—Somebody!
> How public—like a Frog—
> To tell your name—the livelong June—
> To an admiring Bog!
>
> (Fr260)

The poem elides the difference between the adult world of publication and a world in which everything has a fixed and identifiable meaning; both are 'dreary', organized by hierarchies, prohibitions, and taboos. The nameless nobodies belong to the post-lapsarian landscape: a conspiratorial pair, whose indefinite names are an act of secret resistance. By contrast, the act of 'say[ing] your name', recalls both the social status and dominion Adam and Eve enjoyed in Eden, the fixed language Adam learned from God, and the world of publication that Dickinson abhorred. Naming herself 'Nobody', Dickinson celebrates errancy as the condition of meaning which is not fixed. As 'Nobody' she is unimportant, ordinary, a nonentity but also more important, extraordinary, and a more powerful poetic entity than the pitifully ribbiting public 'Frog' or the sycophantic 'admiring Bog'. Milton has Eve besotted with her own reflection; Dickinson's twist is to darken the landscape. The 'admiring Bog' is an absurd and ignominious image of narcissistic self-love.[26]

Dickinson's colloquial 'Don't Tell! They'd banish us—you know!' irreverently exploits the subversive implications of post-lapsarian concealment as she announces her refusal to publish. 'Banish' recalls the exile from Eden. Dickinson includes 'advertise' as a variant for 'banish us' (Thomas Johnson in fact chooses 'advertise' for his reading edition). The world of advertising suggests a kind of promiscuity, in which public appeal is the endgame. To 'advertise' Adam's and Eve's sin would also be to effect their banishment. So, she converts the sanctity of the pre-lapsarian garden to a post-lapsarian space of secrecy and errancy which allows for greater narrative possibilities than the adult, public world which lies outside of it. Post-lapsarian language, with its emphasis on multiplicity and secrecy, liberates her poetic voice from the repetitive and formulaic utterances, absurd roles, and ridiculous expectations that define being grown up. Her reading of the Fall, here, debunks the mythology of sin and salvation as surely as it rejects the false judgements of a society that prizes status and reputation above all else. It celebrates childish transgressions as narrative possibility and associates pre-lapsarian language with the dull rigidity of renown. Naming herself 'Nobody', Dickinson jovially asserts her poetic voice, taking pleasure in errancy, and subverting the fixed narratives of God and man that are rendered equally absurd in the frog's repetitive and narcissistic singing to his own muddied reflection.

Accidental Falls: Circumstance and the Limits of Authorship

One of the major nineteenth-century tensions in the myth of the Fall was between providence and circumstance; events that were always going to

[26] For more on the darkening of the Edenic landscape in nineteenth-century American literature see: David Miller, *Dark Eden: The Swamp in Nineteenth-Century American Literature* (Cambridge: CUP, 1989).

happen and events that just happen. In a poem which begins 'I am afraid to own a Body', Dickinson's resistance to divine authorship marries with the narrative of circumstance in the image of the frontier.

> I am afraid to own a Body—
> I am afraid to own a Soul—
> Profound—precarious Property—
> Possession, not optional—
>
> Double Estate—entailed at pleasure
> Upon an unsuspecting Heir—
> Duke in a moment of Deathlessness
> And God, for a Frontier.
>
> (Fr1050)

The rhythm of this poem, which runs together 'Duke in a moment of deathlessness' and asks us to pause after 'God', as if to think about what 'God' is, suggests a certain logic to reading 'God' as a 'frontier'. God locates epistemic limit, but here the image of God as a frontier also speaks to the poem's concern with the competing narratives of providence and circumstance. In Dickinson's lifetime, the frontier was associated with the divinely authored narrative of manifest destiny, which allowed pioneers of westward expansion to believe that they were proceeding hand-in-hand with God. But the frontier also belongs to the conditions of history and circumstance. Frontier narratives are replete with accidents and chance encounters. The frontier became a symbol of human vulnerability: a physical and epistemological threshold, beyond which lay unknown territories of savagery and wildness. The frontier is both limit and possibility. But here there is no one to test the narrative, no Christ-like 'Tender Pioneer' (Fr727) to tread the path for the speaker to follow. Invoking the frontier, Dickinson implies an epistemological quest, but she also sets providence against circumstance, suggesting, perhaps, that neither leave us much agency.

The key to unlocking the exegetical meaning of this poem is found in book X of *Paradise Lost*. Newly fallen, Milton's Adam laments his disastrous condition: 'Why am I mocked with death, and lengthened out to deathless pain?' (*PL*, book X, l. 756). Milton's Adam is disbelieving of his fate, accusing God of petty vengeance:

> Can he make a deathless death?
> [...]

> Will he draw out,
> For anger's sake, finite to infinite,
> In punished man, to satisfy his rigor,
> Satisfied never.
> (*PL*, book X, ll. 779–85)

Dickinson's elusive and seemingly contradictory 'moment of Deathlessness' derives from Milton's term for the condition of relentless misery Adam confronts after he falls. For Walt Whitman deathlessness was expressive of expansive possibility and poetic longevity: 'I know I am deathless', he declares in the final edition *Leaves of Grass.*[27] But Dickinson stays closer to Milton. For Milton's Adam, the sin which brought death into existence has disclosed the puppet-show of dominion in Eden and revealed him to be entirely at the mercy of God. Adam fears an excess of authorial control: a vengeful severity, which allows him no ability to shape his own ends, no release from misery and suffering. Milton's reflexive vocabulary drives the point home. The finite is undone by the infinite; the release of ending mocked by the unstoppable force of divine anger.

Dickinson's 'moment' heightens the frustrated loss of control which is inherent in the myth of the Fall. This works two ways. There is a frustration in the idea that there was *a moment* when it all went wrong, an instant when the spatio-temporal order of Paradise was put out of joint by the arrival of death, a suddenness with which humanity was rudely displaced from the garden. But, in the long span of evolutionary time, where disasters feel as if they come upon us with overwhelming suddenness because they happen so slowly, there is also some consolation in the fiction that there *was* a moment where everything went wrong. Dickinson may also have drawn her language of entail from Milton. Milton's Adam announces himself 'disinherited' of posterity and subject to death 'in perpetuity' (*PL*, book X, ll. 802 and 794). Dickinson's Duke, like Milton's Adam, feels himself to be the 'unsuspecting heir' of a narrative he cannot control. For Milton's Adam, the duality of body and soul is thrust upon him with the fact of mortality: 'the spirit of man, which God inspired, cannot together perish / With this corporeal clod' (*PL*, book X, ll. 765–7). Dickinson's Duke, like Milton's Adam, faces this 'double estate' with a sense of powerlessness: 'Possession not optional'. The body also

[27] Walt Whitman, 'Song of Myself', *Leaves of Grass* (1891–2) https://whitmanarchive.org/published/LG/1891/poems/27

gestures towards more secular predetermined narratives: the sexual and social constraints of being in a body. For Dickinson, body and soul might also indicate the textual form of poetry.[28] The idea of a narrative which is imposed and an ending over which one has no control recalls, for the poet who refused to publish, the auction house of publication. 'Possession' starts to read as a pun: to possess body and soul is also to be possessed by various narratives one does not own.

'I am afraid to own a Body' suggests that the deliberately silly, childish, and playful poem in which Dickinson rebelliously names herself 'Nobody' ironically occupies its own kind of pre-lapsarian fiction in its celebration of errancy and infancy as forms of poetic self-actualization. Like the cheeky child who 'Diagnos[es]' the Bible, Dickinson's 'Nobody' is sure that her disobedience is empowering. But, as she elides the difference between the narrative of providence and the narrative of circumstance in the figure of God as a frontier, she implies that any claim to self-actualization is always pushing against narratives we don't control. Like 'Diagnosis of the Bible, by a Boy', 'I'm Nobody' protects a space of childish play, an innocently wicked refusal to conform, as an arena in which to rehearse the potential disruption of the adult world of received exegetical wisdoms and rigid social hierarchies. By contrast, 'I am afraid to own a Body' is a coming-of-age story in which Dickinson's 'Duke' faces 'Possession not optional', just as Milton's Adam feels uncontrollable 'misery / . . . begun / Both in me, and without me' (book X, ll. 791–3).

The keystone of Adam and Eve's story is loss; its first chapter is grief. So it is fitting that Dickinson begins her greatest Fall poem with a funeral, a moment of painful disruption and reordering. 'I felt a Funeral, in my Brain' has not been read as a Fall poem but several critics have noted its religious relevance. Aliki Barnstone sees it as part of Dickinson's 'revisionary theology of self-conversion'; Jane Eberwein recognizes a 'condition of emotional arrest', which Dickinson derived, in part, from her Calvinist heritage.[29] Cristanne Miller observes that the aural qualities of this poem work by setting rising and falling rhythms against each other and notes an epistemological reflection in these sound patterns. The ending is anti-climactic; the moment of revelation occurs just before the predictable plunge of the fall 'down and down'. Thus, Miller

[28] See Shira Wolosky, 'Emily Dickinson: Being in the Body', in *The Cambridge Companion to Emily Dickinson*, ed. Wendy Martin (Cambridge: CUP, 2002), 129–41, 129–30.

[29] Aliki Barnstone, *Changing Rapture: Emily Dickinson's Poetic Development* (Hanover, NH: University Press of New England, 2002), 75, Jane Donahue Eberwein, *Emily Dickinson: Strategies of Limitation* (Amherst, Mass.: University of Massachusetts Press), 141.

describes the real breakthrough in consciousness as the moment of aural lingering in the fourth stanza in which 'Being' is 'But an Ear'.[30]

Another way of thinking about that moment is in terms of horizontal levelling. In Dickinson's brilliant rendering of the Fall into Knowledge as a fall into unknowing, the vertiginous descent of the received exegetical reading is juxtaposed with moments of levelling awareness as she interrogates the processes of being and becoming while radically rethinking Milton's providential worldview.

I felt a Funeral, in my Brain,
And Mourners to and fro
Kept treading—treading—till it seemed
That Sense was breaking through—

And when they all were seated,
A Service, like a Drum—
Kept beating—beating—till I thought
My mind was going numb—

And then I heard them lift a Box
And creak across my Soul
With those same Boots of Lead, again,
Then Space—began to toll,

As all the Heavens were a Bell,
And Being, but an Ear,
And I, and Silence, some strange Race,
Wrecked, solitary, here—

And then a Plank in Reason, broke,
And I dropped down, and down—
And hit a World, at every plunge,
And Finished knowing—then—

(Fr340)

One way of reading this poem is as an allegory of the Fall, which is both deeply in tune with, and strongly resistant to, the narrative implicit in falling.

[30] Cristanne Miller, *Reading in Time: Emily Dickinson in the Nineteenth Century* (Amherst, Mass.: University of Massachusetts Press, 2012), 39–42. Miller also observes that readers of this poem debate the extent to which the poem's funeral is metaphorical. It is interpreted variously as a poem about consciousness, death, a migraine, and a psychic break, but also as a poem which recalls a real funeral, possibly that of Frazer Stearns, who was killed in action in the Civil War (38).

For if 'I felt a Funeral' is a poem about the Fall into Knowledge, it is also a poem that resists falling and resists knowledge. The spatial dynamics turn on a tension between the vertical 'drop' and the horizontal 'to and fro'. The violent 'plunge' is marked by sudden moments of arrest. The heavy repetition of 'treading' and 'beating' agonizingly expands our sense of time. The vertiginous fall is punctuated by the flattening experiences of pain and grief as the poem comes to terms with the loss of a metaphysical worldview that grounded Being: the 'creak across' and the disorienting expanse of 'space' and 'solitary' 'wreck' of the third and fourth stanzas suspend and expand our sense of time and space. These levelling movements work against the downward trajectory to suggest the difficult process of becoming, an adjustment to the newly destabilized ontology of Being. The poetic 'I' is subject to a sickening verticality which ends with a deliberately ambiguous suspension of meaning and obfuscation of place: 'And Finished knowing—then—.' The line can be read in two seemingly contradictory ways: the beginning and the end of knowledge. The graphic silence of her characteristic dash and unfinished sentence spread outwards as the Fall plateaus. Dickinson's variant for 'Finished' is 'Got through', a phrase that emphasizes survival through a traumatic rupture of the old order of existence.

With the dissolution of the old order comes a new reality where the aesthetics of loss have a different role to play. The key change is at the end of the third stanza, when 'Space began to Toll'. Crucially, this is not a moment of vertiginous collapse but a moment of suspension which feels more horizontal. As the sounding of the funeral bell consumes her Being, the claustrophobic live-burial gives way to a kind of agoraphobic isolation. Silence and difference accompany the poetic voice, whose articulations of being and becoming are partial and incomplete. The violent plunge is presented as aftermath: as the 'plank in Reason' breaks, the speaker's descent into the grave is catapulted into freefall but Dickinson's anaphoric 'And then' absorbs this catastrophic collapse into a poetic pattern of repetition, which both sets up and undermines expected narrative.

Knowledge, here, is not born of 'sense' or 'Reason' but the bruising realities of accident and chance. 'And hit a World, at every Plunge' is far from the controlled and stifling movements which open the poem. The enclosed funeral parlour has given way to a galactic setting of 'Space' and 'World[s]'. The 'Silence' and 'strange[ness]' of the shipwrecked 'I' (a pun perhaps on the eye-opening trauma of the Fall) recurs in the disorientation of the last line. Perhaps the most literal reading of this poem is that the speaker has fallen unconscious after a violent accident in which she has hit, and hurt, her head.

There is a certain absence of knowledge at the end, a blanking out of sense and meaning, carried by this narrative. The Fall into Knowledge is, in that sense, conveyed as an abandonment of those forms of knowledge associated with stability and certainty, a dramatic shift in the worldviews which ground our 'Being' and govern our behaviour. But it is not a change born of sin, or part of a providential history of salvation. It is an accidental slip.

Writing to Asa Gray, shortly after the publication of *On the Origin of Species*, Darwin had expressed unhappiness at the thought that 'everything is the result of brute force'. He wanted to hold onto a faith in 'designed laws', accepting, unwillingly, that ends may be accidentally worked out. Darwin falls back on an individual and affective faith in the face of the radical uncertainty of an evolutionary worldview, finding the subject too intellectually overwhelming: 'Let each man hope and believe what he can', he says.[31] The brute force of a bump to the head, which precipitates a shipwreck of the soul, leaves Dickinson's poem on similarly uncertain ground. Like Darwin, Dickinson recognizes that epistemic limits exert a strong shaping force on our way of being in the world. This is a fortunate fall into knowledge only because it is a fall into unknowing—an acceptance of the terms of uncertainty, a process of self-actualization that feels fraught with risk. It bears comparison with George Levine's theorization of secularism as a 'falling upward' into a beautiful and dangerous earthly, and earthy, world.[32] Rather like Levine, Dickinson is not explicit about the recourse to faith in this situation. There is no clear 'hope' or 'belief' here. But there is a sense of a future, a new departure and a new sort of 'knowing' that embraces risk and holds onto the temperament of faith.

Dickinson's presentation of the Fall as a traumatic rupturing of certainty, which is also a welcome release from the Enlightenment graveyard of 'sense' and 'Reason', forges an integral connection between ontology and epistemology, or 'Being' and 'Knowing', in the events of Genesis 3. The poem's resistance to falling, its arrests, plateaus, and eye- (or I-) opening expansions of the self, suggest that what interested Dickinson about the Fall here was the serendipitous narrative of accident and initiation and the possibilities opened by error. As such, the endpoint of the poem may not be one where the speaker has been separated from God but one where, cut adrift from 'sense' and 'Reason', she is on more level, but more uncertain, ground. The one certainty

[31] Charles Darwin to Asa Gray, 22 May 1860, *Correspondence*, vol. 6, 504.

[32] George Levine, 'Introduction', *The Joy of Secularism; Eleven Essays for How we Live Now* (Princeton: Princeton University Press, 2011), 13.

here is that forms of knowledge, the worldviews we hold and the narratives that convey them, ground our being. To rupture them may be as necessary and liberating as it is traumatic and terrifying. As Adam and Eve head into the uncertain territory east of Eden, so the poem 'finish[es]' in an unknown place which might be construed as the start of the story. The final 'then—' both modifies the finish and subverts repetition with continuation, echoing the anaphoric 'And then', which opens the third stanza.

Towards the beginning of this chapter, I suggested that all exegesis is a selective and story-building activity and that Dickinson recognized it as such. While many of her contemporaries either forged a new way of being religious through poetry or turned to history to authenticate their exegetical narratives, Dickinson did not. As she invites us to encounter biblical narratives in her poetry, she directs us away from the 'untold Volume' of sermonizing or historicizing tales she encountered as a child and towards exegesis as a version of figural realism which both reflects and shapes our way of being in the world. Her image of God as a capricious child is both a form of criticism and identification as she, too, assumes the paradoxical voice of the fallen, yet innocent, 'Boy' and celebrates a mischievous space of irresponsible play. The youthful space is levelling, stripping God of his paternal authority and blurring the boundaries between innocence and wickedness. It is a trope through which her playful poems can pose a serious challenge to God's justice and providence. In her depiction of the Fall as a slip or trip, the ontological importance of accident, which is implicit in childhood blunders, comes to the fore. The lingering question is whether narratives of circumstance function that differently to the received narrative of providence.

Dickinson's reworking of the Fall implies that accidents can occasion a fundamental rupture of the nature of 'Being' and its relation to forms of knowledge. The bump to the head, which precipitates a shipwreck of the soul, leaves no more control over processes of becoming than the 'Double Estate—entailed at pleasure / Upon an unsuspecting Heir' who echoes Milton's fallen and despairing Adam. What evolutionary narrative removes is not the ordering of accident (chance replaces design) but the consolation that comes with salvation theology: the Redeemer that Dickinson knows Darwin had not quite thrown away. The 'unsuspecting Heir' echoes Milton's Adam but he is also a type of Christ promising eternal life. With providence, the ending is foretold: Adam's sin is redeemed by Christ's sacrifice. With circumstance, the ending is unknown. Dickinson makes a play for new world-making fictions through poetic errancy and the wayward pull of desire, and her dialogues with Milton and Darwin undercut the authority of providence. She realizes that exegesis might build the stories by which we live (and sometimes die) and so she lampoons the vertical structures of a narrative that 'condemns' with the 'captivat[ing]' distractions of playful poetics. But she also recognizes that these received narratives are not the only limit on human agency. In the face of uncontrollable circumstance, 'thrilling' tales and disobedient fictions may provide little more than a pre-lapsarian illusion of agency.

4
'This World of Mistakes'
Eliot and Moral Choice

'Now mamma, don't interfere with me. If you have ever had any trouble in your own life, remember it, and don't interfere with me. If I am to be miserable, let it be my own choice.'[1] So speaks Gwendolen Harleth, the spoiled, magnetic, archly flirtatious, fiercely independent, and ultimately unhappy heroine of *Daniel Deronda*, George Eliot's last novel. Gwendolen is a gambler, first seen at the roulette-table where she catches the eye of Deronda, while 'deposit[ing] her stake with an air of firm choice' (*DD* 5). In this opening scene Eliot foregrounds one of the major themes of the book: every choice is, to some extent, a gamble. Gwendolen's spirited declaration to her mother is poignant because, as her story unfolds, it becomes clear that, not only are her choices limited, and sometimes defined, by the conditions of her sex, there will also be no right or wrong choice, no straight decision over whether to be happy or miserable, no just desserts or welcome redemption. Like most wilful and disobedient children, including those in Genesis 3, Gwendolen resents parental direction because she wants to be grown up: an author of her own universe.[2]

In an 1856 essay on Sophocles' *Antigone*, Eliot wrote eloquently about the difficulties of clear moral choice:

> It is a very superficial criticism which interprets the character of Creon as that of a hypocritical tyrant, and regards Antigone as a blameless victim. Coarse contrasts like this are not the materials handled by great dramatists. The exquisite art of Sophocles is shown in the touches by which he makes us

[1] George Eliot, *Daniel Deronda*, ed. Graham Handley (Oxford: OUP, 2014), 128. All further references are to this edition, included in the text.

[2] As George Levine and Nancy Henry explain, modern feminism has had its problems with Eliot: 'Feminist criticism, for example, long complained that Eliot never created a woman like Marian Evans, who resisted the conventions of society, and made a creative and original life for herself, living outside of wedlock with moral confidence', 'Introduction: George Eliot and the Art of Realism', in *The Cambridge Companion to George Eliot*, ed. George Levine and Nancy Henry (Cambridge: CUP, 2019), 1–18, 10.

The Myth of the Fall in Nineteenth-Century Literature. Linda Freedman, Oxford University Press.
 DOI: 10.1093/oso/9780198969570.003.0005

> feel that Creon, as well as Antigone, is contending for what he believes to be the right, while both are also conscious that, in following out one principle, they are laying themselves open to just blame for transgressing another; and it is this consciousness which secretly heightens the exasperation of Creon and the defiant hardness of Antigone.[3]

Here, choice depends on a bifurcated and inadequate account of reality that cannot be right without also being knowingly wrong. To understand the relation between worldview and action had become, several years before she published her first work of fiction, what Eliot believed to be the function of great art and the skill of the great dramatist.

This chapter explores the way the myth of the Fall drives questions of moral choice in *The Mill on the Floss* and *Daniel Deronda*. When Eve makes the wrong choice in Genesis 3, she is condemned to bring forth children 'in sorrow', and her body opens a space between error and consequence. In Eliot's novels, consequences often become real even before any error has occurred. Maggie Tulliver feels the shock of her fall before it has completed externally: 'She had said she would rather die than fall into that temptation. She felt it now—now that the consequences of such a fall had come before the outward act was completed' (*MOTF* 436). Eliot undermines the vital moment of choice with the overwhelming fluidity of desire; choice is felt as a rush or internal collapse, enacted within an already fallen and entangled world. Maggie and Gwendolen sometimes seem resonant of Milton's Eve, guilty of a wilful fluency, or fall into fancy; often, they simply drift into error, get caught up and carried away.

In the evangelical tradition in which Marian Evans was raised, salvation was found in a narrative of sacred return. In Eliot's domestic fictions, the longing for home functions as a secular version of this narrative. Eliot knew what it was to want a home. When her father threatened to throw her out for refusing to go to church, she wrote desperately to a friend: 'I must have a home, and not a visiting place' (*GEL*, vol. 1, 134).[4] At the end of *Silas Marner*, she indulges a fantasy of Edenic wish-fulfilment around the idea of home. Eppie rejects the very fallen and social world of her lawful father, Godfrey Cass, and his plans for an advantageous marriage, and chooses to stay with Silas, the father who has always given her a home, and marry Aaron, the

[3] George Eliot, 'The Antigone and its Moral', *Leader* 7 (29 Mar. 1856), 306.
[4] See Phillip Davies, *The Transferred Life of George Eliot* (Oxford: OUP, 2017), 45.

honest gardener, who will help her in her duty of love and care. The novel ends with a marriage and homecoming that has the flavour of Edenic return:

> The garden was fenced with stones on two sides, but in front there was an open fence, through which the flowers shone with answering gladness, as the four united people came in sight of them.
>
> 'O father', said Eppie, 'what a pretty home ours is! I think nobody could be happier than we are.' (*SM* 161)

Maggie Tulliver similarly longs to discover some great meaning and divine harmony that both makes sense of her small world and dull sufferings and offers her 'a sense of home' that gives some refuge from it: 'with an ear straining after dreamy music that died away and would not come near to her; with a blind, unconscious yearning that would link together the wonderful impressions of this mysterious life, and give her soul a sense of home in it.' (*MOTF* 219). A divinely willed, harmonious, universe was the retreating horizon in Eliot's secular vision, not forgotten, but sometimes going against the grain of her more committed thought.[5]

The myth of the Fall survives partly as a foil to the generous and forgiving form of realism that she develops in her novels. But fallenness also becomes a self-reflective artistic lens, a way of imagining that forgiving form, which she implied, in a defence of Goethe's widely condemned *Wilhelm Meister*, was *more* ethical than narratives of sin and punishment: 'Everywhere he brings us into the presence of living, generous, humanity—mixed and erring, and self-deluding... the line between the virtuous and vicious, so far from being a moral safeguard, is itself an immoral fiction.'[6] In *Adam Bede*, she declared her aesthetic ambitions optimistically, though acknowledging the limits of her reach:

> to give a faithful account of men and things as they have mirrored themselves in my mind. The mirror is doubtless defective; the outlines will sometimes

[5] The harmonic resonance of Eden was a more widely felt phenomenon in Victorian literature. In Charlotte Brontë's 1853 novel, *Villette*, Lucy Snowe tells Polly de Bassompierre: 'In all that mutually concerns you and Graham there seems to me promise, plan, harmony... Some lives *are* thus blessed: it is God's will: it is the attesting trace and lingering evidence of Eden.' Charlotte Brontë, *Villette*, ed. Helen Cooper (London: Penguin, 2004), 417–18. Of Jude, in *Jude the Obscure*, Thomas Hardy writes, in 1894: 'Nature's logic was too horrid for him to care for. That mercy towards one set of creatures was cruelty towards another sickened his sense of harmony.' Thomas Hardy, *Jude the Obscure*, ed. Dennis Taylor (London: Penguin, 1998), 18.

[6] George Eliot, 'The Morality of Wilhelm Meister', *Leader* 6 (21 July 1855), 703.

> be disturbed, the reflection faint or confused; but I feel as bound to tell you as precisely as I can what that reflection is, as if I were in the witness-box, narrating my experience on oath.[7]

'Notes on Form in Art', written in 1868 but unpublished, makes more of the idea of the limit and opacity of fallen forms, which are perspectival, entangled, pressured, and often mistaken: 'what is form but the limit of that difference by which we discriminate one object from another?—a limit determined partly by the intrinsic relations and composition of the object,—& partly by the extrinsic action of other bodies upon it'.[8] *Daniel Deronda* opens with ever-growing scepticism:

> Men can do nothing without the make-believe of a beginning. Even Science, the strict measurer is obliged to start with a make-believe unit, and must fix on a point in the stars' unceasing journey when his sidereal clock shall pretend that time is Nought. His less accurate grandmother Poetry has always been understood to start in the middle; but on reflection it appears that her proceeding is not very different from his; since Science, too, reckons backwards as well as forwards, divides his unit into billions, and with his clock-finger at Nought readily sets of *in media res*. No retrospect will take us to the true beginning: and whether the prologue be in heaven or in earth, it is but a fraction of that all-presupposing fact with which our story sets out. (*DD* 3)

The strategies of realism, far from providing an objective truth, reiterated the intensely fallible perspectivism of human beings. In this opening epigraph, Eliot invokes Genesis, 'the true beginning' and, by implication, the myth of the Fall, from which the Gwendolen and Deronda story sets out. Myth, as she frames it here, is not a key to unlocking the truth of the universe but something akin to the 'make-believe unit' of Science, a hypothesis, forever collapsing under the weight of experiment and history but giving shape and meaning to narrative time. Long after she rejected the binary of right and wrong choice, the myth of the Fall retained its hold on her fiction, underlying, but not defining, the moment of moral choice in a world in which error was a more fluid, entangled, and forgivable notion than sin.

[7] George Eliot, *Adam Bede*, ed. Carol A. Martin (Oxford: OUP, 2008), 159. All further references are to this edition, included in the text.

[8] George Eliot, 'Notes on Form in Art', *Essays of George Eliot*, ed. Thomas Pinney (London: Routledge & Kegan Paul, 1963), 431–6, 434.

'Unstable as Water, Thou Shalt Not Excel': Maggie's Fluency

'We are Adam and Eve unfallen', Stephen Guest declares to Lucy Deane, shortly before he meets, and falls for, Maggie (*MOTF* 339). Maggie is a second Eve, but she belongs to an entangled and fallen world. 'If life were quite easy and simple, as it might have been in paradise,' she says to Stephen, after they run away together,

> and we could always see that one first being towards whom . . . I mean, if life did not make duties for us before love comes,—love would be a sign that two people ought to belong to each other. But I see—I feel it is not so now: some of us must resign love. Many things are difficult and dark for me; but I see one thing quite clearly, that I must not, cannot seek my own happiness by sacrificing others. Love is natural, but surely pity and faithfulness and memory are natural too. And they would live in me still, and punish me if I did not obey them. (*MOTF* 414)

Invoking the myth of the Fall, Eliot emphasizes that choices are never as simple as in Genesis 3. Maggie's choice comes upon her in a confusing rush of feeling, in which new desires clash with old ties and affections. On the one hand, she finds in duty, pity, faithfulness, and memory the residually religious forms of behaviour that anchor morality in a world where what feels 'natural', the expression of a subject, has assumed a godlike status. But Maggie's speech is also halting, broken, and unsure. She is convincing herself of the right action that should follow a known duty—'I must not, cannot'—a quick shift from obligation to emotional choice.

For evangelicals the production of godly character was a constant effort; an unrelenting suppression of instinctive response; an unfailing determination to make the right choices.[9] Marian Evans was taught to see character as individual moral responsibility, strengthened by continual effort and resistance to baser instinct, weakened and corrupted by selfish desires. Her early letters convey a strong sense of a young girl consistently failing in the desired self-discipline. On 6 February 1839, she wrote to her aunt: '"Unstable as water, thou shalt not excel" seems to be my character, instead of that regular progress from strength to strength that marks even in this world of mistakes the people that shall in the heavenly Zion stand before God.' (*GEL*, vol. 1, 14).

[9] Taylor, *A Secular Age*, 395.

Even in this pious mode, she is already bringing a secular vocabulary to bear on her religious schema. It is not 'this world of sin' but 'this world of mistakes'. A mistake is a misjudgement, an error in interpretation. It is a phrase that well describes the more forgiving and generous secular worldview she would later develop through fiction.

She aligns herself with Reuben, Jacob's first-born son who loses his birthright by sleeping with his father's concubine. Jacob admonishes him thus:

> Reuben, thou art my firstborn, my might, and the beginning of my strength, the excellence of dignity and the excellence of power:
>
> Unstable as water, thou shalt not excel; because thou wenteth up to thy father's bed; then defiledst thou it.[10]

Reuben is often troubled, he vacillates, and he ultimately offends his father. He is the promising child who disappoints. His major fault is a lack of self-discipline. At the time of Jacob's remonstrance, Reuben's sin is long past. But, for his father, the transgression has deformed and defined the child's character and its root cause become the core of his very being. Marian Evans was taught to see this instability as the defining trait of fallen humanity. As Avrom Fleischman observes, for evangelicals: 'The nature of human existence... is to live an unstable life in a realm of mutability, though a realm of permanence exists and is at least emotionally accessible.'[11] The young girl saw, in her own character, a transgressive fluidity.

Years after Eliot had abandoned her evangelical faith self-discipline in the face of near unbearable pressure remained, for her, an admirable quality of character. She liked words like 'shrink' and 'writhe' that implied individual action was physical reaction: an instinctive response to pain. In *Adam Bede*, the vain and selfish Arthur Donnithorne, who easily seduces pretty Hetty Sorrel but cares only about his own image and reputation, 'shrink[s] strongly from incurring... disapprobation' (*AB* 185). Hetty, who falls easily, has 'the timidity of a luxurious, pleasure-seeking nature which shrinks from a hint of pain' (*AB* 240). Maggie Tulliver 'writhe[s] under the demonstrable truth of the character he [her brother, Tom] had given to her conduct' (*MOTF* 319). She leaves Stephen Guest with an involuntary touch from which he 'shrank... as if from burning iron' (*MOTF* 444). The most significant, and impressive, choice Gwendolen makes, as she surrenders her agency to chance

[10] Gen. 49: 3–4.

[11] Avrom Fleischman, *George Eliot's Intellectual Life* (Cambridge: CUP, 2010), 13.

at the gaming table, is the decision not to 'flinch': 'she controlled her muscles…showed no tremor of face and hands' (*DD* 6).

Evangelicalism drew from, and influenced, eighteenth-century cultures of sensibility: fluid vacillations and abundant tears could be seen as the necessary abasement preceding conversion. In *Adam Bede,* Hetty's response to the new and unfamiliar pressure of fear is to cry. Dinah Morris, a Methodist preacher modelled on Eliot's aunt, misinterprets Hetty's distress as a sign of the fallen women's passage to spiritual redemption. The narrator observes:

> Dinah had never seen Hetty affected in this way before and, with her usual benignant hopefulness, she trusted it was the stirring of a divine impulse. She kissed the sobbing thing, and began to cry with her for grateful joy. But Hetty was simply in that excitable state of mind in which there is no calculating what turn the feelings will take from one moment to another, and for the first time she became irritated under Dinah's caress. (*AB* 240–1)

Faithful Dinah, convinced of her salvific duty and the promise of divine redemption, misreads Hetty's emotional volatility as evidence of her own triumph in saving the poor girl's soul. In her devoted worldview, she is as limited as Hetty 'in her narrow fantastic calculation of her own pleasures and pains' (*AB* 306). Eliot makes it clear that this is not a moment of religious conversion; it is movement without meaning, a vacillating fluidity of feeling, a fearful, instinctive, reaction to uncontrollable circumstance and the sensation of pain.

While Eliot never lost her evangelical admiration for self-discipline, she came to realize the value of sensitive instincts. The duplicitous Tito, in *Romola*, is her most unforgiven character, and Eliot describes his lack of residually religious 'dread' and 'terror' as the most severe moral failing:

> Tito's thought showed itself as active as a virulent acid, eating its rapid way through all the tissues of sentiment. His mind was destitute of that dread which has been erroneously decried as if it were nothing higher than a man's animal care for his own skin: that awe of the Divine Nemesis, which was felt by religious pagans, and, though it took a more positive form under Christianity, is still felt by the mass of mankind simply as a vague fear at anything which is called wrong-doing.[12]

[12] George Eliot, *Romola,* ed. Dorothea Barratt (London: Penguin, 1996), 116. All further references are to this edition, included in the text.

She emphasizes that moral laws are instinctively felt rather than dutifully learned: 'Such terror of the unseen is so far above mere sensual cowardice that it will annihilate that cowardice: it is the initial recognition of a moral law restraining desire, and checks the hard bold scrutiny of imperfect thought into obligations which can never be proved to have any sanctity in the absence of feeling.' (*R* 116). Without sensitive instincts, Tito makes unforgivably selfish and bad moral choices.

Although she was taught to see the instability of water as a trope which represented human weakness, Eliot learned also to align it with divine strength. In 1854, she published her translation of Ludwig Feuerbach's *Essence of Christianity*: 'for what God reveals', she translated, 'is a quality of God himself, that of which the heart is full overflows the lips'.[13] And, then:

> everything which is the substance of this world is yielding, soft and thin, is flowing, and gives itself forth, and the ground and origin of it is in the eternal Unity, for unity ever flows forth from itself, for in the nature of things not dense, as water and air, we can understand no susceptibility or pain, they being one in themselves.[14]

'With the ideas of Feuerbach I everywhere agree', she declared enthusiastically as she translated (*GEL*, vol. 2, 153). But she came also to recognize the limits of his optimism, admitting, in 1859: 'One would like one's life to be borne on the onward wave and not the receding one—the flow not the ebb. Yet somebody must live in the bad times.' (*GEL*, vol. 3, 228). An evangelical view of suffering was not easily abandoned. In 1839 she confessed: 'I set such a high value on "the sweet uses of adversity" that I am in danger of failing in sympathy for those who are experiencing it.' (*GEL*, vol. 1, 15). The 'bad times' were always more interesting to write about and Eliot struggled to rid herself of the residual feeling that something could be gained from suffering. She stopped believing that God wanted us to endure it. But she never lost interest in the aftermath: the 'receding wave' and the 'blessings derived from that endurance' (*GEL*, vol. 3, 228; vol. 1, 15).

[13] Ludwig Feuerbach, *The Essence of Christianity*, tr. Marian Evans (London: Chapman & Hall, 1856), 55. For further reading on Feuerbach's influence on Eliot's treatment of sensitive response and sympathetic ethics, see Christina Richieri Griffin, 'Senses, Sympathy, Omniscience and Secularism', *ELH* 84.2 (Summer 2017): 475–502. Richieri explains (p. 479) that Feuerbach's notion of sympathy remained deeply rooted in human physiology, and he insists on the authority of the senses throughout *Essence of Christianity*. For an introduction to Eliot's translation of and interest in Feuerbach, see Rosemary Ashton, *The German Idea: Four English Writers and the Reception of German Thought 1800–1860* (Cambridge: CUP, 1980), 155–66.

[14] Feuerbach, *Essence of Christianity*, tr. Evans, 132–3.

In Maggie, she explores the possibility that 'sorrow' might create the conditions for divine outpouring and spiritual growth. 'Maggie, with all her keen susceptibility, yet felt as if the sorrow made larger room for her love to flow in, and gave breathing space to her passionate nature.' (*MOTF* 242). Fluidity began to give structure and meaning to secular experiences of pain under pressure, holding onto the religious idea that suffering might be *for* something—that it could still belong to that which was ultimately for the good.

Water does not choose where it flows; it fills available space; is checked by external bounds; but, if powerful enough, it breaks those bounds. The extended conceit around water becomes a way of representing the forces that press, internally and externally, on the boundaries of being and circumscribe voluntary choice. *The Mill on the Floss* opens with a tender and intimate paean to the unstable character of water:

> A wide plain, where the broadening Floss hurries on between its green banks to the sea, and the loving tide, rushing to meet it, checks its passage with an impetuous embrace. On this mighty tide the black ships—laden with the fresh-scented fir planks, with rounded sacks of oil-bearing seed, or with the dark glitter of coal are borne along to the town of St Ogg's, which shows its aged, fluted red roofs and the broad gables of its wharves between the low wooded hill and the river brink, tinging the water with a soft purple hue under the transient glance of the February sun...Just by the red-roofed town the tributary Ripple flows with a lively current into the Floss. How lovely the little river is, with its dark, changing, wavelets! It seems to me like a living companion while I wander along the bank and listen to its low placid voice, as to the voice of one who is deaf and loving. (*MOTF* 7)

Eliot emphasizes the multi-directional energy of physical and emotional movement. Nothing stays still or goes straight. The narrator's perspective focuses in and fans out again, darting at unpredictable angles across an animate landscape. The 'broadening Floss' does not hold its shape but expands and narrows to fit the available space. Its meeting with the sea is not the restful homecoming that Augustine imagined finding in God but a joyful reunion of equals, intensely and wildly human in its display of impetuous feeling and eager embrace. Through the residually religious conceit of the instability of water, Eliot makes an important point about secular ethics. We may be more changed by circumstance than design; more 'checked' by love than fear; our affections drawn by what is living, vital, fluid, and changing; our actions determined by those affections rather than a self-disciplined devotion to perfection.

Like the rushing tide, whose impetuous, loving, embrace checks the flow of the river, Maggie 'rushe[s] to her deeds with passionate impulse' (*MOTF* 61). As a child she is frequently in trouble and, sensitive to both the judgements and injuries of others, she is often in tears. When her brother, Tom, is in distress, Maggie 'sob[s] for company' (*MOTF* 170). 'They're such children for the water mine are', declares Mrs Tulliver ominously, when Maggie goes missing, 'they'll be brought in dead and drownded some day. I wish the river was far enough.' (*MOTF* 97–8). It is Maggie, not Tom, who 'pour[s] out all that indignant remonstrance, against which Tom's mind was closed, in bitter tears' (*MOTF* 323). Tom, in his fury at discovering his sister's clandestine meetings with Philip Wakem, the son of his father's enemy, declares: 'there is no consistency in you' (*MOTF* 318). He might as well have said: 'unstable as water, thou shalt not excel'. It is partly this quality of inner fluency that makes Maggie seem, as Nina Auerbach puts it: 'a fallen woman by nature, in whom any activity is secondary to the intense ambiguous impact of what she *is*'.[15]

Maggie's fall is a fluid motion—a lack of resistance rather than wilful disobedience:

> Maggie felt as if she was being led down the garden, among the roses, being helped with firm and tender care into the boat, having the cushion and cloak arranged at her feet and her parasol opened for her (which she had forgotten)—all by this stronger presence that seemed to bear her along without any act of her own will. (*MOTF* 430)

The crucial tension that Eliot sets up, here, is between different kinds of will. Feuerbach derided the dictatorial, egoistic will of Genesis 1:

> which has unlimited command, which requires no means in order to attain its end, which immediately, by itself, i.e. by pure will calls into being whatever it pleases. It pains the egoist that the satisfaction of his wishes and need is only to be attained immediately, that for him there is a chasm between the wish and its realisation, between the object in imagination and the object in reality. Hence in order to relieve this pain, to make himself free from the limits of reality, he supposes as the true, the highest being, one who brings forth an object by the mere I WILL. For this reason, Nature, the world, was

[15] Auerbach, 'Rise of the Fallen Woman', 29–52, 50.

> to the Hebrews, the product of a dictatorial word, of a categorical imperative, of a magic fiat.[16]

He emphasized a better will, rooted in an incarnational aesthetic and belonging to the reciprocal relations of the fallen world: 'My fellow man is my objective conscience. He makes my failings a reproach to me, even when he does not expressly mention them, he is my personified feeling of shame.'[17]

Maggie falls for an egoist. Having broken his understanding with her cousin, Lucy, in order to indulge his desires for Maggie, Stephen tries to persuade her that her own desires for him accord with the natural order of things, that by wanting something she has not made it happen but made it right that it happens to her:

> See, Maggie, how everything has come without our seeking—in spite of all our efforts. We never thought of being alone together again: it has all been done by others. See how the tide is carrying us out—away from all those unnatural bonds that we have trying to make faster around us—and trying in vain ... Everything has concurred to point it out to us. We have contrived nothing, we have thought nothing of ourselves. (*MOTF* 431)

Just as she had once felt herself 'shaken by the invisible influence' of Stephen's fairly second-rate singing in her cousin's parlour and 'borne along on a wave too strong for her', Maggie wants to allow herself to surrender: 'to the yearning after that belief, that the tide was doing it all—that she might glide along with the swift, silent stream, and not struggle any more' (*MOTF* 386 and 431). It would be easier to make that narrative decision, to allow herself to believe that she has no choice: that the flow of desire is too strong to be checked by any counter-currents. Eliot lets us feel Maggie's potential fall as the wearied sinking of relief, and welcome oblivion, which foreshadows her death.

But Maggie does not go through with it, and her decision to resist is the right one. Not because it makes anyone happy—everyone is miserable. But it checks a diabolic force of fluency: the 'stealing influence' and 'fatal intoxication' that threatens to turn her will to the execution of another's narrative. Maggie's cry of 'angry resistance' cuts with shrill emotional energy across the soothing, soporific melody of Stephen's mellifluous tones as she accuses him of depriving her of choice: '"Let me go!" she said, in an agitated tone, flashing

[16] Feuerbach, *Essence of Christianity*, tr. Evans, 156.

[17] Feuerbach, *Essence of Christianity*, tr. Evans, 209.

an indignant look at him and trying to get her hands free. "You have wanted to deprive me of any choice. You knew we were come too far—you have dared to take advantage of my thoughtlessness. It is unmanly to bring me into such a position."' (*MOTF* 431). 'In following out one principle, they are laying themselves open to just blame for transgressing another', Eliot had written of Antigone and Creon, four years earlier. Maggie immediately feels the hurt that her principled decision has done, finding it harder to resist Stephen's looks of misery than she had his tenderness:

> This yielding to the idea of Stephen's suffering was more fatal than the other yielding, because it was less distinguishable from that sense of others' claims which was the moral basis of her resistance…They glided along in this way, both resting in that silence as in a haven, both dreading lest their feeling should be divided again. (*MOTF* 432)

In making her principled choice, Maggie is also forced into going against those principles. Her feeling for Stephen's misery quickly cuts across her feeling for Philip and Lucy. The world is too complex, too peopled, the ties of duty and tides of feeling too multi-directional, to afford a simple binary of right and wrong action, or of Feuerbach's *I* and *Thou*.

In *The Mill on the Floss*, a sense of home becomes the anchor in a world where stories do not run in straight lines and the promise of salvation has receded. When Maggie finally walks away, she is 'not conscious of a decision'. Her moment of choice is again undermined, but this time by memory and not desire: 'it was like an automatic action, that fulfils a forgotten intention' (*MOTF* 444). What Feuerbach imagined as an 'objective conscience', or 'personified feeling of shame', remains tied, for Maggie, to the old anchors of love and home. Love for her brother, Tom, displaced onto her childhood affection for Philip, acts as the real pull on her conscience when in a fit of 'vivid dreaming', aboard the vessel with Stephen, she imagines herself fallen and lost: 'Philip,—no, not Philip, but her brother who rowed past without looking at her; and she rose to stretch out her arms and call to him, and their own boat turned over with the movement, and they began to sink' (*MOTF* 436). In another quick shift, this time from Philip to Tom, there is a movement from what Rousseau termed 'supplement' to origin as the betrayed lover becomes the beloved brother, whose place he has always kept open and never quite managed to fill. 'Should you like me to kiss you as I do Tom?' she asks Philip as a little girl. And then, to her father: 'O father! Philip Wakem is so very good to Tom—he is such a clever boy, and I *do* love him!' (*MOTF* 173). Eliot's syntax admits the confusion of brother and future lover. Who is it that Maggie declares she loves, here: Philip or Tom? Turning and sinking, Maggie's fall becomes the metonymic extension of her fluid instability and her love for Tom, rehearsed through Philip, the anchor that Hetty, in her vacillating, formless, fear, does not have.

In the novel's tragic dénouement, Tom, for the first time, experiences the overwhelming, 'rush[ing]', feeling that is so familiar to Maggie:

> It was not until Tom had pushed off—and they were on the wide water—he face to face with Maggie—that the full meaning of what had happened rushed upon his mind. It came with so overpowering a force—it was such a new revelation to his spirit, of the depths in life, that had lain beyond his vision which he had fancied so keen and clear—that he was unable to ask a question. They sat mutely gazing upon each other: Maggie with eyes of intense life looking out from a weary, beaten, face—Tom pale with a certain awe and humiliation. Thought was busy though lips were silent: and, though he could ask no question, he guessed a story of almost miraculously divinely-protected effort. But at last a mist gathered over the blue-grey eyes, and the lips found a word they could utter: the old childish—'Magsie'.
>
> Maggie could make no answer but a long deep sob of that mysterious wondrous happiness that is one with pain. (*MOTF* 482)

The moment when the brother who, 'like every one of us, was imprisoned within the limits of his own nature' feels as she feels, sees as she sees, is a longed-for moment of connection (*MOTF* 462). Tom's severity—the hard questions by which he always seeks to elicit a hard truth from his sister—has no place in this new bond of fluid feeling. His linguistic tyrannies fail him: he has interrogated and forced her into stark choices many times before but now he is 'unable to ask a question'.[18] Powerless to check the rush that metaphorically—and then, literally—overpowers him, Tom can only submit. The rush comes from within as much as from without, compromising the parameters of his being. The only language that Eliot can make recourse to, here, is religious. 'Revelation', 'awe and humiliation' comes, as it does for Paul, face-to-face: 'For now we see through a glass darkly; but then face to face:

[18] The most significant example is Tom's interrogation of Maggie after her meeting with Phillip Wakem in the Red Deeps. After questioning her, he declares: 'Now, then, Maggie, there are but two courses for you to take: either you vow solemnly to me, with your hand on my father's Bible, that you will never have another meeting or speak another word in private with Philip Wakem, or you refuse, and I tell my father everything... Choose!', *Mill on the Floss*, 316–18, 317.

now I know in part; but then I shall know, even as I am known.'[19] It is not *what* Tom understands—'he guessed a story'—but *how* he understands that matters. To use Feuerbach's phrasing, he has become not 'I' but 'Thou'.[20]

In this final scene, Eliot both invokes and undercuts the egoistic will of the God of Genesis who sends a flood to cleanse the fallen world of sin. The deaths of the two Tulliver children are foreshadowed in a description of the Rhone earlier in the novel: 'which once rose, like an angry, destroying god, sweeping down the feeble generations whose breath is in their nostrils, and making their dwellings a desolation' (*MOTF* 251). In this earlier allusion, Eliot clearly invokes Genesis 7: 22: 'All in whose nostrils *was* the breath of life, of all that was in the dry *land*, died'. In the final flood scene, she sets the drowning in opposition to the near total destruction of Genesis 7 even as she echoes the biblical narrative:

> Nature repairs her ravages—repairs them with her sunshine, and with human labour. The desolation wrought by that flood, had left little visible trace on the face of the earth, five years after. The fifth autumn was rich in golden corn-stacks, rising in thick clusters among the distant hedgerows, the wharves and wharehouses on the Floss were busy again, with the echo of eager voices, with hopeful lading and unlading.
>
> And every man and woman mentioned in this history was still living—except those whose end we know. (*MOTF* 483)

The biblical flood story becomes a heightened and melodramatic vocabulary for an event which belongs to a very different world in which nothing is total or consuming. The flood of St Oggs is a tragedy of circumstance, which has both its architecture and foil in the wilful destruction of the God of Genesis 7. The apocalyptic flood of Genesis 7 is the result of a temper tantrum, a furious fit of self-loathing from a Creator-God whose creation has gone beyond his control: 'And the Lord said, I will destroy man whom I have created from the face of the earth; both man and beast, and the creeping thing, and the fowls of the air; for it repenteth me that I have made them.'[21] Published one year after *On the Origin of Species*, Eliot's turning of the biblical myth clearly reflects Darwin's influence. In Genesis 7, God gives Noah and his family a clean slate. The exit from the ark echoes the creation story of Genesis 1, a moment of cyclical return to a state of emergent life: 'Every beast, every

[19] 1 Cor. 13: 12. [20] Feuerbach, *Essence of Christianity*, tr. Evans, 209.
[21] Gen. 6: 7.

creeping thing, and every fowl, and whatsoever creepeth over the earth, after their kinds, went forth out of the ark.'[22] For Eliot, time is evolutionary, with no prospect of beginning again or stopping the count. History moves forward, instead of returning to primordial origins. There is no tabula rasa and losses are real, felt, and recorded in the texture of experience.

> Nature repairs her ravages—but not all. The uptorn trees are not rooted again; the parted hills left scarred: if there is new growth, the trees are not the same as the old, and the hills underneath their green vesture bear the marks of the past rending. To the eyes that have dwelt on the past, there is no thorough repair. (*MOTF* 483)

Tom's revelation, which is imagined in terms of Feuerbachian outpouring and identification, holds onto the feeling of redemption in a secular and distinctly non-biblical world. It is a moment of hope and tenderness, a brief hiatus in the chaotic drowning of the flood scene. In this moment, Eliot suggests that human interdependencies, early and formative attachments and generous feelings, provide secular stand-ins for salvation, anchors in a world in which it is easy to drift into error and in which the right choice is sometimes just a matter of resisting that diabolic and seductive force of fluency that allows one to get caught up, and carried away.

'Why Should Not a Woman Have a Little Supremacy?' Gwendolen's Gamble

In the opening scene of *Daniel Deronda*, Eliot uses the myth of the Fall teasingly to suggest a desire for power and the limits of female agency. Gwendolen fantasizes about usurping male supremacy as she hits a winning streak in the casino: 'She had begun to believe in her luck, others had begun to believe in it: she had visions of being followed by a *cortège* who would worship her as a goddess of luck and watch her play as a directing augury. Such things had been known of male gamblers; why should not a woman have a little supremacy?' (*DD* 6). Eliot satirizes Gwendolen's vanity, but her satire is not without affection for the determined and powerless young woman who wants a commanding authority, and freedom from subjection, that she will never be able to have. The conceit of gambling, in which every decision surrenders agency

[22] Gen. 8: 19.

to chance and luck, emphasizes Gwendolen's lack of narrative control and the stakes of her gambling 'choice' feel particularly high. The consequences of error press on Gwendolen's being even before any mistake has been made.

Eliot plays with some degree of irony on the trope of the fallen woman, framing Gwendolen's character in terms of the mythic archetype derived from Genesis 3 while undermining its judgements. The novel opens with a line which invokes both the Darwinian context of sexual selection and frames Deronda as the unfallen Adam who might have just encountered his temptress:[23]

> Was she beautiful or not beautiful? And what was the secret form or expression which gave the dynamic quality to her glance? Was the good or the evil genius dominant in those beams? Probably the evil; else why was the effect that of unrest rather than undisturbed charm? Why was the wish to look again felt as coercion and not a longing in which the whole being consents? (*DD* 3)

Even as she invokes the Fall, Eliot mocks the staleness such interpretative codes can confer. Deronda is deprived of the satisfaction of easy judgements: beautiful or not beautiful, good or evil. Gwendolen's attractiveness resists the subjection to trope and archetype, even as it affirms it. She is the only lively thing in the room: transfixing precisely because her character will not be fixed.

Eliot will not commit to the myth of the Fall, but she also will not let it go. Gwendolen, one of the older ladies observes to her male companion: 'has got herself up as a sort of serpent now, all green and silver, and winds her neck about a little more than usual' (*DD* 7). She is, he observes, the kind 'a man might risk hanging for... Woman was tempted by a serpent, why not man?' (*DD* 7–8). Like the image of Deronda as an unfallen Adam, the image of Gwendolen as a beautiful serpentine temptress lingers even as Eliot wryly undercuts it: 'The remark that Gwendolen wound her neck about more than usual this evening was true. But it was not that she might carry out the serpent idea more completely: it was that she watched for any chance of seeing Deronda, so that she might enquire about this stranger, under whose measuring glance she was still wincing.' (*DD* 8). Eliot mocks the prejudicial judgements and baroque elaborations that immediately cast an attractive woman as

[23] For further discussion of the Darwinian context for this scene, see: Kaye, *Flirt's Tragedy*, 118–50, 119.

a viper and yet we do still feel as if a fall narrative is being set up, even as it is being undermined.

This intensifies the sexual tension. Gwendolen and Deronda are instantly caught in erotic dynamics. Gwendolen's winning streak is broken, and her powerlessness brought home, when she catches Deronda's eye:

> her eyes met Deronda's, and instead of averting them as she would have desired to do, she was unpleasantly conscious that they were arrested—how long? The darting sense that he was measuring her and looking down on her as an inferior, that he was of a different quality from the human dross around her, that he felt himself in a region outside and above her, and was examining her as a specimen of a lower order, roused a tingling resentment which stretched the moment with conflict. It did not bring the blood to her cheeks, but sent it away from her lips. (*DD* 6)

This moment of heightened sexual tension and emotional arrest compounds our growing sense that Gwendolen might be playing a high stakes game. The extended conceit of gambling, which amplifies Gwendolen's helpless desire for agency, is also felt in Eliot's disconcerting play on scale. Time is 'stretched' and untrackable—'how long' she wonders, did this moment last? But, like a hunted animal, Gwendolen also has an instinctive 'darting sense', here a quickening awareness—in the animal world, a sharp physical dash in response to danger. The speed of reaction shrinks that timeless elongation to a split-second. As time both expands and contracts, so does space: Deronda's presence is felt as both uncomfortably close and immeasurably far away, 'in a region outside and above her'. Emotional charge becomes the stretching and narrowing of cosmic fabric. 'Tingling' also recalls the shock of an electric current. Gwendolen and Deronda are, for this moment, co-ordinates in a radically uncertain material universe, in which the laws of time and space are destabilized and narrative direction far beyond individual control.

And then Gwendolen makes what seems to be a choice: 'She controlled herself by the help of an inward defiance, and without other sign of emotion than this lip-paleness turned to play.' (*DD* 6). So, the stillness of the expanded moment is broken by a turn away, which feels at once deliberate and coerced. Eliot manages to satirize Gwendolen's vanity while making us acutely aware of her vulnerability. Gwendolen's angry pride holds her together, but it also reveals her fragility in the face of circumstances beyond her control. Deronda's gaze is a synecdoche of the commanding structures that only in her fantasies has she overthrown. As she loses her stake, and starts to feel intensely self-conscious and embarrassed with 'that man still watching her', she ramps up her performance, holding onto dignity as a substitute for agency: 'when her next stake was swept away, she felt the orbits of her eyes getting hot, and the certainty she had (without looking) of that man still watching her was something like a pressure which begins to be torturing. The more reason to her why she should not flinch but go on playing as if she were indifferent to loss or gain.' (*DD*, p. 6).

Here is both a girl on the verge of tears and a world on the brink of collapse. Gwendolen's determined coolness becomes a desperate defence against the hot pricking around 'the orbits of her eyes'. Holding back tears becomes contiguous with maintaining the boundaries of self and world. External pressure is met with internal pressure. Weight pushes on both sides of Gwendolen's being; in the mounting tension of this scene, it feels impossible that lines will hold. The elongated moment when eyes meet and dice roll feels stretched because it is fraught with risk. 'Such a drama takes no long while to play out', Eliot's narrator observes as she describes Gwendolen's increasingly reckless gaming at the table, 'development and catastrophe can often be measured by nothing clumsier than the moment-hand' (*DD* 6). Here, again, is the double trope of the fortunate or catastrophic fall. In the moment of play, there is everything to play for, but no real control.

Embedding the conceit of gambling within the mythic structures of the Fall, Eliot makes us feel as if the stakes for Gwendolen are extraordinarily high. As in Genesis 3, a woman's choice might be a world-making, or world-breaking, event. But the binary operation of the Fall, in which a single decision sets an incontrovertible narrative in motion, is something which Eliot works deliberately and determinedly to undermine with repeatedly shifting stakes, unpredictable outcomes, and mutable circumstances:

> Since she was not winning strikingly, the next best thing was to lose strikingly. She controlled her muscles, and showed no tremor of mouth or hands. Each time her stake was swept off, she doubled it. Many were watching her, but the sole observation she was conscious of was Deronda's, who, though she had never looked towards him, she was sure had not moved away. (*DD* 6)

The object has shifted but the goal is still to win. The gamble, now, is that Deronda will find her attractive. The more dramatic her losses at the table, the more dramatic her success in the room. There is an endearing, and desperate, recklessness in the way in which Gwendolen tries to keep hold of a narrative that is running away from her and a bluntness of plot which exposes her foolishness. She returns to her bedroom to find that the monetary loss, which she so swiftly rendered unimportant, is of sudden, absolute, importance. Her family are ruined. She can no longer stay in pleasant dissipation abroad. The sudden change in economic circumstance gives her no choice. She must return home. In these opening scenes, Eliot sets the architecture of the Fall, in which choice is a right or wrong action, against the shifting, multiple and uncontrollable economies of circumstance and chance, in which every win might also be an unpredictable loss.

In *The Mill on the Floss*, Stephen tries to persuade Maggie that by wanting something she has not made it happen but made it right that it happens to her. In *Daniel Deronda*, Eliot exposes the frighteningly mixed feelings of pleasure, guilt, and terror that accompany the egoistic will. In another dreamy boat sequence, in which Gwendolen's cruel husband, Grandcourt, drowns, Gwendolen experiences an overwhelming fluidity of feeling, which seems, terrifyingly, to be the most forceful architect of reality:

> They were taken out of the port and carried eastward by a gentle breeze. Some clouds tempered the sunlight, and the hour was always deepening towards the supreme beauty of the evening. Sails larger and smaller changed their aspect like sensitive things, and made a cheerful companionship, alternately near and far. The grand city shone more vaguely, the mountains looked out above it, and there was stillness as in an island sanctuary. Yet, suddenly, Gwendolen let her hands fall, and said in a scarcely audible tone, 'God help me!' (*DD* 574)

In the passive surrender of her hands and the dreadful realization of her whispered prayer, there is a feeling of internal collapse, a symbolic relinquishing of agency, which seem to compromise the boundary between inner want and outer reality. The landscape becomes dreamily inconsistent, as if it too has taken on the unstable quality of water. Sunlight is 'tempered' by cloud; 'the hour was always deepening'. The sails also have a distinct fluidity, 'alternately near and far'. In the painterly quality of the scene lies the error that John Ruskin, whom Eliot admired for his realism, termed 'pathetic fallacy': the incorrect attribution of human emotions to nature.[24] For one, false,

[24] Eliot wrote: 'the truth of infinite value that [Ruskin] teaches is realism—the doctrine that all truth and beauty are to be attained by a humble and faithful study of nature, and not by substituting vague forms, bred by imagination on the mists of feeling, in the place of definite, substantial, reality'. Unsigned review of *Modern Painters III* in *The Westminster Review* 9 (Apr. 1856). Reprinted in J. L. Bradley, *Ruskin: The Critical Heritage* (New York: Routledge, 1984), 179–83, 180. For further reading, see Darrell Mansell, 'Ruskin and George Eliot's Realism', *Criticism* 7.3 (1965): 203–16.

moment, the whole world seems an extension of Gwendolen's inner being, as if the dreadful events begun in her imagination have already, in some sense, completed.

Eliot emphasizes the terror implicit in the idea that imagining something makes it real, that there could be no distinction between imagination and reality in the action of choice. In this sense, the scene stages a dramatic conflict with the egoistic will of the Creator-God, who can simply say or touch something and it be. Gwendolen is filled with dread that, by desiring Grandcourt dead, she has brought his death into being. 'It is come, it is come!' she gasps to Deronda, 'He is dead!' (*DD* 578). 'It has all remained in your imagination. It has gone on only in your thought', Deronda insists, as he reassures her that her momentary murderous will cannot have manifested as reality. But even he has doubts, slipping into a question: 'To the last the evil temptation has been resisted?' (*DD* 583). 'I only know', says Gwendolen, 'that I saw my wish outside me.' (*DD* 586).

Gwendolen, overcome with guilty feeling, retrospectively constructs a 'beginning', taking us back to the 'make-believe' beginning of the novel's opening, and finding, in the myth of the Fall, a narrative frame for psychological breakdown:

> 'Perhaps you don't quite know the beginning of it all,' said Gwendolen, slowly, as if she were overcoming her reluctance. 'There was someone else he ought to have married. And I knew it, and I told her I would not hinder it. And I went away—that was when you first saw me. But then we became poor all at once, and I was very miserable, and I was tempted. I thought, "I shall do as I like and make everything right." I persuaded myself. And it was all different. It was all dreadful. Then came hatred and wicked thoughts. That was how it all came. I told you I was afraid of myself. And I did what you told me—I did try to make my fear a safeguard. I thought of what I would be if I—I felt what would come—how I should dread the morning—wishing it would be always night—and yet in the darkness always seeing something—seeing death. If you did not know how miserable I was, you might—but now it has all been no use. I can care for nothing but saving the rest from knowing—poor mamma, who has never been happy.' (*DD* 589)

What was once seen as a separation from God is now viewed as a dislocation of selfhood. 'Ourself behind ourself—concealed / Should startle most', wrote Dickinson in 1862. '[T]he strife within her seemed like her own effort to escape from herself', writes Eliot of Gwendolen. Gwendolen's fragmented narrative resonates with desperate loneliness, the gaps in sense and meaning reflective of an overwhelming feeling of vulnerability and compensated by an instinctive reaching for protective buffers in the absence of salvation.

Maggie articulates a basic principle of secular ethics, which Eliot derived, in part, from Feuerbach: 'the real ties lie in the feelings and expectations we have raised in other minds' (*MOTF* 416). But in the overlapping and unequally interdependent stories of the realist novel, Eliot was also able to expose the feeling of loss, limit, and uncertainty that underpinned secular ethics. Like a frightened animal, or infant child, Gwendolen 'clung to the thought of Deronda: she persuaded herself that he would not go away while she was there—he knew that she needed help' (*DD* 574). His kindness becomes the substitute for salvation. But even as Eliot paints him as the embodiment of moral goodness and generous response, she allows him his human selfishness, his own wants and needs and limits:

> His strong feeling for this stricken creature could not hinder rushing images of future difficulty. He continued to meet her appealing eyes as he spoke, but it was with the painful consciousness that to her ear his words might carry a promise which one day would seem unfulfilled: he would make an indefinite promise to an indefinite hope. (*DD* 590)

In an entangled world of overlapping lives, attractions, duties, and feelings we do not want or need each other equally nor, perhaps, can we always know what expectations we are raising or avoid raising expectations that cannot be fulfilled. Such dependency again makes choice feel like coercion: a falling into narrative that is not a deliberate decision and yet cannot be ethically avoided. '"It will be better for me to go now," said Deronda, worn in spirit by the perpetual strain of this scene. "Remember what we said of your task—to get well before other friends come."' (*DD* 591).

Deronda manifests to Gwendolen as her Feuerbachian 'feeling of personified shame': 'the sense that he was there would save her from acting out the evil within' (*DD* 574). The girl who had once longed for agency and excitement now longs for the consolations of benevolent dictation and the relief of known ends, while the man who has become her Saviour makes a slightly embarrassed, exhausted, withdrawal from her claims: '"I will lead any life you tell me…You will always live at the Abbey—or at Diplow?" "I am quite uncertain where I will live", said Deronda, colouring.' (*DD* 590). Maggie knows she is going home when she leaves Stephen. But it feels, for Gwendolen, as if the script has run out: 'It is impossible for me to think how my life will go on' (*DD* 590). Tom and Maggie drown in each other's arms and Eliot allows her reader a tender comfort in the tragic resolution and biblical echo of their foreshadowed end. In Gwendolen's story, Eliot returns to the dynamics of the will without offering that narrative consolation. In the moment that Deronda tells her he can't be the anchor she wants and displays the desires and affections which will take his story in a different direction, Gwendolen is forced to grow up.

In the casino, in thrall to her own fantasies of agency, Gwendolen did not flinch. Now, action has become reaction, an instinctive response to pain and pressure: 'sunk back with closed eyes, like a lost, weary, storm-beaten white doe, unable to rise and pursue its unguided way. He rose and stood before her. The movement touched her consciousness, and she opened her eyes with a slight quivering that seemed like fear.' (*DD* 587). The threat of overwhelming fluidity, which she controls in the casino, and which overtakes her in the boat, erupts in floods of tears:

> when he had left her, she sank on her knees, in hysterical crying. The distance between them was too great. She was a banished soul—beholding a possible life which she had sinned herself away from.
>
> She was found in this way, crushed on the floor. Such grief seemed natural in a poor lady whose husband had been drowned in her presence. (*DD* 591)

Even as Gwendolen imagines herself irredeemably fallen, Eliot takes us away from sin and back to 'this world of mistakes', in which no one ever seems to be able to know another person's reality and no interpretative choice is free of error. The wry comment on misinterpretation comes as a corrective to the biblical melodrama of Gwendolen's self-image. As in the casino, the mythic architecture of the Fall makes the stakes seem incredibly high. But in the soft shock of the scene's ending, Eliot turns to a satire of everyday mistakes. This both makes Gwendolen seem more alone and gives us a more generous frame for reading her fallenness. Gwendolen's error seems less disastrous, more commonplace than catastrophic. If the novel could expose the shortcomings of sympathy and human interdependence as stand-ins for salvation, it could also help build a more forgiving aesthetic.

In Gwendolen, Eliot suggests that the collapse of the boundary between imagination and action, a parody of the egoistic will of Genesis 1, is a form of psychological breakdown, which results in an intense and devastating loneliness. We never see Grandcourt's death, and it remains a lacuna, a strangely volatile and uncertain moment of the possible and impossible, refracted through desire and guilt. The inaction of the decisive moment has a precedent in Grandcourt's proposal to Gwendolen, where he offers himself with withdrawal and she accepts with a negative:

> 'Do you command me to go?' No familiar spirit could have suggested to him more effective words.
>
> 'No,' said Gwendolen. She could not let him go: that negative was a clutch. She seemed to herself to be, after all, only drifted towards the tremendous decision:—but drifting depended on something besides the currents, when the sails have been set beforehand. (*DD* 254)

Even as Eliot dramatizes the madness that lies in collapsing the distinction between imagined and enacted will, she also allows that action is sometimes inaction: surrender not just to circumstance but to a current that could equally be desire or despair.

For Gwendolen, there is no pleasure in the proposal itself, and no real freedom in the hurried moment of supposed choice:

> A fish honestly invited to come and be eaten has a clear course in declining, but how if it finds itself swimming against a net? And apart from the network, would she have dared at once to say anything decisive? Gwendolen had not time to be clear on that point. As it was she was compelled to silence. (*DD* 252)

But there is, in its aftermath, the quick thrill that she gets from gambling. As in the casino, Gwendolen deludes herself with a fantasy of agency in the very moment such power is lost:

> she thought she was entering on a fuller power of managing circumstance—with all the official strength of marriage, which some women made so poor a use of...with her erect head and elastic footstep she was walking amid illusions; and yet, too, there was an under-consciousness in her that she was a little intoxicated. (*DD* 296–7)

For Gwendolen, caught up in her desired self-image, these moments have the thrill of flirtation. Flirtation, as Adam Phillips observes, offers the pleasure of contingency.[25] It keeps possibility in play through its very lack of narrative

[25] Adam Phillips, *On Flirtation* (London: Faber, 1994), p. xvii.

commitment. We can flirt with ideologies without wholeheartedly embracing their worldview. We can flirt with versions of ourselves as much as with other people. Imagining herself as a 'directing augury' in the casino, she flirts with the same powerful version of herself that she imagines here. The other self, the 'under-consciousness', does not disappear. Thus, on her winning streak: 'she looked round her with a survey too markedly cold and neutral not to have in it a little of that nature which we call art concealing an inward exultation' (*DD* 5). Acting a part becomes a means of survival when the self seems so very alone. It is a narrative decision, which sets the sails as much as it preserves the drifting boat from sinking. 'But do your work and I shall know you. Do your work and you shall reinforce yourself', wrote Ralph Waldo Emerson in 1844, as he railed against conformity.[26] Eliot similarly suggests that we make ourselves a reality through action. In order to be what we are, we must claim it, stake it, enact it. But there is also a fear that we live in a state of perpetual theatre, continually watched and judged by others and acting out a reality which then commits us to a sense of self.[27] 'You can play the madwoman', Grandcourt says scornfully to his mistress as she threatens to expose his duplicity (*DD* 292). But he is also unnerved by 'the strange mixture of acting and reality in her passion', turning quickly to threats in order to regain his dictatorial control: 'Be quiet and hear what I tell you. I will never forgive you if you present yourself again and make a scene.' (*DD* 293–4). Eliot, like Emerson, understood the risk of performance. In acting out a reality, we might commit ourselves to its truth.

The worst risk, for Eliot, lay in anaesthetic action. In the casino, everyone is living out their own inadequate version of reality. A 'respectable London tradesman, blonde and soft-handed', convinces himself that 'the vice of gambling lay in losing money at it' and that 'Providence had never manifested any disapprobation of his amusement' because he never lost enough. An inert 'deposit of newcomers' watch passively on the fortunes of others: 'one of them, usually a woman, might now and then be observed putting down a five-franc piece with a simpering air, just to see what the passion of gambling really was' (*DD* 6). The gamblers are anaesthetized. Drugged by a miserable compulsion, they have no aesthetic, and therefore no real ethical, capacity: 'while every single player differed markedly from every other, there was a certain uniform negativeness of expression which had the effect of a mask—as if

[26] Ralph Waldo Emerson, 'Self Reliance', *Selected Essays* ed. Larzer Ziff (Harmondsworth: Penguin, 1982), 175–203, 181.

[27] For a fuller discussion of this in relation to Emerson, see Stanley Cavell, *Emerson's Transcendental Etudes* (Stanford, Calif.: Stanford University Press, 2003), 84–99.

they had all eaten of some root that for the time compelled the brains of each to the same narrow monotony of action' (*DD* 5). In 1872, Eliot had described her horror at seeing Byron's grand-niece gambling: 'The saddest thing to be witnessed is the play of Miss Leigh, Byron's grand niece, who is only 26 years old, and is completely in the grasp of this mean, money-raking demon. It made me cry to see her young fresh face among the hags and brutally stupid men around her' (*GEL*, vol. 5, 514). The beautiful Miss Leigh gave her some inspiration for Gwendolen, the only lively and sensitive thing amidst the horribly anaesthetized habitual gamblers in the casino.

'O this masquerade of a world', Marian Evans had written to her aunt in 1842, aghast at her growing awareness of limited feeling and insincere, performed virtue (*GEL*, vol. 1, 128). Aesthetic capacity became, for her, the basis of moral choice but not its endgame. The lines between imagination and action need to hold: their undoing is psychological collapse. But a poor imagination and narrow range of feeling made action more likely to be governed by the anaesthetic of habit. Commenting on the parochial religion of the Dodsons and the Tullivers in *The Mill on the Floss*, Eliot observes: 'Their religion was of a simple, semi-pagan, kind, but there was no heresy in it—if heresy properly means choice—for they didn't know there was any other religion, except that of chapel-goers, which appeared to run in a family, like asthma.' (*MOTF* 253). She pokes fun at their mistaken prejudices, but she also emphasizes the ethical restrictions of the conforming, unimaginative, anaesthetic mind. We cannot choose to do something we cannot imagine. Drawing our attention to the etymology of heresy (Greek *αἵρεσις*, 'choosing, choice, course taken') Eliot implies that there is no room for moral choice in conformity.

'Varying in the Right Direction': Fortunately Fallen Forms

'Fundamentally, form is unlikeness', Eliot wrote in 1868, '...every difference is form.'[28] If Blake saw form as an ethical decision, an encounter with difference, so did Eliot. But unlike Blake, and perhaps influenced again by her reading of Emerson and certainly by her reading of Darwin, Eliot described

[28] George Eliot, 'Notes on Form in Art', in *Essays of George Eliot*, 431–6, 432–3.

superior form in terms of organic growth, natural affinities, and microscopic differences:[29]

> And as knowledge continues to grow by its alternating processes of distinction & combination, seeing smaller and smaller unlikenesses & grouping or associating these under a common likeness, it arrives at the conception of wholes more and more multiplied & highly differenced, yet more & more absolutely bound together by various conditions of common likeness or mutual dependence…The highest form, then, is the highest organism, that is to say the most varied group of relations bound together in a wholeness which again has the most varied relations with other phenomena.[30]

In *On the Origin of Species*, Darwin had framed the shock of real existential loss within a tragedy of maladaptation. But he had also left space for an optimistic theory of organic growth: 'Natural selection will always tend to preserve all the individuals varying in the right direction, though in different degrees, so as to better fill up the unoccupied place.'[31] Eliot draws inspiration from the comic, as well as tragic, architecture of Darwin's thought: the joyful celebration of varied life, crammed, vibrant existence, pushing, struggling, living, and dying in a vast organic network of interconnectedness, a world awaiting fulfilment. As Gillian Beer puts it: 'originating is an activity not an authority. And deviation, not truth to type, is the creative principle.'[32] Eliot's subtext is also Darwinian. There will be tragedies of maladaptation, like Maggie's, unequal dependencies and partial withdrawals as with Gwendolen and Deronda. The 'growing good of the world', which Eliot hopes for at the end of *Middlemarch*, does not preclude real loss and unequal, unmet, need.[33]

A superior form, for Eliot, is that which varies in the right direction. Emotion continually readjusts to circumstance and condition. Mistakes are inevitable and hypothesis forever collapses under the weight of experience: 'Poetic form was not begotten by thinking it out, or framing as a shell which should hold emotional expression any more than the shell of an animal arises before the living creature.'[34] Somewhere in between anaesthetic conformity

[29] In his 1844 essay, 'The Poet', Emerson wrote: 'it is not metres but metre-making argument that makes a poem,—a thought so passionate and alive that like the spirit of a plant or animal it has architecture of its own and adorns nature with a new thing'. Emerson, *Selected Essays*, 259–84, 263–4.

[30] George Eliot, 'Notes on Form in Art', *Essays of George Eliot*, 433.

[31] Darwin, *Origin*, 79.

[32] Beer, *Darwin's Plots*, 59.

[33] George Eliot, *Middlemarch* ed. Rosemary Ashton (London: Penguin, 2003), 838. All further references to this edition, included in the text.

[34] Eliot, 'Notes on Form in Art', in *Essays of George Eliot*, 435.

and aesthetic form varying in the right direction is the everyday limitation of 'thinking it out, or framing': the imagined set-pieces, identikits, self-delusions, and fantasies that both create the conditions of mistaken choice and allow people to live with their mistakes. Maggie and Gwendolen both fall too easily into fictions, too quickly into fantasies. But it is also their means of survival. Errors were not purely intellectual. They belonged to character. As Eliot had written to her friend, Sara Hennell: 'we cannot...wrench them away without destroying vitality'.[35]

Eliot forgives Gwendolen, who, even as she makes her choice—a choice that has both the excitement of authorship and the feel of coercion—feels that dreadful moral limit as an instinctive, shrinking reaction:

> A few minutes before she was looking along an inescapable path of repulsive monotony, with hopeless inward rebellion against the imperious lot which left her no choice: and lo, now, a moment of choice was come. Yet—was it triumph she felt most or terror? Impossible for Gwendolen not to feel some triumph in a tribute to her power at a time when she was first tasting the bitterness of insignificance: again she seemed to be getting a sort of empire over her own life. But how to use it? Here came the terror. Quick, quick, like pictures in a book beaten open with a sense of hurry, came back vividly, yet all in fragments, all that she had gone through in relation to Grandcourt—the allurements, the vacillations, the resolve to accede, the final repulsion; the incisive face of that dark-eyed lady with the lovely boy; her own pledge (was it a pledge?) not to marry him?—the new disbelief in the worth of men and things for which that scene of disclosure had become a symbol. That unalterable experience made a vision at which in the first agitated moment, before tempering reflections could suggest themselves, her native terror shrank. Where was the good of choice coming again? What did she wish? Anything different? No! and yet in the dark seed-growths of consciousness a new wish was forming itself—'I wish I had never known it!' Something, anything she wished for that would have saved her from the dread to let Grandcourt come. (*DD* 245)

Gwendolen's feeling of dread, 'her native terror', is the closest she will get to a saving grace, but it comes with none of the remembered consolations of a religious worldview. Eliot's skill is to make us realize that feelings and duties don't run in straight or singular lines. Triumph and terror are hard to

[35] George Eliot to Sara Hennell, 19 October 1843, *GEL*, 1, 162.

distinguish and may be felt simultaneously and unequally in the same moment. Contradictory feelings crowd, but don't cancel, each other out. Images form hurriedly, in pressured moments of overwhelming and conflicting emotion and desperate instability of feeling. If Eliot draws her optimistic vision of superior aesthetic form from the comic architecture of evolutionary theory 'varying in the right direction', she alerts us, here, to the precarity and unreliability of every aesthetic and evolutionary movement and the uncertainty of its ends. Eliot's organic metaphor, a wish forming in 'the dark seed-growth of consciousness', mixes the image of organic resilience and pressing, fertile desire with a profound sense of a hijacked narrative and furtive rebellion. Gwendolen wishes she could go back to a moment before the beginning and set a different story in motion. As in her other key moments of choice, her only action is inaction: 'the dread to let Grandcourt come'.

The shift from a divinely willed to humanly enacted world feels perpetually risky and potentially lonely. Maggie and Gwendolen's bad choices are often felt as a fluid fall from within, and into entangled circumstances, sometimes a wearied relief and sometimes the result of paralysed inaction and foregone conclusion. But choice can also be a narrative decision, a desire to act a part. Imagination, far from being the handmaiden of sympathy, often traps others in the selfish weave of individual ambition and frustrated desire for agency. 'We are all of us imaginative in some form or other,' writes Eliot in *Middlemarch*, 'for images are the brood of desire' (*M* 324). Yet, imagination is also the basis of moral choice; and without it, choice is limited. In this context, the myth of the Fall becomes both dramatic architecture and foil for the inevitably fallible misjudgements that belong not to a world of sin but to 'this world of mistakes'.

Understanding that the moment of moral choice is not straightforward, Eliot recognizes that the myth of the Fall is often pernicious and overly judgemental. But it also becomes a way of framing a very human desire for solace and anchors in an uncertain world and of giving meaning to everyday suffering. The myth of the Fall helps construct a secular narrative of return, where goodness is directed by early ties and generous feelings. It emphasizes the consolations that are lost in a secular worldview, informing Eliot's sense of the loneliness of growing up in an uncertain and open-ended secular world, where the script suddenly seems to run out, interdependencies are unequal, and needs are often unmet. She also developed a form of realism which drove a more generous and optimistic secular vision, suggesting that hope lies in varying in the right direction: a version of the fortunate fall which forgives some mistakes.

PART II
NATION

5

Textures of a New Eden

Cole, Emerson, Whitman

Towards the end of a century that saw the full effects of the industrial revolution, Gerard Manley Hopkins aligned distance from nature with separation from God:

> And all is seared with trade; bleared, smeared with toil;
> And wears man's smudge and shares man's smell: the soil
> Is bare now, nor can foot feel, being shod.[1]

It is not just that the heavy human footprint destroys the beauties of nature. It is also that unfeelingness is the source of modern alienation; humanity is cut off by material and technological advancement from an organic skin-to-skin relation with world. This version of the Fall, the single imagined moment where it all went wrong, is the moment we lost the right kind of touch. As Erin Goss puts it: 'things will only announce God if one knows how to touch them.'[2]

In 1836, the British-born American landscape painter, Thomas Cole, had tried to inspire his American audience with a sense of religious and moral urgency, telling them all was not yet lost in the new world and locating hope for the future in the ability to 'see and feel' the beauty of nature and stop the relentless 'march' of industrialization he had witnessed as a child in England:

> what is sometimes called improvement in its march makes us fear that the bright and tender flowers of the imagination shall all be crushed beneath its iron tramp...Nature has spread for us a rich and delightful banquet. Shall we turn from it? We are still in Eden; the wall that shuts us out from the garden is our own ignorance and folly.[3]

[1] Gerard Manley Hopkins, 'God's Grandeur', in *The Poetical Works of Gerard Manley Hopkins*, ed. Norman H. MacKenzie (Oxford: OUP, 1990), 139.

[2] Erin M. Goss, '"Almost Unmade": Hopkins and the Body Apocalyptic', *Victorian Poetry* 49.1 (Spring 2011): 83–103, 87.

[3] Thomas Cole, 'Essay on American Scenery', *American Monthly Magazine* 1 (Jan. 1836), 1–2.

The Myth of the Fall in Nineteenth-Century Literature. Linda Freedman, Oxford University Press.
 DOI: 10.1093/oso/9780198969570.003.0006

Like Hopkins, Cole imagines the Fall as the moment we collectively and overwhelmingly lose the right kind of touch; put on a shoe; build a wall; crush all the 'tender flowers of the imagination'. He presents this moment as a change in the texture of experience, a hardening of the bounding line between inner and outer, a self-imposed exile.

This change in the texture of experience is also the story that Charles Taylor tells about secularization. The lost porousness of the bounding line belongs to what Taylor identifies as an earlier, enchanted, world. This was a world in which, Taylor believes, atheism was close to impossible, a world in which 'it just seems so obvious that God is there, acting in the cosmos, founding and sustaining societies, acting as a bulwark against evil'.[4] At this point in history, Taylor maintains, the boundary between mind and world was much more blurred. By contrast, Taylor sees the modern self as buffered. For the modern subject, he suggests, selfhood is consonant with interiority; the beyond (whether spiritual or material) does not need to intrude. 'This self', he concludes, 'can see itself as invulnerable, as master of the meanings of things for it.'[5] Both Taylor and Cole express a religious feeling of loss, but they also acknowledge the way in which secular narratives of progress might feel empowering. As God retreats, humanity imagines itself more able to author its own existence.

Thomas Cole expresses a longing to restore an earlier, enchanted, world and condemns what he sees as the unfeelingness of modern alienation and 'improvement'. He attacks industrialization as a tyrannical, and deluded, hijacking of divine authorship, urging his audience not just to 'see' but to 'feel' the beauty of American landscape and so restore a religious appreciation of divine creation and human creativity. In an essay on J. G. Herder, Niklaus Largier elucidates a similar quality of vision, describing the eye as 'the organ of touch'.[6] In Largier's theorization, the sense of touch helps define a quality of vision rooted in collections, experiences, and transfigurations before or below the moment of formation and fixity. He brings the nostalgia of touch to the fore: 'the eye sees determined, limited, defined shapes, forms, and colors. Touch, however, appears as a moment of liberation from this determination, as a reminiscence of something decidedly more open.'[7] The moral force of Cole's seer is rooted in precisely this kind of nostalgia, which, for him, is a

[4] Taylor, *Secular Age*, 26. [5] Taylor, *Secular Age*, 38.

[6] Niklaus Largier, 'Figure, Plasticity, Affect', in *Touching and Being Touched: Kinesthesia and Affect in Dance and Movement,* ed. Gabrielle Brandstetter, Gerko Egert, and Sabine Zubarik (Berlin: De Gruyter, 2013), 23–34, 27.

[7] Largier, 'Figure, Plasticity, Affect', 31.

version of pre-lapsarian fantasy. The eye as the organ of touch both remembers and restores creative possibility; as Largier puts it, 'the plasticity of the soul in its relations with itself, things, works of art, and the world'.[8] Cole's moral urgency derives from the twin religious principles of faith and hope: faith in a lost moment of beginning and hope that the seer might restore, and not just recognize, the innocent possibility and plasticity that preceded the determined logic of the Fall.

The myth of America as a New Eden is rooted in the plasticity and possibility of pre-lapsarian beginning. When R. W. B. Lewis encouraged a return to nineteenth-century sensibilities in the context of cold war threat, he described an 'antagonism to nature' as one of the cardinal defects of modern hopelessness: 'for the very language of literature evaporates when it loses faith in and hence touch with natural objects; and from a distrust of experience'.[9] New world mythology was distinctive because the recovery narrative, the desire to restore a lost innocence, turned on the belief that America was the Eden of the future. Early settlers were motivated by more than topographical optimism as they colonized and cultivated the land. Seventeenth- and eighteenth-century colonists frequently believed in both the historical reality and prophesied futurity of Eden. The default model for everything from planting trees to educating children was the perfect pattern of Paradise.[10] The myth of America as a New Eden thus became associated with the kind of active moral, civic and artistic enterprise that both Lewis and Cole encourage, as well as the nostalgic vision of innocence that they idealize; it reinforced the virtuous endeavours of culture as much as the pure beginnings of nature.

In the 1830s, 1840s, and 1850s, white American artists and writers renewed the colonial myth with a mixture of enthusiasm and anxiety. Before it is about the damage we have done to nature, Cole's 'Essay on American Scenery' is about the good we might do through culture: 'Poetry and Painting sublime and purify thought, by grasping the past, the present, and the future', he declares.[11] The job of the artist, as Cole expresses it here, is mythic speech: a dynamic and prophetic mode of expression. With their capacity to feel, Cole's ideal painters and poets will be path-builders. But he also cannot conceal a rising scepticism. He seems confused about the direction in which America might move. We are still in Eden but we have shut ourselves out. We must not

[8] Largier, 'Figure, Plasticity, Affect', 31.
[9] Lewis, *American Adam*, 196.
[10] See Zachary McLeod Hutchins, *Inventing Eden: Primitivism, Millennialism and the Making of New England* (Oxford: OUP, 2014), 3.
[11] Cole, 'Essay on American Scenery', 1.

turn from Eden, and yet we must return. We have fallen through 'ignorance and folly' ('the march of improvement' is the curse of ignorance that sells itself as the fruit of the tree of knowledge) but the banquet that Nature has spread is rich and tempting (is this another invitation to eat?). The question Cole struggles to articulate is not whether America can enclose itself in the mythical moment of beginning, but whether the artist can hold onto the creative openness of touch and restore the plasticity of innocence from within the fallen conditions of history.

This chapter revisits the idea that Eden is more than a symbol for America; it is part of its self-mythologization. In Roland Barthes's terms, it is a formal metalanguage, or mythic speech, which asserts itself as a grammar, inflexion, or mode of meaning.[12] The ease with which myth moves across media, its claim to universality, means that its formal quality becomes particularly apparent in interdisciplinary comparisons. Once we are talking not just about words and images, but the binding together of words and images, the way composition and feel makes narrative sense, the shared formal vocabulary of the visual and verbal arts, which is implicit in the shared etymology of texture and text (Latin, *textus*, to weave), comes to the fore. I discuss Cole's paintings alongside two of Ralph Waldo Emerson's most significant essays and Walt Whitman's 1855 version of *Leaves of Grass*. If the Fall becomes the moment we lost the right kind of touch, the myth of a New Eden reinforces itself both in the feel of dominion, and through the plasticity of possibility and original world-making force.

In the same year as 'Essay on American Scenery', Emerson anonymously published his long essay on 'Nature', in which he asked: 'why should we not also enjoy an original relation to the Universe?'[13] Emerson also wanted to reinvent the myth of America as a New Eden. Like so many of his contemporaries, he was looking for a way of living that felt free from received error and he put his faith in the arts. 'America is a poem in our eyes', he went on to write in 1844: 'its ample geography dazzles the imagination, and it will not wait long for metres'.[14] But he also knew that he was too late for the possibility and potentiality to which he laid claim. His investment in pre-lapsarian fantasy is countered by an ever-rising scepticism, a feeling of being shut out and detached from original world-making force. In 1855, Walt Whitman self-consciously and deliberately presented himself as the answer to Emerson's

[12] Barthes, 'Myth Today', *Mythologies*, 141.
[13] Emerson, 'Nature' (1836), *Selected Essays*, 35–83, 36.
[14] Emerson, 'The Poet' (1844), *Selected Essays*, 259–85, 281.

call for a poet and prophet of a new American Eden. In Whitman's 1855 poem, most of which becomes 'Walt Whitman' and 'Song of Myself', we can read a far more confident ideology of dominion: 'I know the hand of God is the elderhand of my own', he declares.[15] He writes against original sin, celebrating libidinous energy. But there are still doubts, scepticisms about his own poetic agency. In the work of Cole, Emerson, and Whitman, volatile shifts between faith and scepticism are felt as shifts in the texture of experience: smoothness and roughness, fluid force and sliding surface, integration and disintegration of form. The job of the artist becomes mythic speech: to recover, renew and reform the textures of Eden from within the fallen world.

Smooth Myths and Rough Histories: *Expulsion from the Garden of Eden* (1828) and *The Oxbow* (1836)

In 1828, Cole painted two pictures with an Edenic theme. One, titled 'The Garden of Eden', was an idyllic pre-lapsarian vision of American landscape (Figure 10). The other was a picture of the Fall, which he titled: *Expulsion from the Garden of Eden* (Figure 11). Like 'Essay on American Scenery', *Expulsion from the Garden of Eden* carries its story at least partly through surface textures. The canvas is sharply divided. On the right-hand side of the painting lies Eden, a carefully constructed sense of the pristine, painted so smoothly and delicately that no brushstrokes can be seen. In both paintings the softness of Eden reflects the influence of the French seventeenth-century painter, Claude Lorraine, who was famous for his idyllic imaginative landscapes. In the nineteenth century, it became popular for artists to paint from nature using a Claude glass, which was a convex shaped reflective tool made from polished onyx or opaque glass. Viewed through a Claude glass, the scene acquired a gentle and removed appearance. As the artist and author William Gilpin wrote, the use of a Claude glass would 'give the object of nature a soft, mellow, tinge, like the colouring of that master [Claude Lorraine]'.[16] It was a

[15] Walt Whitman, *Leaves of Grass* (1855), https://whitmanarchive.org/published/LG/index.html. Unless otherwise stated, all references are to the 1855 poem. All versions of *Leaves of Grass* can be found on the Walt Whitman archive, via the above link.

[16] William Gilpin, *Observations on the Highlands of Scotland* (Richmond: Richmond Publishing, 1973), 124.

Figure 10 Thomas Cole, *The Garden of Eden*, 1828. Amon Carter Museum of American Art. Fort Worth, Texas.

Figure 11 Thomas Cole, *Expulsion from the Garden of Eden*, 1828. Gift of Martha C. Karolik for the M. and M. Karolik Collection of American Paintings, 1815–65. Museum of Fine Art, Boston.

deliberately distancing technique, removing the scene from the immediacy of experience.

By contrast, the fallen world is a tribute to Salvator Rosa, a seventeenth-century Italian baroque painter, who, by the early nineteenth century, had a reputation as the ultimate fallen man. In 1824, a rather lurid and fanciful biography by the Irish novelist Lady Sydney Morgan cemented Rosa's image as a Byronic hero. In her preface, Lady Morgan admitted a romantic fascination with 'the character of the man': 'I estimated still more highly the qualities of the Italian patriot, who, stepping boldly in advance of a degraded age, stood in the foreground of his times, like one of his own spirited and graceful figures.'[17] William Hazlitt wrote scathingly about Lady Morgan's preference for 'fabulous and apocryphal…*conjecture*' over 'details…[and] *data*.'[18] But he, too, emphasized a rough sensibility and opposed it with the Claudian ideal:

> There is not, in Salvator's scenes, the luxuriant beauty and divine harmony of Claude…but there is a deeper seclusion, a more abrupt and total escape from society, more savage wildness and grotesqueness of form, a more earthy texture, a fresher atmosphere, and a more obstinate resistance to all the effeminate refinements of art…the very violence and untractableness of his temper threw him with instinctive force upon those objects in nature which would be most likely to soothe and disarm it.[19]

In 1860, John Ruskin described him as a 'fallen soul', claiming: 'The misery of the earth is a marvel to him; he cannot leave off gazing at it. The religion of the earth is a horror to him. He gnashes his teeth at it, rages at it, mocks and gibes at it.'[20]

Salvator and Claude were major influences on Cole and helped shape his reputation. As Allan Wallach explains:

> When Cole left for England in 1829, the American art public tended to think of him as the American Salvator Rosa on account of his penchant for the sublime. (In the 1830s he produced a small painting entitled Salvator sketching banditti, a playful homage to a preferred artist and perhaps a fantasy self-portrait). By the time he returned to the United States in 1832,

[17] Lady Morgan, *The Life and Times of Salvator Rosa,* 2 vols (London: Printed for Henry Coburn, 1824), vol. 1, pp. iii–iv.

[18] William Hazlitt, 'Lady Morgan's Life of Salvator', *Edinburgh Review* (July 1824), 316–349, 317.

[19] Hazlitt, 'Lady Morgan's Life of Salvator', 323.

[20] John Ruskin, *Modern Painters*, vol. 5 (London: Smith, Eder & Co., 1873), 241–2.

> Claude, so central to the English landscape tradition, had become his favourite, and during the 1830s as a new tranquility began to manifest itself in his art, he acquired a reputation as the 'American Claude',—or, as one writer put it 'our American Claude'.[21]

These contrasting influences helped Cole develop a style of landscape painting which registered moral meaning. Tim Barringer writes: 'The Eden paintings offer a contrast between a world of nature without sin and a world defined by it; aesthetically, they juxtapose the beautiful (*Eden*) with the sublime (*Expulsion*), relying respectively on Claude and Rosa.'[22] Barringer draws attention to the contrast between the two different paintings that Cole produced in 1828, but the soft textures in *The Garden of Eden* (Figure 10) are also reproduced in the idyllic right-hand side of the *Expulsion.* Claude and Salvator gave Cole the visual vocabulary he needed to represent the Fall as a dramatic rupture in the texture of experience.

Unlike, Cole's 'Essay on American Scenery', which seems confused about the direction of travel, the narrative movement of the *Expulsion* is unequivocally from right to left, Claude to Salvator, pristine and intangible Eden to the rough textures of the fallen world. Bent and broken, Adam and Eve are propelled out of the garden by strong shafts of light. Their swamped frames are emblematic of limited agency. Clearly, there is no way back. Cole has painted a lost world: the bisected canvas marks a temporal as well as physical displacement. Knowing the sensational effects of binary composition, he wrote to his patron: 'I have introduced the more terrible effects of nature and have endeavoured to heighten the effect by giving a glimpse of the Garden of Eden in its tranquillity.'[23] Compare this 'glimpse', and its sense of the fleeting

[21] Allan Wallach, 'Thomas Cole and Transatlantic Romanticism', in *Transatlantic Romanticism: British and American Art and Literature 1790–1860, ed.* Andrew Hemingway and Allan Wallach (Amherst, Mass.: University of Massachusetts Press, 2015), 206–26, 215. See also Richard Wallace, *Salvator Rosa in America* (Wellsey, Mass.: Jewish Arts Centre, 1979) and, for a discussion of 'Our American Claude', Ellwood C. Parry, *The Art of Thomas Cole: Ambition and Imagination* (Newark and London: Associated University Presses, 1988), 188–225. Robert Gilmore emphasizes Cole's affinity with Rosa in his correspondence with the artist. See 'Correspondence between Thomas Cole and Robert Gilmore Jr', in *Studies on Thomas Cole: An American Romanticist,* ed. Howard S. Merritt, special issue, *Baltimore Museum of Art Annual* 2 (1967): 41–81. For a general introduction to European influences on Cole's landscape painting, including Salvator and Claude, see Tim Barringer and Jennifer Raab, '"An Inheritance in Print": Thomas Cole and the Aesthetics of Landscape', in *Picturesque and Sublime: Thomas Cole's Transatlantic Inheritance,* ed. Tim Barringer, Gillian Forrester, Sophie Lynford, Jennifer Raab, and Nicholas Robbins (Catskill, NY: Thomas Cole National Historic Site, 2018), 1–49.

[22] Tim Barringer, 'Thomas Cole's Atlantic Crossings', in *Thomas Cole's Journey: Atlantic Crossings,* ed. Elizabeth Mankin Kornhauser and Tim Barringer (New York: Metropolitan Museum of Art, 2018), 20–61, 30.

[23] Thomas Cole to Robert Gilmore, 1828. Thomas Cole Papers 1821–63. Box 3, Folder 8. New York State Library.

intangibility of idealized perfection, with the 'grasp' that Cole hopes poetry and painting might have in his 'Essay on American Scenery'. The Claudian idyll, with its softened textures, and sense of removal, gives Cole a vocabulary for a state he knows is irrecoverable and intangible, a mythical moment of beginning. This is emphatically *not* an Eden we can grasp.

The focus is on the fallen world. Although the narrative movement is unequivocally from right to left, Adam and Eve enter the world with a slightly confused compass. Cole's homage to Salvator results in a more historically situated, and complicated, landscape than the secluded and ravaged wilderness that Hazlitt saw in his paintings. Partly, the two exiles are going back to the industrialized landscape of Bolton, Lancashire, where Cole was born. As a child, he witnessed the violent anti-industrial campaigns of the Luddites who burned mills and broke machines to defend the skilled workforce that was being usurped by factories. He grew up in an environment of religious dissent and heard sermons by millenarian preachers who often saw the end of the world prefigured in the fires of the Luddite rebellion.[24] The volcano Cole paints in the upper left mixes allusions to these anti-industrial protests with Miltonic iconography of Hell. Cole had been inspired by Milton when he painted *The Garden of Eden* and he was clearly thinking about Milton when he composed this picture because he drew so precisely from John Martin's illustrations of *Paradise Lost* that he could be accused of plagiarism (Figure 12).[25] If Adam and Eve are going east to the Old World and back in historical time, they are also going west across America and forward into futurity.

[24] Barringer, 'Thomas Cole's Atlantic Crossings', 21–3.

[25] J. Bard McNulty shows how Cole's language in his letters to his patron echoes the description of Eden in book IV, ll. 216–63 of *Paradise Lost. The Correspondence of Thomas Cole and Daniel Wadsworth: Letters in the Watkinson Library*, ed. J. Bard McNulty (Albany, NY: Connecticut Historical Society, 1983), 20. See also Franklin Kelly and Claire M. Barry, *Thomas Cole's Paintings of Eden* (Fort Worth, Tex.: Amon Carter Museum, 1994), 22–3. Allan Wallach notes that when Cole arrived in London, he was already an admirer of John Martin and that Martin's mezzotints of scenes from *Paradise Lost* inspired both *Expulsion from the Garden of Eden* and *The Garden of Eden*, painted in the same year. The charge of plagiarism, which Cole vehemently denied, was made by a newspaper reviewer, writing under the pseudonym 'Middle Tint the Second'. Wallach, 'Thomas Cole and Transatlantic Romanticism', 215–16. Tim Barringer also explains: 'For this first foray into historical landscape, Cole relied heavily on British visual precedents, particularly Martin's illustrations to Milton's *Paradise Lost* (1824–27), published as mezzotints, readily available in New York. Cole's *Expulsion* took as its starting point Martin's *Adam and Eve Driven Out of Paradise*. When the paintings were exhibited at the National Academy of Design in 1828, a hostile critic accused Cole of plagiarism, claiming that "the whole of the expulsion is a literal copy of the celebrated MARTIN'S picture". Though Cole hotly denied these charges, the similarity is undeniable.' Barringer, 'Thomas Cole's Atlantic Crossings', 31–2. Barringer notes that the newspaper reviewer was called John Browere (260 n. 46). See also Christopher Kent Wilson, 'Rediscovered Thomas Cole Letter: New Light on the Expulsion from the Garden of Eden', *American Art Journal* 18.1 (Winter 1986): 73–4, and Parry, *Art of Thomas Cole*, 73.

Figure 12 John Martin, *Adam and Eve Driven out of Paradise*, 1824–7. Gift of Samuel Glazer. Museum of Fine Art, Boston.

The *Expulsion* was painted in 1828, the year that Andrew Jackson became President of the United States. Jackson pursued and encouraged a policy of westward expansion across America, which Cole hated.[26] The myth of America as a New Eden, which allowed Puritan settlers to imagine that they were proceeding hand-in-hand with their God, also allowed Jacksonian democrats to believe they were fulfilling a divine right to the land.[27] The myth asserts itself in the pristine garden, a place of eternal beginning, an untouched

[26] See Angela Miller, 'Thomas Cole and Jacksonian America: The Course of Empire as Political Allegory', *Prospects* 14 (Oct. 1989): 65–92. Miller notes (p. 67) that 'Cole's conservative critique of American culture intensified during the latter part of his career, bearing out his opposition to Jacksonian democracy in the 1930s.' Barringer and Forrester note that, by the 1830s, Cole was painting 'allegorical landscapes that offered incisive critiques of Jacksonian America', *Picturesque and Sublime*, 135. Barringer also observes that Jackson's 'sweeping platform of commercial growth and imperial expansion' played strongly into Cole's fear of the 'inexorable forces of change', and that, after 1832, 'he began to equate the destruction of the wilderness with Jackson's expansionist policies', 'Thomas Cole's Atlantic Crossings' 29, 78. See also Christine Stansell and Sean Wilentz, 'Cole's America: An Introduction', in *Thomas Cole: Landscape into History*, ed. William H. Truettner and Alan Wallach (New Haven: Yale University Press, 1994), 3–21.

[27] John W. Ward explains: 'It was under the auspices of nature and providence that the cult of the self-made man prospered in America. By making God's favor depend upon each man's exertion, the people of the Age of Jackson easily reconciled personal striving with cosmic determinism, as determinists have done from Puritanism', 'Andrew Jackson: Symbol for an Age', *Jacksonian Democracy: Myth or Reality*, ed. James L. Bugg Jr (New York: Holt, Rinehard & Winston, 1962), 107–11, 108.

and untouchable wilderness. The reality is better represented in the scarred earth of the fallen world. It feels deliberate that Cole lets us see the marks on his surface as he asks us to read our marked world, mixing literary allusions to *Paradise Lost* with historical narratives of seventeenth-century colonialism and nineteenth-century westward expansion, as well as contemporary transatlantic fears about growing industrialization and the mechanization of labour. Advancing across America, westward expansion invoked divine Providence as part of a policy which Cole thought was deeply fallen. In *Expulsion from the Garden of Eden*, Cole holds the myth of America as a New Eden up to the light: Jacksonian democrats are fallen.

In addition to the publication of 'Essay on American Scenery', 1836 saw the completion of Cole's masterpiece, *View from Mount Holyoake, Northampton, Massachusetts after a Thunderstorm—The Oxbow* (Figure 13), which can be seen as a late companion piece for the *Expulsion*. Both paintings are composed around a dividing line. In the *Expulsion*, the division is stark and the movement is unequivocally from right to left, innocence to sin, invoking Milton's providential narrative while simultaneously critiquing its co-option to Jacksonian expansionism. In *The Oxbow*, both the division and direction are far more ambiguous. Visually, the story seems to reverse the narrative of

Figure 13 Thomas Cole, *View from Mount Holyoke, Northampton, Massachusetts, after a Thunderstorm—The Oxbow*, 1836. Gift of Mrs Russell Sage, 1908. Metropolitan Museum of Art, New York.

the *Expulsion*. We begin in the rough textures of the foreground and look towards smoother surfaces. No part of this painting resembles the untouched and temporally displaced landscape of the *Expulsion* in which, as Sarah Burns observes: 'it is as if the bridge back into Eden had collapsed after Adam and Eve made their way into the fallen world'.[28]

The foreground depicts a precipitous place inscribed with theological history and the valences of moral choice. The wilderness in which the painter sits is one that Cole had been painting since the mid-1820s. *Lake with Dead Trees* (1825) was his first serious attempt at a full-scale painting of the American wilderness (Figure 14). In 1835, Cole remembered his early fascination with dead trees and described their reflection in the lake as being 'like immense glittering serpents playing in the deep'.[29] The withered trees tell a different story to the lopped trunks that Cole would paint into his satire of

Figure 14 Thomas Cole, *Lake with Dead Trees (Catskill)*, 1825. Bequest of Charles F. and Abigail L. Olney. Allen Memorial Art Museum.

[28] Sarah Burns, *Painting the Dark Side: Art and the Gothic Imagination in Nineteenth-Century America* (Berkeley, Calif.: University of California Press, 2004), 15.

[29] Thomas Cole, 'Thoughts and Occurrences', 5 July 1835, cited in Burns, *Painting the Dark Side*, 2.

'progress' in the second of his major series titled *The Course of Empire*. In the latter painting, cut trees quite clearly bear testimony to humanity's violent encounter with the land: the narrative of imperial 'progress' is ironic. The blasted, as opposed to cut, tree, marks an encounter between God and man not man and nature. That encounter is felt, and marked, in the body of the earth.

Produced in the same year as his *Essay on American Scenery*, *The Oxbow* provides a way of reinterpreting Cole's claim that 'we are still in Eden'. Positioning himself in the roughened foreground of spiritual encounter, Cole implies that we are not in an untouched, and untouchable, landscape or the mythically enclosed moment of eternal beginning, but a state belonging to the temporal world: a beginning which gains meaning from the conditions which precede and follow it, a beginning from within, rather than before time. The bottom left foreground of *The Oxbow* is variously marked. The brushstrokes are visible, the paint thick, and the landscape again recalls the influence of Salvator Rosa. The artist is seated at the easel, engaged in plein air oil sketching. There is a parasol, planted like a flag in the ground; perhaps a reference to Jacksonian expansionism, perhaps to American colonial history more generally. Unlike the *Expulsion*, which moves uncompromisingly from left to right, it is not quite clear which direction this painting moves. The dividing line reflects this narrative difference. In the *Expulsion*, sharp peaks of light bisect the landscape. In *The Oxbow*, the curvature provides a softer delineation of difference; and the river looks remarkably like a question mark. Within this narrative structure, the repercussions of mark-making in the painting's meta-narrative are more ambiguous. America is not an untouched land, but neither is its destiny decided.

It is difficult to know both where we begin and which way we are going. Perhaps in the thinly painted agrarian scene on the left-hand side of the canvas, there is a vision of redemption. In his 'Essay on American Scenery', Cole favourably described culture as the metonymic extension of cultivation. So, there may be a symbolic goodness in the ordered and measured control of the land. But there is also a warning. The marks of deforestation resemble the Hebrew letters that would spell out Noah. The twenty-first-century artist, Ed Ruscha, whose series *The Course of Empire* pays homage to Cole's series of the same name, has claimed that artists never make their letters into clearly readable words (Ruscha uses Korean letters in one of his paintings).[30]

[30] Ed Ruscha in conversation with curator Chris Riopelle in a talk given around the exhibition of his series, *The Course of Empire*, alongside an exhibition of *Thomas Cole: Eden to Empire* at the National Gallery, London, 2017.

Even the suggestion that these letters spell 'Noah' may encode a warning of the Flood. Such manifest warnings recall the millenarianism of Cole's youth. The storm on the left-hand side of the painting has passed, but the flood may be coming.

So perhaps the movement is from right to left. The wilderness is vanishing as agrarianism inevitably spreads across the west. If we read the painting in this way then the artist takes the place of the 'Vanishing Indian'. Cole's pictures were produced at a time when the newly declared United States of America was seeking to remove indigenous people from land, memory, and history. The Indian Removal Act of 1830 confirmed these noxious activities as legal objectives of the new nation. The trope of the 'vanishing Indian' became part of the armoury of westward expansion. Asher Brown Durand's 1853 painting titled *Progress (The Advance of Civilisation)* depicted a vision of manifest destiny and painted indigenous people into the bottom left-hand corner in a romanticized depiction of their passing away from the American landscape. Cole, placing himself in that position, suggests both the inability of the artist to work against the forces of change and, perhaps, the hope of artistic agency to change the expected narrative.

What it means to 'view' is arguably one of the painting's primary concerns. If the artist is in the middle of the foreground, the viewer is positioned somewhere above it. The painting developed from a topographical sketch but Cole, always more interested in composition than topography, made some important adjustments to the landscape. Cole may have started thinking about the painting as early as 1829 (one year after he painted the *Expulsion*) when he traced Basil Hall's topographical sketch of the view from Mount Holyoake in *Forty Etchings Made with the Camera Lucida in North America in 1827 and 1828* (1829). In an 1833 sketch, he widened the angle of vision while raising the viewer's perspective. The finished painting further elevated the viewpoint and tilted the valley upward towards the picture plane. When the painting was first hung, there was a direct instruction to place it as low as possible so that the viewer might be afforded a vantage point. Cole sold the painting to Charles Nicoli Talbot who asked how it should be exhibited. Cole responded: 'the only advice I can offer is that it should have a side light & that it should be hung as low as can be conveniently'.[31]

[31] David Bjelajac, 'Thomas Cole's *Oxbow* and the American Zion Divided', *American Art* 20.1 (Spring 2001): 60–83, 63.

Allan Wallach reads Cole's composition in relation to Jeremy Bentham's panopticon, offering its viewers a feeling of power and omniscience in its panoramic breadth and telescopic focus on distant details which he terms the 'panoptic sublime'.[32] David Bjelajac suggests that: 'the artist intended spectators to view his *Oxbow* and other landscapes through what he referred to as "the mind's eye." "The mind's eye" sees through both time and space, reading nature's forms as prophetic types of providential signs of a future state of being.'[33] But there is a stark contrast between the ordered narrative implicit in this reading and the more equivocal and ambivalent narrative of the curved and questioning river and the uncertain position of the painter. The mastery of the 'panoptic sublime' collapses if we put ourselves in the picture. Making marks from within a marked landscape, the artist of *The Oxbow* illuminates a vital difference between the unmarked Eden of the *Expulsion*, which like the 'panoptic sublime' is viewed from afar, and the Eden that may be in danger of passing away here. If the former denotes a pernicious myth, the latter suggests a place of spiritual encounter in the fallen world. Salvator, not Claude, tells us where we are in Cole's paintings. Like Adam and Eve in the *Expulsion*, the artist is a tiny figure, swamped by the forces operating outside his being. The forces that press on both sides of the questioning river all but obscure the figure of the artist. The lingering uncertainty revolves around the desired good of culture. How significant are the marks the artist makes?

When Cole declares 'we are still in Eden' in 'Essay on American Scenery', his assertive panoptic moralism attempts to suppress the scepticism that rises more forcefully in *The Oxbow*. Cole may not be deliberately punning on 'stillness' but the pun resounds in our ears. The prophetic moment, which holds all time in its grasp, occasions a certain kind of disembodied stillness. But 'still' also suggests something ongoing, temporal, contingent, emerging from, and committed to, history. In the *Expulsion*, Eden lies decidedly out of reach. In *The Oxbow*, Eden has to be made somewhere within the marked textures of the earth if it is to be made at all. Cole is not at all sure that ends are decided by beginnings and not at all sure that redemption lies in artistic touch.

[32] Allan Wallach, 'Making a Picture of the View from Mount Holyoake', in *American Iconology: New Approaches to Nineteenth-Century Art and Literature*, ed. David C. Miller (New Haven: Yale University Press, 1993), 80–92.

[33] Bjelajac, 'Thomas Cole's *Oxbow*', 61.

Fluid Force and Sliding Surface: 'Nature' (1836) and 'Experience' (1844)

Like Cole, Emerson maintains that 'to see' is first and foremost 'to feel'. In 'Nature', published in the same year as 'Essay on American Scenery', Emerson invests, excitedly and assertively, in the transformative and redemptive potential of such vision, which is rooted in the plasticity and possibility of touch before the moment of formation and fixity: 'Standing on the bare ground, my head bathed by the blithe air, and uplifted into infinite space,—all mean egotism vanishes. I become a transparent eye-ball. I am nothing; I see all; the currents of the Universal Being circulate through me; I am part or parcel of God.'[34] Inspiration comes from a feeling of contact with the earth, which then dissolves into porousness. Air transmutes into spirit. Divinity is characterized by blitheness; weightlessness; transparency; elevation; electric currents and Feuerbachian flow.[35] And at the centre of it all is a disembodied 'eye-ball', a synecdoche for the Transcendentalist visionary, which turns entirely, and not without a little corporeal grotesquerie, on the eye as an organ of touch.

This moment in Emerson is joyful and seems, perhaps, a little silly. Lawrence Buell ascribes to it a 'deliberately comic bubbliness' and an 'over the top ecstasy', pointing to its history of caricature—a cartoon from the notebook of Transcendentalist poet-artist, Christopher Cranch, depicts him as a single, bulging, eye-ball, a match-stick body with top-hat and tails atop long, spindly, stilt-like, legs. Sockless and shoeless, his bare feet protrude absurdly from his trousers, standing, indeed, on the bare ground.[36] The joke is on the citified scholar, who exhorts his readers to manual labour and emphasizes the body as a means of communion with nature and mental transcendence, extolling the loss of ego, while really dictating the superior values of intellectual liberation as defined by his own supercilious, skinny, over-cultivated, urban, self. But Emerson, like Cole, was serious in his desire for renewed contact between nature and culture, and he idealized this contact as a feeling of fluid force before the moment of formative fixity.

Emerson's questions are cultural but they are also theological. He was ordained as a minister in 1829 and resigned the post in 1832, writing in his journal: 'I have sometimes thought that, in order to be a good minister, it was necessary to leave the ministry. The profession is antiquated. In an altered

[34] Emerson, 'Nature' (1836), *Selected Essays*, 35–82, 39.

[35] For an explanation of Feuerbach's notion of divinity as fluidity see my discussion in Chapter 4, 122.

[36] Lawrence Buell, *Emerson* (Cambridge, Mass.: Harvard University Press, 2003), 94.

age, we worship in the dead forms of our forefathers.'[37] 'Why should not we also enjoy an original relation to the Universe?' he asks, with similar impatience, in 'Nature'.[38] The theological answer to Emerson's question is the 'original sin' that banishes Adam and Eve from the garden, the Fall that introduces distance and discord into their relations with each other and their relations with the earth. Original relation belongs to Eden, as Emerson, with his theological training, understood perfectly well. Emerson's question, however, is not about divine prohibition but human agency. He is less interested in the proscribed barrier, the punishment of exile, than the ways in which it might be poetically and imaginatively overcome. Emerson's desire for 'an original relation to the Universe' is another resurgence of the colonial myth: America as a New Eden, a reborn world.

In 'Nature', Emerson's mood is optimistic and he is full of energetic insistence and rallying exhortation. He can make the renewal of Eden sound absurdly easy: 'the problem of restoring to the world original and eternal beauty is solved by the redemption of the soul'.[39] Emerson's faith that conversion can happen instantaneously and miraculously is partly a result of his New England training in religious and political eloquence. Truths appear as divinely revealed and self-evident, rather than hidden and obscure. Emerson wants to rouse and startle us to assent, a preacher turned teacher. 'The whole secret of a teacher's force', he wrote in 1834, 'lies in the conviction that men are convertible'; 'and they are', he added, with cheerful confidence.[40] Conversion happens in the instant of revelation, not by a slow process of argument. Emerson's Platonism is also in evidence:

> A man conversing in earnest, if he watch his intellectual processes, will find that a material image more or less luminous arises in his mind, contemporaneous with every thought, which furnishes the vestment of the thought. Hence good writing and brilliant discourse are perpetual allegories... It is the working of the Original Cause through the instruments he has made.[41]

This is one version of Emerson's desired 'original relation'. The world is full of connections and correspondences between immutable truths and the language

[37] Cited in Wilson Sullivan, *New England Men of Letters* (New York: Macmillan, 1972), 6.

[38] Emerson, 'Nature', *Selected Essays*, 35.

[39] Emerson, 'Nature', *Selected Essays*, 79.

[40] Cited in Robert Richardson, *Emerson: The Mind on Fire* (Berkeley, Calif.: University of California Press, 1995), 169.

[41] Emerson, 'Nature', *Selected Essays*, 52.

of material forms. 'It appears to men, or it does not appear', Emerson says.[42] But it is always there. Learning from Rousseau and Wordsworth, he celebrates youthfulness as a quality of uncluttered perception, finding in it a vocabulary for pre-lapsarian beginning. God is not only seen, but felt, and fully integrated in the texture of Eden: what Emerson described, after reading an essay by Frederic Hedge on Coleridge and the new German thought, as a 'living, leaping, logos'.[43] The Edenic fantasy that Emerson constructs in 'Nature' is a world in which divinity not only embraces humanity, it is the primary and most natural state of man: 'Infancy is the perpetual Messiah, which comes into the arms of fallen men, and pleads with them to return to Paradise.'[44]

In the preface to the *Second Discourse*, Rousseau had used Plato's image of the ruined statue of Glaucus to describe the fall into culture.[45] Emerson writes similarly: 'A man is a God in ruins'.[46] Also like Rousseau, Emerson sees fallenness as a state of self-alienation: 'The reason why the world lacks unity, and remains broken and in heaps, is because man is disunited with himself.'[47] In the autumn of 1829, Emerson had encountered Coleridge's *Aids to Reflection* in an American edition, published with a long introduction by James Marsh. Through Coleridge, and guided by Marsh, Emerson was exposed to Kantian ideas of Reason and the Understanding. If Understanding was rooted in fallen sensory impressions, Reason was the power of self-determination that would get us closer to truth. Marsh praised the dynamism of Coleridge's language for enacting the very force it described: 'a living power, consubstantial with the power of thought that gave birth to it, and answering and calling into action a corresponding power in our minds'.[48] This, as Emerson's biographer, Richardson argues, had an 'electric effect' on the young minister, especially as he also reread J. G. Herder's *Outlines of a Philosophy of the History of Man* around the same time.[49] Herder described man as: 'a power in the universal system of powers, a being in the inconceivable harmony of some world of God'.[50]

The renewal of Eden will come, Emerson maintains in 'Nature', through the recovery of God in man. The self-determining power that he encountered as Kantian reason in Coleridge became the fluid force of spirit he celebrated as a world-making power in 'Nature': 'That which intellectually considered

[42] Emerson, 'Nature', *Selected Essays*, 53.
[43] Emerson in a letter to his brother, Edward, in 1833. Richardson, *Emerson: Mind on Fire*, 166.
[44] Emerson, 'Nature', *Selected Essays*, 77.
[45] Rousseau, *Discourse on the Origin of Inequality*, 14.
[46] Emerson, 'Nature', *Selected Essays*, 77.
[47] Emerson, 'Nature', *Selected Essays*, 79.
[48] Richardson, *Emerson: Mind on Fire*, 93.
[49] Richardson, *Emerson: Mind on Fire*, 93.
[50] Richardson, *Emerson: Mind on Fire*, 94.

we call Reason, considered in relation to Nature we call Spirit. Spirit is the Creator.'[51] Yet, he wrote: 'At present, man applies to nature but half his force. He works on the world with his understanding alone…Meantime, in the thick darkness, there are not wanting gleams of a better light,—occasional examples of the actions of man upon nature with his entire force—with reason as well as understanding.'[52] Emerson's vocabulary is both religious and textural. Thought is prayer: the reaching towards epistemic limit, which is felt as a stirring of depths before and below the moment of formation. What Emerson understands as original relation—here between devotion and thought—is meltingly fluid and opposed with the fixed and frozen superficiality of the relations that make sense to the Understanding:

> In the uttermost meaning of the words, thought is devout and devotion is thought. Deep calls unto deep. But in actual life, the marriage is not celebrated. There are innocent men who worship God after the tradition of their fathers, but their sense of duty has not yet extended to the use of all their faculties. And there are patient naturalists, but they freeze their subject under the wintry light of the understanding. Is not prayer also a study of truth,—a sally of the soul into the unfound infinite? No man ever prayed heartily without learning something. But, when a faithful thinker, resolute to detach every object from personal relations and see it in the light of thought shall, at the same time, kindle science with the fire of the holiest affections, then will God go forth anew into the creation.[53]

'Deep calls unto deep' recalls the creation of form in Genesis 1: 2: 'And the earth was without form, and void; and darkness *was* upon the face of the deep. And the Spirit of God moved upon the face of the waters.' The marriage of thought and devotion, the intellectual disposition to faith, taps into the fluid potential of this original moment before the first act of formation. Emerson suggests that, in the fallen world, it is this intellectual disposition to faith that keeps the plasticity and possibility of creativity alive. He also suggests that fallenness can be a sort of timid innocence, a state of dutiful conformity to received wisdom—or error. Like Blake, he has a Romantic resistance to fixed forms, suggesting that the fluid force of original creativity is frozen by the wintry light of the understanding but discovered by the soul that makes itself vulnerable through an affectionate and adventurous faith in

[51] Emerson, 'Nature', *Selected Essays*, 49.
[52] Emerson, 'Nature', *Selected Essays*, 78.
[53] Emerson, 'Nature', *Selected Essays*, 79–80.

the unknown. God must be felt first in the 'unfound infinite', and then in the divinely integrated texture of experience.

Emerson had been reading Thomas Carlyle's anonymously published essays for years before he visited England in 1833 and travelled to Scotland to meet him. Carlyle's 1827 essay, 'The State of German Literature', is rightly seen as a primary source of inspiration for the young American preacher, who, licensed though not yet ordained, was already searching for a form of religious practice that felt free from received error a decade before he wrote 'Nature'.[54] Anti-utilitarian Carlyle emphasized the dynamism of 'spiritual commerce', enabled by new modes of material exchange: 'a true thought, or a noble creation, passes lightly to us from the remotest countries, provided only our minds are open to receive it'.[55] He quoted Schiller and Fichte, claiming that literary men were a 'perpetual priesthood', the appointed interpreters of the 'Divine Idea', an underlying unity and unchanging essence in all things.[56] Emerson would echo him closely in his address to Harvard Divinity School in 1838, when he announced an equivalence between the office of 'priest or poet'.[57] Carlyle's priestly poet was a prophet, chosen to speak the truth: 'To seize character, even that of one man, in its life and secret mechanism, requires a philosopher; to delineate it with truth and impressiveness, is work for a poet'.[58] Emerson also declared that the vocation of 'priest or poet' was to articulate divinely revealed truths: 'always the seer is a sayer'.[59]

In 'Nature', Emerson imagines this figure as an 'Orphic Poet', a prophet-artist who, like the God of Genesis 2, finds matter open and responsive to the shaping force of spirit: 'Then shall come to pass what my poet said: "Nature is not fixed but fluid. Spirit alters, moulds, makes it."'[60] Emerson's visionary poet becomes a path-builder, just like Cole's ideal poets and painters in his 'Essay on American Scenery'. With triumphant ease, he extends world-making possibility to the shaping force of spirit in every individual:

> The immobility or bruteness of nature is the absence of spirit; to pure spirit it is fluid, it is volatile, it is obedient. Every spirit builds itself a house and beyond its world a heaven. Know then that the world exists for you. For you is the phenomenon perfect. What we are, that only we can see. All that

[54] Richardson, *Emerson: Mind on Fire*, 146.
[55] Thomas Carlyle, 'The State of German Literature', *Edinburgh Review* (Oct. 1827304–51, 307).
[56] Carlyle, 'German Literature', 329.
[57] Emerson, Divinity School Address, *Selected Essays*, 117.
[58] Carlyle, 'German Literature', 309.
[59] Emerson, Divinity School Address, *Selected Essays*, 116.
[60] Emerson, 'Nature', *Selected Essays*, 80.

> Adam had, all that Caesar could, you have and can do. Adam called his house, heaven and earth. Caesar called his house, Rome; you, perhaps, call yours a cobbler's trade; a hundred acres of ploughed land; or a scholar's garret. Yet line for line, and point for point, your dominion is as great as theirs, though without fine names. Build therefore your own world.[61]

Emerson's 'Orphic Poet' is proudly anthropocentric and unapologetically colonial. 'Line for line, and point for point', he exhorts us to build this new Eden as an illimitable extension of ourselves.

Do we take Emerson at his Orphic Poet's word? For Emerson's Puritan ancestors, God's Word was degraded in poetic language. Edward Taylor traced poetic language back to sound exiting from the body:

> Unclean, Unclean: My Lord, Undone, all vile
> Yea all Defild: What shall thy Servant doe?
> Unfit for thee: not fit for holy Soile,
> Nor for Communion of Saints below.
> A bag of botches, Lump of Loathsomeness:
> Defild by Touch, by Issue: Leproust flesh.[62]

The squelchy sounds and rotting flesh convey the full force of the degradation of the Logos in the corporeality of fallen man. The burden of shame is felt in the way language is inextricably and pleasurably bound to body. For Taylor, as for other Puritan writers, shame becomes the pivotal point of both salvation and the enjoyment of poetry. Taylor anticipates the problem of Emerson's 'original relation to the Universe' because he describes a being sullied by articulation. For a writer of Emerson's religious inheritance, to achieve an original relation to the Universe meant overcoming the resistance of post-lapsarian language to God.[63]

When Emerson's Orphic Poet exhorts us to build a new world 'line for line, and point for point', he is constructing a linguistic logic of dominion, which overwrites the chiaroscuro of the Fall with linear extensions of power and meaning. We can see Emerson's own scepticism rising occasionally in 'Nature', when he acknowledges the way in which sensory impressions might be

[61] Emerson, 'Nature', *Selected Essays*, 80–1.

[62] *Edward Taylor's God's Determinations and Preparatory Meditations: A Critical Edition*, ed. Daniel Patterson (Kent, O.: Kent State University Press, 2003), 'Meditation 26', 253.

[63] See Elisa New, *The Regenerate Lyric: Theology and Innovation in American Poetry* (Cambridge: CUP, 2009), 15–56.

mistaken for spiritual truth, and nature might be a more resistant medium than the poet wants to find it:

> But this beauty of Nature which is seen and felt as beauty is the least part. The shows of day, the dewy mornings, the rainbow, mountains, orchards in blossom, stars, moonlight, shadows still in water, and the like, if too eagerly hunted, become shows merely, and mock us with their unreality. Go out of the house to see the moon and 't is mere tinsel; it will not please as when its light shines upon your necessary journey. The beauty that shimmers in the yellow light of October, who ever could clutch it? Go forth and find it, and it is gone. "t is only a mirage as you look from the windows of diligence.[64]

Like Blake's prophet-artist, Los, frenziedly hurling orbs into Urizen's void, Emerson finds that beauty slips away, retreating before artistic effort and creative enterprise.

In his 1844 essay, 'The Poet', Emerson presented a slightly different model, closer to the God of Genesis 1, or his mouthpiece, Adam: 'the poet is the Namer, or Language-Maker, naming things sometimes after their appearance, and sometimes after their essence, and giving to every one its own name and not another's, thereby rejoicing the intellect, which delights in detachment and boundary'.[65] Fallen poetic language becomes the archive and tomb of forgotten original relation: 'fossil poetry'.[66] 'Genius', Emerson declares, 'repairs the decays of things'.[67] Emerson is still invested in wholeness, unity, and the fluid depths of original relation, claiming: 'It is dislocation and detachment from the life of God that makes things ugly, and the poet, who re-attaches things to Nature and the Whole.'[68] But, there is, perhaps, a greater worry that the 'language-maker' might not be the original sculptor of Genesis 2, or even the ordering deity of Genesis 1, but a Frankenstein, who reanimates dead forms and belongs to a compromised, post-lapsarian world, 're-attaching even artificial things, and violations of nature, to nature, by a deeper insight'.[69]

Carlyle particularly praised German literature for restoring simplicity, both to the character of the poet and to the quality of poetic language.[70] Following Carlyle, Emerson also praised simplicity, bringing post-lapsarian loss to the fore: 'A man's power to connect thought with its proper symbol, and so utter it, depends on the simplicity of his character, that is, upon his love of truth

[64] Emerson, 'Nature', *Selected Essays*, 44–5.
[65] Emerson, 'The Poet', *Selected Essays*, 271.
[66] Emerson, 'The Poet', *Selected Essays*, 271.
[67] Emerson, 'The Poet', *Selected Essays*, 272.
[68] Emerson, 'The Poet', *Selected Essays*, 269.
[69] Emerson, 'The Poet', *Selected Essays*, 269.
[70] Carlyle, 'German Literature', 336.

and his desire to communicate it without loss. The corruption of man is followed by the corruption of language.'[71] Emerson ascribes the Orphic Poet of 'Nature' the simplicity that eludes fallen man. His creativity is plastic possibility, forging connections from the fluid depths of original relation. As Stanley Cavell argues in his writings on moral perfectionism, this kind of pre-lapsarian fantasy, which Cavell refers to, more secularly, as 'the utopian moment', expresses a sense that a transcendental element is indispensable in the motivation for a moral existence. Cavell notes that this has become part of the conversation on moral perfectionism because philosophy has become estranged from theology; it is theological in origin. For Emerson, the moral conversation was still anchored in a theological imagination to which the juxtaposition of a transcendental, atemporal point of fixity and a mutable temporality was axiomatic. Cavell concludes: 'our sense of an unattained self is not an escape from, it is rather an index of, our commitment to the unattained city, one within the one that we sustain, one we know there is no good reason we perpetually fail to attain.'[72]

If Emerson's sense of the original shaping force of spirit is carried by images full of fluid potential, his metaphors for the fallen world turn on frozen surfaces, and the slipping and sliding of meaning. In 'The Poet', the energetic exhortations to world-building and the bubbling enthusiasm of Emerson's transcendent egoless eye-ball have given way to a more tired desire for porousness and guidance in a world where difference and disconnect is everywhere felt and apparent: 'The condition of true naming, on the poet's part, is his resigning himself to the divine aura, which breathes through forms, and accompanying that.'[73] The spirit Emerson longs for is not the Apollonian principle of order and control that belongs to 'language-maker' of Genesis 1, but the fluid Dionysian gifts of abandonment and intoxication: 'For if in any matter we can stimulate this instinct, new passages are opened for us into nature, the mind flows into and through things hardest and highest, and the metamorphosis is possible…the quality of the imagination is to flow, and not to freeze…all language is vehicular and transitive.'[74] As in 'Nature', he is aware of how easily truth might be confused with illusion and quick to warn against 'counterfeit excitement and fury': 'The spirit of the world, the great calm presence of the creator, comes not forth to the sorceries of opium or of wine. The sublime vision comes to the pure and

[71] Emerson, 'Nature', *Selected Essays*, 51.

[72] Stanley Cavell, *Cities of Words: Pedagogical Letters on a Register of the Moral Life* (Boston: Harvard University Press, 2005), 18.

[73] Emerson, 'The Poet', *Selected Essays*, 274.

[74] Emerson, 'The Poet', *Selected Essays*, 274–9.

simple soul in a clean and chaste body.'[75] But the pun on 'spirit' is deliberate. Emerson knows that the counterfeit lies ready-to-hand, while his longed-for truth slips and slides away: 'I look in vain for the poet whom I describe', he admits.[76]

'The Poet' appeared in the same collection as Emerson's essay, 'Experience', which draws attention to this slipperiness of meaning as a quality of fallenness: 'What opium is instilled into all disaster! It shows formidable as we approach it, but there is at last no rough, rasping friction, but the most slippery, sliding surfaces. We fall soft on a thought.'[77] In 'Nature', Emerson imagines the Edenic quest in terms of the 'unfound infinite' of the self: the fluid, fertile, interior, clay with which we might build a new world. In 'Experience', he returns us to that narrative of quest, beginning: 'where do we find ourselves?'[78] If 'Nature' celebrates the generative possibility of depth in the 'unfound infinite', 'Experience' makes clear that we 'find ourselves' in a fallen world of slippery, sliding surfaces. Things feel disconnected and unfamiliar, detached and uncertain: 'Ghostlike we glide through nature, and should not know our place again.'[79] He explains: 'I take this evanescence and lubricity of all objects, which lets them slip through our fingers then when we clutch hardest, to be the most unhandsome part of our condition.'[80] Such lubricity is the very opposite of the elasticity Emerson celebrates as original world-making potential in 'Nature'. 'That immobility and absence of elasticity which we find in the arts, we find with more pain in the artist', he writes with disappointment.[81] The inertness of the world follows directly from the inertness of thought. Thus, he writes: 'There is no power of expansion in men.'[82] The slipperiness of experience was not a new concern for Emerson. 'There is a devil of lubricity in the universe', he had written, in his notebooks of 1837, 'The thought is not married to the act.'[83]

Emerson acknowledges that our desire for a connection that feels real and palpable sometimes leads us to hold onto pain. Writing about the death of his infant son, he confessed:

[75] Emerson, 'The Poet', *Selected Essays*, 275.
[76] Emerson, 'The Poet', *Selected Essays*, 281.
[77] Emerson, 'Experience' (1844), *Selected Essays*, 287.
[78] Emerson, 'Experience' (1844), *Selected Essays*, 285.
[79] Emerson, 'Experience' (1844), *Selected Essays*, 286.
[80] Emerson, 'Experience' (1844), *Selected Essays*, 288.
[81] Emerson, 'Experience' (1844), *Selected Essays*, 293.
[82] Emerson, 'Experience' (1844), *Selected Essays*, 293.
[83] *The Journals and Miscellaneous Notebooks of Ralph Waldo Emerson,* vol. 6. *1824–1838*, ed. Ralph H. Orth (Cambridge, Mass.: Harvard University Press, 1966), 276.

> There are moods in which we court suffering, in the hope that here at least we shall find reality, sharp peaks and edges of truth. But it turns out to be scene-painting and counterfeit. The only thing that grief has taught me, is to know how shallow it is. That, like all the rest, plays about the surface, and never introduces me to the reality, for contact with which we would even pay the costly price of sons and lovers…something which I fancied was a part of me,—which could not be torn away without tearing me, nor enlarged without enriching me, falls off and leaves no scar. It was caducous. I grieve that grief can teach me nothing, nor carry me one step into real nature.[84]

In his 1838 lecture series on human life, he devoted talks to comedy and tragedy. Both were reprised in essays in *The Dial*, in 1844, where he wrote of 'The Tragic':

> Tragedy is in the eye of the observer, and not the heart of the sufferer. It looks like an insupportable load under which the earth moans aloud, but analyse it, it is not I, it is not you, it is always another person who is tormented. If a man says, lo I suffer,—it is apparent that he suffers not, for grief is dumb. It is so distributed so as not to destroy. That which would rend you, falls on tougher textures.[85]

Suffering is not the sharp feeling of catastrophic ruin that we think of as tragedy. It is a cushioned exclusion from divine truth: the everyday slips of meaning and thought, the caducous losses that build falsity and grief into the fallen texture of the world. Emerson is often criticized for callousness in this passage. It is deeply unpalatable to describe feelings on the loss of any child, let alone one's own child, as 'shallow', and downright offensive to suggest trading sons and lovers for some feeling of authentic contact. But it is the distaste of a devotion to theological truth. We can recognize Emerson's source in the near-sacrifice of Isaac by Abraham: 'Take now thine son, thine only son Isaac, whom thou lovest, and get thee into the land of Moriah, and offer him there for a burnt offering.'[86] Abraham's obedience is a sign of his commitment to God. In his retelling of the story, Søren Kierkegaard suggested that Abraham becomes the Father of Faith not just because he will sacrifice his beloved son, but because he will sacrifice the love his son has for him to preserve the child's love of God: 'But below his breath Abraham said to himself:

[84] Emerson, 'Experience' (1844), *Selected Essays*, 287–8.

[85] Emerson, 'The Tragic', *The Dial* 4 (Apr. 1844): 515–21.

[86] Gen. 22: 2.

"Lord in Heaven I thank Thee; it is after all better that he believe I am a monster than he shall lose his faith in thee." '[87] Like Kierkegaard's man of faith who longs only to witness this sacrifice with fear and trembling, Emerson laments the loss of a world in which God is so closely integrated in the texture of experience that suffering might bring us closer to truth.

In 'Experience', Emerson extends his earlier conceit of 'wintry understanding' and 'freez[ing]' forms to more icy exteriors, which emphasize partiality and disconnect. The ductile, mouldable, earth, celebrated by the Orphic Poet of 'Nature', is here a frozen skating-pond. The enthusiasm for original sculpting and the perfectibility of matter by spirit has given way to a sceptical appreciation for tact: 'We live amid surfaces, and the true art of life is to skate well on them. Under the oldest, mouldiest conventions, a man of native force prospers just as well as in the newest world, and that by skill of handling and treatment.'[88] As David Russell observes, tact—the skill of handling—'is an art of redirection and revaluation, working within the terms it seeks to critique in order—by handling a shift in mode, or tone, or approach—to open up new avenues for relation.'[89] For Russell, tact reflects present ambivalence rather than a commitment to future perfection. Emerson, in a poem entitled 'Tact', concluded similarly: 'It has no tomorrow / It ends with today.'[90] Discussing the Victorian essay, Russell suggests that the nineteenth-century emphasis on tact was, partly, a response to population growth, especially in cities:

> At a time when people were living in closer proximity than ever before, and among ever more different people, tactful essays proposed a new mode of feeling one's way in society, which depended less on knowing other people, and placing them in hierarchical categories of status and instead inventing new ways to value others and live with them.[91]

Tact can be seen as a strategy of adaptation in the face of increased epistemic uncertainty and variability: a democratization of the essay form. Experience may demand that we adapt, rather than build, our own world.

But even as Emerson admits the uses and necessity of tact his real admiration is still for a more original sounding 'native force'. He draws his

[87] Søren Kierkegaard, *Fear and Trembling: Dialectical Lyric by Johannes de Silentio*, tr. Alastair Hannay (London: Penguin, 1985), 46.

[88] Emerson, 'Experience' (1844), *Selected Essays*, 294–5.

[89] David Russell, *Tact: Aesthetic Liberalism and the Essay Form in Nineteenth-Century Britain* (Princeton: Princeton University Press, 2018), 2.

[90] Emerson, 'Tact', *Poems* (Boston: James Munroe & Co., 1847), 51.

[91] Russell, *Tact*, 6–7.

vocabulary, here, from the same developments in material science that inspired him when he wrote: 'the currents of the Universal Being circulate through me. I am part and parcel of God.' As early as 1828, he read Humphrey Davy's *Elements of Chemical Philosophy*. He read Davy's *Elements of Agricultural Chemistry* in 1832, and by 1833 he was praising Davy for approaching: 'the elemental law, the *causa causans*, the supernatural force'.[92] In 1831, he read John Herschel's *Preliminary Discourse on the Study of Natural Philosophy*. He found in Herschel an account of almost universal correspondences in the material world: scientific evidence of a unifying force. Davy and Herschel prepared Emerson to receive the full import of Michael Faraday's discoveries for his poetic theories. In his journals of 1833, Emerson wrote of the 'great long expected discovery of the identity of electricity & magnetism lately completed by Dr. Faraday, obtaining the spark from the magnet & opening almost a…door to the secret mechanisms of life & sensation in the relation of the pile of Volta to the electrical fish'.[93] For Emerson, Faraday had revealed the underlying principle of life: its 'native force'. Electricity generated a vocabulary for mental forces and energies that was widely used in nineteenth-century psychology, and that resonated with the principles of dynamism that Emerson had found in Carlyle, Coleridge, and Kant.

Where the Orphic Poet finds the world responsive, the poet of the fallen world, still, for Emerson, a 'man of native force', finds it resistant, but not dead to his touch. In his 1841 essay, 'Circles', Emerson portrays the thinker as a divine disruption, and sliding becomes a metaphor of possibility: 'Beware when the great God lets loose a thinker on this planet. Then all things are at risk…this surface on which we now stand is not fixed, but sliding'.[94] In 'Experience', he uses the image of a 'sliding scale' to reinforce a Platonic view of consciousness: 'If I have described life as a flux of moods, then I must now add, that there is that within us which changes not, and which ranks all sensations and states of mind. The consciousness in each man is a sliding scale, which identifies him now with the First Cause and now with the flesh of the body.'[95] Sliding surfaces suggest a world, and a language, frozen by 'wintry understanding', and exiled from 'original relation', but they also keep us moving.

Emerson's sense of sliding reality also manifests in the slipperiness of his style: a sign of the resistance he encounters in his own world-building tool of

[92] Eric Wilson, *Emerson's Sublime Science* (Basingstoke: Palgrave Macmillan, 1999), 89.

[93] Wilson, *Emerson's Sublime Science*, 91.

[94] Emerson, 'Circles' (1844), *Selected Essays*, 230–3.

[95] Emerson, 'Experience' (1844), *Selected Essays*, 302.

language. It is the catch-22 of any writing on Emerson that the critic can never quote him without finding a contradictory quote. Emerson gives us a get-out: 'a foolish consistency', he maintains, 'is the hobgoblin of little minds'.[96] For all his apparent injunctions, Emerson, as Adam Phillips observes, favours provocation over instruction, and 'there is no provocation without inconsistency'.[97] Postures, poses, voices, and moods are the constitutive features of Emerson's style. The 'try-out' of the essay appeals to him (French, *essayer*, 'to try'). Phillips emphasizes the way in which Emerson idealizes moments of transition, and focuses on the staccato rhythms, jumps, and conflicts of meaning that build growth, adventure, aspiration, and provocation into his verbal texture: 'Could he write a new world out of the language of the old world? Could he write moments of transition in a transitional style, without being too impressed by his conclusions, without having to stop?'[98] At their most optimistic, Emerson's aesthetics encode the ascendant movement of a divine comedy: 'our greatness is always in a tendency or direction', he declares, employing the same poetic architecture that would console Darwin for the loss in extinction, and inspire Eliot with the hope of 'varying in the right direction'.[99] He looks, as I have said, to startle us into assent: a preacher-born teacher. But he is also intensely conscious of downward movements, the slipping away, and sliding of meaning that denote the resistance of his medium and tools. Without original relation, after original sin, all language is fallen, even the language of nature.

So, he writes in 'Experience':

> It is very unhappy, but too late to be helped, the discovery we have made, that we exist. That discovery is called the Fall of Man. Ever afterwards, we suspect our instruments. We have learned that we do not see directly but mediately, that we have no way of correcting these coloured and distorting lenses, which we are, or of computing the amount of their errors. Perhaps these subject-lenses have a creative power: perhaps there are no objects. Once we lived in what we saw; now, the rapaciousness of this new power, which threatens to absorb all things, engages us. Nature, art, persons, letters, religions, objects successively tumble in, and God is but one of its ideas.[100]

[96] Emerson, 'Self-Reliance' (1841), *Selected Essays*, 183.

[97] Adam Phillips, 'Emerson and the Impossibilities of Style', in *Thinking through Style: Non-Fiction Prose of the Long Nineteenth Century*, ed. Michael D. Hurley and Marcus Waithe (Oxford: OUP, 2018), 135–148, 145.

[98] Phillips, 'Emerson and Impossibilities', 143.

[99] Emerson, 'Experience' (1844), *Selected Essays*, 303; Darwin, *Origin*, 79.

[100] Emerson, 'Experience' (1844), *Selected Essays*, 304–5.

In his 1841 essay, 'Self-Reliance', Emerson builds the resistance of fallen language into his provocations. At the centre of the essay is an exhortation to immediate speech, which is also a quotation of Descartes: 'Man is timid and apologetic; he is no longer upright; he dares not say "I think," "I am", but quotes some saint or sage.'[101] In 'Nature', Emerson puts his faith in 'unfound infinite' of the self to overcome the resistance of language and build the world anew. In 'Self-Reliance', he issues a similar provocation: 'Trust Thyself'.[102] The allusion is to the motto of the oracle at Delphi: 'Know Thyself.' Emerson is still in thrall to notions of divine possession and articulation. But, slipping from knowledge to trust, and sliding between self-assertion and direct quotation, he implicitly questions whether we are able to 'know' or 'say' anything with the absolute certainty historically attributed to the divine. Thus, he asks, with greater scepticism and doubt: 'Who is the Trustee? What is the aboriginal Self on which a universal reliance may be grounded?'[103] In 'Experience', he acknowledges: 'the individual texture holds its dominion.'[104]

Self-trust, Stanley Cavell argues, is not hard to do, but hard to let yourself do. It requires taking back into yourself an authority you have been compelled to invest elsewhere.[105] It is made harder for Emerson because, like George Eliot, he realizes that our notion of self is, to some extent, a socially negotiated performance to which we then feel committed: 'The other terror that scares us from self-trust is our consistency; a reverence for our past act or word because the eyes of others have no other data for computing our orbit than past acts, and we are loth to disappoint them.'[106] Here again is Emerson's rejection of consistency, and a tacit acknowledgement that sliding from one position to another might be a more honest approximation of self-trust than faith in fluid force. He concludes, with some sense of despair: 'the man must be so much that he must make all circumstances indifferent.'[107] Like Cole and Dickinson, Emerson came to realize that the shift from Providence to circumstance, the major impact of secularization on the myth of the Fall, inspired human authorship with no greater sense of agency and felt impossible to master. 'One we thought positive power is all', he wrote, in an 1860 essay on

[101] Emerson, 'Self-Reliance' (1841), *Selected Essays*, 189.
[102] Emerson, 'Self-Reliance' (1841), *Selected Essays*, 177.
[103] Emerson, 'Self-Reliance' (1841), *Selected Essays*, 187.
[104] Emerson, 'Experience' (1844), *Selected Essays*, 290.
[105] Cavell, *Emerson's Transcendental Études*, 31.
[106] Emerson, 'Self-Reliance' (1841), *Selected Essays*, 182.
[107] Emerson, 'Self-Reliance' (1841), *Selected Essays*, 185.

'Fate': 'now we learn, that negative power, or circumstance, is half.'[108] 'Reality', he concludes in his journals of 1871–2, 'has a sliding floor.'[109]

Whitman's Uncommon Smoothness: *Leaves of Grass* (1855)

In 'Nature', Emerson had declared: 'there is a property on the horizon which no man has but he whose eye can integrate all parts, that is, the poet.'[110] In 'The Poet', he announced: 'the poet is representative. He stands among partial men for the complete man.'[111] Answering Emerson's call for an integrating 'eye' and a representative 'I', Walt Whitman presented himself as the poet who would ventriloquize the nation, and whose woven song would hold it together in integrated unity. In the years preceding the American Civil War, the recently declared independent United States presented itself as an experiment in democracy; and Whitman declared himself its representative democratic bard. 'I weave the song of Myself', he announced in the final edition of *Leaves of Grass*. Writing as weaving employs a common metaphor for authorial craft, but Whitman moves beyond its familiar use. Coming at the end of a career that had seen *Leaves of Grass* go through six editions, this claim made the formal metalanguage of thirty-seven years of textual revisions and additions explicit. From the very first edition of the *Leaves*, Whitman made the texture of a woven song, a leafy book, and messy, living, endlessly reconstituting organic matter, essential to negotiating the problematic binary of unity and multiplicity: the sinew of his democratic vision.

Antebellum America was always far from the democratic triumph to which it laid claim. Slavery continued, the franchise was limited to free, white, men, and the Indian Removal Act of 1830 enshrined the ongoing barbarism of colonial expansion in law. Yet, the 1855 poem, most of which becomes 'Walt Whitman' and then 'Song of Myself', prides itself on democratic inclusivity. 'I will not have a single person slighted or left away', Whitman declares. He sets out to ventriloquize the voices of the oppressed, excluded, unnoticed and silenced:

> Through me many long dumb voices
> Voices of the interminable generations of slaves,

[108] Emerson, 'Fate' (1860), *Selected Essays*, 369.

[109] *The Journals and Miscellaneous Notebooks of Ralph Waldo Emerson*, ed. Ronald A. Bosco and Glen M. Johnson (Cambridge, Mass.: Belknap Press, 1982), vol. 16. *1866–1882*, 251.

[110] Emerson, 'Nature' (1836), *Selected Essays*, 38.

[111] Emerson, 'The Poet' (1844), *Selected Essays*, 260.

Voices of prostitutes and of deformed persons,
Voices of the diseased and despairing, and of thieves and dwarfs,
Voices of cycles of preparation and accretion,
And of the threads that connect the stars—and of wombs, and of
the fatherstuff,
And of the rights of them the others are down upon,
Of the trivial and flat and foolish and despised,
Of fog in the air and beetles rolling balls of dung.[112]

But there is an irony. In its laudable democratic imperative, Whitman's ventriloquial voice risks once more naturalizing the ideology of dominion, this time in the solar poetic self who strives to 'contain multitudes'.

In the years preceding the publication of the 1855 edition of *Leaves of Grass*, Whitman wrote extensively about the visual arts: thirty-seven articles published between 1849 and 1855 commented on them and five were devoted solely to them.[113] On the evening of 31 March 1851, he gave an invited address to the Brooklyn Art Union. He presented the artist as the restorer of Eden in America. In his praise of contemporary art, he was responding partly to Cole's depictions of untouched beauty but more directly to the smooth brushstrokes and picturesque stillness of his disciples, who would become known as the Hudson River School. Whitman declared: 'When God, according to the myth, finished Heaven and Earth—...God looked forth and saw everything that he had made, and pronounced it good. Good because ever reproductive of its first beauty, finish and freshness...With this freshness—and with that which the Lord called good—the Artist has to do.'[114]

Whitman was a great champion of contemporary art in the 1840s and 1850s. But the irony of Cole's artistic legacy is that the painters who would be bracketed as the Hudson River School, those he had done much to

[112] Whitman, *Leaves of Grass* (Brooklyn, NY, 1855). University of Iowa Libraries, Special Collections & University Archives, FOLIO PS3201 1855, copy 1. Accessed via the Walt Whitman Archive. https://whitmanarchive.org.

[113] David S. Reynolds, *Walt Whitman's America: A Cultural Biography* (New York: Vintage, 1996), 279.

[114] *Walt Whitman's Selected Journalism*, ed. Douglass A. Novar and Jason Stacey (Ames, Ia.: University of Iowa Press, 2015), 153–4. His artistic opinions were very much in vogue. An anonymous contributor to the *National Academy of Design Catalogue* in 1837 declared: 'Painting leads the mind to contemplation of the infinite and varied beauties of creation, and directs the thoughts of Nature up to Nature's God.' A contributor to *The Crayon* wrote: 'the Creed of art is the parallel of that of true religion, the reverence of God in one case becoming reverence of Nature in another, and the same spirit of love being the vitality of both'. A series of articles by William Stillman on 'The Nature and Use of Beauty', published in *The Crayon*, described the constant battle to unite the beauty of art with the spirituality of God in man. Examples cited in Sandra Langer, 'The Aesthetics of Democracy', *Art Journal* 39.2 (Winter 1979–80): 132–5, 132–3.

encourage, and whom Whitman admired, produced avowedly nationalistic works in which the rough historical textures of the *Expulsion* and the narrative ambiguity of *The Oxbow* were nowhere to be seen. The political vision of the Hudson River School aligned strongly with the dogma of 'manifest destiny', which, by the 1850s, was explicitly used to justify westward expansion. In Cole's paintings, the image of America as a pristine land was a temporal displacement, knowingly situated outside the realities of history and the corruptions of empire and exposed, in the *Expulsion*, as a pernicious myth. In the paintings of his followers, it was a colonialist manifesto. In his address to the Brooklyn Art Union, Whitman emphasized the role of the artist as a restorer of Eden, reinforcing the myth of perfect beginning that Cole had begun to critique.

David Reynolds suggests that something of that critique remains in Whitman's address to the Art Union. He ended with lines from his poem 'Resurgemas' in which the corpses of murdered young rebels nurture the seeds of revolution against tyranny. Reynolds observes: 'There was a philosophical and social complacency behind the prevailing style, which seemed to announce that nature, God, and humanity could be neatly summed up and delivered to the viewer in optimistic packages…He wanted picturesqueness, but also explosiveness, rebelliousness, grotesqueness.'[115] This ambiguity, born of a desire to encompass everything, is also characteristic of Whitman's poetry. He gives a lengthy roll call of examples of explosiveness, rebelliousness, and grotesqueness in the 1855 *Leaves of Grass*: 'howls restrained by decorum / Arrests of criminals, slights, adulterous offers made, acceptances, rejections with convex lips'. The packaging of a collection of poems that Whitman extended, revised, and re-edited six times was not 'neat', though, in 1855, it was avowedly optimistic.

Whitman answers Emerson's call for the integrating poetic eye with a texture, and text, which makes Design both an object of satire and desire. The integrated, woven, texture of his song finds a correlation in the papery, leafy texture of the book, and another in the jingoistic 'flag of [his] disposition', which extends metonymically to the 'handkerchief of the Lord', a synecdoche for the argument from Design. Here is a key passage:

> A child said, 'What is the grass?' fetching it to me with full hands;
> How could I answer the child? I do not know what it is any more than he.

[115] Reynolds, *Walt Whitman's America*, 298.

I guess it must be the flag of my disposition, out of hopeful green
 stuff woven.

Or I guess it is the handkerchief of the Lord,
A scented gift and remembrancer designedly dropt,
Bearing the owner's name someway in the corners, that we may see
 and remark, and say *Whose?*

The woven flag and scented handkerchief hold their integrity and sustain their legibility only briefly, but, for the time that they do, they ask to be read as marks of authorship. The handful of grass obviously recalls *Leaves of Grass*, the book, mark, or 'flag' of the well-disposed poetic self, which reflects the well-disposed (poetically ordered or integrated) nation. The handkerchief, artfully dropped to encourage a lover's designs on its owner, plays on the argument from Design, which encouraged Christians to read the Book of Nature as evidence of divine providence. The unrecognized name implies the retreating legibility of this narrative; a 'remembrancer' also suggests a relic of something past. But, in the lingering scent and the finder's curious attraction, Whitman acknowledges a seductive hold. There is more affinity than difference between the texture of handkerchief and flag.

If the flag draws from these various iterations of the Genesis creation myth, its disintegration reflects the counter-narratives of material science. Whitman's ecumenical genius fed as hungrily off contemporary science as it did off religious myth. Whitman read Lucretius, *On the Nature of the Universe*, and he enthusiastically reviewed Justus von Liebig's *Organic Chemistry and its Application to Agriculture and Physiology* when it first appeared in America in 1847 and he was editor of the *Brooklyn Daily Eagle*. For Whitman, Liebig was an 'elevating' and 'beautiful' artist, offering in his practice: 'the essences of creation, and the changes, and the growths, and formations and decays, of so large a constituent part of the earth, and the things therof'.[116] At the same time, Faraday was demonstrating the principles of indestructible energy in physics and Robert Chambers offered a proto-Darwinian geological challenge to the hierarchies established by Genesis. Whitman liked the idea that nothing would ever be lost. He could find an energetic solace in 'materialism first and last imbuing' because he imagined disintegration was only ever a process of reintegration and growth. So, the flag and handkerchief dissolve back into the grass, which is read, now, not as a multitudinous handful of

[116] See Mark Noble, *American Poetic Materialism from Whitman to Stevens* (Cambridge: CUP, 2014), 49–51.

parts, absorbed in the unified whole, but the legibility of the whole in the part. The grass is a great leveller: 'itself a child...a uniform hieroglyphic...the beautiful uncut hair of graves'. Moving cyclically from birth to death to sprouting birth in death, the disintegration of flag and handkerchief deliberately works against the linear trajectory of Design, the Emersonian integrating eye, and the jingoism of contemporary visual art.

This kind of philosophic materialism works against real loss. Thus, Whitman writes:

> All goes onward and outward...and nothing collapses,
> And to die is different from what anyone supposed, and luckier.

Disintegration is transformative as opposed to reductive: a process of creative alchemy. The emphasis on constant levelling and endless renewal provides a model for Whitman's hopeful democratic vision. But it also poses a threat to his desired authorial agency. In the poem's opening lines, the democratizing principle of the 'atom' that Whitman declares belongs 'to me as good as...to you' casts doubt on whether anything, especially authorial agency, can ever really belong to anyone:

> I celebrate myself,
> And what I shall assume you shall assume
> For every atom belonging to me as good as belongs to you.

There is an intrinsic scepticism in philosophic materialism, which works against faith in authorial agency. In a world in which structures are forever shifting and narrative outcomes are unpredictable and unknowable, agency is difficult to claim. Whitman, like Gwendolen in the casino, the embedded artist of *The Oxbow*, and the sliding poet of 'Experience', risks becoming caught in the uncertainty of narrative flux, even as he tries to contain it.[117]

In order to fight the intrinsic scepticism of philosophic materialism, Whitman imagines himself as the centrifugal and centripetal force in his poetic universe.

> To me the converging objects of the universe perpetually flow,
> All are written to me, and I must get what the writing means

[117] See Chapter 4, 131.

The centripetal and centrifugal force of the poet works to preserve authorial agency in the alchemical process. This is how Whitman combats the potentially overwhelming fluidity of materialism and narratives of circumstance and chance. It is how he preserves the 'Me, myself' that allows him to declare 'Apart from the pulling and the hauling stands what I am', even as he also maintains 'Nothing is original with me', claiming ownership over the process of creative alchemy: 'Voices indecent by me clarified and transfigured'.

'Nothing is original with me' refutes original sin as much as it supports the recombinatory theory of matter. Whitman presents a version of Eden in which the Fall is simply not a possibility because nothing is forbidden. The 1860 edition of *Leaves of Grass* included the collection *Enfans d'Adam*, titled 'Children of Adam' in 1867, which retells the first few chapters of Genesis as a celebration of fertility:

> To the garden, the world, anew ascending
> Potent mates, daughters, sons, preluding,
> The love, the life of their bodies, meaning and being

Whitman undoes the judgement of the Fall, in which sex is identified with original sin, and aligns it instead with new world possibility. He also undoes the hierarchical reception of Genesis which gives men dominance over women, declaring an easy equivalence:

> By my side, or back of me, Eve following,
> Or in front, and I following her just the same.[118]

In the 1881-1882 edition of the *Leaves*, he declared himself 'Nature without check with original energy.'[119] He undoes the narrative that begins with prohibition: the check on nature that converts Emerson's 'original relation' into original sin. The line is notably free of punctuation, which is another way in which Whitman signals the absence of a divisive and punctuating moment of Fall. This is more generally reflected in Whitman's frequent use of parataxis and anaphora. Whitman's lists extend, rather than check, meanings. Like Emerson's Orphic Poet, he forges seemingly endless connections, which, 'line for line, and point for point', build a new world as an illimitable extension of himself.

[118] Walt Whitman. Enfans d'Adam, "Leaves of Grass (1860–1861)." The Walt Whitman Archive. Gen. ed. Matt Cohen, Ed Folsom, & Kenneth M. Price.

[119] Whitman, 'Song of Myself' *Leaves of Grass* (Boston: James R. Osgood and Company, 1881–1882), 29. Albert and Shirley Small Special Collections Library, University of Virginia, PS3201 1882a, copy 2. Accessed via The Walt Whitman Archive.

In his 1855 vision of America as a New Eden, Whitman smooths away the divisive difference of the Fall that we see in a painting such as Cole's *Expulsion*. He replaces this difference with equivalence, announcing: 'By God! I will accept nothing which all cannot have their counterpart of on the same terms.' Whitman's equivalence has a democratic, anti-hierarchical imperative, which makes conservatism look like radicalism. But Whitman, who wants to find a 'place' for everything, draws comfort from conservative fixity even as he celebrates diversity.

> I resist anything better than my own diversity,
> And breathe the air and leave plenty after me,
> And am not stuck up, and am in my place.
>
> The moth and the fisheggs are in their place,
> The suns I see and the suns I cannot see are in their place,
> The palpable is in its place and the impalpable is in its place.

Roland Barthes observes that: 'the form [of myth] does not suppress the meaning, only impoverishes it, puts it at a distance, it holds it at one's disposal.'[120] Here, diversity does not dissolve but it is impoverished, and held at a distance, by the sameness of poetic representation. Whitman's Edenic texture, the 'hopeful green stuff' of his woven song, asserts itself in the mode, rather than the literal meaning, of his utterance, which not only finds a place for everything, but keeps everything in its place.

Whitman masters the narratives that counter present perfection. He undoes the myth of the Fall, which tells us we had something perfect and lost it. He writes against judgement of the Fall which casts sexual desire as 'sin.' He also counters Providence, which tells us that our return to that happy state lies with God's will; and he manages the forces of scepticism by preserving the 'Me, myself' of authorial agency '[a]part from the pulling and hauling' of the world. Such logic allows Whitman to hold history at a distance and declare the myth of eternal beginning:

> There was never any more inception than there is now,
> Nor any more youth or age than there is now;
> And will never be any more perfection than there is now,
> Nor any more heaven or hell than there is now.

[120] Barthes, 'Myth Today,' *Mythologies*, 141.

The continuously smooth, yet oddly motionless, equivalence, which makes difference look like sameness, holds onto the stillness of perfect beginning in the 'now' of the present. It keeps check and chiaroscuro, the rupture of choice and the meaning of difference, at bay. This correlates, thematically, with Whitman's celebration of the libidinous, insistently ascendant, though curiously atemporal, 'procreant urge of the world'. The 'procreant urge of the world' reflects a model of creation drawn from Lucretius not Genesis. For Lucretius, the earth gave birth; it was not created by God. The implicit affirmation of sexual freedom is also another way of asserting 'Nature without check': Eden without prohibition, sin, or Fall.

In his Preface to the 1855 poem, Whitman responds directly to Emerson's call for a new age of poet-priests: 'As if it were necessary to trot back generation after generation to the eastern records! As if the beauty and sacredness of the demonstrable must fall behind that of the mythical. As if men do not make their mark out of any times.' *Leaves of Grass* renews the myth of America as a New Eden by rooting it again in 'demonstrable' history. Whitman's freshness lies largely in his sense of living history: 'To him enter the essences of real things'. But, as the polyvalence of history becomes subject to the grammar of commensurate being and absorbed into the smooth texture of Whitman's mythic speech, it becomes preserved, and simultaneously attenuated, in the perfect present tense. In his 1855 poem, Whitman declares: 'I help the auctioneer...the sloven does not know half his business'. In the 1860 edition, this identification follows an expression of lust:

> The female form approaching—I, pensive, love-flesh
> tremulous, aching;
> The slave's body for sale—I, sternly, with harsh
> voice, auctioneering[.][121]

This gives his utopic vision an oddly dystopic quality. In Whitman's disturbingly easy identifications and equivalences, a world without moral limit or checked desires starts to feel a deeply unpleasant and unerotic thing.

Through the textural narratives of *The Expulsion* and *The Oxbow*, Cole discards the myth of perfect beginning in favour of moral choice. In the former

[121] Whitman, 'Enfans d'Adam', 289.

painting, the pristine landscape, influenced by the Claudian idyll, is a dangerous fantasy. Cole's *Expulsion* acknowledges the ways in which the survival of the myth of perfect beginning has depended on, and reinforced, the settler impulse. Cole's revisiting of Eden in *The Oxbow* deals with the same moral choice he presents in 'Essay on American Scenery', but it is more explicitly sceptical about authorial agency, less sure that those who 'see and feel' might restore the texture of innocence to the marked surfaces of the earth without the guiding hand of Providence. In his painting, if not in his writing, Cole has let go of the myth that tells us America can be the land of perfect beginning and decided futurity.

While the poet of the 1855 *Leaves* can claim 'I know the hand of God is the elderhand of my own', the artist of *The Oxbow* can make no such declaration. The painting suggests that cosmic forces are active in the world (the blasted trees and stormy skies tell a story of spiritual presence). But the ambiguity of narrative direction, and the overwhelmed aspect of the painter, suggests that, unlike Whitman, Cole does not claim mastery over their meanings. 'Who need be afraid of the merge?' Whitman asks. Certainly not his 1855 poet who buffers himself most powerfully in the resulting mythic speech. Cole, on the other hand, does seem frightened. He takes refuge in distinction; and, by the end of his career, Edenic texture denotes precipitous choice not eternal beginning. What he has lost, in the 1836 painting, is the linear trajectory of the Fall, the confidence that right and wrong choices set incontrovertible and knowable narratives in motion. The mark of beginning might not decide the end. The nostalgia of touch, the way in which it harks back to a moment below or before formation, is reassuring for Cole only when it lies securely within a religious framework of faith and hope, providence and redemption. Losing the certainty of narrative direction and the clarity of textural distinction, *The Oxbow* is a worried meditation on the creative, and perhaps destructive, possibilities of touch *without* the consolations of reminiscence.

For Emerson, the vitality and possibility of America as a New Eden turns on the extent to which matter remains hospitable to spirit. Edenic texture is fully integrated with divinity and the Orphic poet, who resembles the God of Genesis 2, finds his medium malleable and responsive. The fallen poet discovers it far more resistant to his touch. Meanings slip and original world-making force—the power of touch before the moment of formation and fixity—has given way to the 'skill of handling' amidst the sliding surface of reality. In Whitman's 1855 poem, new world utopia starts to feel even more dystopic; a commitment to present perfection which disallows sin but continues to permit a horrible violence.

6

The Violence of Cain

Wilson, Brown, Truth

In 1963, one hundred years after Abraham Lincoln issued the Emancipation Proclamation, and as President Kennedy proposed new civil rights legislation amidst violent and endemic racism, James Baldwin wrote: 'In the same way that we, for white people, were the descendants of Ham, and were cursed for ever, white people were, for us, the descendants of Cain.'[1] The religious origins of divisive stereotyping are found in early purification rituals, where it becomes a way of ordering existence, avoiding spiritual corruption and maintaining the integrity of forms against the impairment or defilement of difference, the shameful, and the undesirable.[2] But Baldwin shows that the biblical stereotyping of race has had the opposite effect. He emphasizes that racist division, in its attempt to preserve the so-called purity of difference, is, in fact, a form of pollution, which infects the self it is supposed to preserve.

Baldwin's essay takes the story of Cain and Abel as a foundational mythic structure for racial violence in America. He urges us to move beyond the racism of biblical stereotype towards a more complex understanding of the fratricide as symbolic of the beginnings of American nationhood. Presented as two letters to his nephew and written on the one hundredth anniversary of the Emancipation Proclamation, Baldwin's essay is poignant, in its timing and in its form. He presents the hatred of one's brother as a form of self-hatred, and fear and distrust become acts of reflexive violence: 'And the passion with which we loved the Lord was a measure of how deeply we feared, and distrusted and, in the end, hated almost all strangers, always, and avoided and despised ourselves.'[3] Racism, bolstered by religious authority and fuelled by feelings of zealotry, is both a social and personal degradation. The deep corruption of racism manifests as a dangerous and distorting mirror in which love reflects as hate and the self is unmade in the image it has of its brother.

[1] James Baldwin, *The Fire Next Time* (London: Penguin, 2017), 41.

[2] For a description of early purification rituals see Robert Parker, *Miasma: Pollution and Purification in Early Greek Religion* (Oxford: Clarendon Press, 1983), 18–32.

[3] Baldwin, *Fire Next Time*, 41.

The Myth of the Fall in Nineteenth-Century Literature. Linda Freedman, Oxford University Press.
 DOI: 10.1093/oso/9780198969570.003.0007

Rewriting the origin myth allows for an exertion of authorial control. It suggests that the future of the world might be changed if the past is told differently. This is a story that is yet to be completed, one in which the senseless murder of Abel, the suffering and death inflicted on millions of Black Americans, might be *for* something. It is this difficult dative that turns suffering into sacrifice where the meaning is held in the future. Baldwin eloquently expresses the problem this poses in American history:

> This past, the Negro's past, of rope, fire, torture, castration, infanticide, rape; death and humiliation; fear by day and night, fear as deep as the marrow of the bone; doubt that he was worthy of life, since everyone around him denied it; sorrow for his women, for his kinfolk, for his children, who needed his protection, and whom he could not protect; rage, hatred, and murder, hatred for white men so deep that it often turned against him and his own, and made all love, all trust, all joy, impossible—this past, this endless struggle to achieve and reveal and confirm a human identity, human authority, yet contains, for all its horror, something very beautiful. I do not mean to be sentimental about suffering—enough is certainly as good as a feast—but people who cannot suffer can never grow up, can never discover who they are.[4]

George Eliot had thought similarly about suffering, struggling to rid herself of the feeling that something could be learned from it, and that it was part of growing up. There is a harm, Baldwin acknowledges, in seeing African-American history in these terms. If we believe that atrocity has a religious dative—that Black people suffered and died *for* something better—we run the risk of creating a theodicy of suffering, and worse, fetishizing it as martyrdom. Baldwin's literary sensibility identifies the dangerous mode of mythic meaning: 'I do not mean to be sentimental about suffering', he says. But he also recalls its value. Sentiment was an important part of the abolitionist armoury. In African-American writing of Reconstruction, sentiment helped build narratives of sacrifice, which advocated racial assimilation into a newly resurrected body politic. Baldwin rejects a sentimental theodicy of suffering, but he also wants to promote a narrative of personal and national growth, which has its literary foundations in the sentimental and religious writing of sacrifice.

'How can the American Negro past be used?' he asks.[5] His answer is partly to reclaim and rewrite the myths of white supremacy. In 1918, the white cultural

[4] Baldwin, *Fire Next Time*, 84.

[5] Baldwin, *Fire Next Time*, 87.

nationalist Van Wyck Brooks had published his essay, 'On Creating a Usable Past', in *The Dial.* It stressed the commonality of experience and considered what Americans might want to remember about their collective history in order to progress. He concluded:

> Knowing that others have desired the things we desire and have encountered the same obstacles, and that in some degree time has begun to face those obstacles down and make the way straight for us, would not the creative forces of this country lose a little of the hectic individualism that keeps them from uniting against their common enemies? And would this not bring about, for the first time, that sense of brotherhood in effort and in aspiration, which is the best promise of a national culture?[6]

Van Wyck Brooks is silent on the subject of race. His fraternal reference points are white American authors. As John Ernest observes, African-American historians have inevitably been metahistorical, questioning the terms of history and the politics of historical writing.[7] Baldwin makes erasure his target, unearthing the body buried by Cain. He invokes, and rejects, the received myths of white American cultural identity. He constructs an alternative lineage, citing and paying homage to W. E. B. Du Bois. Echoing, and revising Emerson, invoking and critiquing the myth of a New Eden, recasting the American 'dream' of prosperity and self-making as a 'racial nightmare', Baldwin ends with a new exhortation to build our own world:

> Everything now we must assume, is in our hands; we have no right to assume otherwise. If we—and now I mean the relatively conscious whites and the relatively conscious blacks [sic], who must, like lovers, insist on, or create, the consciousness of others—do not falter in our duty now, we may be able, handful that we are, to end this racial nightmare, and achieve our country, and change the history of the world. If we do not now dare everything, the fulfilment of that prophecy, recreated from the song of a slave, is upon us: *God gave Noah the rainbow sign, No more water, the fire next time!*[8]

[6] Van Wyck Brooks, 'On Creating a Usable Past', *The Dial* (11 Apr. 1918): 337–41, 341.

[7] John Ernest, *Liberation Historiography: African American Writers and the Challenge of History 1794–1861* (Chapel Hill, NC: University of North Carolina Press, 2004), 4.

[8] Baldwin, *Fire Next Time*, 89. James Truslow Adams, in his best-selling book, *Epic of America* (1931) coined the phrase 'American dream' to describe the colonialist ideology of progressive self-making.

To 'change the history of the world' suggests we might shape a different future, but it also implies a rewriting of the way the past has been told.

For Black Americans, fighting for freedom and civil rights, the dream of a new beginning was not the spotless landscape of Eden; it was rooted in resurrection from sin. In this context, the myth of America's Fall was not Genesis 3 but Genesis 4: the violence that set brother against brother, white against Black, in the violent beginnings of American history. The fratricide asserts itself in slavery, revolution, and Civil War. It informs images of sacrifice and substitution, violence and resistance, which construct various versions, and rejections, of Black citizenship. It lingers in the tens of thousands of murderous lynchings, described by Ida B. Wells as a mark of Cain on white America: 'dehumanizing brutality which fixes upon America the blot of a national crime'.[9] But even as it is used to mark the origin and continuation of evil, the story of Cain and Abel invests hope. It signifies the double within, explored through the invocation and resistance of type. Blood and brotherhood become ways of thinking, too, about the bleeding, and interdependence, of worlds. The hope of resurrection is represented by Abel, a type of Christ, whose blood becomes symbolic of shared foundational sacrifice in the new republic and vocal resistance to white supremacy as it cries from the ground.

This chapter begins with a discussion of the white Cain as a subversive stereotype which circulated in Africa and America from at least the early decades of the nineteenth century. It focuses on William J. Wilson's *Afric American Picture Gallery*, serialized in 1859. Wilson was a Brooklyn schoolteacher, activist, and journalist who wrote regularly for *Frederick Douglass' Paper*. The *Afric American Picture Gallery* consciously undermined the myth of America as a New Eden, seeking to tell a different story of origins and shape a different future. Wilson satirized white supremacy in the arts and imagined an alternative Black pantheon, countering received error to demand a better future. Through its engagingly imaginative and errant structures, the *Picture Gallery* profoundly resists conformity and refuses to surrender allegory to the racist division of type.

The final part of the chapter offers two brief discussions of works which reflect on the narrative of sacrifice in the context of Reconstruction. The difficult dative of sacrifice, the belief that suffering and death must be *for* something better, comes to the fore in African-American writing of Reconstruction

[9] Ida B. Wells, 'A Red Record: Tabulated Statistics and Alleged Causes of Lynchings in the United States, 1892–1893–1894', in *The Light of Truth: Writings of an Anti-Lynching Crusader*, ed. Mia Bay (London: Penguin, 2014), 220–312, 228.

precisely because claims to a better future relied on a past imagined in terms of foundational sacrifice and blood-letting. William Wells Brown's 1867 version of the 1850 novel *Clotel* (retitled *Clotelle*) resists the sentimental strain, while also seeking to turn it towards a narrative of national resurrection and racial integration. In his use of realism, Brown warns us against the risk of platitude in sentimental constructions, but he also invests in the narrative of sacrifice and resurrection to advocate for racial uplift. The 1875 publication of Sojourner Truth's *Book of Life*, together with a republication of her 1850 *Narrative*, offered a compelling emblem of resurrection, refusing to tolerate the sentimental treatment of suffering, just at the moment when Jim Crow legislation took hold in the South. The *Narrative of Sojourner Truth* and the *Book of Life* fiercely resist a sentimental portrayal of suffering. Reviving the zealous spirit of antebellum reform just at the moment when Reconstruction was about to collapse, the *Narrative* presented Truth's sincere faith in miraculous transformation as the life-blood of the new nation and her *Book of Life* as the foundation of a new world order.

Stereotype and Subversion: The White Cain

The stereotyping of white people as Cain began as a deliberate subversion of white supremacism.[10] It was common, in the nineteenth century, for white Europeans and Americans to preach that Black skin was the mark of Cain, and Ham his direct descendant. Gus Rogers, who had been enslaved in North Carolina and Alabama, explained the genesis of his race by referring to the story of Ham in terms of white pro-slavery apologia:

> God gave it [religion] to Adam and took it away from Adam and gave it to Noah, and you know miss, Noah had three sons, and when Noah got drunk on wine, one of his sons laughed at him, and the other two took a sheet and walked backwards and threw it over Noah. Noah told the one who laughed, 'Your children will be hewers of wood and drawers of water for the other two children, and they will be known by their hair and their skin being dark.' So Miss, there we are, and that is the way God meant us to be.[11]

[10] For a more extensive discussion and series of examples of the mark of Cain as a symbol of white violence see: Nyashi Junior, 'The Mark of Cain and White Violence', *Journal of Biblical Literature* 139.24 (2020): 661–73.

[11] 'Interview with Gus Rogers' in Mary A. Poole, *Slave Narratives: A Folk History of Slavery in the United States from Interviews with Former Slaves*, vol. 1. *Alabama Narratives* (Delhi: Prabhat Publishers, 2019), 259 Kindle Version.

Frederick Douglass invoked the oppressive use of the myth in his *Narrative*, observing, rather bleakly, that children born of rape would make it harder to sustain:

> it is nevertheless plain that a very different looking class of people are springing up at the south, and are now held in slavery, from those originally brought to this country from Africa; and if their increase will do no other good, it will do away the force of the argument that God cursed Ham, and therefore American slavery is right. If the lineal descendants of Ham are alone to be scripturally enslaved, it is certain that slavery in the South must soon become unscriptural; for thousands are ushered into the world annually, who, like myself, owe their existence to white fathers, and those fathers most frequently their own masters.[12]

Mary Kingsley, who travelled extensively in West Africa in the 1890s, recalls asking a 12-year-old girl in the Cameroons why she was Black. The answer she received was the one taught: 'One of my pa's pas saw dem Patriark Noah wivout his clothes'.[13] Kingsley was more struck, however, by another story, which she said was often told to her: after Cain killed Abel, he carried the body around with him for years, trying to hide it from God, growing gradually whiter with fear, until he saw a crow scratching a hole in the desert and buried the body there: 'but all his children were white, and from Cain came the white races, while Abel's children are Black, as were all men before the first murder'.[14] In 1859, the white Baptist preacher and Southern Humourist writer, Harden E. Taliaferro, published his observations of *Fisher's River (North Carolina) Scenes and Characters*, which included a reference to racial origin debates.

> Naturalists have for ages been trying to account for the different forms and complexions of men. Some of them will have to be of different races, not all descended from the same pair, Adam and Eve. Others contend that all have descended from the same pair, but climate and accidental cause have made the difference; hence Professor A and Professor B have their diverse theories

[12] *Narrative of the Life of Frederick Douglass, an American Slave* [1845], ed. Deborah E. McDowell (Oxford: OUP, 2009), 17.

[13] Mary Kingsley, *West African Studies*, 328, cited in Lawrence W. Levine, *Black Culture and Black Consciousness: Afro-American Folk Thought from Slavery to Freedom* (Oxford: OUP, 2007), 85.

[14] Mary Kingsley, *Travels in West Africa*, 430–1, cited in Levine, *Black Culture*, 85.

> and their disciples and admirers. When one leaves the plain teachings of the Bible and go into vague speculations, one man's hypothesis is nearly as good as another's.[15]

With this introduction, he presented his readers with a 'new theory', which he recalled from the teachings of the Revd Charles Gentry, a Black preacher, whom he had known growing up in rural North Carolina in the 1820s:

> Adam, Cain, Abel, Seth was all ob 'um black as jet... Cain he kill his brudder Abel wid a great big club... and God he cum to Cain, and say, 'Cain, whar is dy brudder Abel?'... Cain he turn white as bleech cambric in de face, and de whole race of Cain dey bin white ebber since. De mark de Lord put on de face ob Cain was a white mark.[16]

The African counter myth, which circulated in America from at least the early decades of the nineteenth century, claimed the mark of Cain was white skin.[17] The idea that the first parents were Black allowed for a subversion of colonial tools of oppression: whiteness could be seen as degenerative Blackness.[18]

The white Cain was also invoked to criticize colonialism and slavery. In 1818, the Haitian intellectual and critic of colonialism, Pompée-Valentin de Vastey published *Le système colonial dévoilé* (*The Colonial System Unveiled*). He condemned the way in which biblical stereotype was used as part of the armoury of colonialism: 'Hannerman maintains that the colour of blacks originates in the curse that Noah pronounced against Ham; others affirm that our colour and our reprobation can be traced back to Cain, for killing his brother Abel'.[19] Inverting the stereotype became a form of resistance to colonial oppression and enslavement, so he declared:

> I have strong reasons for believing that it is actually the whites who are the race of Cain, for I find in them primitive hatred, that spirit of envy and

[15] Harden E. Taliaferro, *Fisher's River (North Carolina) Scenes and Characters* (New York, 1859), 187.

[16] Taliaferro, *Fisher's River*, 188, cited in Levine, *Black Culture*, 85.

[17] For comparative sources see: Levine, *Black Culture*, 85–6.

[18] Theories around the skin colour of Adam and his family persisted throughout the nineteenth century. The most developed was J. F. Dyson, *A New and Simple Explanation of the Human Race and the Origin of Color* (1886). See Mia Bay, *The White Image in the Black Mind: African American Ideas about White People* (Oxford: OUP, 2000), 79.

[19] Baron Valentin de Vastey, *The Colonial System Unveiled*, tr. and ed. Chris Bongie (Liverpool: Liverpool University Press, 2014), 104.

> arrogance, and that passion for riches of which scripture speaks and which led him to sacrifice his brother; it is this same spirit which animates those who traffic in human flesh and feeds their predilection for persecuting us as the descendants of Abel.[20]

In 1829, David Walker similarly invoked the white Cain in his attack on the institution of slavery. He wrote:

> some ignorant creatures hesitate not to tell us that we, (the blacks) are the seed of Cain the murderer of his brother Abel. But where or of whom those ignorant and avaricious wretches could have got their information, I am unable to declare: Did they receive it from the Bible? I have searched the Bible as well as they, if I am not as well learned as they are, and have never seen a verse which testifies whether we are the seed of Cain or of Abel. Yet those men tell us that we are the seed of Cain, and that God put a dark stain upon us, that we might be known as their slaves!!! Now I ask these avaricious and ignorant wretches, who act more like the seed of Cain by murdering the whites or the blacks? How many vessel loads of human beings have the blacks murdered in cold blood, to make them work in wretchedness and ignorance, to support them and their families?[21]

In these formulations, whiteness was not just seen as degenerative Blackness, but the mark of evil and greed.

If Genesis 3 locates the source of modern misery in the sin of disobedience, Genesis 4 finds it in jealousy and the desire for supremacy. In the family drama of Genesis, Cain and Abel are equals, two brothers fighting for fatherly approval:

> And the Lord had respect unto Abel and his offering: But unto Cain and his offering he had not respect. And Cain was very wroth, and his countenance fell. And the Lord said unto Cain, why art thou wroth? And why is thy countenance fallen? If thou doest well, shalt thou not be accepted? And if thou doest not well, sin lieth at the door. And unto thee *shall* be his desire, and thou shalt rule over him. And Cain talked with Abel his brother: and it came to pass, when they were in the field, that Cain rose up against his brother and slew him.[22]

[20] Vastey, *Colonial System Unveiled*, 104.

[21] David Walker, *Appeal to the Coloured Citizens of the World*, ed. Peter P. Hinks (Philadelphia: Pennsylvania State University Press, 2000), 63.

[22] Gen. 4: 4–8.

In the context of American slavery, depicting the white man as Cain was both an indictment of white violence and a tacit subversion of the master–slave hierarchy and broader notions of white supremacy. While the disobedience of Genesis 3 punches up in an act of resistance to authority, the fratricide stages a violent confrontation with one's equal, and double.

Early theologians observed that projection, and suicidal self-division, are part of the biblical myth. Philo exclaims of Cain: 'What have you done?…You have proven to be your own murderer!'[23] Philo understands Cain's murder of his brother as a form of suicide because he kills off the better part of himself, his own access to the ideal. Cain becomes emblematic of reflexive violence. He stains the earth with blood, which becomes a permanent blot on his relationship with the land: 'And now art thou cursed by the earth, which hath opened her mouth to receive thy brother's blood from thy hand. When thou tillest the ground, it shall not henceforth yield unto thee her strength; a fugitive and a vagabond shalt thou be on the earth.'[24]

Baldwin invokes the emotional betrayal of fratricide—'the very depths from which love springs, or murder'—to similar effect, presenting the history of racial conflict in America as the continuously reflexive violence of Cain:

> These tensions are rooted in the very depths from which love springs, or murder. The white man's unadmitted—and apparently to him, unspeakable—private fears and longings are projected onto the Negro. The only way he can be released from the Negro's tyrannical power over him is to consent, in effect, to become black himself, to become a part of the suffering, dancing, country that he now watches wistfully from the heights of his lonely power and, armed with spiritual traveller's cheques, visits surreptitiously after dark.[25]

In murdering Abel, Cain makes himself an exile from all that his brother represents. Cain will always raise the shadow of Abel; and Abel remains the better part of himself—the locus of Cain's desires. As Ricardo Quinones puts it: "Abel represents an ideal of right conduct and true being that can never die; Cain represents the depravity that is ever dying and never dead.'[26] Baldwin turns the Cain myth into a version of G. W. F. Hegel's master–slave dialectic. In a famous passage in *The Phenomenology of Spirit*, Hegel had described the

[23] Philo, 'The Posterity and Exile of Cain', 255. Cited in Ricardo Quinones, *The Changes of Cain: Violence and the Lost Brother in Cain and Abel Literature* (Princeton: Princeton University Press, 2016), 29.

[24] Gen. 4: 12.

[25] Baldwin, *Fire Next Time*, 82.

[26] Quinones, *Changes of Cain*, 29.

way in which self-consciousness is formed by encounter and dominance undoes its own power. For Hegel movement of recognition turns into a 'struggle to the death', in which one makes a slave of the other, only to find that the recognition he sought can no longer be given by the enslaved.[27]

Baldwin's subtle and lyrical reworking of the myth of Cain into the history of racial violence rejects racist stereotyping in favour of a nuanced vision of racial interdependence and reflexive violence in the national mythology of America. 'We', he writes, 'the black and the white deeply need each other here if we are really to become a nation.'[28] Unlike the myth of a New Eden, which remains in thrall to pre-lapsarian innocence, the story of Cain and Abel announces itself as post-lapsarian history. Cain and Abel are already fallen. For Hobbes, the fratricide was a paradigmatic example of the state of nature as a state of conflict.[29] Byron's Cain laments that he was born too late for Eden:

> I judge but by the fruits—and they are bitter-
> Which I must feed on for a fault not mine.[30]

Used repeatedly to signify the origins of evil, Cain is also a type of its continuing historical presence. Genesis 4 includes a list of Cain's descendants, connecting him, finally, with the reflexive violence of Lamech, who confesses: 'I have slain a man to my wounding, and a young man to my hurt. If Cain shall be avenged sevenfold, truly Lamech seventy and sevenfold.'[31] Cain's reflexive violence proliferates throughout history. He comes to represent social irresponsibility, self-interest, hypocrisy, and religion without humanity. In 1849, Douglass's *North Star* attacked the Christian apologist argument that slavery was a matter between a man and his God, calling it the philosophy and morality of Cain:

> What is it to us that Abel is slain or brutalised; that our poor brother has fallen among thieves; that our country is polluted and disgraced by hideous barbarisms; that the world—God's beautiful world—is turned into a charnel-house, or dungeon of torture to millions of its children? That is a

[27] *Hegel's Phenomenology of Spirit,* tr. A. V. Miller, foreword by J. N. Findlay (Oxford: OUP, 1977), 111–18.

[28] Baldwin, *Fire Next Time*, 83.

[29] See Helen Thornton, 'Cain, Abel and Thomas Hobbes', *History of Political Thought* 24.4 (Winter 2002): 611–33.

[30] Lord Byron, *The Major Works,* ed. Jerome McGann (Oxford: OUP, 2008), 886.

[31] Gen. 4: 23–4.

> matter between the oppressor and his God? Out upon such doctrines! They are rank atheism or worse than atheism![32]

Cain also situates a shift from the agricultural to the urban: he builds the first city, and names it after his first child. The Cain myth thus became formative on notions of citizenship. Quinones explains: 'The legend of the fratricidal foundation of the state, or of a people, becomes a parable. It comes to stand for the inevitable sacrifices and losses that are part of the condition of life.'[33] As Black writers theorized and practised versions of American citizenship in the middle and late decades of the nineteenth century, the Cain myth reiterated the bloody beginnings of American nationhood and emphasized the violent injustice underpinning white narratives of self-making, growth, prosperity, and progress.

'We Must Begin to Tell Our Own Story': *The Afric American Picture Gallery* (1859)

In 1859, the *Anglo-African Magazine* serialized a work of fiction by the Brooklyn schoolteacher, journalist and activist, William J. Wilson, titled *The Afric American Picture Gallery by Ethiop*. In March 1853, Wilson, writing under the pseudonym 'Ethiop' as the 'Brooklyn Correspondent' for *Frederick Douglass' Paper*, had reported on a visit to a Brooklyn art gallery. He wrote:

> there stood Franklin and Adams, Lafayette and Jefferson, and Clay and Webster; the gods and goddesses were there, and the Queen of England was there, and so was the Emperor of France; but I found not the Emperor of Hayti [sic], nor of Dohomey, nor the President of Liberia, nor any other distinguished *black*. I inquired for one or two—Toussaint L'Ouverture, Boyer and Faustin 1…I asked for some who had distinguished themselves in this country. 'They no sell' was the same reply…No demand has been made, thought I, as I rushed out of his place into the street.
>
> The result of this, upon my mind, may be summed up in a few words. A radical change in the process of our development is here demanded…we must begin to tell our own story, write our own lecture, paint our own picture, chisel our own bust.[34]

[32] *North Star* (Rochester, NY, 1 June 1849).
[33] Quinones, *Changes of Cain*, 39.
[34] 'Communications from our Brooklyn Correspondent', *Frederick Douglass' Paper* (11 Mar. 1853), 3.

In *The Afric American Picture Gallery*, Wilson answered his own call. Printed in seven consecutive instalments, the work imagines a tour of a fictional gallery—a pantheon of African-American art which holds likenesses of great Black figures as well as paintings which depict the brutal history of colonization and enslavement. Wilson chose visual art partly because it was a medium with political force. In a 'Lecture on Pictures', delivered to Boston's Tremont Temple in 1861, Frederick Douglass would praise photography as a real index of human progress: 'the picture plays an important part in our politics', he declared, 'and often explodes political shams more effectively than any other agency'.[35] For Douglass the way we react to art was a measure of social standards and Wilson's text used the imagined space of the gallery to stage and satirize contemporary debates on culture and self-reliance that privileged white artists. Painting and sculpture also had a reputation as media that would last. The piece was not illustrated, partly because the pantheon was largely invented and no doubt partly because images cost more than *The Anglo-African* could afford. But Wilson used the press, with its growing reach and relatively cheap means of production, to tell a story which laid claim to the vocabulary of permanence. The language of visual culture allows Wilson to imagine a *lasting* record of Black history. He establishes monuments to greatness, a catalogue of terror, and a living history, speaking pictures which construct a future-facing narrative where progress is made through permanently changing the way the past has been told.

Wilson's 'Ethiop' persona had a strong political character, committed to the future of Black people in America, and this would already have been familiar to readers of the Black press from his regular column in *Frederick Douglass' Paper*. The pseudonym paid homage to Phillis Wheatley, who, in 1773, had lectured white male students on the sin, the 'deadly serpent', that lay waiting to ensnare every one of them: 'An *Ethiop* tells you "tis your greatest foe".'[36] Wheatley's portrait was included in the imaginary gallery as a model for all women.[37] Between 1851 and 1854, *Frederick Douglass' Paper* had staged a running debate between Wilson, writing under the pseudonym, 'Ethiop', and James McCune Smith, writing under the pseudonym, 'Communipaw', over the theory and practice of Black citizenship. As Derrick Spires observes, the

[35] Frederick Douglass, 'Lecture on Pictures', in *Picturing Frederick Douglass: An Illustrated Biography of the Century's Most Illustrated American*, ed. John Stauffer et al. (New York: Liveright, 2015), 126–41, 130.

[36] Phillis Wheatley, 'To the University of CAMBRIDGE in NEW-ENGLAND', 1773, *Complete Writings* (London: Penguin, 2001), 11–12, 12.

[37] William Wilson, 'Afric American Picture Gallery, Fifth Paper, by Ethiop', *Anglo-African Magazine* 1 (1859; New York: Arno Press and the New York Times, 1969), 216–19, 217–18.

literary strengths of both writers were essential to the project. Smith and Wilson explored the kinds of subjectivities needed for Black citizens to navigate the developing economic structures of middle-class America, and they attacked each other's versions of truth using the strategies of literary criticism.[38]

In *The Afric American Picture Gallery*, Wilson developed the character of Ethiop beyond the persona of the Brooklyn correspondent. Ethiop is an explorer, guide, and curator of Black history, directing us to see, and feel, as he moves our eye around an imaginary pantheon of African-American art: 'let the reader, with me enter into this almost unknown Gallery', he says. 'Well, here we are, and looking about us…But let us take a survey, and speak only about what strikes us most forcibly in our present mood.'[39] Ethiop presents himself as an Emersonian instructor in order to invoke, and critique, the dominant white Northern discourse of self-culture. In 1844, Emerson had written: 'the secret of the illusoriness of life is the necessity of a succession of moods or objects…[life is a] train of moods like a succession of beads.'[40] Emerson maintains that this 'flux of moods' colours the world, and shapes its meaning for us as we slide from one position to another: 'they prove to be many-colored lenses which paint the world their own hue, and each shows only what lies in focus.'[41] For Emerson, the imperative of the shifting self is to find itself in its moods. For Wilson, mood-curation turns on a critique of the subjectivity and self-centredness of such vision, which continuously remakes the world in the vein of its own temperament and feeling.

Directly repudiating the Edenic ideal in contemporary art—the 'finish and freshness' that Whitman so admired—Ethiop takes us, first, to a forgotten corner of the gallery and the dark, 'unfavourable', side of American history: 'Picture Number 1. The Slave Ship.'[42] He begins by assuming a Ruskinian 'truth to nature' aesthetic: 'faithful to every shrub, crag and nook.'[43] He quickly undercuts any idealism with sardonic wit. The real truth is not the beauty of the American landscape but the violence such doctrines of beauty conceal. This is a hellscape, reminiscent of John Martin's illustration of Satan summoning his legions in *Paradise Lost*:

[38] Derrick Spires, *The Practice of Citizenship: Black Politics and Print Culture in the Early United States* (Philadelphia: University of Pennsylvania Press, 2019), 121–60, 123.
[39] Wilson, 'Afric American Picture Gallery', 53.
[40] Emerson, 'Experience' (1844), *Selected Essays*, 288–9.
[41] Emerson, 'Experience' (1844), *Selected Essays*, 289.
[42] 'The picture hangs near the entrance on the South Side of the Gallery, and in a rather unfavourable light', Wilson, 'Afric American Picture Gallery', 53.
[43] Wilson, 'Afric American Picture Gallery', 53.

> The small boat struck by, and contending with, a huge breaker, is so near the shore, that you can behold, and startle as you behold, the emaciated and death-like faces of the unfortunate victims and the hideous countenances of their captors; and high and above all, perched upon the stern, with foot, tail and horns, and the chief insignias of his office, is his Satanic Majesty, gloating over the whole scene.
>
> What is more truthful than that the devil is ever the firm friend and companion of the slave ship.[44]

America is no pre-lapsarian Paradise for the artist to restore. It is deeply fallen, and the artist has exposed its diabolic condition. Wilson's sudden shift from the observation of nature to the grotesque encounter subverts the aesthetic of revelation, which suggested God's truth would reveal itself if the world was handled correctly. Here, the revelation is horrific: a face-to-face encounter with evil. This would be an absurd and exaggerated scene, Wilson implies, were it not for the awful fact of its spiritual and physical truth.

A later picture reveals George Washington's Mount Vernon—a shrine to white people's history of freedom—as a site of profound corruption. 'The consuming fingers of decay and dilapidation mark each and every house. Every old slave hut, like so many spectres, shadows forth decay. Decay stands staring in the gate-ways, staring in the porches, staring in the cellars.'[45] The Gothic mode emphasizes the skeletons in the closet of white history. Ethiop continues:

> The first thing here that arrests the eye is the recently dug up coffin of Washington; just behind which stands the body of his faithful old slave and body servant; while in front a living slave of today stands, with the bones of Washington gathered up in his arms and labelled 'For Sale' 'Price $200,000; this negro included.' 'Money wanted.'—A number of other slaves, men, women, and children, are placed in a row along the bank, just beyond, bearing about the neck of each the following inscription: *These negroes for sale. Money wanted.*[46]

Wilson's skill is to expose the absurdity of American hagiography, and the idealizing drives of its history, which treat Washington as a founding father of

[44] Wilson, 'Afric American Picture Gallery', 53.
[45] Wilson, 'Afric American Picture Gallery', 88.
[46] Wilson, 'Afric American Picture Gallery', 88.

freedom. In 1856, Edward Everett had delivered an 'Oration on the character of Washington' at the Mercantile Library in Boston, calling Washington 'the brightest ornament' from 'an age of wonders'.[47] 'Edward Everett, the distinguished limner of Washington, should see it [this picture]', Ethiop says, sarcastically, 'and point out its defects'.[48] Digging up Washington's coffin, and placing his bones on sale in the arms of a slave 'included in the price', Ethiop unearths the grim truth of the enslaver behind Everett's idealizing myth. Wilson's use of the Gothic and grotesque turns a mocking and resistant eye on white versions of history, and blames both Washington, and the kind of hero-worship he receives, for the origin and continuity of evil. The Cain myth lingers in the exposé of buried horror, not explicitly invoked, but latent in Wilson's stark condemnation of the violence the white man has done to his Black brothers.

Ethiop's mood-curation undercuts American idealism and visions of 'manifest destiny' with grim and uncompromising horror. These pictures are a satirical exposé of the prevailing white artistic culture of perfection and an attack on white supremacist versions of American history, disclosing the harm of pre-lapsarian fantasy. But then Ethiop takes us to a picture where the mood changes dramatically, emphasizing that such fantasy is not only the failing of white Americans. Picture No. 4 depicts 'Sunset in Abeokuta', which shows the Nigerian city as part of an unfallen world. The soft and fluid textures of Eden are everywhere apparent, and the radiant beauty of the sky is unmatched even by the sign of God's post-lapsarian covenant with Noah: 'The landscape is rich, varied and beautiful. The sky has all the warmth of hue and softness of tint, all that gorgeousness (changing seemingly with every instant,) for which an African sky is so much noted. No rainbow with us, in its full splendour, is so variegated or so wide in its range of colours.'[49] Ethiop paints a real picture of freedom. He evokes the idyllic landscape painting of Thomas Cole's followers, but he also borrows his aesthetic partly from the panoramas of anti-slavery, which used aerial perspective to give Northern viewers a feeling of unfettered moral superiority over their Southern, slave-holding, counterparts.[50] Here, instead of looking down on a tortured procession of enslaved and labouring individuals, the lofty artistic eye observes distant 'dusky' bodies

[47] Edward Everett, *Oration on the Character of Washington* (Mount Vernon, Va.: Mount Vernon Press, 1913), 9.

[48] Wilson, 'Afric American Picture Gallery', 89.

[49] Wilson, 'Afric American Picture Gallery', 54.

[50] See: Theresa A. Goddu, 'Anti-Slavery's Panoramic Perspective', *MELUS* 39.2 (Visual Culture and Race) (Summer 2014): 12–41. In *Selling Antislavery* (Philadelphia: University of Pennsylvania Press, 2002), Goddu discusses the influence of anti-slavery panoramas on Wilson's 'Picture Gallery', 212–18.

at leisure: 'The last touches of the artist's pencil has made the glow of the coming evening to softly spread itself over here and there a dusky inhabitant reclining upon the banks of an unrippled lake.'[51] Nothing troubles the still waters of this unfallen Paradise. It is, Ethiop observes, a 'scene so charming that one could almost wish to be there.'[52] But, the caveat—'almost'—is key. Wilson urges his reader to resist the seductive lure of pre-lapsarian fantasy and the illusive feeling of panoramic control. This is partly an attack on the complacency of contemporary American landscape painting, which offered the viewer neatly packaged Edenic visions; it is partly an attack on the self-satisfied quality of anti-slavery panorama, which offered viewers a feeling of moral superiority; and it is partly an attack on the emigrationist ideologies espoused by some contemporary Black writers and activists.

The Afric American Picture Gallery appeared in *The Anglo-African Magazine* alongside instalments of Martin Delaney's *Blake, or the Huts of America*, a novel about slave rebellion, which functioned as a polemic for emigration. Delaney had joined the staff of Frederick Douglass's *North Star* in 1848, but, unlike Douglass, he saw no future for Black people in white America. In 1836, Emerson had used his figure of the 'Orphic Poet' to urge his fellow Americans to 'build therefore [their] own world': 'all that Adam had, all that Caesar could, you have and can do.'[53] Delaney saw no reason to believe Black people could own this privilege in a land where they were, or ever had been, enslaved. But, as Paul Gilroy observes, he sought a version of power for the Black man in the white world that was similarly rooted in patriarchal structures.[54] Delaney propagated an avowedly separatist, anti-Emersonian, narrative of dominion and self-making. In 1852, he published *The Condition, Elevation, Emigration, and Destiny of the Colored People of the United States*, which made him one of the best-known public advocates for mass emigration: 'we are a nation within a nation,' he declared, 'all that is left for us to do is to *make* ourselves the "lords of terrestrial creation." The land is ours, there it lies with inexhaustible resources; let us go and possess it. In Eastern Africa must rise up a nation to whom all the world must pay commercial tribute.'[55] In 1859, Delaney led an emigration commission to West Africa to explore possible sites for settlement along the Niger River.

[51] Wilson, 'Afric American Picture Gallery', 54.

[52] Wilson, 'Afric American Picture Gallery', 54.

[53] Emerson, 'Nature', *Selected Essays*, 80–1.

[54] See Paul Gilroy, *The Black Atlantic: Modernity and Double Consciousness* (London: Verso, 1993), 25–6.

[55] Martin R. Delaney, *The Condition, Elevation, Emigration and Destiny of the Coloured People of the United States* (Clifton, NJ: African Tree Press, 2015), 11 and 203.

In Wilson's *Picture Gallery*, the image of Africa as a New Eden is a seductive delusion: a distraction from the fight for freedom and citizenship. Wilson makes his point partly through Ethiop's mood-curation. 'Sunset in Abeokuta' is positioned between two pictures that construct, as well as critique, a narrative of belonging. Immediately beforehand, Ethiop shows us 'Picture No. 3. The First Martyr of the Revolution'. The painting is of Crispus Attucks, shot twice in the chest during the Boston Massacre of 1770. Ethiop narrates:

> This is the head of Attucks. It may not be generally known, and it may not be desirable that the public should know that the first martyr of the American Revolution was a colored man; that the first bosom that was bared to the blast of war was black; the first blood that drenched the pathway which led up to the path of liberty was from the veins of a colored man.
>
> And yet such is the fact.[56]

This was not, in fact, a fact. Crispus Attucks was commonly regarded as the first casualty of the American Revolution because he was thought to be the first person killed in the Boston Massacre. But 11-year-old Christopher Seider had been shot a few weeks earlier. Historians disagree on whether Attucks was enslaved or free but it is agreed that he was of Wampanoag and African descent. Here, as with all origin myths, the claim to the 'first' carries immediate authority and a sense of authenticity and validation. Black writers of the antebellum period frequently invoked the first 'martyrs' of the revolution as a symbol of shared foundational blood sacrifice and the fraternal right to citizenship.[57]

The Convention of Colored Citizens, held at Albany, in 1840, declared that Black people had been made Cain in a land where they had truly been Abel: 'we were made aliens and strangers in the country of our birth; a disenfranchised class in the very land where lie the bones of our fathers... whose soil is enriched by their purest and noblest blood'.[58] In Ezekiel, the valley of dry

[56] Wilson, 'Afric American Picture Gallery', 54.

[57] Attucks's active resistance against the British prompted some white Americans to treat him as a hero and 'martyr' for independence, but others resisted that narrative as potentially threatening to white supremacy. See Jennifer C. James, *A Freedom Bought with Blood: African American War Literature from the Civil War to World War II* (Durham, NC: University of North Carolina Press, 2007), 1–3.

[58] Minutes of the State Convention of Colored Citizens, Held at Albany, on the 18th, 19th, and 20th of August, 1840, for the purpose of considering their political condition, 30. All convention records accessed via the *Coloured Conventions Project* (https//colouredconventions.org).

bones, invoked in the reference to 'the very land where lie the bones of our fathers', holds the promise of spiritual and national resurrection:

> Son of Man, these bones are the whole house of Israel: behold they say: Our bones are dried, and our hope is lost: we are cut off from our parts...Thus sayeth the Lord GOD, Behold I will take the children of Israel from among the heathen, whither they be gone, and will gather them on every side, and bring them into their own land. And I will make them one nation...and they shall be no more two nations.[59]

Mixing images of blood-sacrifice, resurrection, reunion, and divine will, the Black citizens of Albany sanctified their claim to the land and their intrinsic belonging in the disconnected American body politic, implying that white and Black should be no more 'two nations' but 'one nation' under God.

In 1848, the Black citizens of Pennsylvania accused white Americans of betraying this foundational sacrifice for freedom. Only with a united, and fully free, body politic, would the sacrifice be redeemed: 'Then, and not until then, will the martyred blood that washed your virgin soil have produced trees of liberty, from which mankind may, without the distinction of complexion, pluck the heaven-born fruit.'[60] The Liberty Tree was the name given to an elm tree that was the site of the first act of colonial defiance against British rule in 1765. Felled by Loyalist Nathanial Coffin Jr, in August 1775, it became a symbol of revolutionary spirit. In this construction, the foundational blood sacrifice of the revolutionary 'martyrs' is the fertile ground of the ideal republic. '[T]rees of liberty' reconstruct the forbidden fruit of the Tree of Knowledge as the 'heaven-born fruit' of democratic freedom. The new Republic is deeply fallen, but it is also able to represent a lost utopian ideal; and it is not without the hope of redemption.

Eighteenth-century discourses of incipience and growth suggest a fortunate fall is still possible as the newly born nation comes to maturity. America is at the point of pubescence. The foundational blood sacrifice of the revolution becomes a sacred moment of common origin, imagined (falsely) as a moment of equality, betrayed by the catastrophic sin of slavery and the fallen condition of racist division. Thus the authors declare: 'we make no foreign issue with you—we place ourselves on your own declaration of rights and principles. On these hang our future hope, and with them we will stand or

[59] Ezek. 37: 11 and 21–2.

[60] 'Appeal to the Voters of the Commonwealth of Pennsylvania', Minutes of the State Convention of the Colored Citizens of Pennsylvania, convened at Harrisburg, Dec 13th and 14th 1848, 8–12, 10–11.

fall.'[61] Like Rousseau, they imply that, if we can get the moment of maturity right, and recover an imagined original wholeness and unity, then the future may be one of progress rather than decline. Foundational sacrifice exerts an old and sacred claim to origin: thus, Black Americans remind their white brothers that they make, and are, 'no foreign issue'.

The 'Appeal to the Colored Citizens of Pennsylvania', also recorded in the minutes of the 1848 convention, makes the fraternal blood betrayal even more explicit:

> and the most humiliating part in the whole drama is the contemplation that we are forced to contend for our rights with the sons of those conquerors who shed their blood and battling with the same enemy and in defence of the same glorious principles, and whose ashes have produced trees of liberty, under which their posterity may not only be protected from the storms of despotism, but may repose in peaceful security beneath their branches...we have marked their issue—and nailed our flag to their complexional standard...we will be found fiercely combating the enemies of natural rights, and Providence...All we ask of them is that they 'take their feet from off our necks', and that we may stand free and erect like themselves...all we desire is that they practice their own professed principles.[62]

The quotation, 'take their feet from off our necks', became, and remains, a powerful refrain of anti-racist campaigning. Its source is women's rights. In 1837, the white Southern abolitionist and women's rights activist, Sarah Grimké, penned a series of *Letters on the Equality of the Sexes*, which set out to undermine and rebut the deliberately sexist exegesis commonly applied to Genesis 1–3. 'All I ask of our brethren', she writes, scathingly:

> is that they will take their feet from off our necks, and permit us to stand upright on the ground which God designed us to occupy. If he has not given us the rights which have, as I conceive, been wrested from us, we shall soon give evidence of our inferiority, and shrink back into that obscurity, from which the high souled magnanimity of man has assigned us our appropriate sphere.[63]

[61] 'Appeal to the Voters of the Commonwealth of Pennsylvania', 11.

[62] 'An Appeal to the Colored Citzens of Pennsylvania', Minutes of the State Convention of the Colored Citizens of Pennsylvania, convened at Harrisburg, Dec 13th and 14th 1848, 12–22, 19–21.

[63] Sarah Grimké, 'Letter II: Women Subject Only to God', in *On Slavery and Abolitionism: Essays and Letters*, ed. Sarah Grimké and Angelina Grimké (London: Penguin, 2014), 35–8, 35–6.

Grimké's address to her oppressive 'brethren' undermines patriarchal authority in the same way as the story of Cain and Abel undermines white supremacism. Brothers are equals. Grimké accuses men of a crime against God in the oppression of women. It became a rallying call of anti-racist campaigners on the same grounds. White supremacy is a corruption of the 'natural rights' for which the foundational sacrifice of the new Republic was made. The 'free and erect' Black man or woman resurrects the symbolic hope of America.[64] The Black body is the body politic.

Positioning the head of Attucks, 'The First Martyr of the Revolution', before 'Sunset at Abeokuta', Wilson draws on this iconography of foundational sacrifice and blood betrayal to heighten his critique of emigration. At the same time, he resists the sentimentality of sacrifice with an abrupt shift in tone: 'the first blood that drenched the pathway which led up to the path of liberty was from the veins of a colored man. And yet such is the fact.'[65] Pictures 5 and 6 then show the Southern and Northern portions of 'The Underground Railroad' and reiterate the symbolic status of the Black body as a synechdoche of the broken body politic, which can be restored only with emancipation and equal rights:

> In the first view we have but the feet and legs; indicating the mysterious manner in which those feet and legs move bodies towards freedom ... The head, the recognised seat of the mind, is useless to the slave or, if of service to him, this thinking apparatus is not his own; it belongs to his owner; hence he makes use of his feet and legs, or the physical machinery; whereas in the second view, at the northern end of this undefinable Road, where liberty is, the head or mental part, is presented to view. The slave—the chattel,—the thing is a *man*.[66]

The escape is a remembering, piecing together body parts to reveal the whole man the slave has always been. Moving from the slave-holding South to the free North, feet to head of body and nation, Wilson remembers the broken body politic by conjoining the Black body and mind. If Delaney saw no future for Black bodies in the American body politic, Wilson saw no future for the American body politic without Black bodies.

[64] 'An Appeal to the Colored Citzens of Pennsylvania', 19–21.
[65] Wilson, 'Afric American Picture Gallery', 54.
[66] Wilson, 'Afric American Picture Gallery', 55.

Mental freedom, the acquisition of knowledge—and particularly literacy—was a frequent trope in emancipation literature and helped construct the narrative of a fortunate fall. Frederick Douglass describes learning to read as: 'a new and special revelation, explaining dark and mysterious things'.[67] 'From that moment', he declares, 'I understood the pathway from slavery to freedom'.[68] Wilson uses the trope to suggest a fortunate fall into knowledge for the reader as well as the fugitive. The reader sees the man as he always was, reduced only by his enslaved condition. '[T]he man must be so much that he must make all circumstances indifferent', Emerson had written, with some sense of despair, in 'Self-Reliance', as he resigned himself to the slipping and sliding of mood.[69] Wilson is uncompromising: a slave cannot make circumstance indifferent. A later picture, titled 'Condition', draws the attention of a crowd of visitors to the gallery. The condition of the figure is 'abject wretchedness...a face marked with ignorance and the indifference of stolid content'.[70] Wilson stages a lively, and familiar, debate on self-making between a doctor, a philosopher, a sceptic, and a 'lady from abroad'. A brisk 'old lady' reprimands them all: 'you young folks' talk is altogether too metaphorical for me'.[71] The scene is partly a satire of Northern intellectualism. It is also a polemic for abolition, which resists the self-indulgent moral superiority of anti-slavery. Abolition is not an Edenic fantasy, Wilson implies. Nor is it enough to philosophize about freedom: conditions can, and must, change.

Wilson's project is satirical and political, but it is also deeply imaginative. Like Dickinson, he invests in the imaginative structures of errancy: the poetic reordering of existence. We feel the wandering aesthetic the minute Ethiop takes us into his gallery, already a secluded and secretly subversive space. Ethiop's behaviour destabilizes the dictated narrative: 'If ever an abiding love for any branch of *Art* is indicative of a fitness to pursue it, then I should have been a painter...Fate marked out a rougher, sterner, destiny for me. But the habit of rambling in search of, and hunting up curious, old, or rare pictures, is as strong as ever'.[72] His rambling curiosity is constructive. It establishes an alternative to Emerson's 1850 collection, *Representative Men*, with the same didactic intent.[73] 'Pictures are teaching by example', declares Ethiop, before taking the reader to a portrait of Toussaint L'Ouverture, the General and

[67] *Narrative of Frederick Douglass*, 39. [68] *Narrative of Frederick Douglass*, 39.

[69] Emerson, 'Self-Reliance' (1841), *Selected Essays*, 185.

[70] Wilson, 'Afric American Picture Gallery', 243.

[71] Wilson, 'Afric American Picture Gallery', 244.

[72] Wilson, 'Afric American Picture Gallery', 52.

[73] The work also bears comparison with Washington Irving's *The Sketchbook of Geoffrey Crayon*, first published serially between 1819 and 1820.

leader of the Haitian revolution, whom Wilson had wanted to see in the Brooklyn gallery and who, Ethiop declares, 'led the breathings of this people after liberty'.[74] A portrait of the Haitian Emperor Souloque and his Court stands as a rejection of minstrelsy and mockery.[75] 'Madam', says Ethiop, to a supercilious lady who sniffs at the paintings: 'these pictures on the whole make no claim to the high artistic merit you look for in them, though I think some of them rather clever as works of *art*; but they serve as simple reminders of what people of color were, now are, and yet will be'.[76] Thus, the second instalment ends, with a selection of strong and successful Black revolutionary figures, who represent a real and possible alternative to the lives depicted in portraits of abject and fugitive slaves. Ethiop's errant rambling and unearthing of seemingly random and jumbled curiosities is quite purposeful. Cain may have buried Abel, but Ethiop has opened the ground.

Wilson both invokes and resists the tyranny of type. The third paper introduces 'A New Picture', the allegorical character of Thomas Onward:

> not an *Old Tom*; nor an *Uncle Tom*, nor a *Saintly Tom*, nor even what is commonly deemed a *good Tom*; but a shrewd little rogue, a real live *Young Tom*, up to all conceivable mischief and equal to all emergencies. He is a perfect model of a little fellow in his way, and a fair representative of his class... The American Nation, if it can, may try its hardened hand a few centuries longer upon our live little Tom; but it will hardly mould him to their liking. Like gold ore he will lose but the alloy and become brighter and brighter in the oft passing through the furnace of their oppression.[77]

Wilson plays on the difficult idea that sacrifice makes suffering worthwhile. Oppression becomes a baptism of fire. The violence Tom suffers tends towards the refinement and strength of the Black race. The material resistance of Thomas Onward turns allegory towards a rejection of racist figures. This is a powerful image of survival: matter that resists the fire of the forge. But Wilson is also struggling here with the *need* for types in visions of progress. 'A real live Young Tom', a flesh and blood figure, comes up against a representative Tom; the life of a man must also tell the story of a people.

The imaginative space of the picture gallery subversively reorders the received reading of the world. Ethiop praises the heresy of 'the unruly, the

[74] Wilson, 'Afric American Picture Gallery', 87.
[75] Wilson, 'Afric American Picture Gallery', 87–8.
[76] Wilson, 'Afric American Picture Gallery', 90.
[77] Wilson, 'Afric American Picture Gallery', 100.

sceptical, the worthless of the flock—the wicked ones'.[78] From this group come the strongest rebels and revolutionaries: 'our Nat Turners...the Margaret Garners...our Douglasses and our Browns'.[79] The revisionary potential of Ethiop's wandering aesthetic comes to the fore when he shows us a picture of 'The Black Forest'. Looking at the painting, he magically, or providentially, receives a mysterious invitation to visit the source and 'examine some pictures and other curiosities'.[80] On meeting his host, Bernice, who emerges later as an artist and the father of Thomas Onward, he experiences another fortunate fall: 'never before did I witness such a flood of knowledge poured forth from the lips of man'.[81] Ethiop makes an astonishing discovery with this man: a tablet 'of brown sand-stone, thirty-six inches square, and three in thickness, engraved on one side only'.[82] The tablet is a clear subversion of Mosaic Law and received wisdom. The layout mirrors biblical chapter and verse and the style apes biblical prosody. Dated to the year 4000, it addresses 'those who live in 'this age of pure light and perfect liberty'.[83] In this early example of Afrofuturism, the message is clear: to change the future one must take hold of, and subvert, the world-shaping discourses of the past. Thus, Ethiop exclaims: 'Is it fiction, is it history, is it prophecy! Who can tell?'[84]

The tablet recounts the history of 'The Amecans, or Milk White Race', and tells of an age of chattel slavery in the nineteenth and twentieth centuries. The portrait of the Amecans draws from nineteenth-century African and African American myths of whiteness as the mark of Cain. Writing as the Brooklyn correspondent for *Frederick Douglass' Paper*, Wilson had criticized the way in which a republican sense of the commonwealth had been hijacked by the greedy and callous self-interest of white supremacism: 'the propensity for *grasping* and *appropriating*', he wrote, 'are as indelibly stamped in every face as the mark of Cain'.[85] The 'milk white' skin of the Amecans is a sign of corruption rather than purity, and associated with exile and wickedness: 'their faces were like the chalk of foreign hills, yea like unto the evil spirit'. Like Cain, they are builders of immoral cities, driven by greed and avarice. Their whiteness becomes a contagion, aligned with the spread of imperialism: 'the seas were whitened with their sails'. Like Cain, before he is cursed, they are, in

[78] Wilson, 'Afric American Picture Gallery', 217.
[79] Wilson, 'Afric American Picture Gallery', 217.
[80] Wilson, 'Afric American Picture Gallery', 101.
[81] Wilson, 'Afric American Picture Gallery', 103.
[82] Wilson, 'Afric American Picture Gallery', 174.
[83] Wilson, 'Afric American Picture Gallery', 174.
[84] Wilson, 'Afric American Picture Gallery', 174.
[85] *Frederick Douglass' Paper* (26 Feb. 1852).

their strength: 'wonderful tillers of the soil, making it yield in its abundance'. In sacrificing their brothers for wealth and power, they have worshipped false Gods, and suffered the price:

> And they wrapped themselves up in their ease and luxury in hopeful security; and their hand slackened; and great physical and mental weakness came over them; and many changes came in among them... And these people dwindled at last to leanness, and their bones became small, and thin, and so did their statues, and their minds became feeble, so much so that they wist not what they did; and finally they disappeared from the children of men.[86]

The Amecans vanish without trace. They have no place in collective memory, no statues, no records, no position in the pantheon of the arts. No one has ever heard of them. Their fate recalls that of the idolatrous Israelites at Sinai: 'And Moses returned unto the LORD and said, Oh this people have sinned a great sin, and have made them gods of gold...And the LORD said unto Moses, Whosoever hath sinned against me, him shall I blot out of my book.'[87] Three thousand die in the camp at Sinai, slain by their brothers upon the order of divine vengeance. Wilson's alternative cosmology is an undisguised threat.

The parallel between the fate of the Amecans and the white slave-holding race of Americans intensifies when Bernice shows Ethiop another living picture: a monstrous captive, the enslaver and murderer of his son, kept chained in retribution. Bernice's revenge is a version of the curse of Cain, which also recalls the punishment of Prometheus:

> I will not harm a hair of his head; but so long as he lives that gloomy cell shall be his prison-house, and these chains he is now bearing about with him in his sleeping moments and in his long waking hours, shall be his only earthly companions, and when he dies, as die he must, I will cast his carcass forth to gorge the *Vultures* that sit upon the mountain peaks of the Black Forest.[88]

Taken from his home and family, the enslaver is condemned to a fate which both echoes the curse of Cain and, in its allusion to Prometheus, puts the enslaver in the position of the Black men, women, and children sacrificed on

[86] Wilson, 'Afric American Picture Gallery', 175.
[87] Exod. 32: 31–3.
[88] Wilson, 'Afric American Picture Gallery', 177.

the altar of American slavery. It recalls Frederick Douglass's outrage at the public delight in the recapturing of the fugitive slave, Anthony Burns, in 1854. Douglass wrote, with heavy sarcasm, of the jubilation, suggesting that the Promethean enterprise of America, the bold new Republic, was devouring its own soul: 'How sweet to the ear and heart of every true American are the shrieks of Anthony Burns, as the American eagle sends his remorseless beak and bloody talons into him! How grateful to the taste and pleasant to the eye, is the warm blood of the sable fugitive. He is now getting his dessert.'[89] The paper also printed a sermon, by Theodore Parker, which compared the brutal violence of the Fugitive Slave Act to the reflexive violence of Cain, and imagined Burns within the sacrificial typology of Abel and Christ: 'Then listen to the voice of the crucified..."Where is Anthony Burns, thy brother? I was a stranger, and you sought my life; naked and you rent away my skin; in prison and you delivered me to the tormentors—fate far worse than death. Inasmuch as you did it to Anthony Burns, you did it to me."'[90] In 1848, William Wells Brown had edited a collection of anti-slavery verse, titled *The Anti-Slavery Harp*. The cover again deployed Promethean imagery, showing the ravening eagle of America attacking a prostrate Black woman, as she attempts to shield her child, in full view of the US Capitol and the American flag. Like the fate of the Amecans, Bernice's revenge is both an Old Testament eye for an eye and another example of the reflexive violence of Cain and an example of the Promethean spirit turned in upon itself.

The Afric American Picture Gallery announces the post-lapsarian origins of American nationhood. It depicts a usable past and demands a better future. Wilson is fully cognizant of the ways in which narratives of belonging depend on notions of foundational sacrifice. Thus, he suggests the blood of Attucks has consecrated the ground. In the character of Thomas Onward, he raises the prospect of suffering as a baptism of fire, which tends towards the refinement and strengthening of the race. But Thomas Onward also becomes an example of material resistance, positioning the historical consciousness of the *Afric American Picture Gallery* as intensely future-facing. 'The Black Forest' episode suggests Wilson understood the risk in religious narratives of sacrifice, which need suffering and death to be *for* something better. Keeping the enslaver and murderer of his son captive until the day when vultures will pluck at his corpse, Bernice turns the sacrificial narrative back on the

[89] 'Anthony Burns Returned to Slavery', *Frederick Douglass' Paper* (9 June 1854): 2.

[90] 'Crime Against Humanity: A Sermon Preached at the Music Hall, Boston, Sunday, June 4th, 1854, by Rev. Theodore Parker', *Frederick Douglass' Paper* (16 June 1854): 1–2, 2.

perpetrators of its violence. Wilson presents the reflexive violence of Cain without sentiment. The Promethean myth is turned in upon itself. Blood will have blood.

Sacrifice without Submission: Brown's *Clotelle* (1867) and Truth's *Book of Life* (1875)

The end of the Civil War was often imagined as a turning point: a possible salvation that, if missed, would be another catastrophic fall and a second national betrayal. In October 1865, the Black citizens of California expressed the deaths of Black soldiers on the battlefield as a blood sacrifice that laid a fundamental claim on the future of the nation: 'we have consecrated every battlefield of the country with our blood . . . This is our land, where we have had our birth, for it we have fought and bled, here we will remain, as a race, until eternities [sic] thunders shake us from this soil.'[91] As in the antebellum period, images of blood-letting helped construct the rights of Black citizens, establishing a sacred claim to a common origin. 'There is nothing new in it', declared the Black citizens of Arkansas, in December 1865: 'we have voted, and we desire to exercise the privilege granted us heretofore, as our inalienable right...we wrote the contract in blood...our future is sure.'[92] Laying claim to the foundations of America was a deliberate strategy, which exposed its hypocrisy. The myth of a New Eden reinforced common origin and insisted on a moment of national redemption and rebirth:

> We dream no more—our country wakes at last
> And reads wise lessons from the stormy past.
> The spirit of the nation, proud and free,
> Might err and wander, reft of memory;
>
> But linked to truth, magnetic poles of yore,
> The dead sense wakens and she sins no more.
> The drama moves, the people fill the stage,
> And virtue will restore the golden age.[93]

[91] Proceedings of the California State Convention of the Colored Citizens, Held in Sacramento on the 25th, 26th, 27th, and 28th of October, 1865, 17, 19.

[92] Proceedings of the Convention of Colored Citizens of the State of Arkansas: held in Little Rock, Thursday, Friday and Saturday, Nov. 30, Dec. 1 & 2. 1865, 192.

[93] Proceedings of the Convention of Colored Citizens of the State of Arkansas,193–4.

America could be the symbol it has falsely claimed, but only with equal rights. The Pennsylvania State Equal Rights' League employed similar tactics, echoing Edward Everett's speech at Gettysburg: 'the unswerving loyalty and patriotism of our colored soldiers and sailors, as evidenced by their unsullied courage, their sacrifice of life, the effusion of blood, and the successful victories they have achieved, demand for them an admission into the arena of true manhood and freedom by giving them the right to vote'.[94] Everett had blamed the South for the war, declaring that: 'the only hope of drawing any of the other slaveholding States into the conspiracy was in bringing about a conflict of arms, and "firing the heart of the South" by the effusion of blood'.[95] He emphasized the tribute due to all those who 'nobly sacrificed their lives'. Using Everett's words, the demand for Equal Rights insisted Black soldiers be included in that collective sacrifice, and in the national resurrection. Blood sacrifice therefore reinforced Black rights to citizenship partly by reclaiming the mythic origins of the nation from the corruption of white supremacist doctrines of 'blood purity'. The blood of Black martyrs had not only consecrated the ground of freedom but had mixed there with the blood of their white brothers.

The demand emphasized the need for solidarity among Black citizens:

> separation in feeling, division in interest and counsel, and a general want of confidence in each other, are the main causes of our inability to obtain redress for the many cruel wrongs of the past, and security against them in the future. These we regard as the causes. The effect needs but little delineation... It is to remain as we are, a stolid mass, with vigor enough to play the part of a second Cain, and insensible of the golden opportunity which presents itself to struggle for our birth-right.[96]

The identification with Cain is deliberately subversive. In this formulation, Cain is not the oppressor, but the wronged brother, unfairly treated by the father. In this way, the story of Cain and Abel anticipates the later story of

[94] Proceedings of the Annual Meeting of the Pennsylvania State Equal Rights' League. Held in the City of Harrisburg, August 9th and 10th, 1865, 145–6.

[95] 'Address by Hon. Edward Everett', in *Address of Hon. Edward Everett at the Consecration of the National Cemetery at Gettysburg, 19th November, 1863, with the Dedicatory Speech of President Lincoln, and the Other Exercises of the Occasion; Accompanied by an Account of the Origin of the Undertaking and of the Arrangement of the Cemetery Grounds, and by a Map of the Battle-Field and Plan of the Cemetery* (Boston: Little, Brown & Co., 1864). 29–82, Edward Everett, *Orations and Speeches on Various Occasions*, vol. 4 (Boston: Little, Brown, & Co., 1885), 622–59.

[96] Proceedings of the Annual Meeting of the Pennsylvania State Equal Rights' League, 138.

Jacob and Esau. The assertive violence of Cain provides a point of comparison and contrast with the stolid and submissive Esau, who, starving after a day's hunting, sells his birthright for a mess of pottage, exploited by his jealous, cunning, brother. The fraternal conflict foreshadows the conflict and inequality of peoples: 'And the LORD said unto her, Two nations are in thy womb, and two manner of people shall be separated from thy bowels; and the one people shall be stronger than the other people; and the elder shall serve the younger.'[97] Arguing that a united body would have 'vigor enough to play the part of a second Cain' and 'struggle for our birth-right', the Address urges Black citizens not to play the part of Esau and subject themselves to a life of second-class citizenship. This is not a call to arms, but it is an uncompromised ultimatum on equal rights with an unconcealed threat. With 'vigor enough to play the part of a second Cain', Black citizens could rise up against their oppressive brethren. As Gregory Laski has argued: 'representing revenge was one part of the process of gaining a foothold as a citizen in the Reconstruction-era nation.'[98]

Revenge is an important counter-narrative to pious and sentimental depictions of self-sacrifice. In Frances Harper's 1892 novel, *Iola Leroy*, Tom Anderson is a Christ-like figure, enlisting in the Union army and sacrificing his life for his fellow soldiers. In an earlier work, *Minnie's Sacrifice*, serialized in *The Christian Recorder* in 1869, the lesson is 'that it is braver to suffer with one's own branch of the human race.'[99] Black writers of Reconstruction faced a difficult task in constructing a usable past. On the one hand, sentimental depictions of the blood shed by Black soldiers, like the blood of Attucks, became an image of foundational sacrifice—a claim to the land. They could also whitewash brutality. William Wells Brown became increasingly cognizant of this risk as he revised his 1850 novel *Clotel, or the President's Daughter* in 1867. In the earlier novel, the white heiress, Georgiana, who is 'in favour of immediate emancipation', invokes the foundational sacrifice of Attucks in support of Black people's right to belong in America.[100] The later version, *Clotelle, or the Colored Heroine: A Tale of Southern States*, treats foundational sacrifice with much more scepticism. Clotelle's husband, Jerome, enlists in the 'Native Guards', the first Black regiment. Brown holds the accepted line,

[97] Gen. 25: 23.

[98] Gregory Laski, 'Reconstructing Revenge: Race and Justice After the Civil War', *American Literature* 91.4 (Dec. 2019): 751–81, 760.

[99] Frances E. W. Harper, *Minnie's Sacrifice, Sowing and Reaping, Trial and Triumph: Three Rediscovered Novels'* (Boston: Beacon Press, 1994), 91.

[100] William Wells Brown, *Clotel, or the President's Daughter* (London: Penguin, 2004), 134.

praising the heroism of the soldiers, and their sacrifice for 'Republican institutions'. But he writes: 'There was, however, one scene, the closing one in the first day's attack on Port Hudson, which, while it reflects undying credit upon the bravery of the negro, pays but a sorry tribute to the humanity of the white general who brought the scene into existence.'[101] The callous white general, who is no virtuous Northern abolitionist, asks his Black subordinates to volunteer to recover the corpse of another (presumably white) officer. Four by four, the men advance, and are 'cut down'.[102] Brown is clear that this is a massacre and a collective suicide. The deaths are purposeless. There is no sacrificial dative: no sense that the men die *for* something better: 'Twelve men had been killed in the effort to obtain the body of the brave Payne, but to no purpose. Humanity forbade another trial, and yet it was made.'[103] Jerome is killed in the final charge. Refusing a sentimental portrayal of his death, Brown turns an ironic eye on narratives of sacrifice: 'His head was entirely torn off by a shell. The body of the deceased officer having been rescued, an end was put to the human sacrifice.'[104]

In *The Negro in the American Rebellion*, also published in 1867, Brown gives the incident an entire chapter. Here, the attitude to sacrifice is more ambivalent. He describes what seems like senseless killing, and then concludes: 'The self-forgetfulness, the undaunted heroism, and the great endurance of the negro, as exhibited that day, created a new chapter in American history for the colored man.'[105] As Jennifer James observes, Brown seems to want to have it both ways: the deaths were both a collective suicide and a senseless massacre but the sentimental narrative of foundational sacrifice preserves them in historical record, constructs a usable past.[106] The point of a usable past is that it is future-facing. Brown implies that the chapter is yet unwritten, the sacrifice unfulfilled, the meaning of suffering and death deferred. In another episode, a soldier of the Fifty-fourth Massacchussetts Volunteers (a Black regiment) asks for fair pay to feed his family: 'Our hearts pine in bitter anguish when we look back to our loved ones at home, and we are compelled to shed many a briny tear. We have offered our lives in a sacrifice for a country that has not the magnanimity to treat us like real men.'[107]

[101] Brown, *Clotel*, appendix C, 236–48, 237. [102] Brown, *Clotel*, appendix C, 238.
[103] Brown, *Clotel*, appendix C, 238. [104] Brown, *Clotel*, appendix C, 238.
[105] William Wells Brown, *The Negro in the American Rebellion, his Heroism and his Fidelity* (Boston: Lee & Shephard, 1867), 172.
[106] See James, *Freedom Bought with Blood*, 35–6. James notes that Brown based the scene on a real incident: a non-commissioned Black officer—Captain Andre Cailloux—was killed in a poorly planned attack on the rebel works at Port Hudson, La.
[107] Brown, *Negro in the American Rebellion*, 251.

Sergeant William Walker, of Company A. Third South-Carolina Colored Troops follows suit, is court-martialled, and shot: the sentimental portrayal of sacrifice undercut by murder.

On the first anniversary of the Emancipation Proclamation, while the war was still ongoing, Brown had presented the bloodshed as an opportunity for national rebirth: 'This rebellion will extinguish slavery in our land, and the Negro is henceforth and forever to be part of the nation. His blood is to mingle with that of his former oppressor, and the two races blended in one will make a more peaceful, hardy, powerful and intellectual race than America has ever seen before.'[108] Like the petition for Equal Rights, made by the Black citizens of Pennsylvania in 1865, this presents foundational blood sacrifice as blood mixing. It is not Black sacrifice, but shared sacrifice, common humanity, that will purge racist divisions and sanctify the ground of the new republic. This was an idealistic vision rooted in a religious sensibility of hope. Real blood mixing happened when white men raped enslaved women and did nothing for the abolitionist cause. In 1867, the idealistic narrative of sacrifice and resurrection already felt precarious.[109] Undercutting the sentimental mode with realism, Brown warns his readers against the too-ready adoption of sentiment, when the reality was senseless murder. But he also suggests that we might make it make sense. Murder, or suicide, would be sacrifice, he implies, if death's dative was complete. In 1867, the 'new chapter' was yet to be written, the sacrifice made real.

Brown is less pious than Harper, less devoted to the religious narrative of sacrifice, which locates a real moral good in suffering, and his treatment of it is decidedly more secular. For both writers, however, sentiment turns religious narrative to social and moral purpose. Like Harper, Brown uses the sentimental religious construction to advocate for racial uplift, not vengeance. He alerts us, however, to the risk of platitude. In 1875, as the efforts of Reconstruction collapsed under Jim Crow, the danger was real. This was the year that Frances Titus published a new edition of the 1850 *Narrative of Sojourner Truth*, along with an edited copy of Truth's scrapbook, the *Book of Life*. Titus had first met Truth in 1856 and began collaborating with her in 1867. The *Book of Life* was an alternative history, assembled from Truth's two-volume scrapbook, selected and positioned alongside recollections and newspaper clippings. The scrapbooks, which Titus tells us Truth carried around

[108] Cited in James, *Freedom Bought with Blood*, 46–7.

[109] See: David Blight, *Race and Reunion: The Civil War in American Memory* (Cambridge, Mass.: Belknap Press, 2002).

with her, are no longer extant, but they were not uncommon ways of recording and creating Black histories of nineteenth-century America. Frederick Douglass made scrapbooks in the late 1880s and 1890s, and it is possible that earlier ones were destroyed along with others of his papers in an 1872 fire. Black civil rights activists, newspaper editors, performers, and celebrities kept scrapbooks of clippings and sometimes their own writings.

Newspaper reading, and clipping, was often promoted as a way of advancing the progress of the race. In 1864, *The Christian Recorder*, an African Methodist Episcopal newspaper based in Philadelphia, presented a dialogue between two sisters whose children fare differently in school. The children who read newspapers are far ahead of their cousins, who do not. Their mother explains that not only has she taught them to read newspapers, but 'to make a scrap-book together, in which they save all the useful, interesting little items that would otherwise be forgotten'. The article's anonymous author takes up this idea, asking: 'Will not every mother take to heart this lesson, and encourage her children to read with care the family paper, and instruct them how to preserve in readable shape the useful items they may find in it'.[110] The 1875 publication of Truth's *Narrative* together with the *Book of Life* arrived on the literary scene at a moment when the progress of the last decade seemed about to collapse and the narrative of sacrifice and resurrection proved ever more of a fallacy.

Born Isabella *c.*1797 and enslaved in the Hudson River Valley of New York until 1827, Truth never learned to read or write. She dictated her *Narrative* to her friend, Olive Gilbert, who told the story in the third person and involved her own views, publishing it in 1850. In 1884, one year after Truth's death, Titus released a final edition, with a memorial chapter. These are, therefore, heavily mediated texts, but Sojourner Truth emerges as a figure with real force and presence. The 1875 publication of the *Narrative of Sojourner Truth* and the *Book of Life* constructed Truth as an emblem of spiritual and social resurrection, recalling the energy of antebellum reform and the victory of abolition, just as Southern Democrats betrayed the hope of racial reconstruction.

The encounter feels like entering into the aesthetic experience of Wilson's *Picture Gallery*, an immersive portrait so intensely animated that it counters the degradation of oppression with mercurial vitality. In its treatment of sacrifice, the *Narrative* emphasizes a very human and compelling resistance to

[110] Ellen Gruber Garvey, *Writing with Scissors: American Scrapbooks from the Civil War to the Harlem Renaissance* (Oxford: OUP, 2012), 135.

suffering. Unlike Harper's Tom or Minnie, Brown's brave soldiers, and Wilson's 'Saintly Tom', Isabella is no willing sentimental martyr, but a woman wanting to live, bargaining with her God:[111]

> She at first commenced promising God, that if he would help her out of all her difficulties, she would pay him by being very good; and this goodness she intended as remuneration to God. She could think of no benefit that was to accrue to herself or her fellow-creatures, from her leading a life of purity and generous self-sacrifice for the good of others; as far as any but God was concerned, she saw nothing in it but heart-trying penance, sustained by the sternest exertion, and this she soon found much more easily promised than performed.[112]

Like Thomas Onward, Truth becomes an example of spiritual and material resistance.

As Nell Irvine Painter observes, Truth often puzzles readers because her narrative does not fit easily into the genre: 'expecting an account of the evils of slavery, they encounter page after page of her religious adventures'.[113] Enslaved and legally emancipated in the North, Truth's story is markedly different from those of fugitive slaves from Southern plantations. Gilbert recounts a number of Truth's experiences in racially integrated but predominantly white religious sects, which characterized the period of religious revival in the early nineteenth century known as the Second Great Awakening. Like many others, Isabella joined groups which gathered around charismatic cult leaders, styling themselves as prophets: one of the most infamous was Robert Matthews, who called himself the Prophet Matthias. The cult allowed sexual and physical violence.[114] Matthews physically abused Isabella, suppressed her preaching and forced her to work for nothing. Yet she remained loyal. Gilbert's retelling keeps Isabella above such humiliations in order to keep the iconic Sojourner Truth free of complicating contradiction, concluding with brisk cheerfulness that she 'happily escaped the contamination that surrounded her'.[115]

[111] Nell Irvin Painter notes that bargaining was an early feature of Isabella's religious practice, before her conversion to Methodism, and that her religious sensibility remained syncretic. *Sojourner Truth: A Life, a Symbol* (London: Norton, 1997), 24–5.

[112] *Narrative of Sojourner Truth: a Bondswoman of Olden Time, with a history of her labours and Correspondence drawn from her 'Book of Life'; Also, a Memorial Chapter* (London: Penguin, 1998), 41.

[113] *Narrative of Sojourner Truth*, p. xiv.

[114] Painter describes the Kingdom of Matthias in more detail in her biography, including the sexual abuse of Isabella by Ann Fogler and Isabella's willingness to testify for Matthews. *Sojourner Truth: A Life, a Symbol*, 48–61.

[115] *Narrative of Sojourner Truth*, 65.

Wanting to portray Truth as a figure of strength and hope, the *Narrative* invests deeply in the literal rendering of the symbol, and in the symbolic power of Truth's chosen name. Isabella rejects the false name of slavery and adopts the allegorical 'Sojourner Truth' on 1 June 1843: the day of Pentecost.[116] In the New Testament, Pentecost is the day that the Holy Spirit descends on the Apostles: 'And there appeared unto them cloven tongues like as of fire, and it sat upon each of them. And they were all filled with the Holy Ghost, and began to speak other tongues, as the Spirit gave them utterance.'[117] The outpouring of spirit foreshadows the Day of Judgment, and holds the promise of resurrection: 'then they that gladly received his word were baptised.'[118] Isabella recalls her religious calling, and second baptism, as a Pentecostal awakening: 'The Spirit calls me there, and I must go.'[119]

Like other inspired laymen and women, Black and white, she took to the roads to preach. Her wandering existence as an itinerant preacher becomes a living allegory of the resistance of Truth to Falsehood. Like Wilson's portrayal of Thomas Onward, both the 1850 and the 1875 editions refuse to surrender either Truth, or truth, to the tyranny of type. The unorthodoxy of true faith, and Truth's compelling resistance to expected behaviours, is everywhere apparent. It comes to the fore in the *Narrative* when Truth castigates the fanaticism of Second Advent preachers, who stir the crowd into meaningless frenzy. She accuses them of being principles of diabolic chaos and perpetrators of idolatry:

> Here you are talking about being 'changed in the twinkling of an eye.' If the Lord should come, he'd change you to *nothing*! for there is nothing to you.
>
> You seem to be expecting to go to some parlor *away up* somewhere, and when the wicked have been burnt, you are coming back to walk in ashes over their ashes—this is to be your New Jerusalem!!...I am going to stay here and *stand the fire*, like Shadrach, Meshach and Abednego! And Jesus will walk with me through the fire, and keep me from harm...Do you tell me that God's children *can't stand fire*?[120]

The Book of Daniel tells the story of these three men, who refuse to worship the false gods of the mad tyrant, King Nebuchadnezzar: 'Is it true, O Shadrach,

[116] *Narrative of Sojourner Truth*, 68. '[S]he informed Mrs. Whiting, the woman of the house where she was stopping, that her name was no longer Isabella, but SOJOURNER; and that she was going east. And to her inquiry, "What are you going east for?" her answer was, "The Spirit calls me there, and I must go".'

[117] Acts 2: 3–4. [118] Acts 2: 41.

[119] *Narrative of Sojourner Truth*, 68. [120] *Narrative of Sojourner Truth*, 76.

Meschach and Abednego, do not ye serve my gods, nor worship the golden image which I have set up?...if ye worship not, ye shall be cast the same hour into the midst of a burning, fiery, furnace; and who *is* that God that shall deliver you out my hands?'[121] Nebuchadnezzar demands that the furnace be seven times hotter than usual. Fully clothed, the men are bound and thrown into the flames. The fire is so hot that it consumes those who throw them, but the three men are miraculously unscathed, protected by a fourth who walks beside them: 'Lo, I see four men loose, walking in the midst of the fire, and they have no hurt; and the form of the fourth is like the Son of God.'[122] The miracle produces a volte-face in the tyrant King:

> Then Nebuchadnezzar spake, and said, Blessed be the God of Shadrach, Meschach and Abednego, who hath sent his angel, and delivered his servants who trusted in him, and have changed the king's word, and yielded their bodies, that they might not serve nor worship any god, except their own God.
>
> Therefore, I make a decree, That every people, nation, and language, which speak anything amiss against the God of Shadrach, Meschach and Abednego, shall be cut in pieces, and their houses shall be made a dunghill: because there is no other God that can deliver after this sort.[123]

The biblical allusion emphasizes resurrection as part of a miracle tradition, which makes an enormous demand on faith. In the eighteenth century, David Hume had placed faith in miracles such as resurrection outside of the domain of rational thought, saying that, 'no testimony for any kind of miracle has ever amounted to a probability, much less to a proof'.[124] In the febrile religious climate of antebellum America, miracles often bore the burden of revealed religion, precisely because of the demand they made on faith, asking for a belief in the immanent and mysterious workings of God in the world, and emphasizing spiritual resurrection in *this* life. Calling on the miracle tradition, the exemplarism of this scene roots revolution in revelation. Confronted with the fire of faith, tyranny and idolatry will miraculously collapse. The scene dramatizes an intense Pentecostalism: the Holy Spirit will baptize the righteous with fire.[125] The *Narrative* concludes with another, contemporary,

[121] Dan. 3: 14–15. [122] Dan. 3: 25. [123] Dan. 3: 28–9.

[124] David Hume, 'An Inquiry Concerning Human Understanding', 1748, *The Philosophical Works of David Hume* (Edinburgh: Port, 1826), vol. 4, section 10, p. 150.

[125] The source for this aspect of Pentecostal faith is Matt. 3: 11. John the Baptist declares: 'I indeed baptise you with water unto repentance, but he that cometh after me is mightier than I, whose shoes I am not worthy to bear; he shall baptise you with the Holy Ghost and with fire.'

miracle: 'A slaveholding master turned to a brother!'[126] The revelation of the brotherhood between master and slave undoes the violence of Cain in a single transformative miraculous moment of grace. Unlike *Clotelle*, which turns the religious construction of sacrifice and resurrection to social purpose, the social transformation in Truth's *Narrative* bears witness to her sincere faith in miracles and develops a version of sacrifice which does not allow for submission. The invocation of Shadrach, Meschach, and Abednego will not allow the glorification of suffering: they experience 'no hurt'.

Truth rejects fanaticism as self-serving idolatry, a nervous delusion, forged in collective fear as opposed to individual and affective faith. Idolaters, as we know from the fate of the Israelites at Sinai, are blotted from God's book. In the Old Testament, this book, the book of life, records the names of all the righteous, who shall live; the blotted, like those at Sinai, shall die. The Book of Revelation transforms this into a narrative of the afterlife: 'And whosoever was not found written in the book of life was cast into the lake of fire'.[127] True life becomes salvation and resurrection through Christ: 'the book of life of the Lamb'.[128] Death thus becomes an undoing of creation: absent names are 'slain from the foundation of the world'.[129]

Nowhere is Truth's literal enactment of the symbol of resurrection as the foundation of a new world order clearer than in her *Book of Life*. The 1875 edition, which included both the *Narrative* and the *Book of Life*, resurrected the fervid religiosity of the reforming antebellum spirit and presented a picture of racial mixing and an emblem of national resurrection just at the moment when racist segregation was becoming more violent. Frances Titus presented the charismatic itinerant preacher and former slave as a second Moses, the spiritual leader of her people:

> Slavery has been swallowed up in a Red Sea of blood, and the slave has emerged from the conflict of races, transformed from a chattel to a man. Holding the ballot, the black man enters the halls of legislation, and his rights are recognised there. 'God was not dead', and in looking back on their captivity, Sojourner sees that her people have been guided through the dark wilderness of oppression by the 'pillar of fire.'
>
> Her race now stands at the Pisgah of freedom, looking into the promised land, where the culture, which has so long been denied them can, by their own efforts, be obtained.[130]

[126] *Narrative of Sojourner Truth*, 85.
[127] Rev. 20: 15.
[128] Rev. 13: 8.
[129] Rev. 13: 8.
[130] *Narrative of Sojourner Truth*, 4.

In a Christian reading, Moses, like Abel, becomes a type of Christ: the sin offering holds the hope of resurrection. Written three years before the Federal withdrawal from the Southern States, amidst widespread lynching and the rising threat of Jim Crow, this narrative of sacrifice and resurrection had a strong, and terrible, dramatic irony. The Civil Rights Act of 1875 was the last of the major Reconstruction statutes and assured African Americans of equal treatment on public transport, public accommodations, and service on juries. The US Supreme Court declared the Act unconstitutional in 1883, and the ruling remained in place until 1964. In the period between 1875 and 1883 it was rarely enforced. Southern States began to pass Jim Crow segregation laws from the early 1870s. In 1892, the anti-lynching crusader and equal rights campaigner, Ida B. Wells, protested: 'As a hewer of wood and a drawer of water—a menial—the Afro-American is welcomed everywhere. As a man—nowhere. The race teacher or preacher who tries to cultivate man or womanhood among his people is mobbed or run away.'[131]

While the *Narrative* depicted Truth's religious wanderings and sincere faith in the miraculous transformation of society by the Holy Spirit, the *Book of Life* presented a social activist, zealously committed to reform and devoted to racial uplift. Inscribing the names of William Lloyd Garrison, Abraham Lincoln, Parker Pilsbury, Lucretia Mott, Lydia Maria Child, and numerous other white abolitionists and advocates for women's rights, Truth elides the difference between spiritual and social transformation and implicitly rejects the idea that the foundation of the new nation could ever be a segregated space. The scrapbook included extracts from newspaper articles on Truth, written by prominent abolitionists, letters she had received, and accounts of her outspoken defiance of regulation and expectation—on one occasion reportedly baring her breasts to someone who dared say she could not be a woman for she spoke as a man.[132]

In an anecdote, told by the white abolitionist Wendell Phillips, Truth listened to Frederick Douglass's stirring call to arms in 1852: 'It must come to blood; they must fight for themselves and redeem themselves, or it would never be done.'[133] According to Phillips, and related by Titus:

> Sojourner was sitting, tall and dark, on the very front seat, facing the platform; and in the hush of deep feeling, after Douglas [sic] sat down, she spoke out in her deep, peculiar voice, heard all over the house:

[131] Ida B. Wells, 'Bishop Tanner's Ray of Light', *Independent* (28 July 1892), in *The Light of Truth*, 52–6, 55.
[132] 'Book of Life', *Narrative of Sojourner Truth*, 95.
[133] 'Book of Life', *Narrative of Sojourner Truth*, 114.

> 'Frederick, is God dead?'
>
> The scene was perfectly electrical, and thrilled through the whole house, changing as by a flash the whole feeling of the audience. Not another word she said or needed to say; it was enough.[134]

'Is God dead?' was the phrase most commonly associated with Truth in the nineteenth century and Titus had it inscribed on her first gravestone.[135] This sincere faith in redemption and miracle worked against a celebration of Black sacrifice. On 14 July 1854, William Lloyd Garrison's *Liberator* reported on a 4 July Anti-Slavery meeting, at which Truth had spoken. 'It was good that white people should sometimes feel the prick', she retorted, to laughter and cheers. Suffering was not to be idealized, and Abel's blood became a sign of the righteous inevitability of divine justice, sacrifice without submission: 'Even the blood of one man, Abel, did not call from the ground in vain…God would recompense them for all their sufferings in this world'.[136]

When Baldwin concluded his heartfelt plea for inter-racial fraternity in America, he drew from the popular spiritual, 'Oh Mary, don't you weep', in a spirit of hope and energetic resistance: *'God gave Noah the rainbow sign, No more water, the fire next time!'* Sung by slaves, it became an anthem of the civil rights movement. The song relates the anguish of Mary of Bethany begging Jesus to raise her brother Lazarus from the dead and instils comfort with the story of the exodus from Egypt: freedom thus becomes a type of resurrection and the promise of new life. The 'rainbow sign' recalls another new beginning: the covenant which gave Noah and his descendants dominion over a newly washed earth and God's promise that water would never again wipe them from it. For their part, humanity were bound to avoid bloodshed: 'Whoso sheddeth man's blood, by man shall his blood be shed: for in the image of God made he man.'[137] Crimes against humanity manifest crimes against God, for in this narrative only God must have the power to create or destroy. The Flood had been a punishment for the audacity of violence: 'And God said to Noah, The end of all flesh is come before me; for the earth is filled with violence through them; and, behold, I will destroy them with the earth.'[138] The spiritual emphasizes that the rainbow is not just a mark of protection, but a warning to maintain the change. Fire, not water, will consume next time.

134 'Book of Life', *Narrative of Sojourner Truth*, 114.

135 *Narrative of Sojourner Truth*, 255 n. 93.

136 'Proceedings at the Anti-Slavery Celebration at Framingham, July 4, 1854', *The Liberator* (Boston, Friday, 14 July 1854), 1.

137 Gen. 9: 7.

138 Gen. 6: 13.

The song brings the post-lapsarian origins of African-American history to the fore. For Wilson, Brown, and Truth, the myth of the Fall was not Genesis 3 but Genesis 4: the violence that set brother against brother in a crime against God. Conceiving of this violence as sin, and of suffering and death as sacrifice, holds onto the hope of redemption. As in the colonialist myth of a New Eden, America becomes a story yet to be written. The sacrifice yet to be fulfilled means that meaning is always deferred. This has an energizing idealism. But it is also always coming up against the demands of realism, the suffering and struggle that might have no greater meaning, the knowledge that pain might not be *for* anything at all. These authors are united not by their optimism so much as their refusal to submit to pessimism. Taking control of the origin myth, and imagining the mark of Cain as white, and not Black, skin, feeds a literary tradition where future hope lies partly in changing the way the past has been told and where sacrifice is an act of resistance precisely because it submits only to God.

7
Tracing the Old Eden
Ruskin, Newman, Hopkins

'Put the print against the window', John Ruskin writes, as he instructs students to learn from Turner, in *The Elements of Drawing*:

> and trace slowly and with the greatest care every black line; retrace this on smooth drawing-paper; and, finally, go over the whole with your pen, looking at the original plate always, so that if you err at all, it may be on the right side, not making the line which is too curved or too straight already in the tracing, more curved or more straight, as you go over it.[1]

Implicit in the instruction to 'err on the right side' is an acknowledgement that the correct line may never be traced, but the effort of obedience allows for greater adherence to its direction, and attention to original source. Tracing, as Ruskin makes repeatedly clear in his pedagogical writings, is an exercise in error and self-improvement, and a discipline which aims to recover an original truth: 'the solitary student can only find out his own mistakes with the help of the traced limit'.[2] Like Blake, Ruskin imbricates aesthetics and theology in his philosophy of the line. The 'traced limit' turns on obedience and fidelity. But it also encodes the probability of error and the likelihood of doubt. As in Genesis 3, the demand for obedience paradoxically enables transgression. Human error becomes possible, and perhaps inevitable, as soon as a definitive line is drawn.

The English myth of the Fall is one in which absolutes seemed to have been lost or forgotten but are always still there, ready to be revealed. Ruskin's emphasis on discipline and obedience in draughtsmanship—tracing the lines that matter—begins from the premise that all human effort is fallen, but its very fallenness is the condition of revelation and redemption. Ruskin is continually alerting his readers to both the importance and precarity of every

[1] John Ruskin, 'The Elements of Drawing', in *Collected Works*, ed. E. T. Cook and A. Wedderburn, 39 vols (London: George Allen & Unwin: 1903–12), vol. 15, 5–233, 99.

[2] Ruskin, 'Elements of Drawing', 15.

The Myth of the Fall in Nineteenth-Century Literature. Linda Freedman, Oxford University Press.
 DOI: 10.1093/oso/9780198969570.003.0008

energetic effort. His prophetic mode anchors the secular treatment of national and personal memory in sacred time: the continuity of an absolute truth, to which we will return, despite generations of secular change. The Fall has happened and will happen; redemption—and the return to the absolute standards of Eden—will arrive only because it is always already there.

In *Modern Painters*, Ruskin stressed the duty of young artists to go to nature with obedience and faithfulness, exhorting them to: 'neither to choose, nor compose, nor imagine, nor experimentalise; but to be humble and earnest in following the steps of nature, and tracing the finger of God'.[3] Recalling a formative experience in Fontainebleau, he described tracing as the first stage in his own artistic and spiritual awakening:

> Languidly, but not idly, I began to draw it; and as I drew, the languor passed away: the beautiful lines insisted on being traced—without weariness. More and more beautiful they became, as each rose out of the rest and took its place in the air. With wonder increasing every instant, I saw that they 'composed' themselves, by finer laws than any known of men. At last, the tree was there, and everything that I had thought before about trees, nowhere![4]

Ruskin presents a very particular kind of work; one of recreative pleasure rather than irksome toil. He was alert to the connection between 'labour' and 'lapse', which share an etymological root (Latin, *labi*, to slide or glide). In an essay on 'Store-Keeping', first published in *Fraser's Magazine* in 1862, and later as the second chapter of *Munera Pulveris*, he probed the tension between post-lapsarian toil and the kind of pleasurable, recreative effort involved in drawing at Fontainebleau:

> Literally, [labour] is the quantity of 'Lapse', loss or failure of human life, caused by any effort. It is usually confused with effort itself, or the application of power (opera); but there is much effort which is merely a mode of recreation, or of pleasure. The most beautiful actions of the human body, and the highest results of the human intelligence, are conditions, or achievements, of quite unlaborious,—nay, of recreative,—effort.[5]

Like Blake, Ruskin is always trying to reconcile his faith in the divine gift of revelation with his strong Protestant work ethic and his sense that effort

[3] Ruskin, 'Modern Painters, vol. 1', in *Collected Works*, vol. 3, 77–635, 623.
[4] Ruskin, 'Praeterita', in *Collected Works*, vol. 35, 5–567, 314.
[5] Ruskin, 'Munera Pulveris', in *Collected Works*, vol. 17, 119–299, 183.

brings reward. As he recalls his experience in Fontainebleau, the beautiful line that insists on being traced appears at the meeting of labour and grace: the touch of the absolute, granted as a gift but received in the condition of recreative effort.

This chapter discusses Ruskin's warning to England in *The Stones of Venice* alongside the Catholic mythologies of a lost Eden of Englishness that emerge in the writings of John Henry Newman and Gerald Manley Hopkins. If the myth of the New Eden was part of the practice of settler colonialism, the myth of the Old Eden was part of the armoury of a broader nineteenth-century English imperialism. Tracing was Ruskin's artistic mode of expression for the imperfect recovery of a grace and truth that he felt was fast departing from the world. Tracing the memory of a great empire in the fallen stones of Venice, Ruskin's vision is strongly imperial but it is also, paradoxically, one which values humility. Before his conversion to Catholicism, John Henry Newman also urged his followers to 'habitually search out and lovingly hang over the traces of God's justice'.[6] But as a Catholic convert, he developed a different, eruptive, vocabulary for revelation and redemption. If the Protestant Eden was to be traced, the Catholic Eden would be resurrected. The scholarly Newman is always forced to tread a difficult path between the invisible trace of grace and the unerasable traces of the accumulated non-Catholic past, the 'old Eve-sin' of knowledge, which enables the intellectual flexibility and philosophical disinterestedness that he values in his quest for truth, even as it remains the mark of the Fall. But in his sermons of national resurrection, Newman preached a far more violent incarnation theology, emphasizing the startling suddenness of redemption that would come with a 'Second Spring' of English Catholicism.[7]

The aesthetic overlaps between Ruskin and Newman are strongly felt in the poetry of Gerard Manley Hopkins. The attention that Ruskin gave to the natural world, his claim that the beautiful line insists on being traced as the mark of God on the earth, had a formative effect on the young Hopkins, who immersed himself in Ruskin's writings on art and architecture and quoted him repeatedly in his journals. Ruskin taught Hopkins that art could be didactic: an index of religious and national principles. 'What are works of art for?' Hopkins wrote to Robert Bridges in 1886:

[6] John Henry Newman, 'On Justice, as a Principle of Divine Government', in *Fifteen Sermons Preached before the University of Oxford Between A.D. 1826 and 1843* (Notre Dame, Ind.: University of Notre Dame Press, 1997), 99–119, 107.

[7] John Henry Newman, 'The Second Spring', in *Sermons Preached on Various Occasions* (London: Longmans Green & Co., 1908), 163–83.

> To educate? To be standards?...A great work by an Englishmen is like a great battle won by England. It is an unfading bay tree. It will even be admired by, and praised by, and do good to those who hate England (as England is most perilously hated), who do not even wish to be benefitted by her. It is then even a patriotic duty...Let your light shine before men that they may see your good works (say, of art) and glorify yr. Father in heaven (that is acknowledge that they have an absolute excellence in them and are steps in a scale of infinite and inexhaustible excellence.)[8]

When Hopkins converted to Catholicism, he was received into the church by Newman. He chose to join the highly disciplined and active Society of Jesus, committed to the movement to win England back to her ancient and, he thought, true, faith. But it was not without struggle. The words Hopkins returns to, in his vision of Edenic recovery, are the visceral 'spring', 'stress', and 'strain'.

Ruskin, Newman, and Hopkins call for absolute standards, authority to counteract the growing trend towards relativism in nineteenth-century thought.[9] For all three, Eden belonged to sacred time: truth and the wholeness of uncorrupted origin. If the new American Eden was yet to be made, the old English Eden lay ready to be revealed. For these writers, revelation comes as a gift of grace, but it is received in the condition of energetic and effortful obedience. For the Protestant Ruskin, art critic and drawing teacher, Eden is always on the move, retreating in the soft folds of national and personal memory, and tracing becomes the mode of imperfect recovery. For Catholic Newman and Hopkins, the revelation of divine truth turns on a more immediate and agonized incarnation theology: the 'spring', 'stress', and 'strain' of the Word made flesh and the erotic drives of sacrifice and submission.

'She Forgot it without Excuse': *The Stones of Venice* and a Warning to England (1851–1853)

Between 1851 and 1853, Ruskin published a three-volume work, titled *The Stones of Venice*, in which he presented Venetian architecture as a national index of lost religious principles. 'Architecture', he declared in the first

[8] Hopkins to Bridges, Dublin, 13 Oct. 1886, in *The Letters of Gerard Manley Hopkins to Robert Bridges*, ed. Claude Colleer Abbott (London: OUP, 1935), 231.

[9] See Christopher Herbert, *Victorian Relativity: Radical Thought and Scientific Discovery* (London and Chicago: University of Chicago Press, 2001).

volume, 'is the work of nations'.[10] Tracing architectural lines became a way of recovering the pre-Reformation spirit of the nation, betrayed in what he saw as a wilful Catholic idolatry in the face of Protestant revelation. As Ruskin's biographer, Tim Hilton, explains, we can start to see Ruskin's ideas for the *Stones of Venice* forming as early as 1840 when the Ruskin family travelled across France to Italy, with the young John interrupting his studies at Oxford to recover from a serious illness. Repulsed by what he saw as the 'shadow of death' upon Rome, Ruskin corresponded eagerly with friends back home on patriotic and anti-Catholic matters. The family kept to English society in both Rome and Naples and made no apparent effort to meet any Italians. Ruskin's ideas about English superiority were easily confirmed by the expatriate prejudice of his social circle.[11]

The story that Ruskin tells of the Fall of Venice is a fall into culture: the collapse of a people who broke religious faith 'for the advancement of...private interests' and chose to worship idols of their own making.[12] The result, as in Rousseau's *Second Discourse*, is the encrustation of falsehood on the living body and soul of the nation: 'vital religion' expired, declares Ruskin, while the 'outward observance was as strict as ever'.[13] He presented Venice as a warning to England and announced his prophetic calling in terms that recalled the skills he had taught in the *Elements of Drawing*: 'to trace the lines of this image before it be forever lost and to record, as far as I may, the warning which seems to me to be uttered by every one of the fast-gaining waves, that beat like passing bells against the STONES OF VENICE'.[14] Tracing becomes a mode of salvific memory: the imperfect recovery of a grace that is fast retreating from the world.

As in New World mythology, pre-lapsarian fantasy belongs to a colonial mentality and becomes part of the armoury of imperialism. Ruskin endorses the pernicious myth of dominion: a God-given right to rule. The Fall turns not on the fact of empire, which Ruskin upholds, but on what he perceives as its idolatry. It is deeply significant, therefore, that Ruskin begins with the example of the biblical empire of Tyre, whose Fall and punishment was also the result of idolatry: the crime of the misplaced absolute:

[10] Ruskin, 'The Stones of Venice', in *Collected Works*, vols 9–11, vol. 9, 289.

[11] Tim Hilton, *John Ruskin* (New Haven and London: Yale University Press, 2002), 58–9.

[12] Ruskin, 'Stones of Venice', *Collected Works*, vol. 9, 24.

[13] Ruskin, 'Stones of Venice', *Collected Works*, vol. 9, 31. In the *Second Discourse*, Rousseau had described the fall into culture as the acceptance of outward show at the cost of inward truth: a 'semblance of peace [purchased] at the price of true felicity'.

[14] Ruskin, 'Stones of Venice', *Collected Works*, vol. 9, 17.

> Since first the dominion of men was asserted over the oceans, three thrones, of mark beyond all others, have been set upon its sands: the thrones of Tyre, Venice and England. Of the first of these great powers only the memory remains; of the Second, only the ruin; the Third, which inherits their greatness, may be led through prouder eminence, to less pitied destruction.[15]

Described in Nehemiah as a successful sea-faring nation of merchants and fishwives, the people of Tyre become greedy, selling even on the Sabbath day.[16] The Prince of Tyre is an over-reacher and an idolater, who worships his own status over God. Ezekiel prophesies his downfall:

> By thy great wisdom and by thy traffick hast thou increased thy riches, and thine heart is lifted up because of thy riches: Therefore, thus saith the Lord GOD; Because thou has set thine heart as the heart of God; Behold, therefore I will bring strangers upon thee, the terrible of the nations: and they shall draw their swords against the beauty of thy wisdom, and they shall defile their brightness.[17]

In his arrogance, the Prince of Tyre commits a version of the 'old Eve-sin'. The serpent in Genesis 3 tempts Eve with the prospect that she and Adam will 'be as gods, knowing good and evil'.[18] Like Eve, the Prince of Tyre destroys his God-given right to dominion because he dares to imagine himself equal. Ezekiel tells him of his sin: 'thou hast said I am a God, I sit in the seat of God, in the midst of the seas, yet thou art a man, and not a God'.[19]

Ezekiel draws another parallel with Genesis when he declares that the Prince of Tyre 'art the anointed cherub that covereth...thou hast walked up and down in the midst of the stones of fire'.[20] The allusion is to the cherubim placed at the east of Eden in the last verse of Genesis 3, 'with a flaming sword, which turned every way, to keep the way of the tree of life'.[21] But the Prince of Tyre, like the fallen angels and humans before him, has collapsed under the sin of vain idolatry: 'Thine heart was lifted up because of thy beauty, thou hast corrupted thy wisdom by reason of thy brightness.'[22] Tertullian explicitly connected the Prince of Tyre with Satan, who was good before he fell.[23]

[15] Ruskin, 'Stones of Venice', *Collected Works*, vol. 9, 17.

[16] 'There dwelt men of Tyre even therein, which brought fish and all manner of ware, and sold on the Sabbath unto the children of Judah, and in Jerusalem.' Neh. 13:16.

[17] Ezek. 28: 5–7. [18] Gen. 3: 5. [19] Ezek. 28: 2.

[20] Ezek. 28: 14. [21] Gen. 3: 24. [22] Ezek. 28: 17.

[23] Hector M. Patmore, *Adam, Satan and The King of Tyre: The Interpretation of Ezekiel 28:11–19 in Late Antiquity* (Leiden: Brill, 2012), 43.

Remembering the 'exaltation, the sin and the punishment of Tyre', Ruskin makes it an example.[24] The Fall of Tyre is a warning: England's empire is also liable to be destroyed if the guiding hand of God is forgotten in arrogance and idolatrous greed.

Like the Israelites at Sinai, who are 'blotted' from the Book of Life, and Wilson's idolatrous slave-owning Amecans, the price paid by Tyre is obliteration, a bleaching of even the memory of greatness: 'the very depth of the Fall of Tyre has blinded us to its reality, and we forget as we watch the bleaching of the rocks between the sunshine and the sea, that they were once "as in Eden, the garden of the Gods"'.[25] The allusion is again to a passage in Ezekiel, which describes Eden in terms of divinely appointed wealth: 'Thou hast been in Eden the garden of God; every precious stone was thy covering, the sardius, topaz, and the diamond, the beryl, the onyx, and the jasper, the sapphire, the emerald, and the carbuncle, and gold: the workmanship of thy tabrets and of thy pipes was prepared in thee in the day that thou wast created.'[26] The splendour that is granted by God stands in stark contrast to the acquired riches of the greedy empire. The people of Tyre have forgotten that dominion is granted on the condition of obedience to God.

They have also forgotten that good workmanship has a divine source: 'prepared in thee in the day that thou wast created'. 'The right thing to be liked', Ruskin declares in the *Stones of Venice*, 'is God's work'.[27] He maintains that, for the noble Christian workman and artist, who knows he is fallen, an awareness of the divine source of his gifts manifests as humility not arrogance: 'ten to one he makes a mistake in the first touch he gives to his work as a thinking being', says Ruskin.[28] But, here, as in *The Elements of Drawing*, erring on the right side is the condition of effortful obedience. Ruskin makes a clear distinction between effortful obedience, which is always conscious of imperfection and aspiration, and the blind obedience of simply doing what one is told: 'the difference between the spirit of touch in a man who is inventing, and of the man who is obeying directions, is often all the difference between a great and common work of art'.[29] So, Ruskin reminds his English readers of the 'old Eve-sin' and the entangling, serpentine, trap of arrogance and idolatry. 'Knowledge is good for [the artist]', Ruskin writes: 'so long as he could keep it utterly, serviley subordinate to his own divine work, and out of his way, the moment it is likely to entangle him'.[30]

[24] Ruskin, 'Stones of Venice', *Collected Works*, vol. 9, 17.
[25] Ruskin, 'Stones of Venice', *Collected Works*, vols. 9, 17.
[26] Ezek. 28: 13.
[27] Ruskin, 'Stones of Venice', *Collected Works*, vol. 9, 70.
[28] Ruskin, 'Stones of Venice', *Collected Works*, vol. 9, 192.
[29] Ruskin, 'Stones of Venice', 200.
[30] Ruskin, 'Stones of Venice', 52.

Ruskin ends the opening chapter of *The Stones of Venice* with an attack on what he sees as the wilful idolatry and concomitant artistic failure of Venice after the Reformation:

> Romanism, instead of being a promoter of the arts, has never shown itself capable of a single great conception since the separation of Protestantism from its side. So long as, corrupt though it may be, no clear witness had been borne against it, so that it still included in its ranks a vast number of faithful Christians, so long its arts were noble. But the witness was born—the error made apparent: and Rome, refusing to hear the testimony, or forsake the falsehood, has been struck from that instant with an intellectual palsy, which has not only incapacitated her from any further use in the arts, which once were her ministers, but has made her worship the shame of its own shrines, and her worshippers their destroyers.[31]

What Ruskin perceives as Catholic idolatry is here presented as stubborn disobedience in the face of Protestant revelation. He depicts post-Reformation Catholicism as a knowing falsehood and wilful self-destruction, a deliberate refusal of truth by a nation sunk so low as to 'worship shame'. Because Ruskin sees art and architecture as an index of religious and national principle, he maintains that nothing of value can be produced by a people who have so determinedly fallen that they have turned their back on the absolute standards of divine truth.

Venice thus appears as a second Tyre, and a warning to England to avoid the fate of idolatrous empires who have misplaced absolute standards and abandoned their God-given right to dominion. Ruskin waxes lyrical as he invites his English reader to enter with him into 'the streets of the Sea city'—a phrase ambiguous enough to recall all three sea-faring empires of Tyre, Venice, and England, and make the stakes of the analogy, and the warning, clear.

> Come, then, if truths such as these are worth our thoughts; come, and let us know, before we enter the streets of the Sea city, whether we are indeed to submit ourselves to their undistinguished enchantment, and to look upon the last changes which were wrought on the lifted forms of her palaces, as we should on the capricious towering of summer clouds in the sunset, ere they sank into the deep of night; or whether, rather, we shall not behold in the brightness of their accumulated marble, pages on which the sentence of her

[31] Ruskin, 'Stones of Venice', 58.

> luxury was to be written until the waves should efface it, as they fulfilled— 'God has numbered thy kingdom, and finished it!'[32]

The biblical quotation alludes to the failure of Belshazzar to learn from the sins and punishment of his father, Nebuchadnezzar, the mad tyrant who forces idolatry on his people, and is made to eat grass like the beasts in order to learn that his place is subordinate to God:

> And he was driven from the sons of men; and his heart was made like the beasts, and his dwelling was with the wild asses: they fed him with grass like oxen, and his body was wet with the dew of heaven; till he knew that the most high God ruled in the kingdom of men, and that he appointeth over it whomsoever he will.
>
> And thou his son, O Belshazzar, hast not humbled thine heart, though thou knewest all this;
>
> But hast lifted up thyself against the Lord of heaven; and they have brought the vessels of his house before thee, and thou, and thy lords, thy wives, and thy concubines, have drunk wine in them; and thou hast praised the gods of silver, and gold, of brass, iron, wood, and stone, which see not, nor hear, nor know: and the God in whose hand thy breath is, and whose are all thy ways, hast thou not glorified:
>
> Then was the part of the hand sent from him; and this writing was written.
>
> And this is the writing that was written, MENE, MENE, TEKEL, UPHARSIN.
>
> This is the interpretation of the thing: MENE; God hath numbered thy kingdom, and finished it.[33]

Unlike Belshazzar, Ruskin can read, and interpret, the writing on the wall.

Yet it is evident that Ruskin feels something of the mirage of the pre-lapsarian notion of empire that he is trying to trace. Tyre is largely forgotten. Eden lies even further away, only the 'as it were' of simile connecting it to the 'bleaching of the rocks, between the sunshine and the sea'. Venice, too, is retreating: 'so weak—so quiet,—so bereft of all her loveliness, that we might well doubt, as we watched her faint reflection in the mirage of the lagoon, which was the City and which the Shadow'.[34] Shadow watching thus becomes part of the vocabulary of recovery: tracing the lost light of Paradise. Ruskin describes a

[32] Ruskin, 'Stones of Venice', *Collected Works*, vol. 9, 59.

[33] Dan. 5: 21–6.

[34] Ruskin, 'Stones of Venice', *Collected Works*, vol. 9, 17.

vision of Eden that appears in the play of light and shadow on the West front of St Mark's Basilica:

> the solemn forms of angels, sceptered and robed to the feet, and leaning to each other across the gates, their figures indistinct among the gleaming of the golden ground through the leaves beside them, interrupted and dim, like the morning light as it faded back among the branches of Eden, when first its gates were angel-guarded long ago.[35]

The long-ago light, a remembrance of unfallen origin and garden paradise, is first felt as animated shadow—'figures indistinct' show up the 'gleaming of the golden ground', a brightness which feels immediately lost, 'interrupted and dim…[and] faded'. Shadows take us to where the light is—or where it once was imagined to be. Shadow watching thus becomes an act of theological mourning, tracing the 'faded' lines of a light which has been lost to the darkness of history. Ruskin, here, echoes Wordsworth's sense of a 'radiance which was once so bright'. As Wordsworth puts it:

> Though nothing can bring back the hour
> Of splendour in the grass, of glory in the flower;
> We will grieve not, rather find
> Strength in what remains behind.'[36]

Comparably, the history of Venice: 'in spite of the labour of countless chroniclers, remains in vague and disputable outline—barred with brightness and shade, like the far away edge of her own ocean, where the surf and the sandbank are mingled with the sky'.[37] A point of origin is implicit in the blurry outline, but it is not immediately available, or even traceable. As Marcus Waithe explains, Ruskin's style is often a guide to his thought.[38] Here, simile and subordination take us towards an epistemic horizon and enact, through the intangible beauty of the image, the feeling of a manifestly absent presence that inheres in shadows and traces. A tracing is a dutiful and obedient effort, but it is also the mark of that which has passed; it is left behind. 'To trace the

[35] Ruskin, 'Stones of Venice', *Collected Works*, vol. 9, 82–3.

[36] William Wordsworth, 'Ode on Immortality from Recollections of Early Childhood', in *Major Works*, 302.

[37] Ruskin, 'Stones of Venice', *Collected Works*, vol. 9, 18.

[38] Marcus Waithe, 'Ruskin's Style of Thought', in *Thinking through Style: Non-Fiction Prose of the Long Nineteenth-Century*, ed. Michael D. Hurley and Marcus Waithe (Oxford: OUP, 2018), 183–201.

image' and 'to err on the right side' marks the loss of the true original, as much as it seeks to preserve or retrieve it. So, 'trace' becomes a keyword of deconstruction, the sign of an absent presence.[39] Tracing the lines of the image of Venice, adhering to a philosophy of effortful obedience to truth from the condition of repetitive error, Ruskin aims to preserve the trace of Eden in the mythology of empire.

Like the myth of the New Eden, the myth of the Old Eden holds the complexity and violence of empire at a distance, naturalizing the ideology of dominion partly via a semiology of landscape. As in America, Eden has a parasitic and pernicious relationship with the history of imperialism and the aggressively assumed superiority of supposedly blessed Christian nations. Ruskin emphasizes the special privilege of the artist; divine purpose and plan become legible in the landscape only when one is able to see it. As Ruskin watches the shadows fall on the West front of St Mark's Basilica and imagines the light 'fad[ing] back' to Eden, his experience mirrors revelation. The prophetic mode connects the Fall with the salvation promised by the death of Christ: 'the shadow, as it steals back from them, revealing line after line of azure undulation, as the receding tide leaves the waved sand; their capitals rich with interwoven tracery, rooted knots of herbage and drifting leaves of acanthus and vine, all mystical signs, all beginning and ending in the Cross.'[40] Following the shadow to trace the 'azure' light, Ruskin believes he discovers the trace of grace. The prophetic moment, which holds all time within it, turns the intangible evanescence of beauty into a gesture beyond the physical—a 'mystical sign'. The loss and decay implicit in 'retreating…rooted…drifting' forms can be read as a promise of resurrection and rebirth.

The vision is 'rich with interwoven tracery' and, for Ruskin, architectural traceries speak to hierarchical structures. 'The subordination of tracery', Ruskin writes: '[is] the expression of the laws of the good government in all fragile and unstable things. All tracery, therefore, which is not subordinate, is barbarous.'[41] Gothic tracery, of the kind seen on St Mark's, is superior, Ruskin emphasizes, because it speaks to a structural truth that is absolute and eternal: 'perfect Gothic tracer[ies]…are eternal forms, based on the laws of gravity and cohesion, and no better, nor any others so good, will ever be invented.'[42] Ruskin imagines tracery in terms which recall his exhortation to young artists to trace the finger of God in the lines of the natural world. Architectural tracery

[39] Jacques Derrida, *Writing and Difference* [1967] (London: Routledge, 2001).
[40] Ruskin, 'Stones of Venice', *Collected Works*, vol. 9, 83.
[41] Ruskin, 'Stones of Venice', *Collected Works*, vol. 9, 223–4.
[42] Ruskin, 'Stones of Venice', *Collected Works*, vol. 9, 226.

becomes a similar mode of revelation, bearing witness to the eternal and harmonious 'laws of gravity and cohesion' in the physical universe.

Ruskin liked to draw these comparisons in order to emphasize that divinity could be inscribed in art that followed the lines, and laws, of nature. But, caught in the revelatory majesty of St Mark's, the distinction between man-made and natural forms becomes blurry, the 'waved sand' recalling 'interwoven tracery', which finds its own visual echo in the entangled vines: 'rooted knots...and drifting leaves'. Ruskin makes it clear that he derives his theories of art and nature from Genesis:

> That sentence of Genesis, 'I have given thee every green herb for meat,' like all the rest of the book, has a profound symbolical as well as literal meaning. It is not merely the nourishment of the body but the food of the soul that is intended. The green herb is, of all nature, that which is most healthy to the spiritual life of man...The proudest architecture that man can build has no higher honour than to bear the image and recall the memory of that grass of the field, which is at once the type and the support of his existence.[43]

But there is also the risk that the lines of nature may just be revealing themselves. Ruskin would later experience an 'unconversion' from Protestantism and be drawn to the more secular Comtean 'religion of humanity'. Writing *The Stones of Venice*, he was still invested in the Book of Nature. But, in the 'drifting vines' there is already some sense of the tricks that beauty can play on the artistic eye, and of imaginative rapture as a correlative to faith. Faith becomes more about attitudes than objects, and the Fall a point of continuity between sacred and secular worldviews.

The shifting and shadowy revelation of St Mark's contrasts with the 'intellectual palsy', and exhausted idolatry, that Ruskin perceives in post Reformation Venice.[44] For Ruskin, the seminal religious change of the early sixteenth century was reanimation not reformation: 'it poured new life into the church, but it did not form or define her anew'.[45] Like Rousseau, Ruskin finds himself drawn to a fantasy of the ripe and volatile moment of pubescence in his understanding of the perfect moment that precedes the fall from grace: 'perfect forms...are always connected, and that closely, either with the massy forms out of which they have emerged, or with the enervated types

[43] Ruskin, 'Stones of Venice', *Collected Works*, vol. 9, 238.
[44] Ruskin, 'Stones of Venice', *Collected Works*, vol. 9, 58.
[45] Ruskin, 'Stones of Venice', *Collected Works*, vol. 9, 122.

into which they are instantly to degenerate'.[46] Ruskin's idea of perfection draws from the transient beauty of budding. The life-cycle confirms the suddenness and precarity of the gift of grace: the fleeting touch of the absolute in a world of fallen form. Perfection is thus associated with a vitality which cannot last, even as it lingers in the memory of organic matter.

In 1843, Ruskin had written to his college friend, the Revd Edward Clayton:

> when you say a preparing thing, a fructifying thing, you mean a *dying* thing...if there were trees in the Garden of Eden there was death; or, if there was not death, they could not have had leaves, nor flowers, nor any of those organs of growth or germination which now constitute the essence of a tree. People will look very grave at you indeed, if you hint that there were no flowers in the garden, and yet the very meaning of the word flower is—something to supply *death*.[47]

Thus, Ruskin concludes that death is not inimical to Paradise, if Paradise rightly means life. It leads him to the unorthodox position that death was not a product of the Fall but a sign of the life that preceded it. Organic form, and the architecture which recalls it, becomes the very opposite of the idolatrous 'palsy' that he sees descended on Venice. Fallen forms lose 'the elasticity and spring of natural curves' when the fallen soul loses:

> the perception of life around it; and could no more distinguish the wave of strong branches, full of muscular strength and sanguine circulation, from the lax bending of a broken cord, nor the sinuousness of the edge of the leaf, crushed into deep folds by the expression of its living growth, from the wrinkled contraction of its decay.[48]

Here again, the error is misinterpretation and the sin is idolatry: the crime of the misplaced absolute. The finger of God cannot be traced by those who are not able to see, and distinguish, its truth.

And so, Ruskin realizes that shadows are sometimes just darkness, and the shifting and volatile lines of grace not easily traced. In the opening passages to the third volume, titled *The Fall*, Ruskin suggests that the decline of Venetian architecture in the early Renaissance period led to a futile retracing of steps, which could not recover the vital promise of the nation's Edenic beginnings:

[46] Ruskin, 'Stones of Venice', *Collected Works*, vol. 9, 226.
[47] Ruskin, 'Letters to a College Friend', in *Collected Works*, vol. 1, 476.
[48] Ruskin, 'Stones of Venice', *Collected Works*, vol. 11, 11.

> the Venetian mind, having carried the Gothic to a point at which it was dissatisfied, tried to retrace its steps, fell back first upon Byzantine types, and through them passed to the first Roman. But in thus retracing its steps, it does not recover its own lost energy. It revisits the places through which it had passed in the morning light, but it is now with wearied limbs and under the shadow of evening.[49]

As vital faith was lost, and truth forgotten, Ruskin implies that obedient and effortful tracing disappeared from art and architecture. In the *First Discourse*, Rousseau had described the fall into culture as a self-made and gilded prison—garlands of flowers over the iron chains, with which they are burdened.[50] Ruskin suggests a similar masking of catastrophe:

> year after year, as the history of the life of Christ sank back into the depth of time, and became obscured by the misty atmosphere of the history of the world…it became daily, almost hourly, a greater effort for the faithful heart to apprehend the entire veracity and vitality of the story of its Redeemer…the dimness of memory was disguised by the fruitfulness of fiction.[51]

In this vision of national fall, the sacred truth that reveals itself so clearly to the young man awakened at Fontainebleau, and that Ruskin exhorts young artists to trace in the lines of nature, becomes harder and harder to see. Ruskin fears the 'fruitfulness of fiction': the way in which confected realities can hijack faith with what seems like serpentine stealth. Moreover, he suggests that the fruitful falsehood of fiction both feeds, and is fed by, the insatiably greedy appetite. The 'fruitfulness of fiction' has no limit. In his 1843 letter to Clayton, Ruskin had imagined a similar fate for Eden, had there really been no death before Adam fell: 'suppose death impossible…long before the flood the sea would have been one mass of potted fish, the air of wedged birds, and the earth of impenetrable foliage.'[52] This packed universe anticipates the teeming, messy, cruel, and violent world that Darwin would present in 1859. 'The only question remaining for determination', says Ruskin, 'would have been—which should be *uppermost*.'[53] In a world without definitive limit,

[49] Ruskin, 'Stones of Venice', *Collected Works*, vol. 11, 6.

[50] Rousseau, 'Discourse on the Sciences and the Arts', in *Rousseau: The Basic Political Writings*, 1–26, 6; 'les Sciences, les Lettres & les Arts…étendent les guirlandes de fleurs sur les chaînes de fer dont ils sont chargés', Jean-Jacques Rousseau, *Discours sur les Sciences et les Arts*, 101–2.

[51] Ruskin, 'Stones of Venice', *Collected Works*, vol. 11, 121.

[52] Ruskin, 'Letters to a College Friend', 484.

[53] Ruskin, 'Letters to a College Friend', 484.

where such procreative drives and hungry appetites run unchecked, there is no space for creative and effortful obedience, only fierce, crammed and chaotic competition.

Paradoxically, the result of such overwhelming and unchecked fullness is profound emptiness: a failure to find meaning—lines that matter—in the chaos and confusion of competitive enterprise. Ruskin regretted that he had not thought of a title that better reflected the hollowness of a world in which the finger of God—the mark of the absolute—could not be traced. 'I almost wish', he wrote to his father in 1853: 'I had thought of Isaiah xxxiv.11 before fixing on the title of the third volume. I think the "Stones of Emptiness" would have so *precisely* fitted the Renaissance architecture.'[54] The biblical source makes the link to Ruskin's aesthetic vocabulary and national mythology more explicit. Isaiah's prophecy is a warning to all the nations that stand against Zion—the people of God. It tells of Armageddon, the destruction they will face when God wreaks vengeance upon them for their faithlessness. After prophesying lakes of fire and brimstone and wastelands filled with thorns and dragons, Isaiah concludes: 'and He shall stretch out upon it the line of confusion, the stones of emptiness.'[55]

The sin of Venice was the sin of pride or vain-glory; the same sin that beset the merchants and fishwives of Tyre when they made an idol of their trade, and that destroyed the nations who set themselves against Zion. Ruskin reminds his readers that the 'sin of Vain-Glory' is never unpunished in the Bible and, he claims, the 'first reason for the fall of Venice was the manifestation of such spirit.'[56] Resisting the 'lines of confusion', he reiterates his prophetic mission in terms that again recall the recreative effort and humble obedience involved in good draughtsmanship: 'We have to trace, be it remembered, the pride of state in its gradual intrusion upon the sepulchre; and the consequent and correlative vanishing of the expressions of religious feeling and heavenly hope.'[57] Ruskin remembers because Venice forgot, and inexcusably forgot, the promise that was inscribed in its stones: 'There is a message written in the dyes…that was once written in blood…"He shall return to do judgement and justice"…she forgot it without excuse. Never had a city a more glorious Bible.'[58] Ruskin alludes, here, to God's covenant with Abraham: 'Abraham shall surely become a great and mighty nation…he will command his children and his household after him, and they shall keep the way of the LORD, to do justice

[54] Ruskin, 'Stones of Venice', *Collected Works*, vol. 9, p. xliv.
[55] Isa. 34: 11.
[56] Ruskin, 'Stones of Venice', *Collected Works*, vol. 11, 146–7.
[57] Ruskin, 'Stones of Venice', *Collected Works*, vol. 11, 103.
[58] Ruskin, 'Stones of Venice', *Collected Works*, vol. 10, 141.

and judgement'.[59] He urges England to remember Abraham's promise—to deserve what he sees, with harmful imperial prejudice, as her God-given right to dominion. And so he writes: 'the London of the nineteenth century may yet become as Venice without her despotism'—an unfallen empire.[60]

'Grace Can, Where Nature Cannot': Newman and 'The Second Spring' (1852)

As Ruskin was developing his sense of himself as an English prophet in the Protestant tradition, a different theology of national fall and redemption was growing in Oxford. When Ruskin had entered the university in 1837, Tractarianism, led by John Henry Newman, was already afoot. In 1832, Newman, then a leading light of the Oxford Movement for High Church Anglicanism, had delivered a sermon to the University on *Justice, as a Principle of Divine Government*. He preached that the 'traces' of God's justice were visible to those who were obedient, faithful and effortful enough to see them:

> If we do not habitually thus search out and lovingly hang over the traces of God's justice, which are around us, it is because we are ourselves sinners; because, having a bad conscience, we have a personal interest in denying them, and a terror in having them forced upon us. In proportion as we grow in habits of obedience, far from our vision of the eternal justice of God vanishing from our minds, and being disowned by our feelings, as if it were but the useful misconception of a less advanced virtue, doubtless it increases, as fear is cast out.[61]

To 'grow in habits of obedience' suggests a gradual process of error and self-improvement similar to the one Ruskin implied in the 'traced limit' that will help the student of discover his own mistakes. Tracing divine justice requires attention and self-discipline, but it is also dependent on the gift of grace that turns effort into something recreative, pleasurable, and 'loving'. Newman was temperamentally averse to sudden conversions and, preaching on the subject in 1832, he warned against the susceptibility of the passionate religious mind, which might be too keen to uncover divine traces and too easily and eagerly seduced by fruitful fictions:

[59] Gen. 18: 18–19. [60] Ruskin, 'Stones of Venice', *Collected Works*, vol.11, 230.

[61] John Henry Newman, 'On Justice, as a Principle of Divine Government', in *Fifteen Sermons*, 99–119, 107.

> For a religious mind is always looking towards God, and seeking His traces and referring all events to him, and desirous of his explanation of them; and when to such a one information is brought that God had in some way shown Himself, he will at first sight be tempted to believe it, and it is only the experience of the number of deceits and false prophecies, which are in the world, his confidence in the Catholic church which he sees before him, and which is his guide into the truth, and (if he be educated) his enlightened views concerning the course and views of God's providence, which keep him steady and make him hard to believe such stories.[62]

Like Ruskin, he turns to the natural world to find support for his theological arguments: 'in the growth of plants, for instance; it is slow, gradual, continual; yet one day by chance they grow more than another...So with our souls: we all, by nature, are far from God; nay, and we have all characters to form, which is a work of time.'[63] Yet, there is a key difference. Ruskin sees God's work in the Book of Nature, but Newman takes organic form purely as example. There is nothing divine in this growth of plants, but there is a comforting feeling of expected and self-evident truth. In Newman's theology, the natural world remains subordinate to the world of faith. Organic metaphors sometimes provide the crutch for our understanding of its operations on the soul, but they can never fully explain or reveal it to us.

This scepticism towards natural theology becomes fundamental to his reading of the Fall. In an 1836 sermon on Genesis 3, he suggested that there was something incommunicably pure about divinity—something that can never be revealed in the communicable world of sense experience. God is able to know evil without becoming part of it. But when Adam and Eve ate the fruit of the Tree of Knowledge, they did not share in God's pure knowledge; they knew evil because they had done it. Newman's exegesis emphasizes the serpent's lie: to 'be *as* gods' is not to be God, but to falsely imagine oneself equal (emphasis added). As in Rousseau's *Second Discourse*, the Fall is presented as the result of a foolish trade, giving up substance for 'shadow'—a version of what Rousseau had called 'semblance':

> It is the incommunicable attribute of God to know evil without experiencing it. But man, when he would be as God, could only attain the shadow of

[62] Newman, 'Sudden Conversions', in *Parochial and Plain Sermons,* vol. 8 (London: Longmans Green & Co., 1908), 217–30, 220–1.

[63] Newman, 'Sudden Conversions', 225–6.

> a likeness which as yet he had not, by losing the substance which he had already. He shared in God's knowledge by losing His image. God knows evil and is pure from it—man plunged into evil and so knew it.[64]

There is a limit not just to what we can know, but to the kind of knowledge we can have. Our knowledge is born of experience and thus it is both contaminated and communicated. To set communicated and contaminated knowledge above faith in the incommunicable rightness of God is the sin of idolatry. That sin repeats in the confident empiricist, who forgets his own ignorance and his place in the order of Being. 'Our happiness, as well as duty, lies in not going beyond our measure', Newman reminds his congregation, 'in being contented with what we are—with what God makes us'.[65]

It is not a great step from thinking of knowledge as contaminated *by* communication to thinking of communication *as* contamination. So, for Newman, the Fall becomes, again, a fall into language and culture: 'No one means exactly what he says, because our words have lost their natural meaning…what, indeed, is the very function of society, as it is at present, but a rude attempt to cover the degradation of the Fall'.[66] But here Newman hits a problem. He thinks of communication as contamination. But, the communicable world of experience and education, effort and struggle, is that on which we paradoxically come to depend for our secular knowledge of right and wrong. 'They lost Eden', Newman says with crystalline insight, 'and gained a conscience'.[67] The questioning and self-reflective conscience belongs to the fallen world (Latin, *con* + *scire*, 'with knowledge'). Pre-lapsarian grace is a condition of unthinking, and almost unthinkable, innocence, for which the only fallen parallel is infancy: 'They do not reflect upon themselves', he says of children, as if observing an alien species.[68] But the innocence of children, like the growth of plants, is not to be confused with pre-lapsarian grace. Sin is original, Newman believes, and children are fallen from birth. What looks like innocence is, therefore, merely ignorance. Newman disparages those who behave ignorantly, 'who boast themselves on what they call their knowledge of the world and life' but have no moral and religious education, no taught principles or expanded conscience.[69] He clearly despises their relativist judgements: 'They have no scruples of conscience hindering them from complying with whatever is proposed; they are of any form of religion, have lax or correct

[64] Newman, 'Ignorance of Evil', in *Parochial and Plain Sermons*, vol. 8, 256–68, 256–7.

[65] Newman, 'Ignorance of Evil', 257.

[66] Newman, 'Ignorance of Evil', 266.

[67] Newman, 'Ignorance of Evil', 258.

[68] Newman, 'Ignorance of Evil', 259.

[69] Newman, 'Ignorance of Evil', 261.

morals, according to the occasion.'[70] Conscience matters in the fight against relativism. Yet, without the revelation by grace, even the strictest conscience will only ever fall short of the absolute standards of truth.

Ruskin saw changefulness as an index of religious principle in Gothic architecture because it felt like a mark of effortful obedience to truth. Bolstered by Protestant imperial self-righteousness, he presented the error of post-Reformation Venice as wilful idolatry: a refusal to recognize the revelation of absolute truth. For Ruskin, Venice fell when she stubbornly turned her back on truth and refused the Reformation. She forgot, and Ruskin emphasizes she forgot 'without excuse', that the right to dominion was found only in effortful obedience to God and not in mercantile self-interest. Newman similarly found philosophical flexibility to be a quality of Christian conscience. 'To live is to change', he wrote in the year that he converted to Catholicism, 'and to be perfect is to have changed often'.[71] It is part of the grammar of assent, because it brings one closer to an unchanging and absolute truth.

Conversion is change that recognizes and values the stability of truth. It is the revelation, by grace, of a truth that was always already there, a truth that existed before, and will exist beyond, the thoughtful shifts of the effortful and conscientious mind. In his own *Apologia*, which defended his conversion to Catholicism, Newman learned from the Catholic convert, Augustine, who finds stability only in God. Continuities speak to the unchanging facts of what he comes to see as Catholic truth. As Andrew Miller observes, Newman is an unsettling writer precisely because of the way in which he 'turns a gimlet eye on our confident belief about what will turn out to matter to us and what will not'.[72] 'Because I have been mistaken in my certitude, may I not at least be certain that I have been mistaken?' he asks in *An Essay in Aid of the Grammar of Assent*.[73] But conversion does also engender distrust—especially among the unconverted. As a Catholic convert, Newman had self as well as national interest at heart when he suggested to his Protestant readers that even beliefs held in good faith can turn out to be wrong.

Conversion is the theological and personal underpinning of Newman's mythology of national Fall and Redemption. England is Catholic at source and Protestant beliefs, even those held in good faith, will turn out to be

[70] Newman, 'Ignorance of Evil', 262.

[71] Newman, *An Essay on the Development of Christian Doctrine* [1845] (London: Longmans Green & Co., 1909), 40.

[72] Andrew Miller, *The Burdens of Perfection: On Ethics and Reading in Nineteenth-Century British Literature* (Ithaca, NY: Cornell University Press, 2008), 143.

[73] John Henry Newman, *An Essay in Aid of the Grammar of Assent*, ed. Ian T. Ker (Oxford: OUP, 1985), 231.

wrong. Ruskin puts his faith in the effortful obedience of tracing to find the lines that matter. But Newman finds the world too heavily marked with errata. In this context, tracing Englishness back through the fallen past becomes something of a burden for the literary-minded Newman who, in his writings on education, is forced to accept that, even if there could be a Catholic English literature, as he desires there should be, English literature could never be defined as having grown up along Catholic lines: 'for by the literature of a Nation is meant its classics, and its classics have been given to England, and have been recognised as such long since'.[74] Like the classical writers, Protestants and sceptics have left their mark and post-Reformation history cannot be erased from the mythology of Englishness: 'I seem to trace [Gibbon's] vigorous condensation and peculiar rhythm at every turn in the literature of the present day', Newman declares with a mixture of admiration and frustration.[75] Gibbon had converted to Catholicism but renounced it in a sceptical return to Protestantism. Elsewhere his frustration was more obvious: 'So tyrannous is the literature of a nation, it is too much for us. We cannot destroy, or reverse it; we may confront or encounter it, but we cannot make it over again.'[76] The power of remaking lies only with God. Fallen language will never have the creative power of God's Word, which not only set the world in motion but redeemed it through the sacrifice and resurrection of Christ, the Word made flesh, which moves in, and redeems, fallen forms.

On 13 July 1852, seven years after his conversion to Catholicism, Newman delivered a sermon to the first Synod of Westminster, the restored hierarchy of Bishops of England and Wales, at St Mary's College, Oscott. It was called 'The Second Spring'. He played on the appeal, and signalled the limits, of empiricist strategies of observation:

> were we not near enough the scene of action to be able to say what is going on,—were we the inhabitants of some sister planet possessed of a more perfect mechanism than this earth has discovered for surveying the transactions of another globe,—and did we turn our eyes thence towards England just at this season, we should be arrested by a political phenomenon as wonderful as any which the astronomer notes down from his physical field of view…what prodigious, what preternatural event is adequate to the burden of so vast an effect?[77]

[74] John Henry Newman, *The Idea of a University, Defined and Illustrated* (London: Longmans Green & Co., 1907), 308.

[75] Newman, *Idea of a University*, 323.

[76] Newman, *Idea of a University*, 314.

[77] Newman, 'The Second Spring', in *Sermons Preached on Various Occasions*, 163–83, 167–8.

Careful observation does not yield evidence of God's design; on the contrary, the watchful eye is overwhelmed, and baffled, by the miracle of God's glory. David Hume had placed miracles squarely outside the domain of rational thought, arguing that they just could not bear the burden of proof. Miracles are amazing. They ask not for reason, but for faith.

Spring, Newman realizes, has a peculiar capacity to startle us afresh each year precisely because renewal and rebirth seem so miraculous, so *unnatural*. 'Man rises to fall', writes Newman with a strong sense of melancholic inevitability, 'is born only to die'. So also do great empires crumble and fade: 'Babylon was great, and Tyre, and Egypt and Nineveh, and shall never be great again.'[78] Spring seems to belong not to the natural order of life and death, but to the miracle of resurrection: 'by its own ultimate return, to triumph over that grave, towards which it resolutely hastened from its first hour'.[79] Newman clearly echoes Paul's doctrine of resurrection here; Paul declares 'Death is swallowed up in victory'.[80] Like Paul, Newman's aesthetic is Christological. He recalls, in the image of material disintegration, the sacrifice that holds the hope of Christian resurrection: 'one death is the parent of a thousand lives'.[81] Three years after Newman delivered this sermon, Whitman imagined himself as the centripetal and centrifugal force in a world of continually disintegrating and reintegrating forms because he wanted to counter the intrinsic scepticism of philosophic materialism and assert authorial agency.[82] For Newman, all such change was an expression of devoted sacrifice and submission to the unchanging and absolute authority of God: 'each hour, as it comes, is but a testimony, how fleeting, yet how secure, how certain, is the great whole. It is like an image on the waters, which is ever the same, though the waters ever flow. Change upon change—yet one change cries out to another, like the alternate Seraphim, in praise and in glory of their Maker.'[83] Like the shifts of the conscientious mind, change becomes part of the vocabulary of effortful obedience to a continuous and absolute standard of truth.

As a moment of miraculous rebirth, spring affirms, for Newman, the continued presence of God in a country which has fallen but not yet been cast away. 'The Second Spring' depicts the Reformation as the degradation and humiliation of the true church:

[78] Newman, 'Second Spring', 169. [79] Newman, 'Second Spring', 164.
[80] 1 Cor. 15: 54. [81] Newman, 'Second Spring', 163–4. [82] See Chapter 5, 178–9.
[83] Newman, 'Second Spring', 164.

> Oh, that miserable day, centuries before we were born! What a martyrdom to live in it and see the fair form of Truth, moral and material, hacked piecemeal, and every limb and organ carried off, and burned in the fire, or cast into the deep! But at last the work was done. Truth was disposed of, and shovelled away, and there was a calm, a silence, a sort of peace;—and such was about the state of things when we were born into this weary world.[84]

Just as Christ was humiliated and degraded, tormented and tortured, so was the truth for which he died unceremoniously and unthinkingly murdered and roughly buried by Protestantism. Newman presents the intervening period as a version of the time between the crucifixion and resurrection, a lacuna of spiritual being, flat, quiet, and disenchanted, but nonetheless part of a continuum. 'They know not what they do', Jesus had said as lots were cast on Calvary.[85] Newman sends his congregants the same message. The closest Protestantism has come to truth is to ignorantly murder and defile it.

Newman insists that Catholicism is not incompatible with Englishness, as many declared it to be. On the contrary, it is its true source and form of being. He depicts the nineteenth-century revival of English Catholicism as a miraculous resurrection that has opened the ground and revealed the presence of God: 'The English church was, and the English church was not, and the English church is once again. It is the coming of a Second Spring; it is a restoration in the moral world such as that which yearly takes place in the physical.'[86] This resurrection, Newman insists, will fulfil the sacrifice of the old Catholic martyrs and restore the pre-Reformation spirit of the nation. Newman presents a vision of idealized unity and wholeness, a swelling choir restoring a lost Edenic harmony: 'I listen, and I hear the sound of voices, grave and musical, renewing the old chant, with which Augustine greeted Ethelbert in the free air upon the Kentish strand.'[87] As Jill Muller notes, the real Catholic revival might better be described as a 'cacophony of warring voices'.[88] But Newman's mythology of national Fall and Resurrection presents it as a return to a perfect beginning: the Eden of Englishness. England's fall was woeful but in the natural order of life and death. Her resurrection is marvellous and belongs to the order of divine grace. If Ruskin's Eden retreats, Newman's erupts in new glory. Ruskin advocates effortful obedience to nature to trace the retreating line of God, and we can see the Anglican Newman wrestling with similar

[84] Newman, 'Second Spring', 171.
[85] Luke 23: 34.
[86] Newman, 'Second Spring', 169.
[87] Newman, 'Second Spring', 175.
[88] Jill Muller, *Gerard Manley Hopkins and Victorian Catholicism: A Heart in Hiding* (London: Taylor & Francis, 2003), 4.

theological difficulties when he exhorts his congregants to 'search out and lovingly hang over the traces of God's justice'. But 'The Second Spring' is the work of a Catholic convert who has embraced the incarnational and miraculous vocabulary of spring. Thus, Newman declares his faith in God to reverse the decline that seems inevitable in the natural order of things and promise startling new life: 'grace can, where nature cannot'.[89]

'Our King Back, Oh, upon Énglish Sóuls!': Hopkins and Pre-lapsarian Strain (1875–1877)

To be a patriotic Catholic in Protestant Britain was a strain. As the Anglican Archbishop and poet, R. C. Trench, put it in 1851: 'it is the anti-national character of the Roman Catholic system which perhaps more than all else revolts all Englishmen'.[90] Newman was always trying to reconcile Catholicism with Englishness—to prove to those around him that going over to Rome did not mean abandoning England but saving it, returning to its truth. Converting to Catholicism in 1866, Hopkins believed intensely in this message of salvation. Like Newman, he came to think that the Reformation was a moment of national Fall and, also like Newman, his desire for national redemption reflected, and was formed by, his frustrations with, and faith in, individual conversion. Hopkins also believed that his conversion was a commitment to truth, and that truth was revealed by the grace of God. Eden became synonymous with the true soul of the nation, which had fallen through ignorance and folly, but lay ready to be revealed and redeemed.

If Ruskin fixates on tracing, and Newman embraces the more eruptive, miraculous, vocabulary of spring, Hopkins turns to the poetics of strain to suggest the continued revelation of pre-lapsarian being in the fallen world. Strain suggests a certain agony or stress: an extreme effort, a material pulling or stretching, a burden or responsibility. It also has a musical resonance. In an 1841 sermon, 'The Cross of Christ as the Measure of the World', Newman had spoken of Christ's sacrifice as 'the tone in which all the strains of this world's music are ultimately to be resolved'.[91] In a Darwinian context, a surviving 'strain' was necessarily superior—a sign of strength and fitness. Strain was, therefore, a term expressive of innocence and experience; fall and redemption; inher-

[89] Newman, 'Second Spring', 176.
[90] R. C. Trench, *On the Study of Words* (London: Routledge, 2018), 243.
[91] Newman, 'The Cross of Christ as the Measure of the World', in *Parochial and Plain Sermons*, vol. 6, 83–94, 85.

itance and direction. For Hopkins, it was able to express the agony and joy of pre-lapsarian innocence alive in the fallen world. 'I thought the air must cut and strain / The windpipe', he wrote in some early lines on a nightingale's song.[92] As Michael Hurley observes, Hopkins also uses the word to express the frustration of poetic impotence, the futile straining of his desire: 'All my undertakings miscarry. I am like a straining Eunuch', he wrote in his retreat notes of 1889. Hurley writes, and I agree: 'the mixed metaphor stops us in our tracks, as the image of aborted life—the male poet as barren mother—degrades into another figure of absolute impotency'.[93] And then, in a letter to Robert Bridges, Hopkins expresses the pain of feeling that his strain might be the will of God: 'Nothing comes:—I am a eunuch—but it is for the kingdom of heaven's sake.'[94]

Strain is also a feature of Hopkins's style. Eric Griffiths has written beautifully on the sense of strain that frequently enters into Hopkins's poetic language. He argues that writers such as Newman and Hopkins faced a particular challenge in making the unfamiliar language of Catholicism sound convincingly English, and that this, in part, accounts for the divergent voices we often encounter—sometimes in the same compound word.[95] The feeling of strain in Hopkins's verbal texture is also connected to his ascetism. As Griffiths notes, 'the ever-fretting shirt of punishment' in the early poem, 'Easter Communion', is clearly a source of pleasure to its wearer.[96] And 'fret' was a word which Hopkins returned to often as his ascetic practices came to inform a poetic texture that expressed a sense of existence under continual strain. In instances of vocal strain, where two or more divergent meanings pull language apart, Griffiths notes a profound feeling of excruciation, but argues that it is not without hope.

The bulk of Hopkins's Edenic revelations came in 1876–7, while he was in his third and final year at St Beuno's College in Wales, studying to become a priest. This was the year in which he wrote 'God's Grandeur' and imagined the Fall as the moment in which we lost touch with both God and nature: 'the soil / Is bare now, nor can foot feel, being shod.'[97] In his youth Hopkins had wanted to be an artist and had developed his artistic skills partly by reading Ruskin. In this poem, he describes the spoiled world as a canvas with a ruined and roughened surface, paint sloppily applied: 'bleared,

[92] Gerard Manley Hopkins, 'The Nightingale', in *The Poetical Works of Gerard Manley Hopkins*, ed. Norman H. MacKenzie (Oxford: Clarendon Press, 1990), 88–9, 89.

[93] Hurley, *Faith in Poetry*, 116.

[94] Cited in Hurley, *Faith in Poetry*, 116.

[95] Eric Griffiths, *The Printed Voice of Victorian Poetry* (Oxford: Clarendon, 1989), 267 and 273.

[96] Griffiths, *Printed Voice*, 273.

[97] Hopkins, 'God's Grandeur', *Poetical Works*, 139. See also Chapter 5, 145.

smeared...smudge[d]'.[98] The hope of redemption becomes embodied in the fantasy of an unspoilt, perennially new earth, which faith will reveal:

> Ánd, for all this, nature is never spent:
>   There lives the dearest freshness deep down things;
> And though the last lights off the black West went
>   Oh, morning, at the brown brink eastward, springs –
> Because the Holy Ghost óver the bent
>   World broods with warm breast and with ah! Bright wings.[99]

Hopkins's vision of redemption is one in which age reveals itself as youth, bleariness as brightness, bare, barren soil as warm brooding breast. Time is more than rolled back. It is undone completely. It is not just that the marks of humanity on the earth have not yet been made. In this vision of salvation, they will never be made, because the mess of human history, the 'smudge' and 'smear' and 'smell' of labour and suffering, is replaced by the perennial present of flawless beginning. We may have ruined the surface, but the foundations are the strong 'springs' of Eden.

Unlike Newman, Hopkins was a young man when he converted to Catholicism and his Catholic education was scholastic. The theological underpinnings to this vision of Edenic recovery are found in the teachings of the thirteenth-century Scottish Catholic priest and Franciscan friar, John Duns—known as Duns Scotus. Hopkins studied him earnestly and found a great deal to admire and like. Scotist Christology arguably provided Hopkins with the most radical and important inspiration for vision of Edenic recovery. Most theologians thought the Word was made flesh to redeem the sin that Adam and Eve had brought on humankind. But Duns Scotus maintained that the incarnation was not simply the product of Divine mercy. On the contrary, the incarnation was God's first intent in creation. Christ would have descended as High King of Eden even if he had not been urgently needed as a Redeemer for fallen man. 'The first outstress of God's power', Hopkins wrote in 1881, 'was Christ'.[100]

So, for Hopkins, Christ was the beginning: the purest intention of God's creation and the absolute standard of pre-lapsarian being. His faith in the

[98] Hopkins, 'God's Grandeur', 139. [99] Hopkins, 'God's Grandeur', 139.

[100] Hopkins, 'Spiritual Writings', in *The Sermons and Devotional Writings of Gerard Manley Hopkins*, ed. Christopher Devlin (London: OUP, 1959), 107–209, 197. For a discussion of Hopkins's academic theology, see Walter J. Ong, *Hopkins, the Self and God* (Toronto: University of Toronto Press, 1986), 89–126.

incarnation was Trinitarian. Christ the Son was united with the Father and the Holy Spirit in the One God. When Hopkins imagines the Holy Ghost bent and brooding over the new-born world, he recalls both the Spirit of God moving over the waters in the opening lines of Genesis and Milton's address to the Holy Spirit in the opening lines of *Paradise Lost*:

> thou from the first
> Wast present, and with mighty wings outspread
> Dovelike satst brooding on the vast abyss
> And mad'st it pregnant
>
> (*PL*, book I, ll. 19–22)

For both Milton and Hopkins, the Holy Spirit was first felt in God's creative movements and continued to be felt in the fallen world through prayer. Milton addresses the opening prayer of *Paradise Lost* directly to the Holy Spirit:

> what me is dark
> Illumine, what is low raise and support;
> That to the height of this great argument
> I may assert the eternal providence
> And justify the ways of God to men.
>
> (*PL*, book I, ll. 22–6)

In 'God's Grandeur', the 'springs' of miraculous rebirth are directly connected to the attitude of prayer. The protective warmth of the Holy Spirit is felt 'deep down' as a love of God and Hopkins builds to a crescendo of praise, wonder, and enchantment, erupting in the kind of overwhelmed gasping amazement familiar from Newman's 'Second Spring' as he ends the sestet in the attitude of prayer and praise: 'and with ah! Bright wings'.

Hopkins—as priest and poet—finds the freshness of God's first intent in the power of the Word made flesh, revealed in explosive utterance at the end of the poem. The primary creation erupts in devotion to God. Recalling the Puritan poet, Edward Taylor, who wrote of himself as a 'lump of loathsomeness', Hopkins also suggests that the full force of the degradation of the Logos is felt in the way poetic articulation is inextricably and pleasurably bound to the body. He savours the taste of fallen language, 'bleared, smeared with toil', even as he is repulsed by what it represents. Like the primary creation, the Fall is not confined to biblical history, but continually re-enacted. If Christ,

God's first intent in creation, registers as explosive utterance, the Fall is felt in the transgressive, physical pleasure of poetic language and the unpleasant savouring of distaste—the way in which words hang and cloy on the tongue. When Hopkins felt most distant from God, most desolate and depressed, he experienced his self-loathing as profound—and forced—unpalatability: 'Bitter would have me taste', he wrote, 'my taste was me'.[101] It is the same bitterness that T. S. Eliot would later evoke in 'The Dry Salvages' in *Four Quartets*: 'The bitter apple and the bite in the apple'.[102] The first taste of forbidden fruit was the bitterness of self-disgust; distaste. The impossibility of true utterance represents a permanent dilemma of the fallen world. Hopkins's incarnational poetics, which turn on the tension between the exulted Word made flesh and the degradation of poetic language, are another example of continual strain.

In a poem dated to the hopeful period at St Beuno's in Wales, and strongly influenced by both Ruskin and Newman, 'strain' expresses the joyful agony Hopkins felt at the brief revelation of Eden in the fleeting miracle of spring:

Nothing is so beautiful as Spring—
  When weeds, in wheels, shoot long and lovely and lush;
  Thrush's eggs look little low heavens, and thrush
Through the echoing timber does so rinse and wring
The ear, it strikes like lightening to hear him sing;
  The glassy peartree leaves and blooms, they brush
  The descending blue; that blue is all in a rush
With richness; the racing lambs too fair have their fling.

What is all this juice and all this joy?
  A strain of the earth's sweet being in the beginning
In Eden garden.— Have, get, before it cloy,

Before it cloud, Christ, lord, and sour with sinning,
Innocent mind and Mayday in girl and boy,
  Most, O maid's child, thy choice and worthy of winning.[103]

Ruskin's influence can be felt in Hopkins's careful tracing of beautiful lines in nature. Hopkins's Ruskinian visual imagination, with its empiricist basis in

[101] Hopkins, 'I wake and feel the fell of dark not day', *Collected Works*, 181.
[102] T. S. Eliot, *Four Quartets*, in *Collected and Uncollected Poems*, 2 vols, ed. Christopher Ricks and Jim McCue (London: Faber & Faber, 2015), vol. 1, 177–211, 197.
[103] Hopkins, 'Spring', *Collected Works*, 142.

observation and feeling, was a formative factor on the theories of inscape and instress that he developed in his undergraduate days.[104] Inscape represents the particularity of divine presence in each individual organic form, revealed by careful tracing of the lines of nature. Instress is a principle of divine connectivity: the recognition of God's pattern or plan in the interwoven character of nature. 'When weeds, in wheels, shoot long and lovely and lush' emphasizes both inscape and instress in the natural world in a distinctly Ruskinian way. Ruskin had described herbs growing in 'whorls'. The 'whorled... Catherine-wheel forms' that Hopkins recognized in oak trees are also found in his sketch of a dandelion weed (called 'Cartwheel' in Somerset) and drawings of medallions of spoke-like twigs and leaves.[105] But Hopkins can express, in writing, the energy and volatility of natural forms that he never managed to convey in his static, though accurate, drawings. The octet is characterized by an overwhelming feeling of fertile movement. It is a distinctive feature of Hopkins's style to use anthimeria (the swapping of parts of speech) and, here, the noun, 'thrush', is placed in the position of a verb, making the bird synonymous with its rush 'through the echoing timber'.

Echo, like trace and shadow, suggests the lingering mark of that which has passed: the resonance of Eden in the natural beauty of Spring. Hopkins moves quickly from the 'echoing timber' to a more visceral and agonised sense of musical strain, which: 'does so rinse and wring / The ear, it strikes like lightening to hear him sing'. 'Rinse and wring' recall the liquidity of 'lush' and the unformed watery earth implied by rush—anticipating the fertile 'juice' of the second stanza. But they also connect the promise of new life with baptismal regeneration and the physical strain of crucifixion and resurrection. Rinse suggests cleansing and, more specifically in religious language, the cleaning of the chalice with wine and water after the Eucharist. The blood and tears of Calvary and the olive press of Gethsemane manifest in the 'wring'—or ring—of the song of new life: sound under strain. The lightning strike recalls Matthew's description of Christ's Transfiguration and his promise of Resurrection.[106] In its piercing intrusion, there is also the feeling of erotic ascetic pleasure that Hopkins takes in the penetrative violence of the Cross. The movement of the first stanza—its rush of new life—is eschatological. The world is born again in the agony of sacrifice.

[104] For more on the combined influence of aesthetic and scientific ideas on Hopkins's poetry see Gillian Beer, *Open Fields: Science in Cultural Encounter* (Oxford: OUP, 1996), chapter 11; Daniel Brown, *Hopkins' Idealism: Philosophy, Physics, Poetry* (Oxford: Clarendon Press, 1997); Jude V. Nixon, *Gerard Manley Hopkins and his Contemporaries: Liddon, Newman, Darwin and Pater* (London: Garland, 1994).

[105] Hopkins, *Collected Works*, 371 n. 2.

[106] Matt. 28: 3.

If Eden is felt in the eruptive presence of Christ, it is also always in retreat. Hopkins takes real poetic pleasure in the erotic exuberance of new life which is yet innocent of consequence. He savours the whimsical, sensual caress of 'brush' and 'fling', the playful eagerness of 'racing' lambs and the explosive joy of 'shoot' and 'bloom'. 'The glassy peartree leaves and blooms' is another example of Hopkins using anthimeria to give a sense of objects not just in motion, but *as* motion. And, like the vocal strain which pulls Hopkins's meanings apart, the motion described by anthimeria is, here, divergent. 'Glassy' situates 'leaves' as a noun (pear tree leaves are glossy); but 'leaves and blooms' makes grammatical sense only as a verb and 'leaves' is also a pun. The image of a blooming pear tree putting forth leaves is thus haunted by the knowledge of the Fall: the bloom has always already departed. The downward trajectory is emphasized by the rush in 'brush'; the enjambement hurries the line too quickly towards 'the descending blue' of the bright spring sky; the story still to be completed is the one that has already slipped away.

Hopkins may have chosen the pear tree at least partly for its connection to the Fall. In one of the most well-known scenes in his *Confessions*, Augustine recounts a teenage escapade in which he, along with friends, stole pears just for the pleasure of sin. Augustine confesses:

> Wickedness filled me. I stole something which I had in plenty and of much better quality. My desire was to enjoy not what I sought by stealing but merely the excitement of thieving and doing what was wrong. There was a pear tree near our vineyard laden with fruit, though attractive in neither colour nor taste. To shake the fruit off the tree, and carry off the pears, I and a gang of naughty adolescents set off late at night after (in our usual pestilential way) we had continued our game in the streets. We carried off a huge load of pears. But they were not for our feasts but merely to throw to the pigs. Even if we ate a few, nevertheless our pleasure lay in doing what was not allowed.[107]

There is a familiar symbolism in the fruit-stealing episode. Here it is pears not apples but the reference to the first naughty fruit-picking episode in Eden is deliberate. Augustine is mired in Adam's sin. His wickedness is simply a manifestation of something which goes much deeper, an original sin, which is the basis of every subsequent act of human transgression.

So, pre-lapsarian Eden withdraws even as it strains through the agonized glory of spring. 'Have, get, before it cloy', Hopkins urges. Getting usually

[107] Augustine, *Confessions*, 29.

precedes having. Hopkins's poetic reversal of expected syntax undermines the security of possession with the urgency of desire. Like many writers and artists, including Blake and Emerson, Hopkins recognizes a quality in beauty that feels profoundly elusive. In the fallen world, beautiful strains slip away, retreating before any artistic effort to capture them. 'That strain again!', exclaims the Duke Orsino in the opening to Shakespeare's *Twelfth Night*, 'it had a dying fall'.[108] As 'A strain of the earth's sweet being in the beginning / In Eden garden', beauty refers back to a lost and perfect origin. Imagining the beauty of spring as a pre-lapsarian 'strain', Hopkins's musical metaphor suggests a shared origin which has not been entirely lost and will break through in agony. The final lines return us to the incarnation. 'Innocent mind and Mayday in girl and boy' aligns the Edenic strain with Christ, the virginal 'Maid's child', God's first and purest intent in creation, who suffered and strained—was rinsed and wrung—for man's 'sinning'.

Like 'God's Grandeur', the poem ends in the attitude of devotion. Addressing Christ, Hopkins also recalls the prayer of national salvation he utters at the end of the 'Wreck of the Deutschland', the masterpiece that broke a seven-year poetic silence and was composed at the beginning of the period at St Beuno's. Hopkins wrote the poem after five Franciscan nuns were exiled from Germany, fleeing Catholic persecution for a new life in America, and drowned when their boat ran aground on the coast of Kent. It was intended, at least partly, as a conversion narrative for Protestant Britain. Heavily encoding the crucifixion in the symbolism of the wrecked ship and ravished souls, Hopkins presents a Catholic England as the fulfilment of the nuns' sacrifice.

> Drówned, and among óur shoals.
> Remémber us in the róads, the heaven-haven of the
> reward:
> Our king back, Oh, upon Énglish sóuls!
> Let him éaster in us, be a dáyspring to the dimness of us,
> be a crimson-cresseted east,
> More brightening her, ráre-dear Britain, as his reign rolls,
> Príde, rose, prínce, hero of us, hígh-príest,
> Oür héart's charity's héarth's fire, oür thóughts' chivalry's
> thróng's Lord.[109]

[108] William Shakespeare, *Twelfth Night, or What You Will*, ed. Roger Warren and Stanley Wells, Act 1, Scene 1, line 4 (Oxford: OUP, 2008), 85.

[109] Hopkins, 'The Wreck of the Deutschland', *Collected Works*, 119–28, 128.

'Our king' frames redemption in Scotist terms. Christ, here, is more than Redeemer. He is High King of Eden, God's first intent in creation and herald of a new Catholic dawn. 'Crimson-cresseted east' colours the new beginning with the blood of the cross, recalling the death on Calvary and echoing Newman's idea that the restoration of the Catholic Church in England will fulfil the sacrifice of the old Catholic martyrs—here, also, the drowned nuns. Hopkins's image of Christological salvation is interpersonal and deeply visceral. National conversion happens not upon English soil but 'upon English souls'. As in 'God's Grandeur', the redemptive movement is felt as an erotic drive, a near intolerable, bursting, pressure from within that is also a desire for union: 'Let him éaster in us, be a dáyspring to the dimness of us'. In 1874, while teaching at Manresa House, Roehampton, Hopkins had composed a series of lecture notes, titled 'Rhythm and other structural parts of Rhetoric-verse'. He had described his incarnational theories of language in terms that emphasized national identity: 'we may think of words as heavy bodies...[E]very visible, palpable, body, has a centre of gravity round which it is in balance and a centre of illumination...up to which it is lighted and down from which it is shaded...English is of this kind, the accent of stress strong'.[110] Stress is both a particular assertion of being and a process of national becoming. The accumulation of stresses here is an example of the eruptive signature style that Hopkins termed 'sprung rhythm': the system of poetic metre that counts the stresses in a line and lets unstressed syllables fall naturally. The stresses, plosives, and alliterative crescendo of sound, which build towards the end of the 'Wreck', register the strain of such explosive utterance: the Word made flesh in every faithful soul.

The difficult dative of sacrifice—the question of what the suffering caused by the Fall is *for*—finds one answer in Hopkins's poetic emphasis on stress, spring, and strain. In the second stanza of the 'Wreck', Hopkins describes 'the midriff astrain, with leaning of, laced with fire of stress'. The stress of Christ's sacrificial gift is felt as divergent strain: a pressing burden that shipwrecks the soul—pulls it apart, or 'astrain'—in the moment of salvation. In the final stanza, Christ as 'prince' echoes the pressure of the sacrificial 'principle' Hopkins describes in the fourth stanza; the dissolving self—'soft sift in an hourglass' is stayed by 'the góspel próffer, a préssure, a prínciple, Christ's gíft'. Christ's gift

[110] Gerard Manley Hopkins, 'Rhythm and Other Structural Parts of Rhetoric-verse', in *The Journals and Papers of Gerard Manley Hopkins*, ed. Humphrey House and completed by Graham Storey (London: OUP, 1959), 267–89, 269.

is his sacrifice but also God's first intent in creation; it is the source, root, origin—the first principle of conversion to truth.

Hopkins, like Newman, sees the return of an English Eden as the fulfilment of a sacrifice yet to be completed, and conversion to an absolute standard of truth, which would redeem every English soul, and, by extension, the soul of England. In 1886, Hopkins wrote to Coventry Patmore, full of praise for the good his Catholic poetry would do the British Empire: 'Your poems are a good deed done for the Catholic Church and another for England, for the British Empire...I hold that fine works of art...are really a great power in the world, an element of strength even to an empire.'[111] Here, as in his letter to Bridges, works of art have a didactic purpose—to educate and set standards. And such didacticism goes hand-in-hand with imperialist claims to national superiority—the God-given right to dominion. Absolute standards and the standards of Englishness become almost interchangeable. Once again, the longing for Eden becomes part of the pernicious armoury of imperialism.

It feels odd, therefore, that Catholic constructions of a national Fall should bear comparison with the mythologies that helped shape ideas of Black citizenship in nineteenth-century America. The former is clearly put to the service of white supremacy; the latter seeks only to resist it. And yet, the sacrifice still to be completed was important to both valorizations of suffering as martyrdom. So, too, was the sense that we have to go back in order to go forward. All these visions of redemption emphasize the recovery of sacred time, a shared true origin, which had been roughly and unceremoniously buried, as Cain buried Abel or Protestantism shovelled away Truth. In all cases, the need is for a foundational myth, a sense of stability and source in an ever-shifting world of relational changes. Like Wilson, Brown, and Truth, though with very different political aims, Newman and Hopkins wanted to ground national and personal identity in a notion of foundational sacrifice. Ruskin similarly laments what he sees as the idolatry of post-Reformation Venice, and searches for an absolute standard, a trace of Eden, that he thinks is fast retreating from the world. And so, writing his autobiography, he longs to find an essential being in his own self, just as he wants to find the anchor of truth in the lines of nature. He begins chapter 2 with an allusion to the permanence of paradise in the Edenic garden of his childhood, 'which remains, in all essential points of character, unchanged to this day'.[112] Without the consolations of faith,

[111] Gerard Manley Hopkins, *Further Letters of Gerard Manley Hopkins Including his Correspondence with Coventry Patmore*, ed. Claude Colleer Abbot (Oxford: OUP, 1938), 218–19.

[112] Ruskin, 'Praeterita', 34.

though, such longing loses the hope of redemption. Looking back on his life, he describes a much more secular sense of revelation, a recognition of the 'stubborn and chemically inalterable' laws of his own individual being, a chastened and exhausted acceptance of the 'structure of the pith', now surrounded by depletion and decay: 'looking back from 1886 to that brook shore of 1837, whence I could see the whole of my youth, I find myself in nothing whatsoever *changed*... I am but the same youth, disappointed and rheumatic.'[113]

[113] Ruskin, 'Praeterita', 220.

Epilogue

'The bitter apple and the bite in the apple'

In the third poem of *Four Quartets*, written and published during the existential threat of the Second World War, as bombs fell nightly on London and battles raged across Europe, T. S. Eliot wrote of 'The bitter apple and the bite in the apple'.[1] The Fall is used here to denote two different orders of time, as well as the relationship between them. The 'bitter apple' is the fruit we are forced to keep eating, the ongoing experiences of suffering, desire, will, and choice. The 'bite in the apple' suggests a decisive moment, a singular point of rupture. In Christian theology, this is the original sin that gives all human pleasures the flavour of distaste; in secular philosophy, it is the imagined moment of collapse that that explains the condition of modern malaise. The decisive 'bite' also carries a sense of the energy and enterprise associated with the fortunate fall: the beginnings of desire, experience and knowledge.

The Fall, catastrophic and fortunate, places enormous pressure on the moment—the decisive 'bite in the apple'. If Eden was lost in that moment, so also in a moment might it be redeemed. If Adam and Eve discover the world when they eat of the forbidden fruit, then the Fall becomes a turning point, the moment when they discover desire and grow up. Towards the end of the nineteenth century, a self-conscious artistic and literary decadence displaced both nostalgic and progressive shapes of time and filled that void with the distilled and beautiful moment, the directionless impression, and pleasurable sensation. In 1893, Arthur Symons published an article on 'The Decadent Movement in Literature', defining the new French-influenced international avant-garde known variously as 'impressionists', 'symbolists', 'aesthetes', and 'decadents' by 'a desperate endeavour to give sensation, to flash the impression of a moment, to preserve the very heat and motion of life'.[2] In 1868, Walter Pater had imagined this 'moment' in a way that undid the myth of the Fall;

[1] T. S. Eliot, 'The Dry Salvages', *Four Quartets, Poems*, 197.

[2] Arthur Symons, 'The Decadent Movement in Literature', *Harper's New Monthly Magazine* 87 (Nov. 1893): 858–68, reprinted in Arthur Symons, *The Symbolist Movement in Literature*, ed. Matthew Creasy (Manchester: Carcanet, 2014), 327–52, 331.

The Myth of the Fall in Nineteenth-Century Literature. Linda Freedman, Oxford University Press.
 DOI: 10.1093/oso/9780198969570.003.0009

it was no longer a dramatic turning point, catastrophic or fortunate, but something which worked against both shapes of time. He wrote: 'art comes to you professing frankly to give nothing but the highest quality to your moments as they pass, and simply for those moments' sake'.[3] In this elevated moment there is a still a latent sense of loss, of beauty felt most intensely and pleasurably in the moment of its retreat but, separated from the myth of the Fall, it does not look back to a lost paradise or hold the hope of a future happiness; it is unapologetically present-tense.

In his provocative '10 o' Clock Lecture', delivered in 1885, James McNeill Whistler parodied the biblical Creation story, poking fun at the myth of the Fall, and concomitant notions of purposeful or redemptive artistic form, and celebrating useless beauty:

> In the beginning, man went forth each day—some to do battle, some to the chase; others, again, to dig and to delve in the field—all that they might gain and live, or lose and die. Until there was found among them one, differing from the rest, whose pursuits attracted him not, and so he stayed by the tents with the women, and traced strange devices with a burnt stick upon a gourd.
>
> This man, who took no joy in the ways of his brethren—who cared not for conquest, and fretted in the field, this designer of quaint patterns—this deviser of the beautiful—who perceived in Nature about him curious carvings, as faces are seen in the fire—this dreamer apart, was the first artist.[4]

Like Pater, Whistler writes against both nostalgia and progressivism, defining beauty and pleasure with an insistently atemporal and anti-nationalist present-tense:

> Listen! There never was an artistic period.
> There never was an Art-loving nation.
> ...
> So Art is limited to the infinite, and beginning there cannot
> progress.[5]

[3] Walter Pater, 'Essay on William Morris', 1868. The line was later included in Pater's 'Conclusion' to *Studies in the History of the Renaissance* [1873], ed. Matthew Beaumont (Oxford: Oxford World's Classics, 2010), 121.

[4] James McNeill Whistler, *The Gentle Art of Making Enemiess* (Elibron Classics reprint of London: Heineman, 1904), 139.

[5] Whistler, *Gentle Art*, 139, 155.

In Whistler's parody of Genesis, the Fall becomes the moment we stopped taking pleasure in beauty: 'the artist's occupation was gone', he writes, 'and the manufacturer and the huckster took his place'.[6]

Oscar Wilde similarly rewrote the myth of the Fall as a celebration of decadent pleasure in 'The Artist', a 'poem in prose' first published in 1893. It tells the story of a man who desires 'to fashion an image of *The Pleasure that Abideth for a moment*', an echo of Pater and Whistler, but he can only find the image of '*The Sorrow that endureth forever*', made with his own hands 'that it might serve as a sign of the love of man that dieth not, and a symbol of the sorrow of man that endureth for ever'.[7] Wilde rejects original sin, throwing the image of sorrow into a 'great furnace' that recalls both Hell and Hephaestos's forge. Sorrow and pleasure become interchangeable, formed from the same matter and collapsing the shape of time: 'And out of the bronze of the image of *The Sorrow that endureth for Ever* he fashioned an image of *The Pleasure that abideth for a Moment*.'[8] The equation between 'for Ever' and 'a Moment' simultaneously invokes and undermines the narrative of sin and redemption. In the myth of the Fall, the world is either lost or found in the moment of pleasure. But, here, that moment is purely sensual, divorced from past and future, displacing original sin, refusing eschatological meaning, and separating instinctive drives from the judgement which surrounds moral choice.

Charlotte Mew's 1916 poem 'Madeleine in Church' both refracts and critiques this decadent sensibility, reimagining the moment of pleasure in relation to the trope of the fallen woman. Angela Leighton calls it 'one of the last poems in which the Fall is internalised as a penalty for passion'.[9] More often discussed in relation to Elizabeth Barrett Browning's *Aurora Leigh* and Dante Gabriel Rossetti's 'Jenny', Madeleine also recalls Maggie and Gwendolen, who feel the consequence of their actions even before the error has occurred:[10]

[6] Whistler, *Gentle Art*, 142.

[7] Oscar Wilde, 'The Artist', in *Complete Short Fiction*, ed. Ian Small (London: Penguin, 1994; 2003), 243.

[8] Wilde, 'The Artist', 243.

[9] Angela Leighton, *Victorian Women Poets: Writing Against the Heart* (Brighton: Edward Everett Root publishers, 1992; 2019), 286.

[10] For comparisons between Mew and other female writers of the fallen woman genre, including Rossetti and Barrett Browning, see Angela Leighton, 'Because Men Made the Laws: The Fallen Woman and the Woman Poet', *Victorian Poetry* 27.2 (Summer 1989): 109–27, and *Victorian Women Poets*; Linda Mizejewski, 'Charlotte Mew and the Unrepentant Magdalene: A Myth in Transition', *Texas Studies in Literature and Language* 26.3 (Fall 1986): 282–302; Jereidth Merrin, 'The Ballad of Charlotte Mew', *Modern Philology* 95.2 (Nov 1997): 200–17.

when I was half a child I could not sit
Watching black shadows on green lawns and red carnations
burning in the sun,
Without paying so heavily for it[11]

Like Maggie, she seems a fallen woman by nature, already paying the price for her extreme sensuality and passion in childhood. But there is also a poetic contrast between the lurid symbolism of the scene, which recalls the highly aestheticized and sensual paintings of Dante Gabriel Rossetti or Edward Burne-Jones and the fetish poems of Algernon Charles Swinburne, and the confessional female voice. Mew seems to be self-consciously invoking and critiquing both her Decadent and Victorian inheritance. As Leighton implies, there is an appealingly serpentine and seductive quality in the speaking voice which 'insinuates itself around the studded symbols of a forbidden, literary sexuality'.[12] But Mew's poem also suggests that sensual pleasure will never be, for women, the elevated and inconsequential moment that decadent aesthetes like Pater, Whistler, Wilde, Rossetti, Burne-Jones, and Swinburne have wanted it to be. '*Et avec ça—*', Madeleine sighs, as she recalls her past lovers and resents her faded youth, '*mais on a vécu, tout se paie*'; [And with that—but we have lived, you pay for everything].[13]

The shift that the poem enacts is twofold. First, Madeleine compares the price of pleasure to the price of duty and concludes that the price she paid was at least worth it:

there was my Mother—(well at least the
dead are free!)
Yoked to the man that Father was; yoked to the woman
I am, Monty too;
The little portress at the Convent School, stewing in
hell so patiently;
The poor, fair boy who shot himself at Aix. And what of me—and
what of me?
But I, I paid for what I had, and they for nothing.[14]

[11] Charlotte Mew, 'Madeleine in Church', in *Selected Poetry and Prose*, ed. Julia Copus (London: Faber, 2017), 35–43, 36.
[12] Leighton, *Victorian Women Poets*, 287.
[13] Mew, 'Madeleine in Church', 38.
[14] Mew, 'Madeleine in Church', 38–9.

Second, she rejects the system of exchange that turns redemption into ransom. As Leighton explains, this is particularly relevant to Victorian depictions of prostitution: 'the fallen women is specifically one who has been paid, but who also, in another scale of values, pays. She exists in a place between the socio-economic and spiritual systems, where the coin of one is easily exchanged for the coin of the other.'[15] Madeleine aligns herself with Mary Magdalene, the biblical prostitute who is saved by Christ. The Magdalen was a very particular type of the fallen woman in Victorian literature, who came to be associated with the redemptive femininity and mother idealism of the Madonna.[16] But Madeleine does not want to be redeemed. Her identification with Mary has the jealous streak of a woman who wants to be noticed by a man. 'I wonder if it was like that kiss that once I knew', she says, reimagining the scene, already drawn as sensual and erotic by Dante Gabriel Rossetti, of Mary kissing Christ's feet.[17] 'It did not matter what they said', Madeleine confesses, as she remembers looking at images of the dead Christ in her convent school:

> He was alive to me, so hurt, so hurt! And most of all in Holy Week
> When there was no-one else to see
> I used to think it would not hurt me too, so terribly,
> If He had ever seemed to notice me
> Or, if, for once, He would only speak.[18]

For Madeleine, the bite in the apple is not without a bitter aftertaste, but it is not the taint of original sin, it is the loneliness of a disappointed woman whose pleasure has not delivered happiness. Even as she rejects the judgement of original sin, Mew exposes the isolated moment of pleasure as a decadent fiction, sustained by the male aesthetes that her dramatic monologue both evokes, and critiques. Like Maggie and Gwendolen, Madeleine's unhappiness is subscribed by the myth of the Fall, consequences that precede actions and circumstances that must be endured. The poem also evokes moments of grief

15 Leighton, *Victorian Women Poets*, 284.

16 Eric Trudgill, *Madonnas and Magdalens* (London: William Heinemann, 1976), 289–90.

17 Dante Gabriel Rossetti, 'Mary Magdalene at the Door of Simon the Pharisee', 1858, pen and India ink, Fitzwilliam Museum, University of Cambridge. Rossetti habitually composed lines of verse to accompany his images. These lines, spoken by Mary, offer a commentary on the drawing: 'O loose me! Seest thou not my Bridegroom's face / That draws me to Him? For his feet, my kiss, / My hair, my tears He craves today:—and oh! / What words can tell what other day and place / Shall see me clasp those blood-stained feet of His? / He needs me, calls me, loves me: let me go!' The idea that Mary Magdalene and Christ had a sexual relationship was further sensationalized after the discovery of the apocryphal Gospel of Phillip in 1945 which mentioned Jesus kissing Mary on the mouth. See Paul Foster, *The Apocryphal Gospels: A Very Short Introduction* (Oxford: OUP, 2009), 47–8.

18 Mew, 'Madeleine in Church', 43.

which, as in Blake's *Urizen* books, hold the promise of other worlds and change forever what her world is. Mew presents redemption as no consolation for the human—and here specifically womanly—experience of loss: 'If there were fifty heavens God could not give us back the child / who went or never came.'[19] 'Madeleine in Church' is a poem about aftermath, which uses the trope of the fallen woman to simultaneously reject original sin and hold decadent distillations of sensual pleasure up to the light.

The legibility of the Fall also worked as a foil to cognate concepts of degeneration, which turned on the unreadable and inchoate violence of suppressed or atavistic drives and desires. In his moralistic diatribe against the degenerate spirit of the age, Max Nordau complained about the loss of moral meaning in a dissolute world: 'Over the earth shadows creep with deepening gloom, wrapping all objects in a mysterious dimness, in which all certainty is destroyed and any guess seems plausible. Forms lose their outlines, and are dissolved in floating mist.'[20] The iconic figure of *fin-de-siècle* degeneration, Robert Louis Stevenson's Mr Hyde, is 'not easy to describe.'[21] Confronting his strange deformity with disgust and loathing, the perplexed Mr Utterson finds a kind of solace in naming it sin:

> There is something more if I could find a name for it. God bless me the man seems hardly human! Something troglodytic shall we say? or can it be the old story of Dr Fell? or is it the mere radiance of a foul soul that transpires through and transfigures its clay continent? This last, I think; for oh my poor old Harry Jekyll, if I ever read Satan's signature upon a face, it is that of your new friend.[22]

'Satan's signature' is a judgement which makes a reassuring amount of sense to Utterson and imposes a degree of legibility on the atavistic darkness of Mr Hyde. Even as he undercuts it, Stevenson suggests a consolatory function in the old religious worldview, which could easily identify evil as sin. In undoing original sin, ideas of degeneration worked against the hope of redemption and the circular shape of sacred time, exciting readers with figures of amorphous, unnameable horror.

[19] Mew, 'Madeleine in Church', 39.
[20] Max Nordau, *Degeneration* [1895] (New York: D. Appleton & Co., 2016), 6.
[21] Robert Louis Stevenson, *The Strange Case of Dr Jekyll and Mr Hyde and Other Tales of Terror*, ed. Robert Mighall (London: Penguin, 2002), 10.
[22] Stevenson, *Dr Jekyll and Mr Hyde*, 16.

By contrast, the religious vision of *Four Quartets* holds onto the hope of redemption and ends by affirming the shape of sacred time:

> At the end of all our exploring
> Will be to arrive where we started
> And know the place for the first time.
> Through the unknown, remembered gate
> When the last of earth left to discover
> Is that which was the beginning:
> At the source of the longest river
> The voice of the hidden waterfall
> And the children in the apple-tree
> Not known because not looked for
> But heard, half-heard in the stillness
> Between the two waves of the sea.[23]

For the converted Augustine, the discovery of sacred time had revealed that he was not the author of his own story. 'You knew', he confessed to God, 'but I did not, what the outcome would be'.[24] For Eliot, the journey involves a decision on how to live; what gate to pass through; what to look and listen for if we are to experience a sense of the fullness of time. The nostalgic revelation comes at the point of exhaustion. At the end of the explorations, errant wanderings, divergences and iterations of time, the march of industrialisation, the bankrupt teleologies of secular progress, we return to the consolations of sacred time in Eden: 'that which was the beginning /... the source of the longest river'.[25] Eliot explicitly recalls the symbol of new life evoked in Genesis 2: 10: 'And a river went out from Eden to water the garden'. The 'children in the apple-tree' represent the joy and innocence of pre-lapsarian grace, always there, ready to be revealed. As Augustine finds salvation by surrendering his sense of self, so Eliot imagines: 'A condition of complete simplicity / (Costing not less than everything)'.[26] Eliot observed in simplicity the baffling quality of grace that Blake had associated with poetic inspiration, 'which seems to be the Labour of a long Life all produced without Labour or Study' (E728–9). Like Blake, he valued hard work, but 'Adam's curse' was not undone through

[23] T. S. Eliot, 'Little Gidding', *Four Quartets*, *Poems*, 208–9.
[24] Augustine, *Confessions*, 146. [25] Eliot, 'Little Gidding', 209.
[26] Eliot, 'Little Gidding', 209.

work alone.[27] 'Costing no less than everything', simplicity is reached only through sacrifice, a belief in the story still to be completed, a self-annihilation that is *for* something greater.

The end that is inscribed in the beginning, the moment that is both timeless and temporal retains a sense of the fullness of time, of something that matters both for what and for more than it is:

> A people without history
> Is not redeemed from time, for history is a pattern
> Of timeless moments. So when the light fails
> On a winter's afternoon, in a secluded chapel
> History is now and England.[28]

Eliot follows in the footsteps of Ruskin, Newman, and Hopkins. History is prophecy, the 'now' that holds all time within it. His notion of 'England', here, is mythical as much as historical. It holds onto the promise of redemption, the fullness of time, recovered in the still, quiet moment of prayer. The Fall also continued to generate a more active political energy. In 1937, Marcus Garvey had urged Black people all over the world to take their bite of the apple in order to overcome the enforced taste of bitterness: 'To master the world, you must know the world', he insisted.[29] Self-actualization, and not sin, was the fruit of the Tree of Knowledge. 'God and Nature first made us what we are', he wrote, 'and then out of our own creative genius we make ourselves what we want to be.'[30] For Garvey, leading an international Pan-African movement, this was still a world to be made.

The more pessimistic strain of the myth of the Fall, familiar from the writings of Rousseau, fundamentally influenced the origin myths of human psychology developed by Sigmund Freud.[31] Like Rousseau, Freud wanted

[27] In 1919, Eliot had written: 'Great simplicity is only won by an intense moment or by years of intelligent effort, or by both. It represents one of the most arduous conquests of the human spirit: the triumph of feeling and thought over the natural sin of language', 'The Post Georgians', in *Poems*, 1043 v40. In a 1937 piece on Shakespeare, he observed: 'Simplicity and naturalness of speech are not necessarily his gift at the beginning; he is more likely to arrive at them in his maturity by years of hard work', *Poems*, 1043 v40.

[28] Eliot, 'Little Gidding', 208.

[29] Marcus Garvey, 'Lesson 12, 1937, School of African Philosophy Curriculum: The Purpose of Institutions', in *Marcus Garvey: Life and Lessons*, ed. Robert A. Hill and Barbara Blair (Berkeley, Calif.: University of California Press, 1987), 266–72, 270.

[30] Lewis, *Marcus Garvey*, 55.

[31] See David Humbert, 'The Return of Adam: Freud's Myth of the Fall', *Religious Studies* 29.3 (1993): 287–93.

to pinpoint a single moment of collapse to account for human badness. He named this the murder of the primal father: 'we cannot get away from the assumption that man's sense of guilt springs from the Oedipus complex'.[32] Like Rousseau, he used this moment to account for the feelings of guilty desire that characterized the discordance of modernity:

> it is very conceivable that the sense of guilt produced by civilisation... remains to a large extent unconscious, or appears as a sort of *malaise*, a dissatisfaction for which people seek other motivations. Religions, at any rate, have never overlooked the part played in civilisations by a sense of guilt.[33]

This guilt belongs to what Freud calls 'the unconscious', never directly accessed, but the source of all our impulses and urges. The 'unconscious' is a damning, as opposed to redemptive, notion of timelessness, committing human beings to a secular teleology of destruction rather than hope. 'We have learnt that unconscious mental processes are, in themselves, timeless', Freud writes, 'the idea of time cannot be applied to them'.[34] As Joshua Dienstag explains in a discussion of Freud's pessimism: 'timelessness is not even a real property of the unconscious, but an adjective applied to it by the conscious mind that can only view it across the gulf created by time-consciousness'.[35] Unconscious Oedipal guilt and desire takes the place of the primary stillness evoked by T. S. Eliot and the original world-making power celebrated by Garvey. In positioning time-bound consciousness against the 'timeless' unconscious, Freud was continuing a version of the myth of the Fall as a source of psychological disconnect. 'It is very unhappy, but too late to be helped, this discovery that we exist', Emerson had written in 1844. 'That discovery is called the Fall of Man'.[36] Emerson had maintained the notion of a beneficent and potentially redemptive native force even through rising scepticism, but Freud's unconscious was a profoundly negative source of repressed and guilty desire.

Without the hope of redemption, the myth of the Fall gives us a depressing sense of personal, political, and historical unravelling. We might call this

[32] Sigmund Freud, 'Civilisation and its Discontents', in *The Standard Edition of the Complete Psychological Works of Sigmund Freud*, vol. 21. *1927–33*, tr. and ed. James Strachey (London: Vintage, 2001), 64–148, 131.

[33] Freud, 'Civilisation and its Discontents', 135.

[34] Freud, 'Beyond the Pleasure Principle', in *Standard Edition of the Works of Freud*, vol. 18. *1920–22*, tr. and ed. James Strachey (London: Vintage, 2001), 7–66, 28.

[35] Joshua Foa Dienstag, *Pessimism: Philosophy, Ethic, Spirit* (Princeton: Princeton University Press, 2006), 91.

[36] Emerson, 'Experience' (1844), *Selected Essays*, 304.

facing reality.[37] George Eliot could never give up on the 'blessings derived from that endurance [of adversity]' and Emerson admitted that he courted suffering to find the 'sharp peaks and edges of truth'.[38] Whitman sang 'Of the trivial and flat and foolish and despised'.[39] Wilson exposed the grotesque truths of colonialism and slavery and Brown treated the Civil War dead with uncompromising realism. Even Ruskin knew that real, living, growing things, especially those touched by grace, inevitably confront us with their own mortality: 'when you say a preparing thing, a fructifying thing, you mean a *dying* thing... if there were trees in the Garden of Eden there was death'.[40] The myth of the Fall brings to the fore the hardness, roughness, slipperiness, messiness and decay that confront us when we take things as they are, not as the idols we might wish them to be.

But reality does not have to be faced with pessimism and of the figures discussed in this book, I think only Rousseau is fundamentally pessimistic.[41] As the myth of the Fall becomes a self-reflective artistic lens, the optimism that holds onto the hope of redemption in the face of the circumstances that limit self-actualization is as much, if not more, about aesthetic value as it is about faith in a particular outcome. George Eliot exposes the shortcomings of sympathy as a stand-in for salvation but she also develops a generous and forgiving form of realism and a version of the fortunate fall which values moral choice, allows for error, and hopes that humanity might vary in the right direction even when the ending is unclear. Dickinson makes a creative bid for authorship in her playful poetic exegesis but she also accepts the limits of her power, reconfiguring the fortunate fall into knowledge as a fall into unknowing, which fundamentally embraces uncertainty. In his 1836 vision of America as a New Eden in *The Oxbow*, Thomas Cole also shifts his optimism to the value of moral choice when outcomes feel so uncertain: America is not the land of new beginning but nor is its destiny decided. Emerson similarly comes to endorse pragmatism over idealism, recognizing that, faced with the 'negative power' of circumstance, we might have to adapt, rather than make, our own world.

[37] For a brilliant discussion of this idea, see David Russell, 'How to Face Reality: Ruskin, Freud, Winnicott', *Raritan* 40.3 (Winter 2021): 119–32.

[38] *GEL*, vol. 1, 15; Emerson, 'Experience' (1844), *Selected Essays*, 287–8.

[39] Whitman, *Leaves of Grass* 1855.

[40] Ruskin, 'Letters to a College Friend', *Collected Works*, vol. 1, 476.

[41] Joshua Foa Dienstag places Rousseau and Freud in his history of pessimism. Maria Van der Lugt views Rousseau more ambivalently in her study, *Dark Matters: Pessimism and the Problem of Suffering* (Princeton: Princeton University Press, 2021), 232–83.

Gianni Vattimo makes the opposite case for Christian notions of salvation as a rejection of reality:

> Christianity only really makes sense if reality is not first and foremost the world of things at hand (*vorhanden*), objectively present; and the meaning of Christianity as a message of salvation consists above all in dissolving the peremptory claims of 'reality'. Paul's sentence, 'Oh death where is thy victory?' can rightfully be read as an extreme denial of the 'reality principle.'[42]

The most deeply religious temperaments—Blake, Ruskin, Newman, Hopkins, Emerson, and Truth—are sustained by this message of salvation, even if they are also sometimes despairing. Perhaps we also recall T. S. Eliot:

> Go, go, go, said the bird, for the leaves were full of children,
> Hidden excitedly, containing laughter.
> Go, go, go, said the bird: human kind
> Cannot bear very much reality.[43]

The myth of the Fall can be pernicious and judgemental. It can be nostalgic. It can be energizing and progressive. But it also keeps precarious hope alive—a faith in the miraculous, the revelatory, and the true. As much as it shapes our sense of time, and forces a confrontation of things as they are, the myth of the Fall inspires the world with grace.

[42] Richard Rorty and Gianni Vattimo, *The Future of Religion*, ed. Santiago Zabala (New York: Columbia University Press, 2005), 49–50.
[43] T. S. Eliot, 'Burnt Norton', *Four Quartets*, *Poems*, 180.

Bibliography

Books and Articles

Acosta, Ana, *Reading Genesis in the Long Eighteenth Century: From Milton to Mary Shelley* (Aldershot: Ashgate, 2006).

Adams, James Truslow, *Epic of America* [1931] (Milton Park: Routledge, 2017).

Anger, Suzy, *Victorian Interpretation* (Ithaca, NY: Cornell University Press, 2005), 95–130.

Archambault, Paul J., 'Rousseau's Tactical Misreading of Augustine', *Symposium* 41 (1987): 6–14.

Ashton, Rosemary, *The German Idea: Four English Writers and the Reception of German Thought 1800–1860* (Cambridge: CUP, 1980).

Auerbach, Nina, *Romantic Imprisonment: Women and Other Glorified Outcasts* (New York: Columbia University Press, 1985).

Auerbach, Nina, 'The Rise of the Fallen Woman', *Nineteenth-Century Fiction* 35.1 (1980): 29–52.

Auerbach, Nina, *Woman and Demon: The Life of a Victorian Myth* (Cambridge. Mass.: Harvard University Press, 1982).

Augustine, *Confessions,* tr. with an introduction and notes by Henry Chadwick (Oxford: Oxford World's Classics, 2008).

Baldwin, James, *The Fire Next Time* (London: Penguin, 2017).

Barnstone, Aliki, *Changing Rapture: Emily Dickinson's Poetic Development* (Hanover, NH: University Press of New England, 2002).

Barthes, Roland, 'Myth Today', in *Mythologies* (London: Vintage, 2019).

Barringer, Tim, 'Thomas Cole's Atlantic Crossings', *Thomas Cole's Journey: Atlantic Crossings,* ed. Elizabeth Mankin Kornhauser and Tim Barringer (New York: Metropolitan Museum of Art, 2018), 20–61.

Barringer, Tim, and Raab, Jennifer, 'An Inheritance in Print: Thomas Cole and the Aesthetics of Landscape', in *Picturesque and Sublime: Thomas Cole's Transatlantic Inheritance,* ed. Tim Barringer, Gillian Forrester, Sophie Lynford, Jennifer Raab, and Nicholas Robbins (Catskill, NY: Thomas Cole National Historic Site, 2018), 1–49.

Bay, Mia, *The White Image in the Black Mind: African American Ideas about White People* (Oxford: OUP, 2000).

Beer, Gillian, *Darwin's Plots: Evolutionary Narrative in Darwin, George Eliot and Nineteenth-Century Fiction,* 3rd edn (Cambridge: CUP, 2009; 1983).

Beer, Gillian, *Open Fields: Science in Cultural Encounter* (Oxford: OUP, 1996).

Bennett, Jane, *The Enchantment of Modern Life: Attachments, Crossings and Ethics* (Princeton: PUP, 2011).

Bernstein, Susan David, 'Dirty Reading: Sensation Fiction, Women and Primitivism', *Criticism* 36.2 (Spring 1994): 213–41.

Bjelajac, David, 'Thomas Cole's *Oxbow* and the American Zion Divided', *American Art* 20.1 (Spring 2001): 60–83.

Blake, William, *Genesis: William Blake's Last Illuminated Work,* ed. Mark Crosby and Robert N. Essick, with an essay by Robert N. Wark (reproduced with permission of the Huntingdon Library, Art Collections and Botanical Gardens, San Marino, California, 2012).

Blake, William, *The Complete Poetry and Prose,* ed. David V. Erdman with a commentary by Harold Bloom (New York: Doubleday, 1988).

Blake, William, *The Urizen Books*, ed. David Worrall (Princeton: Princeton University Press, 1995).

Blight, David, *Race and Reunion: The Civil War in American Memory* (Cambridge, Mass.: Belknap Press, 2002).

Bonea, Amelia, Dickson, Melissa, Shuttleworth, Sally, and Wallis, Jennifer, *Anxious Times: Medicine and Modernity in Nineteenth-Century Britain* (Pittsburgh, Penn.: University of Pittsburgh Press, 2019).

Bosco, Ronald A., and Johnson, Glen M., *The Journals and Miscellaneous Notebooks of Ralph Waldo Emerson*, (Cambridge, Mass.: Belknap Press, 1982).

Bradley, John L., *Ruskin: The Critical Heritage* (New York: Routledge, 1984).

Brandstetter, Gabrielle, Egert, Gerko, and Zubarik, Sabine eds, *Touching and Being Touched: Kinesthesia and Affect in Dance and Movement* (Berlin: De Gruyter, 2013).

Brantley, Richard E., *Transatlantic Trio: Empiricism, Evangelicism and Romanticism* (Ames, Iowa: Culicidae Press, 2017).

Brontë, Charlotte, *Villette,* ed. with an introduction and notes by Helen Cooper (London: Penguin, 2004).

Brooks, Van Wyck, 'On Creating a Usable Past', *The Dial* (11 Apr. 1918): 337–41.

Brown, Callum, *The Death of Christian Britain: Understanding Secularisation 1800–2000* (London: Routledge, 2001).

Brown, Daniel, *Hopkins' Idealism: Philosophy, Physics, Poetry* (Oxford: Clarendon Press, 1997).

Brown, William Wells, *Clotel, or the President's Daughter* (London: Penguin, 2004).

Brown, William Wells, *The Negro in the American Rebellion, his Heroism and his Fidelity* (Boston: Lee & Shephard, 1867).

Buell, Lawrence, *Emerson* (Cambridge, Mass.: Harvard University Press, 2003).

Burns, Sarah, *Painting the Dark Side: Art and the Gothic Imagination in Nineteenth-Century America* (Berkeley: University of California Press, 2004).

Bush, George, *Notes, Critical and Practical on the Book of Genesis*; *Designed as a General Help to Biblical Reading and Instruction,* 2 vols (New York: Ivison, Phinney & Co., 1838).

Byron, Lord George Gordon, *The Major Works,* ed. Jerome McGann (Oxford: OUP, 2008).

Calder, Simon, 'The Art of Conduct, the Conduct of Art and the "Mixed Science" of Eliot's Ethics: "Sympathetic Impulse" and "The Scientific Point of View" in *The Mill on the Floss*', *George Eliot Review: Journal of the George Eliot Fellowship* 41 (2010): 60–74.

Caretta, Vincent, 'Olaudah Equiano, Phillis Wheatley Peters and the Black Evangelical Experience', in *The Oxford Handbook of Early Evangelicism,* ed. Jonathan Yeager (Oxford: OUP, 2022), 603–21.

Carlyle, Thomas, 'The State of German Literature', *Edinburgh Review* (Oct. 1827).

Castiglia, Christopher, *The Practices of Hope: Literary Criticism in Disenchanted Times* (New York: New York University Press, 2017).

Cavell, Stanley, *Cities of Words: Pedagogical Letters on a Register of the Moral Life* (Boston: Harvard University Press, 2005).

Cavell, Stanley, *Emerson's Transcendental Etudes* (Stanford, Calif.: Stanford University Press, 2003).

Chadwick, Owen, *The Secularisation of the European Mind in the Nineteenth Century* (Cambridge: CUP, 1975).

Clark, Steve, and Worrall, David, eds, *Blake in the Nineties* (Basingstoke: Macmillan, 1999).

Cogan, Lucy, *Blake and the Failure of Prophecy* (London: Palgrave Macmillan, 2021).

Cogan, Lucy, 'William Blake's *The Book of Los* and the Female Prophetic Tradition', *Romanticism* 21.1 (2015): 48–58.

Cole, Thomas, 'Essay on American Scenery', *American Monthly Magazine* 1 (January 1836).

Condillac, Etienne Bonnot de, *Essay on the Origin of Human Knowledge,* tr. and ed. Hans Aarsleff (Cambridge: CUP, 2001).

Constantinesco, Thomas, *Writing Pain in the Nineteenth-Century United States* (Oxford: OUP. 2022).

Cox, Jeffrey, 'Towards Eliminating the Concept of Secularisation: A Progress Report', in *Secularisation in the Christian World*, ed. Callum Brown and Michael Snape (Farnham: Ashgate, 2010), 12–26.

Crary, Jonathan, *Techniques of the Observer: On Vision and Modernity in the Nineteenth Century* (Cambridge, Mass.: MIT Press, 1990).

Csengei, Ildiko, *Sympathy, Sensibility and the Literature of Feeling in the Eighteenth Century* (Basingstoke: Palgrave, 2012).

Cuvier, Georges, *Essay on the Theory of the Earth* [1813] (London: Routledge, 2018).

Dart, Gregory, *Rousseau, Robespierre and English Romanticism* (Cambridge: CUP, 1999).

Darwin, Charles, *On the Origin of Species* (Oxford: OUP, 2008).

Darwin, Charles, *The Correspondence of Charles Darwin,* ed. Frederic Burkhardt and Sydney Smith, 30 vols (Cambridge: CUP, 1985–).

Davies, Phillip, *The Transferred Life of George Eliot* (Oxford: OUP, 2017).

Delaney, Martin R., *The Condition, Elevation, Emigration and Destiny of the Coloured People of the United States* (Clifton, NJ: African Tree Press, 2015).

Deppman, Jedd, Noble, Marianne, and Stonum, Gary Lee, *Emily Dickinson and Philosophy* ed. (Cambridge: CUP, 2013).

Derrida, Jacques, *Of Grammatology,* tr. Gayatri Chakravorty Spivak with an introduction by Judith Butler (Baltimore: Johns Hopkins University Press, 2016).

Derrida, Jacques, *Writing and Difference* [1967] (London: Routledge, 2001).

Dickinson, Emily, *Emily Dickinson's Poems as she Preserved Them*, ed. Cristianne Miller (Cambridge, Mass.: Harvard University Press, 2016).

Dickinson, Emily, *Letters of Emily Dickinson*, ed. Thomas H. Johnson (Boston: Belknap Press, 1997).

Dickinson, Emily, *The Poems of Emily Dickinson: Variorum Edition*, ed. R. W. Franklin (Cambridge, Mass.: Harvard University Press, 1998).

Dienstag, Joshua Foa, *Pessimism: Philosophy, Ethic, Spirit* (Princeton: Princeton University Press, 2006).

Douglass, Frederick, *Narrative of the Life of Frederick Douglass, an American Slave* [1845], ed. Deborah E. McDowell (Oxford: OUP, 2009).

Eberwein, Jane Donahue, *Emily Dickinson: Strategies of Limitation* (Amherst, Mass.: University of Massachusetts Press, 1987).

Eliot, George, *Adam Bede,* ed. Carol A. Martin (Oxford: OUP, 2008).

Eliot, George, *Daniel Deronda,* ed. Graham Handley (Oxford: OUP, 2014).

Eliot, George, *Essays of George Eliot*, ed. Thomas Pinney (London: Routledge & Kegan Paul, 1963).

Eliot, George, 'Introduction to Genesis', *Leader* 7 (12 Jan. 1856): 41–2.

Eliot, George, 'Mackay's Progress of the Intellect', *Westminster Review* 54 (Jan. 1851).

Eliot, George, *Middlemarch,* ed. Rosemary Ashton (London: Penguin, 2003).

Eliot, George, *Romola,* ed. Dorothea Barratt (London: Penguin, 1996).

Eliot, George, *Silas Marner,* ed. Juliette Atkinson (Oxford: OUP, 2017).

Eliot, George, 'The Antigone and its Moral', *Leader* 7 (29 Mar. 1856).

Eliot, George, *The George Eliot Letters*, ed. Gordon S. Haight, 9 vols (New Haven: Yale University Press, 1954–78).
Eliot, George, *The Mill on the Floss*, ed. Juliette Atkinson (Oxford: OUP, 2015).
Eliot, George, 'The Morality of Wilhelm Meister', *Leader* 6 (21 July 1855).
Eliot, T. S., *Collected and Uncollected Poems*, 2 vols, ed. Christopher Ricks and Jim McCue (London: Faber & Faber, 2015).
Eliot, T. S., *The Complete Prose of T. S. Eliot: The Critical Edition*, vol. 5. *Tradition and Orthodoxy 1934–39*, ed. Imam Javadi, Ronald Schuchard, and Jayme Stayer (London: Faber, 2017).
Eliot, T. S., *The Complete Prose of T. S. Eliot: The Critical Edition*, vol. 6. *The War Years 1940–46*, ed. David E. Chinitz and Ronald Schuchard (London: Faber, 2017).
Emerson, Ralph Waldo, *The Journals and Miscellaneous Notebooks of Ralph Waldo Emerson*, ed. Ralph H. Orth, vol. 6. *1824–1838* (Cambridge, Mass.: Harvard University Press, 1966).
Emerson, Ralph Waldo, 'The Tragic', *The Dial* 4 (Apr. 1844): 515–21.
Emerson, Ralph Waldo, *Poems* (Boston: James Munroe & Co., 1847).
Emerson, Ralph Waldo, *Selected Essays*, ed. Larzer Ziff (Harmondsworth: Penguin, 1982).
Equiano, Olaudah, *The Interesting Narrative and Other Writings*, ed. with an introduction and notes by Vincent Caretta (London: Penguin, 2003).
Erdozain, Dominic, *The Soul of Doubt: The Religious Roots of Unbelief from Luther to Marx* (Oxford: OUP, 2016).
Ernest, John, *Liberation Historiography: African American Writers and the Challenge of History 1794–1861* (Chapel Hill, NC: University of North Carolina Press, 2004).
Eron, Sarah, '"Bound by their Narrowing Perceptions": Sympathetic Bondage and Perverse Pity in *The Book of Urizen*', *Blake: An Illustrated Quarterly* 46.3 (Winter 2012–13): 1–13.
Essick, Robert, *William Blake and the Language of Adam* (Oxford: Clarendon, 1989).
Everett, Edward, *Oration on the Character of Washington* (Mount Vernon: Mount Vernon Press, 1913).
Federico, Annette, 'Being Torn: *The Mill on the Floss*', *Literature, Interpretation, Theory* 12.4 (2001): 359–79.
Felski, Rita, *The Limits of Critique* (Chicago: Chicago University Press, 2015).
Fessenbecker, Patrick, 'Sympathy, Vocation and Moral Deliberation in George Eliot', *ELH* 85.2 (Summer 2018): 501–32.
Feuerbach, Ludwig, *The Essence of Christianity*, tr. Marian Evans (London: Chapman & Hall, 1856).
Fleischman, Avrom, *Figures of Autobiography* (Berkeley: University of California Press, 1983).
Fleischman, Avrom, *George Eliot's Intellectual Life* (Cambridge: CUP, 2010).
Foster, Paul, *The Apocryphal Gospels: A Very Short Introduction* (Oxford: OUP, 2009).
Frank, Waldo, *Our America* (New York: Boni & Liveright, 1919).
Frank, Waldo, *The Jew in our Day*, with an introduction by Reinhold Niebuhr (London: Victor Gollancz, 1944).
Franklin, R. W., *The Editing of Emily Dickinson* (Madison, Wis.: University of Wisconsin Press, 1967).
Freedman, Linda, *Emily Dickinson and the Religious Imagination* (Cambridge: CUP, 2011).
Freedman, Linda, *William Blake and the Myth of America: From the Abolitionists to the Counterculture* (Oxford: OUP, 2018).
Freud, Sigmund, *The Standard Edition of the Complete Psychological Works of Sigmund Freud*, 24 vols, tr. and ed. James Strachey (London: Vintage, 2001).
Friedman, Richard Elliot, *Who Wrote the Bible?* (New York: Simon & Schuster, 2019).

Garvey, Ellen Gruber, *Writing with Scissors: American Scrapbooks from the Civil War to the Harlem Renaissance* (Oxford: OUP, 2012).

Garvey, Marcus, *Life and Lessons,* ed Robert A. Hill and Barbara Blair (Berkeley: University of California Press, 1987).

Garvey, Marcus, *Selected Writings and Speeches of Marcus Garvey,* ed. Bob Blaisdell (Newburyport: Dover Publications, 2005).

Gates, Henry Louis, *The Signifying Monkey: A Theory of African American Literature* (Oxford: OUP, 1989).

Genovese, Eugene D., and Fox-Genovese, Elizabeth, *Fatal Self-Deception: Slaveholding Paternalism in the Old South* (Cambridge: CUP, 2011).

George, Andrew, ed., *The Epic of Gilgamesh: The Babylonian Epic Poem and Other Texts in Akkadian and Sumerian* (London: Penguin, 2000).

Gibbon, Edward, *The History of the Decline and Fall of the Roman Empire,* 6 vols (London: Strahan & Cadell, 1776–89).

Gillespie, Neal C., *Charles Darwin and the Problem of Creation* (Chicago: University of Chicago Press, 1979).

Gilmore, Robert, 'Correspondence between Thomas Cole and Robert Gilmore Jr', in *Studies on Thomas Cole: An American Romanticist,* ed. Howard S. Merritt, special issue, *Baltimore Museum of Art Annual* 2 (1967): 41–81.

Gilpin, William, *Observations on the Highlands of Scotland* (Richmond: Richmond Publishing, 1973).

Gilroy, Paul, *The Black Atlantic: Modernity and Double Consciousness* (London: Verso, 1993).

Glausser, Wayne, *Locke and Blake: A Discussion across the Eighteenth Century* (Jacksonville, Fla. University Press of Florida, 1998).

Goddu, Theresa A., 'Anti-Slavery's Panoramic Perspective', *MELUS* 39.2 (Visual Culture and Race) (Summer 2014): 12–41.

Goddu, Theresa A., *Selling Antislavery* (Philadelphia: University of Pennsylvania Press, 2002).

Goodman, Dena, *Criticism in Action: Enlightenment Experiments in Political Writing* (Ithaca, NY: Cornell University Press, 1989).

Goss, Erin M., '"Almost Unmade": Hopkins and the Body Apocalyptic', *Victorian Poetry* 49.1 (Spring 2011): 83–103.

Goss, Erin M., 'What is Call'd Corporeal': William Blake and the Question of the Body', *The Eighteenth Century* 51.4 (Winter 2010): 413–30.

Green, Matthew I. A., *Visionary Materialism in the Early Works of William Blake* (London: Palgrave, Macmillan, 2005).

Griffiths, Devin, *The Age of Analogy: Science and Literature between the Darwins* (Baltimore: Johns Hopkins University Press, 2016).

Griffiths, Eric, *The Printed Voice of Victorian Poetry* (Oxford: Clarendon, 1989).

Grimké, Sarah, and Grimké, Angelina, *On Slavery and Abolitionism: Essays and Letters* (London: Penguin, 2014).

Haggarty, Sarah, *Blake's Gifts: Poetry and the Politics of Exchange* (Cambridge: CUP, 2010).

Haggarty, Sarah, and Mee, Jon, eds, *Blake and Conflict* (Basingstoke: Palgrave Macmillan 2009).

Hamilton, Ross, *Accident: A Philosophical and Literary History* (Chicago and London: University of Chicago Press, 2007).

Hardy, Thomas, *Jude the Obscure,* ed. with an introduction and notes by Dennis Taylor (London: Penguin, 1998).

Harper, Frances E. W., *Iola Leroy, or Shadows Uplifted* (London: Penguin, 2010).

Harper, Frances E. W., *Minnie's Sacrifice, Sowing and Reaping, Trial and Triumph: Three Rediscovered Novels* (Boston: Beacon Press, 1994).

Hartle, Ann, *The Modern Self in Rousseau's Confessions: A Reply to St Augustine* (Notre Dame, Ind.: University of Notre Dame Press, 1983).

Hathaway, Heather, Jarab, Joseph, and Melnick, Jeffrey, *Race and the Modern Artist* (Oxford: OUP, 2003).

Hazlitt, William, 'Lady Morgan's Life of Salvator', *The Edinburgh Review* (July 1824): 316–49.

Hegel, G. W. F., *Phenomenology of Spirit*, tr. A. V. Miller, with an analysis of the text and foreword by J. N. Findlay (Oxford: OUP, 1977).

Herbert, Christopher, *Culture and Anomie: Ethnographic Imagination in the Nineteenth Century* (Chicago and London: University of Chicago Press, 1991).

Herbert, Christopher, *Victorian Relativity: Radical Thought and Scientific Discovery* (London and Chicago: University of Chicago Press, 2001).

Higgins, Lesley, 'T. S. Eliot and the Poetry of Gerard Manley Hopkins', *Southern Review* 24.2 (Spring 1988): 291–302.

Hilton, Tim, *John Ruskin* (New Haven and London: Yale University Press, 2002).

Hirschman, Albert O., *The Passions and the Interests: Political Arguments for Capitalism Before its Time* (Princeton: Princeton University Press, 2013).

Hook, Della, *Trees in Anglo-Saxon England: Literature, Lore and Landscape* (Woodbridge: Boydell &Brewer, 2010).

Hopkins, Gerard Manley, *Further Letters of Gerard Manley Hopkins Including his Correspondence with Coventry Patmore*, ed. Claude Colleer Abbot (Oxford: OUP, 1938).

Hopkins, Gerard Manley, *The Journals and Papers of Gerard Manley Hopkins*, ed. Humphrey House and completed by Graham Storey (London: OUP, 1959).

Hopkins, Gerard Manley, *The Letters of Gerard Manley Hopkins to Robert Bridges Abbott*, ed. Claude Colleer (London: OUP, 1935).

Hopkins, Gerard Manley, *The Poetical Works of Gerard Manley Hopkins*, ed. Norman H. MacKenzie (Oxford: Clarendon Press, 1990).

Hopkins, Gerard Manley, *The Sermons and Devotional Writings of Gerard Manley Hopkins*, ed. Christopher Devlin (London: OUP, 1959).

Humbert, David, 'The Return of Adam: Freud's Myth of the Fall', *Religious Studies* 29.3 (1993): 287–93.

Hume, David, *The Philosophical Works of David Hume* (Edinburgh: Port, 1826).

Hurley, Michael, *Faith in Poetry: Verse Style as a Mode of Religious Belief* (London: Bloomsbury, 2018).

Hurley, Michael D., and Waithe, Marcus, *Thinking through Style: Non-Fiction Prose of the Long Nineteenth Century* (Oxford: OUP, 2018).

Hutchins, Zachary McLeod, *Inventing Eden: Primitivism, Millennialism and the Making of New England* (Oxford: OUP, 2014).

Jager, Colin, 'Romanticism/Secularisation/Secularism', *Literature Compass* 5.4 (2011): 791–806.

Jager, Colin, 'The Secular and the Literary', *Christianity and Literature* 67.3 (2018): 411–18.

Jager, Colin, *The Book of God: Secularisation and Design in the Romantic Era* (Philadelphia: University of Pennsylvania Press, 2007).

Jager, Colin, *Unquiet Things: Secularism in the Romantic Age* (Philadelphia: University of Pennsylvania Press, 2014).

James, Jennifer C., *A Freedom Bought with Blood: African American War Literature from the Civil War to World War II* (Durham, NC: University of North Carolina Press, 2007).

Jenks, William, *The Comprehensive Commentary on the Holy Bible: Supplement Containing an Accordance to the Holy Scriptures...Carpenter's Biblical Companion Condensed... Biographical Notices...Weymiss' Symbol Dictionary: Chronological and Other Tables* (Brattleboro, Vt.: Brattleboro Typographical Co., 1838).

Jones, Robert Bevan, *The Ancient Yew* (Oxford: Oxbow Books, Windgather Press, 2017).
Junior, Nyashi, 'The Mark of Cain and White Violence', *Journal of Biblical Literature* 139.24 (2020): 661–73.
Kalikoff, Beth, 'The Falling Woman in Three Victorian Novels', *Studies in the Novel* 19.3 (Fall 1987): 356–67.
Kaye, Richard, *The Flirt's Tragedy: Desire without End in Victorian and Edwardian Fiction* (Charlottesville, Va.: University Press of Virginia, 2002).
Kelly, Franklin, and Barry, Claire M., *Thomas Cole's Paintings of Eden* (Fort Worth, Tex.: Amon Carter Museum, 1994).
Kelly, J. N. D., *Early Christian Doctrine* (London: Adam & Charles Black, 1968; 1955).
Kierkegaard, Soren, *Fear and Trembling: Dialectical Lyric by Johannes de Silentio*, tr. Alastair Hannay (London: Penguin, 1985).
Kittel, Harald A., 'The Book of Urizen and An Essay Concerning Human Understanding', in *Interpreting Blake*, ed. Michael Phillips (Cambridge: CUP, 1978), 111–44.
Knight, Mark, and Mason, Emma, *Nineteenth-Century Religion and Literature: An Introduction* (Oxford: OUP, 2006).
Lamb, Jonathan, *The Evolution of Sympathy in the Long Eighteenth Century* (London: Pickering & Chatto, 2009).
LaPorte, Charles, 'Victorian Literature, Religion and Secularisation', *Literature Compass* 10.3 (2013): 277–87.
LaPorte, Charles, *Victorian Poets and the Changing Bible* (Charlottesville, Va.: University of Virginia Press, 2011).
Langer, Sandra, 'The Aesthetics of Democracy', *Art Journal* 39.2 (Winter 1979–80): 132–5.
Laqueur, Thomas W., *Solitary Sex: A Cultural History of Masturbation* (New York: Zone Books, 2003).
Laski, Gregory, 'Reconstructing Revenge: Race and Justice After the Civil War', *American Literature* 91.4 (Dec. 2019): 751–81.
Lee, Maurice S., *Uncertain Chances: Science, Skepticism and Belief in Nineteenth-Century American Literature* (Oxford: OUP, 2013).
Leighton, Angela, '"Because Men Made the Laws": The Fallen Woman and the Woman Poet', *Victorian Poetry* 27.2 (Summer 1989): 109–27.
Leighton, Angela, *Victorian Women Poets: Writing Against the Heart* (Brighton: Edward Everett Root, 1992; 2019).
Levine, George, *Realism, Ethics and Secularism: Essays on Victorian Literature and Science* (Cambridge: CUP, 2009).
Levine, George, *The Joy of Secularism: Eleven Essays for How we Live Now* (Princeton: Princeton University Press, 2011).
Levine, George, and Henry, Nancy, eds., *The Cambridge Companion to George Eliot* (Cambridge: CUP, 2019).
Levine, Lawrence W., *Black Culture and Black Consciousness: Afro-American Folk Thought from Slavery to Freedom* (Oxford: OUP, 2007).
Lewis, R. W. B., *The American Adam: Innocence Tragedy and Tradition in the Nineteenth Century* (Chicago: University of Chicago Press, 1955).
Lewis, Rupert, *Marcus Garvey* (Kingston, Jamaica: University of West Indies Press, 2018).
Locke, John, *An Essay Concerning Human Understanding* [1689], ed. Roger Woolhouse (London: Penguin, 1997).
Loesberg, Jonathan. 'Aesthetics, Ethics and Unreadable Acts', in *Knowing the Past: Victorian Literature and Culture*, ed. Suzy Anger (Ithaca, NY, and London: Cornell University Press, 2001), 121–51.

Lyons, Sara, 'The Disenchantment and Enchantment of the World: Aesthetics, Secularisation and the Gods of Greece from Friedrich Schiller to Walter Pater', *Modern Language Review* 109.4 (Oct. 2014): 873–95.

McAlpin, Mary K., 'Innocence of Experience: Rousseau on Puberty in the State of Civilisation', *Journal of the History of Ideas* 71.2 (Apr. 2010): 241–261.

McGann, Jerome J, 'The Idea of an Indeterminate Text: Blake's Bible of Hell and Dr. Alexander Geddes', *Studies in Romanticism* 25.3 (Fall 1986): 303–24.

McLeod, Hugh, *Secularism in Western Europe, 1848–1914* (New York: St Martin's Press, 2000).

McNulty, J. Bard, ed., *The Correspondence of Thomas Cole and Daniel Wadsworth: Letters in the Watkinson Library* (Albany, NY: Connecticut Historical Society, 1983).

Mansell, Darrell, 'Ruskin and George Eliot's Realism', *Criticism* 7.3 (1965): 203–16.

Marx, Leo, *The Machine in the Garden: Technology and the Pastoral Ideal in America* (Oxford: OUP, 1964).

Maxwell, William J., ed., *Complete Poems* (Chicago: University of Illinois Press, 2004).

Mee, Jon, *Dangerous Enthusiasm: William Blake and the Culture of Radicalism in the 1790s* (Oxford: OUP, 1992).

Merrin, Jeredith, 'The Ballad of Charlotte Mew', *Modern Philology* 95.2 (Nov. 1997): 200–17.

Mew, Charlotte, *Selected Poetry and Prose*, ed. Julia Copus (London: Faber, 2017).

Miller, Andrew, *The Burdens of Perfection: On Ethics and Reading in Nineteenth-Century British Literature* (Ithaca, NY: Cornell University Press, 2008).

Miller, Angela, 'Thomas Cole and Jacksonian America: The Course of Empire as Political Allegory', *Prospects* 14 (Oct. 1989): 65–92.

Miller, Cristanne, *Reading in Time: Emily Dickinson in the Nineteenth Century* (Amherst, Mass.: University of Massachusetts Press, 2012).

Miller, David C., ed., *American Iconology: New Approaches to Nineteenth-Century Art and Literature* (New Haven: Yale University Press, 1993).

Miller, David C., *Dark Eden: The Swamp in Nineteenth-Century American Literature* (Cambridge: Cambridge University Press, 1989).

Milton, John, *Paradise Lost*, ed. Alastair Fowler (London: Routledge, 2007).

Mizejewski, Linda, 'Charlotte Mew and the Unrepentant Magdalene: A Myth in Transition', *Texas Studies in Literature and Language* 26.3 (Fall 1986): 282–302.

Morgan, Lady, *The Life and Times of Salvator Rosa*, 2 vols (London: Printed for Henry Coburn, 1824).

Muldoon, Mark S., *Tricks of Time: Bergson, Merleau-Ponty and Ricoeur in Search of Time, Self, and Meaning* (Pittsburgh, Penn.: Duquesne University Press, 2006).

Muller, Jill, *Gerard Manley Hopkins and Victorian Catholicism: A Heart in Hiding* (London: Taylor & Francis, 2003).

Mutter, Matthew, *Restless Secularism: Modernism and the Religious Inheritance* (New Haven: Yale University Press, 2017).

Myrone, Martin, *The Blake Book* (London: Tate, 2007).

Nazar, Hina, 'Facing Ethics: Narrative and Recognition from George Eliot to Judith Butler', *Nineteenth-Century Contexts* 33.5 (Dec. 2011): 437–50.

New, Elisa, *The Regenerate Lyric: Theology and Innovation in American Poetry* (Cambridge: CUP, 2009).

Newman, John Henry, *An Essay in Aid of the Grammar of Assent*, ed. Ian T. Ker (Oxford: OUP, 1985).

Newman, John Henry, *An Essay on the Development of Christian Doctrine* [1845] (London: Longmans Green and Co., 1909).

Newman, John Henry, *Fifteen Sermons Preached before the University of Oxford between A.D. 1826 and 1843,* with an introduction by Mary Katherine Tillman (Notre Dame, Ind.: University of Notre Dame Press, 1997).

Newman, John Henry, *Parochial and Plain Sermons,* 8 vols (London: Longmans Green & Co., 1908).

Newman, John Henry, *Sermons Preached on Various Occasions* (London: Longmans Green & Co., 1908).

Newman, John Henry, *The Idea of a University, Defined and Illustrated* (London: Longmans Green & Co., 1907).

Niimi, Hatsuko, 'The Book of Ahania: A Metatext', *Blake: An Illustrated Quarterly* 34.2 (Fall 2000): 46–54.

Nixon, Jude V., *Gerard Manley Hopkins and his Contemporaries: Liddon, Newman, Darwin and Pater* (London: Garland, 1994).

Noble, Mark, *American Poetic Materialism from Whitman to Stevens* (Cambridge: CUP, 2014).

Nordau, Max, *Degeneration* [1895] (New York: D. Appleton & Co., 2016).

Ong, Walter J., *Hopkins, the Self and God* (Toronto: University of Toronto Press, 1986).

Ovid, *Ovid's Metamorphoses,* ed. Madeleine Forey, tr. Arthur Golding (London: Penguin, 2002).

Painter, Nell Irvin, *Sojourner Truth: A Life, A Symbol* (London: Norton, 1997).

Parker, Robert, *Miasma: Pollution and Purification in Early Greek Religion* (Oxford: Clarendon Press, 1983).

Parry, Ellwood C., *The Art of Thomas Cole: Ambition and Imagination* (Newark and London: Associated University Presses, 1988).

Pater, Walter, *Studies in the History of the Renaissance,* ed. Matthew Beaumont (Oxford: Oxford World's Classics, 2010).

Patmore, Hector M., *Adam, Satan and The King of Tyre: The Interpretation of Ezekiel 28:11–19 in Late Antiquity* (Leidan: Brill, 2012).

Pettit, Clare, *Serial Forms: The Unfinished Project of Modernity 1815–1848* (Oxford: OUP, 2020).

Pettit, Clare, *Serial Revolutions 1848: Writing, Politics, Form* (Oxford: OUP, 2022).

Poirier, Richard, *A World Elsewhere: The Place of Style in American Literature* (New York: OUP, 1966).

Poole, Mary A., *Slave Narratives: A Folk History of Slavery in the United States from Interviews with Former Slaves*, vol. 1. *Alabama Narratives* (Delhi: Prabhat Publishers, 2019).

Poole, William, *The World Makers: Scientists of the Restoration and the Search for the Origins of the Earth* (Oxford: Peter Lang, 2010).

Pratt, Lloyd, *Archives of American Time: Literature and Modernity in the Nineteenth Century* (Philadelphia: University of Pennsylvania Press, 2009).

Puskar, Jason, *Accident Society: Fiction, Collectivity and the Production of Chance* (Stanford, Calif.: Stanford University Press, 2012).

Pykett, Lyn, *The Improper Feminine: The Women's Sensation Novel and the New Woman Writing* (London: Routledge, 2003).

Quinones, Ricardo, *The Changes of Cain: Violence and the Lost Brother in Cain and Abel Literature* (Princeton: Princeton University Press, 2016).

Richieri Griffin, Christina, 'Senses, Sympathy, Omniscience and Secularism', *ELH* 84.2 (Summer 2017): 475–502.

Reynolds, David S., *Walt Whitman's America: A Cultural Biography* (New York: Vintage, 1996).
Richardson, Robert, *Emerson: The Mind on Fire* (Berkeley: University of California Press, 1995).
Ricoeur, Paul, *Time and Narrative,* vol. 3 (Chicago: University of Chicago Press, 1988).
Riley, Patrick, 'The Inversion of Conversion: Rousseau's Rewriting of Augustinian Autobiography', *Studies in Eighteenth-Century Culture* 28 (1999): 229–55.
Rix, Robert, 'In Infernal Love and Faith: William Blake's "The Marriage of Heaven and Hell"', *Literature and Theology* 20.2 (June 2006): 107–25.
Rix, Robert, *William Blake and the Cultures of Radical Christianity* (Aldershot: Ashgate, 2007).
Roberts, Charlotte, *Edward Gibbon and the Shape of History* (Oxford: OUP, 2014).
Rorty, Richard, and Vattimo, Gianni, *The Future of Religion,* ed. Santiago Zabala (New York: Columbia University Press, 2005).
Rosenblatt, Helena, *Rousseau and Geneva: From the First Discourse to the Social Contract, 1749–1762* (Cambridge: CUP, 1997).
Rousseau, Jean-Jacques, *Confessions,* tr. Angela Scholar and ed. Patrick Coleman (Oxford: Oxford World's Classics, 2000).
Rousseau, Jean-Jacques, *Discourse on the Origin of Inequality* [1755], tr. Franklin Phillip (Oxford: OUP, 2009).
Rousseau, Jean-Jacques, 'Discourse on the Sciences and the Arts', in *Rousseau: The Basic Political Writings* (2nd edn), tr. and ed. Donald A. Cress, introduction and new annotation by David Wootton (Cambridge: Hackett, 2011).
Rousseau, Jean-Jacques, *Discours sur l'origine at les fondements d l'inégalité parmi les hommes,* ed. Gérard Mairet (Paris: Le Livre de Poche, 1996).
Rousseau, Jean-Jacques, *Discours sur les Sciences et les Arts,* ed. George R. Havens (London: OUP, 1946).
Rousseau, Jean-Jacques, *Du contrat social, ou Principes du Droit Politique,* introduction, commentary and notes by Gérard Mairet (Paris: Le Livre de Poche, 1996).
Rousseau, Jean-Jacques, *Émile, or On Education (includes Émile and Sophie; Or, The Solitaries),* in *The Collected Writings of Rousseau,* vol. 13, ed. Christopher Kelly (Hanover, NH: Dartmouth College Press, 2010).
Rousseau, Jean-Jacques, *Émile, or on Education* [1763], tr. Allan Bloom (London: Penguin, 1991).
Rousseau, Jean-Jacques, *Émile, ou de l'Éducation, nouvelle edition avec les variants et des notes* (Paris: Charpentier, Libraire-Éditeur, 1848).
Rousseau, Jean-Jacques, *Les Confessions,* édition et introduction de Bernard Gagnebin, Annotation de Jean Balsamo, annexes et notes complémentaires de Michèle Crogiez (Paris: Le Livre de Poche Classique, 1988).
Rousseau, Jean-Jacques, *The Social Contract, or Principles of Political Right,* tr. and introduced by Maurice Cranston (London: Penguin, 1968).
Rowland, Anna Wierda, *Romanticism and Childhood: The Infantilisation of British Literary Culture* (Cambridge: CUP, 2012).
Rowland, Christopher, *Blake and the Bible* (New Haven: Yale University Press, 2011).
Ruskin, John, *Collected Works,* ed. E. T. Cook and A. Wedderburn, 39 vols (London: George Allen & Unwin, 1903–12).
Ruskin, John, *Modern Painters,* vol. 5 (London: Smith, Eder & Co., 1873).
Russell, David, 'How to Face Reality: Ruskin, Freud, Winnicott', *Raritan* 40.3 (Winter 2021): 119–32.
Russell, David, *Tact: Aesthetic Liberalism and the Essay Form in Nineteenth-Century Britain* (Princeton: Princeton University Press, 2018).

Shakespeare, William, *Twelfth Night, or What You Will,* ed. Roger Warren and Stanley Wells (Oxford: OUP, 2008).

Sheehan, Jonathan, 'When was Disenchantment? History and the Secular Age', in *Varieties of Secularism in a Secular Age,* ed. Michael Warner et al. (Cambridge, Mass.: Harvard University Press, 2011), 217–42.

Shelley, Mary, *Frankenstein, or the Modern Prometheus* [1818], ed. D. L. Macdonald and Kathleen Scherf (London: Broadview, 2012).

Smallwood, Osborn T., 'John Ruskin and the Oxford Movement', *CLA Journal* 3.2 (Dec. 1959): 114–18.

Smith, Henry Nash, *Virgin Land* (Cambridge, Mass.: Harvard University Press, 2018; 1950).

Spires, Derrick, *The Practice of Citizenship: Black Politics and Print Culture in the Early United States* (Philadelphia: University of Pennsylvania Press, 2019).

Stansell, Christine, and Wilentz, Sean, 'Cole's America: An Introduction', in *Thomas Cole: Landscape into History,* ed. William H. Truettner and Alan Wallach (New Haven: Yale University Press, 1994), 3–21.

Starobinski, Jean, *Transparency and Obstruction* (Chicago and London: University of Chicago Press, 1971).

Stauffer, John, Trodd, Zoe, Bernier, Celeste-Marie, Gates, Henry Louis, and Morris, Kenneth B., *Picturing Frederick Douglass: An Illustrated Biography of the Century's Most Illustrated American* (New York: Liveright, 2015).

Stevenson, Robert Louis, *The Strange Case of Dr Jekyll and Mr Hyde and Other Tales of Terror,* ed. Robert Mighall (London: Penguin, 2002).

Sullivan, Wilson, *New England Men of Letters* (New York: Macmillan, 1972).

Symons, Arthur, *The Symbolist Movement in Literature,* ed. Matthew Creasy (Manchester: Carcanet, 2014).

Taliaferro, Harden E., *Fisher's River (North Carolina) Scenes and Characters* (New York, 1859).

Tannenbaum, Leslie, 'Blake's Art of Crypsis: *The Book of Urizen and Genesis*', *Blake Studies* 5.1 (Fall 1972): 141–64.

Taylor, Charles, *A Secular Age* (Cambridge, Mass.: Harvard University Press, 2007).

Taylor, Edward, *God's Determinations and Preparatory Meditations: A Critical Edition,* ed. with an introduction by Daniel Patterson (Kent, O.: Kent State University Press, 2003).

The *Atlantic Monthly* 21 (Boston: Ticknor & Fields, 1868).

Thoreau, Henry David, *Walden,* ed. with introduction and notes by Stephen Fender (Oxford: OUP, 1997).

Thornton, Helen, 'Cain, Abel and Thomas Hobbes', *History of Political Thought* 24.4 (Winter 2002): 611–33.

Tondre, Michael, *The Physics of Possibility: Victorian Fiction, Science and Gender* (Charlottesville, Va.: University of Virginia Press, 2018).

Trench, R. C., *On the Study of Words* (London: Routledge, 2018).

Trudgill, Eric, *Madonnas and Magdalens* (London: William Heinemann, 1976).

Truth, Sojourner, *Narrative of Sojourner Truth: A Bondswoman of Olden Time, with a History of her Labours and Correspondence drawn from her 'Book of Life'; Also, a Memorial Chapter*, ed. Nell Irvine Painter (London: Penguin, 1998).

Van der Lugt, Maria, *Dark Matters: Pessimism and the Problem of Suffering* (Princeton: Princeton University Press, 2021).

Vance, Norman, *Bible and Novel: Narrative Authority and the Death of God* (Oxford: OUP, 2013).

Vastey, Baron Valentin de, *The Colonial System Unveiled,* tr. and ed. Chris Bongie (Liverpool: Liverpool University Press, 2014).

Vaughan, Alden T., and Clark, Edward W., eds, *Puritans among the Indians: Accounts of Captivity and Redemption 1676–1724* (Cambridge, Mass.: Belknap Press of Harvard University Press, 1981).

Viscomi, Joseph, 'Blake's "Annus Mirabilis": The Productions of 1795', *Blake: An Illustrated Quarterly* 41.2 (Fall 2007): 52–84.

Walker, David, *Appeal to the Coloured Citizens of the World,* ed. with an introduction and annotations by Peter P. Hinks (Philadelphia: Pennsylvania State University Press, 2000).

Wallace, Richard, *Salvator Rosa in America* (Wellsey, Mass.: Jewish Arts Centre, 1979).

Wallach, Allan, 'Making a Picture of the View from Mount Holyoake', in *American Iconology: New Approaches to Nineteenth-Century Art and Literature,* ed. David C. Miller (New Haven: Yale University Press, 1993), 80–92.

Wallach, Allan, 'Thomas Cole and Transatlantic Romanticism', in *Transatlantic Romanticism: British and American Art and Literature 1790–1860,* ed. Andrew Hemingway and Allan Wallach (Amherst, Mass.: University of Masssachussets Press, 2015), 206–26.

Ward, John W., 'Andrew Jackson: Symbol for an Age', *Jacksonian Democracy: Myth or Reality,* ed. James L. Bugg Jr (New York: Holt, Rinehard & Winston, 1962), 107–11.

Watt, George, *Fallen Women in the Nineteenth-Century English Novel* (London: Routledge, 1984).

Weber, Max, *The Protestant Ethic and the Spirit of Capitalism,* tr. Talcott Parsons (London: Routledge, 2005).

Wells. Ida B., *The Light of Truth: Writings of an Anti-Lynching Crusader,* ed. Mia Bay (London: Penguin, 2014).

Wendy Martin, ed., *The Cambridge Companion to Emily Dickinson* (Cambridge: CUP, 2002).

Wheatley, Phillis, *Complete Writings* (London: Penguin, 2001).

Whistler, James McNeill, *The Gentle Art of Making Enemiess* (Elibron Classics reprint of London: Heineman, 1904).

White, Hayden, *Figural Realism: Studies in the Mimesis Effect* (Baltimore and London: Johns Hopkins University Press, 1999).

Whitman, Walt, *Leaves of Grass* [1855] and later versions, https://whitmanarchive.org

Whitman, Walt, *Walt Whitman's Selected Journalism,* ed. Douglass A. Novar and Jason Stacey (Ames, Ia.: University of Iowa Press, 2015).

Wilde, Oscar, *Complete Short Fiction,* ed. Ian Small (London: Penguin, 1994; 2003).

Williams, Arnold, *The Common Expositor: An Account of the Commentaries on Genesis 1527–1633* (Chapel Hill, NC: University of North Carolina Press, 1948).

Wilson, Christopher Kent, 'Rediscovered Thomas Cole Letter: New Light on the Expulsion from the Garden of Eden', *American Art Journal* 18.1 (Winter 1986): 73–4.

Wilson, Eric, *Emerson's Sublime Science* (Basingstoke: Palgrave Macmillan, 1999).

Wilson, William, 'Afric American Picture Gallery, by Ethiop', *Anglo-African Magazine* [1859] (New York: Arno Press and the New York Times, 1969).

Winnifrith, Tom, *Fallen Women in the Nineteenth-Century Novel* (Basingstoke: Palgrave, 1994).

Wollstonecraft, Mary, *A Vindication of the Rights of Woman* and *A Vindication of the Rights of Man,* ed. Janet Todd (Oxford: OUP, 1993).

Wordsworth, William, *The Excursion,* ed. Sally Bushell, James A. Butler, and Michael C. Jaye with the assistance of David Garcia (Ithaca, NY, and London: Cornell University Press, 2007).

Wordsworth, William, *The Major Works,* ed. Stephen Gill (Oxford: OUP, 2008).

Wright, D. G., 'Rousseau's *Confessions*: The Tragedy of Teleology', *Journal of Social and Political Thought* 1.4 (Jan. 2003). http://www.yorku.ca/jspot/4/rousseau.html

Wright, T. R., 'George Eliot and Positivism: A Reassessment', *Modern Language Review* 76.2 (Apr. 1981): 257–72.
Yousef, Nancy, *Romantic Intimacy* (Stanford, Calif.: Stanford University Press, 2013).

Archives

Coloured Conventions Project. https://coloredconventions.org/
Frederick Douglass Newspapers. https://www.loc.gov/collections/frederick-douglass-newspapers/about-this-collection/
George Eliot Archive. https://georgeeliotarchive.org/
Thomas Cole Papers. 9 boxes. New York State Library.
Walt Whitman Archive. https://whitmanarchive.org/
William Blake Archive. http://www.blakearchive.org/

Index

Note: Figures are indicated by an italic "(*f*)" following the page number.

Books of the Bible are indicated in italics

For the benefit of digital users, indexed terms that span two pages (e.g., 52–53) may, on occasion, appear on only one of those pages.